Transforming
U.S. Intelligence

Transforming U.S. Intelligence

JENNIFER E. SIMS AND BURTON GERBER, EDITORS

In cooperation with the
Center for Peace and Security Studies
Edmund A. Walsh School of Foreign Service
Georgetown University

Georgetown University Press WASHINGTON, D.C.

Georgetown University Press, Washington, D.C.
© 2005 by Georgetown University Press. All rights reserved.

10 9 8 7 6 5   2005

This book is printed on acid-free paper meeting
the requirements of the American National Standard
for Permanence in Paper for Printed Library Materials.

As of January 1, 2007, 13-digit ISBN numbers will replace the current 10-digit system.
Paperback: 978-1-58901-069-7

Library of Congress Cataloging-in-Publication Data

Transforming U.S. intelligence / Jennifer E. Sims and Burton Gerber, editors ; in cooperation with
the Center for Peace and Security Studies, Georgetown University.
   p. cm.
  Includes bibliographical references and index.
  ISBN 1-58901-069-8 (pbk. : alk. paper)
1. Intelligence service—United States.   I. Title: Transforming US intelligence.   II. Title:
Transforming United States intelligence.   III. Sims, Jennifer E. IV. Gerber, Burton L.V. Georgetown
University. Center for Peace and Security Studies.
  JK468.I6T67 2005
  353.1'7'0973—dc22

                                                  2005008373

CONTENTS

PREFACE

THIS BOOK was initially intended to provide a broad overview of the central issues of U.S. intelligence reform at the start of the twenty-first century. It began with our assumption that the intelligence community had failed significantly in its responsibility to warn against surprise attack and that this failure demanded an exploration into the reasons why. However, as the project evolved, our purposes became both grander and more limited than initially envisioned. Beyond identifying fixes to the problems exposed by September 11, 2001, we have sought to discern those challenges other than terrorism that U.S. intelligence will face in the coming decades. We propose changes in national intelligence practices that might allow flexible response to the full panoply of threats and opportunities these challenges might entail. Given the expansiveness of U.S. interests and yet the limited resources likely to be available, this volume focuses on identifying "transformative solutions" that combine technology with creative tactics and strategies such that exponential growth in capabilities might be possible.

The authors selected for this volume have all had experience within the intelligence community as well as time for reflection on its troubles and strengths. These authors are "insiders" who have lived with these problems, struggled to overcome them, and seen both success and failure. And while they may differ on what these experiences mean in some specific matters, they agree that the most important requirements for reform of the U.S. intelligence community concern its policies and practices more than its structure. Whereas structure can affect practice in positive ways, form should follow function, not the reverse. Moreover, in the spirit of "first do no harm," the authors are unanimous in their view that much of what U.S. intelligence has done since the end of the cold war has been right and good, and that identifying these positive features must be part of a responsible reform process — one that seeks to confirm smart practices even as it fixes bad ones.

This volume focuses on national intelligence — support for the highest forms of policymaking within the U.S. government — rather than reform of military intelligence. As a result of two recent wars, in Afghanistan and Iraq, the Defense Department and U.S. war colleges have given considerable attention to the issues of intelligence support to military operations. Much less effort has been spent on intelligence support for national security strategy writ large and, specifically, support for overarching foreign and defense policy. This volume seeks to restore some balance to the debate.

The editors are grateful to the authors for their written contributions as well as for their generous participation in our authors' conference and roundtables designed to flesh out individual and collective views on this important topic. To aid these collegial discussions, we invited a number of experts to review the draft chapters. For their sharp and insightful commentary, we would like to thank Dr. Richard Betts of Columbia University, Dr. Roger George of the National War College and the Central Intelligence Agency, Dr. Daniel Byman, Georgetown University, Dean Robert Gallucci, Georgetown University, the Honorable Keith Hall, former director of the National Reconnaissance Office and currently a senior vice president with Booz Allen, Ms. Deborah Barger and Mr. Michael Warner of the director of national intelligence's community management staff, Mr. Mark Shaheen, formerly of the U.S. State Department, and Dr. Michael Brown, director of the Center for Peace and Security Studies (CPASS) and the Security Studies Program at Georgetown University. They have all made valuable contributions to the intellectual discussions that have helped shape this volume. Of course the authors take full responsibility for the views expressed in this volume. The editors are fully accountable for any errors in their presentation.

The project as a whole could not have been undertaken without the tremendous financial and logistical support of CPASS at Georgetown University. In addition to the director, Michael Brown, we wish to thank Christina Zechman-Brown, Sara Yamaka, Rebecca Goldberg, Desi Burns Porter, and Erin Roussin. CPASS also provided essential support for research assistance. We would like to thank Matthew Walker, Uday Ram, Andrew Amunson, Peter Fitzgerald, and Michael Yerushalmi for the valuable intellectual and logistical support they provided. The book could not have been completed without them.

We would also like to thank the CIA's Publication Review Board for its expeditious review of chapters prior to publication. And, of course, we wish to thank Richard E. Brown and the staff of Georgetown University Press for their assistance in bringing this project to completion. It has been a pleasure working with them.

Finally, we have dedicated this book to our spouses, Robert Gallucci and the late Rosalie Prokarym Gerber, who have encouraged our commitment to public service. They have been deep sources of strength and wisdom for us. This volume is a small token of our gratitude.

Jennifer E. Sims
Burton Gerber

Introduction

Jennifer E. Sims and Burton Gerber

INTELLIGENCE FAILURES prior to the terrorist attacks of September 11, 2001, and the "missing" weapons of mass destruction (WMD) in Iraq have reminded Americans that good intelligence is crucial for national security. Indeed, the report of the National Commission on Terrorist Attacks upon the United States[1] led quickly to the enactment of legislation restructuring the intelligence community, underscoring both the capacity of American citizens to change their most secretive governmental institutions and their appreciation of the importance of the intelligence mission. The families of the victims of September 11 recognized their opportunity to reform the U.S. government's intelligence service and, remarkably, they did so. At the end of 2004 President George W. Bush signed into law the first strategically significant changes in the American intelligence system since it was created at the end of World War II.[2]

But if the restructuring accomplished at the end of 2004 is widely regarded as the end of U.S. intelligence reform rather than its beginning, this historic moment will have been misused. Now that the Iraq WMD Commission has reported on how the world's most sophisticated intelligence system went from the surprise of September 11 to the surprise of Iraq's missing WMD, reasoned debate on intelligence reform must continue. After all, a new structure for intelligence in Washington does not mean that the process for improved warning, intelligence analysis, and decision making has been fixed.

In fact, some intelligence experts, including former Director of Central Intelligence (DCI) George Tenet, have cautioned that rewiring efforts may actually damage a group of agencies that has had more successes than failures. They argue that failure is a routine hazard of even sound intelligence enterprises and that what is most needed is lower expectations about what U.S. intelligence can be expected to do.[3] Caught between the structural changes legislated at the end of 2004 and the argument that intelligence is not broken, national security managers may be inclined to split the difference, implementing the new structure but not correcting much else.

The Meaning of Transformation

Despite the sobriety of arguments to "stay the course" and the comfort offered by bureaucratic redesign, there is a third course worth exploring: transformation of U.S. intelligence more through practice and policy than through bureaucratic fix. Examining this third way is the purpose of this book. True intelligence transformation fuses wit, creative business practices, and selected technologies for the purpose of achieving strategic advantage. It implies reform—the ability to beat adversaries faster, more efficiently, and with less cost to civil liberties than might otherwise be possible. But its trademark is the marriage of selected technologies with innovative strategies and practices such that revolutionary capabilities emerge. Common and cutting-edge technologies are put to uncommon use; tradecraft and business practices, habits of thought, and technologies are refashioned to gain dramatically new advantages against adversaries.

According to this view, transformation involves less the editing of blueprints for where intelligence officers should sit than the description of what they might best seek to accomplish. In this sense, this volume is a direct response to what the 9/11 Commission identified in its report as "the four principal failures: in imagination, policy, capabilities, and management."[4] In the view of the authors, these four areas are the keystones of intelligence transformation, the end result of which should be a system that offers decision makers a capacity for both precise targeting and strategic perspective, a decisive edge for both negotiation and battle, and options for both defensive and offensive countersurprise.

Central Premises

Perhaps the most important premise shared by most authors in this volume is related to the nature of strategic surprise: the next one is unlikely to look like the last. Although both the surprise of September 11 and the surprise of finding no WMD in Iraq suggest that U.S. intelligence needs fixing, efforts to fix it ought not to focus obsessively on past mistakes. The danger in allowing the press's and public's attention to rest on what went wrong with intelligence on September 11 is that this catastrophe may ironically end up *limiting* reform and reorganization. Truly transformed intelligence requires forward thinking and creativity about all the issues affecting U.S. security, including the intentions of other great and emerging powers such as China, Russia, and India; the security of energy supplies; the instability in many Islamic nations; weapons proliferation; trafficking in women and children; and the aggressive intentions of rogue or failing states.

It follows that transformation of U.S. intelligence should not necessarily be about jettisoning the old in favor of the new, largely because the core features of international politics have been enduring ones: the existence of states and, unfortunately, conflict among them. States will remain challenging adversaries for the United States in part because transnational groups pose new threats to state structures. Allied states and competitors alike will augment their defenses—often with our assistance—against common transnational threats. Both may also make accommodations with terrorist adversaries in order to pass threats on to others. States, even allies, are likely in certain circumstances to take positions adversarial to U.S. interests. They are as likely to be important intelligence targets in the future as they have been in the past.

Similarly, transformation cannot be wisely accomplished without reference to the constraints that bound it, in terms of both the international system and domestic culture. For example, U.S. dependence on worldwide information systems means that an attack on an adversary's communications risks damaging one's own. A second constraint concerns those bureaucracies and management tiers that recent reform legislation arguably thickened. Reputable defense analysts have argued that it takes networks to fight nimble networks of terrorists, criminals, or traffickers in nuclear weapons. Given that Washington's bureaucracies are not likely to go away, the question is how they can best be configured to engage in modern international politics and war. Increased centralization and more management layers are unlikely to be the answer.

Of course, Americans have hotly debated one of the most obvious constraints since September 11: the need to reconcile intelligence requirements with the protection of civil liberties. In democracies the state's interest in maximizing power for national security purposes must be balanced with its interest in preserving the public trust. In the U.S. case, this trust requires protection of constitutional freedoms and the American way of life. History teaches us that intelligence practices unsuited either to the temperament of American political culture or to the new threats embedded in the international system will probably trigger more failures, and all too swiftly. Thus national security decision makers face a conundrum: the best intelligence systems involve state secrecy, deception, and clandestine efforts to steal; yet such systems, when turned inward to address foreign threats to vital domestic interests, can threaten the very institutions of democracy and representative government that they were set up to protect in the first place.

Making such constraints on reform explicit underscores a point suggested earlier. Structure—that is to say, the configuration of departments and agencies—may be far less important than policies, practices, and leadership. This premise seems largely validated by the historical record. Those who made remarkable advances during World War II in breaking German codes, in employing radar to counter German missile attacks, or in developing the art of strategic deception, often annoyed their colleagues, bucked bureaucracy, and felt uncomfortably daring in their pursuits. Their behavior transformed intelligence capabilities during World War II and helped secure Allied victory well before the lessons of Pearl Harbor were fully learned or intelligence institutions rebuilt for the cold war. This volume seeks less to prove this point than to accept it as a premise: intelligence policies and practices matter—perhaps decisively so.

The Nature of Intelligence Policy

In the United States, intelligence policy is largely about managing the conundrums involved in gathering and keeping secrets. For example, how does the intelligence establishment earn the trust and cooperation of the American people in its domestic fight against transnational threats while simultaneously expanding intrusive domestic surveillance authorities — including those that now may lead to criminal prosecutions on unrelated matters? As intelligence is transformed, it will have to grapple with some of the hardest questions democracy puts to the national security state: whether, when, and how the government may consort with criminals, influence elections, listen in on private conversations, eliminate adversaries, withhold information from the public or, alternatively, release it at some cost to the sources and methods used to collect it.

Intelligence policy also concerns how priorities for intelligence collection and analysis are set, with whom the results will be shared, and how the process will be funded. It describes who has authority for declassifying secrets or sharing them, what kinds of cover may be used by intelligence officers, and how covert action proposals are vetted within the government.

Intelligence policy also guides how the intelligence process is managed. For example, it may regulate how intelligence may be released and by whom. Intelligence policy is, therefore, not the exclusive domain of the intelligence professional. It involves decisions about risk versus gain, the adjustment of means to ends, embedding innovation within proven tradecraft, and questions of public tolerance. In fact, decisions about how intelligence policy will be formulated and who will be responsible for it determine, in large measure, whether a given set of intelligence institutions and the democratic system it serves can safely and productively coexist.

Many significant challenges facing the U.S. intelligence community are issues of policy and practice that predate September 11 and have quietly persisted, such as:

- How to reconcile "need-to-know" security procedures with faster-paced, decentralized, and networked decision making;
- How rapidly to identify new decision makers needing intelligence support when urgent issues or crises arise, and how to ensure that dissemination systems are available to reach them (a particular problem now with respect to first responders such as fire, police, and medical authorities at the state and local levels);
- How to ensure that closer analytic support for clandestine collection and covert action programs does not lead to biased analysis of the prospects for those programs — whether they are run by the military or by the Central Intelligence Agency (CIA);
- Whether to integrate to a greater extent unclassified sources and Internet tools into traditional business practices and, if so, how to protect them from corruption;

- How to penetrate terrorist organizations to collect actionable intelligence without excessive involvement in them;
- How to upgrade strategic support for national security decision makers while simultaneously satisfying the intelligence needs of a growing number of tactical operators in the field;
- How to coordinate U.S. intelligence capabilities when important resources, such as the availability of U.S. government facilities overseas, lie outside the control of an intelligence chief or beyond the purview of intelligence budgeting and oversight committees in Congress;
- How to satisfy national security decision makers' current priorities while simultaneously meeting the requirement to warn — that is, to alert clients to impending disasters that require the *reordering* of their priorities;
- How to retain the efficiencies and accountability associated with the various collection agencies while overcoming the problems associated with bureaucratic culture, stovepipes, and turf consciousness.

One might reasonably suppose that changing intelligence policies is no harder than legislating changes in budgets or institutions. If policy is regulation, then strong leaders should be able to change them relatively quickly.

However, long-standing policies both reflect and engender practices that may be deeply ingrained. Intelligence practice often entails art—what is sometimes called "craft" or "strategy," depending on the discipline.[5] "Art," in turn, requires skill and develops out of standard procedures and even habits of thought about what works and doesn't work in the pursuit of one's objectives. These "rules" may be deeply embedded in agency cultures that have long histories and may include, for example, the "scientific" way evidence is gathered to support analytic judgments, or the extent to which overseas ambassadors depend on the CIA, the Bureau of Diplomatic Security, or the State Department's Bureau of Intelligence and Research for their intelligence support. Such standard practices sometimes reflect "habits of thought" that determine how things are done even if no regulation, law, or rule exists to enforce them.

If transformation imperils many of these past policies and practices, and it often does, then to be useful it must offer up workable new ones. Identifying deleterious practices and then suggesting ways to amend them is far more difficult than legislating structural change, partly because it takes "insiders" to really know and understand such faults. Integral to this book's purpose is an exploration of what an intelligence transformation should entail in terms of practical and constructive policies and practices that will be the profession's responsibility to adopt. Doing so will take time and will require patience and perseverance.

The Art of the Possible, Not the Perfect

Transformation of U.S. intelligence is an ambitious but appropriate goal at this time for several reasons. First, the international system, for all its enduring features, has changed dramatically since the end of the cold war as a result of the breakup of the Soviet Union, the rise of transnational threats to U.S. security, the impact of global economic investment and decision making, and the consequences of the information revolution. When changes of this magnitude occur, governments are tested in their relative abilities to monitor developments and act decisively in the national defense and diplomatic arenas. The U.S. government has begun the adaptation process. Over the past decade, the Pentagon has made military transformation an urgent priority in order to prepare for new adversaries, work with unfamiliar allies on unfamiliar terrain, apply rapidly changing technologies, and operate at a faster tempo.

The intelligence community is also making significant efforts to adapt to the new requirements of military modernization, changing communications architectures, rapidly evolving commercial imagery markets, and the rise of transnational threats. Terrorism prompted the 9/11 Commission to recommend greater centralization of authority—a proposal that has now been turned into a statutory requirement. The new leadership of the U.S. intelligence community is engaged in a government-wide effort to modernize the intelligence business. Just as modern war requires joint improvement of all services in a single enterprise, so intelligence must go beyond modernization within each agency to transformation of the whole. This volume seeks to support the newly appointed director of national intelligence in this mission of transformative change.

Second, the political context for intelligence transformation is propitious precisely because significant success has accompanied significant failure. The intelligence failure of Pearl Harbor combined with the intelligence successes of World War II provided the impetus and political will President Truman needed to create the CIA and the position of director of central intelligence in 1947. The stunning achievements of signals intelligence and covert operations against Germany and Japan convinced President Truman, Secretary of War Henry Stimson, and others that U.S. intelligence capabilities were so important that they required significant re-engineering. Similarly, today's successes against much of the leadership of al-Qaeda indicate that intelligence remains vital; they do not mean that intelligence is where it needs to be for the decades ahead. The question is whether there are ways to do the job of intelligence *significantly better* and whether we can implement those improvements before the political will to do so is lost.

Third, slow reform of foreign intelligence practices would be inconsistent with the dramatic changes under way in domestic intelligence. The U.S. government has created the Department of Homeland Security, the Northern Command, and, most recently, the National Counter Terrorism Center, three large new endeavors to protect the homeland through the use of national intelligence. If September 11 demonstrated that domestic and foreign intelligence must be linked, how can significant change in the U.S. intelligence business not be in store? U.S. citizens have been willing to accept much greater domestic surveillance, unexplained incarcerations, and significant inconvenience at airports because the government has suggested that, with such measures, intelligence collection and warning can be significantly improved. If this is true, then the U.S. intelligence system must make meaningful progress in handling significant new volumes of domestic intelligence for use at the local as well as the federal level. Old business practices will have to be transformed, or new tools for intelligence collection, including the new bureaucratic arrangements legislated in 2004, will not result in new capabilities to warn.

Although these arguments for the timeliness of intelligence transformation have much merit, they also suggest that workable proposals will be shaped by the times. Some intelligence experts have argued that the legislation signed into law in 2004 is deeply flawed. This may be true. The changes that this legislation requires, however, are the product of extensive debate and messy compromises, and this, simply put, is how representative democracies get things done. It is a beginning on which the U.S. government can and must build.

The Structure of the Book

The book is divided into three sections: new requirements, new capabilities, and management challenges. This structure reflects the nature of transformation, which requires, first, an understanding of U.S. national interests and the government's strategy for defending them; second, consideration of how technologies can be applied and policies modified to generate capabilities that significantly improve performance; and third, management practices that maximize the chances that improved capabilities will be applied in practice. The volume ends with a conclusion that draws together common themes and the study's most significant findings.

The authors are "insiders" in the sense that they have served in intelligence agencies, relevant parts of the State or Defense Department, and on the staffs of congressional oversight committees. Their experience as insiders has not blinded them to the need for change in intelligence programs, procedures, and policies; in fact, it has made them more acutely informed and determined to promote the kind of transformation that will enhance the security of the nation.

Although the book strives to be as comprehensive as possible, the topic is impossible to cover completely in a single volume. Inevitably some issues of pressing concern to intelligence professionals or theorists have been left out. However, the book does incorporate what, in the editors' view, are the most urgent issues of the day. The hope is that national debate on intelligence policies and reorganization will be enriched as a result.

Notes

1. Also known as the 9/11 Commission, the shortened name used throughout this volume.

2. In 1947 President Truman signed the National Security Act, thereby creating a centralized intelligence service and the position of director of central intelligence to oversee it.

3. See Paul R. Pillar, "Intelligence," in *Attacking Terrorism: Elements of a Grand Strategy*, ed. Audrey Kurth Cronin and James M. Ludes (Washington, D.C.: Georgetown University Press, 2004), 115–39.

4. National Commission on Terrorist Attacks upon the United States, *The 9/11 Commission Report: Final Report of the National Commission on Terrorist Attacks upon the United States* (New York: W. W. Norton, 2004), 339.

5. Although political scientists may be uncomfortable with the notion that art, as opposed to science, shapes business practice, the distinction is crucial. In intelligence, intuition, finesse, style, and imagination must coexist with discipline. This is true in the realm of human intelligence as well as in photoanalysis, cryptanalysis, and the best Foreign Service reporting.

PART ONE New Requirements

ONE # The Twenty-first Century Challenge for U.S. Intelligence

ERNEST R. MAY

FROM THE late 1940s to the late 1980s, the chief test of the quality of U.S. intelligence agencies was their capacity to gauge the capabilities and intentions of the Soviet Union and the People's Republic of China. Retrospective grading of the agencies' performance ranged from their own "OK" to Senator Daniel Patrick Moynihan's flat "F," based largely on their failure to forecast the collapse of the Soviet Union.

Moynihan's grade was too harsh. His criterion was too narrow. Year after year, the U.S. intelligence community had been right on the mark in counting, locating, and describing Soviet military forces capable of a nuclear strike against the U.S. homeland. Though they had not predicted that the Soviet empire would splinter at the end of the 1980s or that the Soviet Union itself would dissolve soon thereafter, they had done better than most nongovernmental Sovietologists—and better than Mikhail Gorbachev and his colleagues on the Soviet Politburo—in identifying weaknesses in the Soviet system and pointing to the possibility of eventual implosion.[1]

"OK" was, however, too generous if applied to overall performance. U.S. intelligence agencies had not done very well at detecting or appraising Soviet military forces other than those positioned for a nuclear strike against the United States. They had failed time and time again to forecast accurately what the Soviet government intended to do. Sometimes this was because a minority in the Politburo overruled the better judgment of its majority, as was the case with the decision to invade Afghanistan in 1979. At other times it was because the agencies' leaders failed to notice or trust information already in their hands, as, for example, in 1980–81, when they persisted in predicting that the Soviets themselves would crack down on Poland instead of leaving it to the Poles to deal with Solidarity. In the case of China, the community had patted itself on the back for predicting accurately that country's first test of a nuclear device, only to learn from a postmortem that it had been wrong about every aspect of the test but its timing.[2] The net performance of the U.S. intelligence community in dealing with major cold war threats probably merits a grade somewhere between B and C.

The Post–Cold War Policy Challenge

Between the fall of the Berlin Wall in 1989 and the terrorist attacks of September 11, 2001, U.S. intelligence agencies faced a very different set of tests. Not only were they challenged to pass judgment on subjects other than the strategic nuclear threat from a rival superpower; they found themselves having to answer to a larger and more varied group of consumers within the "policy community" and to do so during a period of dizzying technological change.

In 1990–91 the chief test for the community had to do with the crisis in the Persian Gulf occasioned by Iraq's invasion of Kuwait. In the past, the community would have been expected to speak mostly about the intentions of Moscow. No longer. Now collectors and analysts had to size up Saddam Hussein as someone acting outside the earlier bipolar framework.

While questions about China continued to be very much those that the community had prepared itself to answer during the cold war, other questions about Asia were new. In particular, intelligence officers were asked about North Korea, not as a pawn between Moscow and Beijing but as an independent power potentially armed with nuclear weapons. They also had to report on and analyze internal conflicts in Pakistan and India and possibilities for a clash between these nations—a clash that after 1998 would be one between two nations that had both tested nuclear weapons.

Similarly, U.S. intelligence agencies found themselves presented with questions about Africa that no longer involved Soviet or Communist maneuvers among African factions but concerned conditions in Africa itself and the dispositions and intentions of indigenous African leaders. In 1993 they were challenged to help U.S. Special Forces trying to get aid to suffering Somalis despite opposition from the country's tribal chieftains. Soon afterward, they had to assess for U.S. policymakers massacres approaching genocide in Rwanda and baffling back-and-forth competition among would-be successors to Mobuto Sese Seko in Zaire.

Even regarding Europe, the questions coming to U.S. intelligence agencies were different from those of the past. From the early 1990s until the end of the decade, these agencies had to focus on following and interpreting events within a disintegrating Yugoslavia. First with regard to Bosnia, then to Kosovo, they had not only to assist U.S. negotiators but also to help U.S. and North Atlantic Treaty Organization (NATO) commanders choose the right targets for air operations and the right mixture of forces for peacekeeping. Meanwhile, they had to field questions about European countries formerly dealt with primarily as Soviet satellites and about former Soviet republics, which they had previously all but ignored.

Western Europe itself became a different target for collection and analysis, for policymakers' questions no longer concerned cooperation against the Soviet Union. Instead these questions had to do with prospects for the European Union's becoming an economic and political competitor and with rumors of European industrial espionage.

On top of many changes in the character of U.S. regional concerns was the emergence of the drastically altered problem that would later become the dominant one—terrorism. The community had concerned itself marginally with terrorism during the 1970s and 1980s. A good deal of both collection and analysis had, however, focused on the Soviet role. Libya's role in the Berlin disco bombing of 1986 came to light largely because Libya had worked hand in hand with the German Democratic Republic, and the United States was collecting signals intelligence in East Germany as part of the coverage of the Soviet target.

The first World Trade Center bombing, in 1993, signaled the rise of a new kind of terrorism, not sponsored by any state, not directed toward any particular political end, but intended just to kill as many Americans as possible. By the late 1990s the community had not only recognized this new problem but had also identified Osama bin Laden as the financier and organizer of an international Islamist terrorist network. After the bombing of U.S. embassies in Kenya and Tanzania in August 1998, Director of Central Intelligence (DCI) George Tenet proclaimed this terrorism the highest priority for the community. The events of September 11, 2001, made it the highest priority issue for the nation.

The decade and a half following the end of the cold war thus put before the U.S. intelligence community a whole range of issues different from those of the cold war era. They called for collection on and analysis of governments, most of which had not been important cold war targets. They called also for collection on and analysis of nongovernmental organizations, particularly in the Muslim world. The community had to reorient some of its collection platforms. It had to develop others anew. Most of all, it had to take a workforce skilled at studying the Soviet Union and strategic weaponry and, by a combination of retraining, new recruitment, and managerial stimulation, give it the skills needed for dealing with altogether different sets of problems.

New Customers—and an Emphasis on Military Operations

Difficult in the best of circumstances, this massive reorientation was made particularly hard by a concurrent change in the population of intelligence consumers. During most of the cold war era, the assiduous readers of intelligence within the U.S. government had been mostly diplomatic negotiators or, in the Pentagon, civilians and military officers preoccupied either with budget planning or with high-level war planning.

This changed with the Gulf War of 1991. From the beginning of time, operational military commanders have wanted to know what was "on the other side of the hill." Improvements in capacity to collect imagery from satellites, combined with improvements in communication between collectors of imagery and collectors of signals intelligence, made it technically possible by 1991 for the U.S. intelligence community to put together actual pictures of the enemy facing U.S. forces opposite Kuwait. The problem was that they could assemble these pictures in Washington but not get them quickly to U.S. commanders in the field.

General Norman Schwarzkopf, in overall charge of operations for the Gulf War, was not known for his even temper. "Stormin' Norman" unleashed on one and all his fury that these pictures were not arriving on the battlefield in real time. Improvisation improved matters somewhat. After the Gulf War the management of the military establishment insisted that managers in the intelligence community give very high priority to technical and organizational improvements, providing future battlefield commanders with the real-time tactical intelligence that Schwarzkopf had demanded. On Capitol Hill, the armed services committees supported this demand even though, at the time, they were clipping the overall defense and intelligence budgets in order to provide a promised post–cold war "peace dividend."

Initially the intelligence community leadership put up resistance. Robert M. Gates, who became DCI under the first President Bush, had been a career analyst in the Central Intelligence Agency (CIA). As deputy national security advisor earlier in the Bush administration, he was intensely aware of how hard it had been for the community to answer new questions such as those about the former Soviet republics, India and Pakistan, and Iraq. He was intent on building new analytic capabilities, both substantial and methodological. The leaders of the intelligence oversight committees in the House and Senate had some sympathy for Gates's objective. But the DCI and the intelligence oversight committees are no match for the military establishment and the armed services committees.

The military establishment itself was in the midst of major internal change. The Goldwater-Nichols Act of 1986 had reduced the autonomy of the separate services, created strong incentives for interservice cooperation, and, among other things, greatly strengthened the chairman of the joint chiefs and the major field commanders in comparison with service chiefs and defense agency chiefs in Washington.[3] The combatant commanders, facing actual or potential operations in Africa, the Balkans, and the Korean peninsula as well as in the Persian Gulf region, put intense pressure on the chairman and the secretary of defense to skew spending for intelligence toward meeting their tactical needs.

After the 1992 presidential election, Gates was replaced by R. James Woolsey, then by John Deutch. Woolsey, who had chaired a study that recommended a new generation of reconnaissance satellites, made action on this recommendation his first priority. This irked senior managers at the CIA who thought personnel should take precedence. That Woolsey pursued his goal by allying himself with the combatant commanders and the armed services committees infuriated his congressional overseers. And his relations with President Clinton were so distant that when a protester landed a little plane on the south lawn of the White House, the joke in Washington was that it was Woolsey trying to get into the Oval Office.[4] Deutch, who had been deputy secretary of defense, made it no secret that his own primary interest remained the military establishment.

The next DCI, George Tenet, who had been Deutch's deputy, had seen the travails of the community first as a staffer, then as staff director for the Senate oversight committee, and, from 1993 to 1995, as senior director for intelligence programs on the National Security Council staff. He became DCI at just the time when the threat from Osama bin Laden and al-Qaeda began to be recognized as one that might match in urgency the threats faced by combatant commanders in the Balkans and elsewhere. Tenet gave priority to rebuilding the CIA's clandestine service.

Having only marginal influence over Defense Department spending for intelligence, Tenet could divert no more than a trickle of funds to serve his own priority. In 2004, long after the terrorist attacks of 2001 had released a flood of new resources for intelligence, Tenet said publicly that the CIA was still five years away from having adequate capability for collecting human intelligence even on its number-one target.[5]

The Technological Challenge

The combination of a rash of new issues and pressure to emphasize tactical military intelligence could alone have been a crippling challenge for the intelligence community. But even if these two challenges had not existed — if the end of the cold war had been postponed for a decade or more and the community had continued to concentrate on the strategic threat from the Soviet Union — the U.S. intelligence community would have found itself struggling with potentially overwhelming problems resulting from technological and technology-driven changes.

Because "information revolution" and "digital revolution" have become such trite phrases, we easily forget how real their results have been. At the beginning of the 1980s, high-powered computation still occurred mostly on mainframes owned and operated by large organizations, with the Defense Department's National Security Agency (NSA) far ahead of all others not only in computational capacity but in research and development. The NSA attracted many of the best mathematicians and programmers in the country. By the turn of the millennium, college students were using personal computers that stored as much data as the NSA had possessed two decades earlier. The Internet had become a medium for global transfer of information on a scale not previously imagined. And right behind the Internet came the cellular telephone, soon so popular that shopping malls began to seem like huge telephone booths.

The implications for intelligence collectors and analysts were obvious and terrifying.

The NSA, swamped with data even in the 1980s, had to try to track communications expanding annually by orders of magnitude, much of it traveling through media previously unfamiliar to the agency's technicians. The agency was hard put to keep up not only with the flow of signals but with techniques of encryption, given that private concerns also spent money to protect their transmissions. General Michael Hayden, the director of the NSA, complained to Congress in 2002 that the terrorist networks the agency was trying to penetrate were the beneficiaries of the $3 trillion global communications industry.[6]

The problem for agencies acquiring imagery was not quite as great, but neither was it trivial. Private concerns and foreign governments put up satellites, acquired imagery, and sold this imagery on the open market. Even if the imagery acquired by the combined resources of the National Reconnaissance Office (NRO) and the National Geospatial-Intelligence Agency (NGA) was of higher resolution, and even if the paths of U.S. reconnaissance satellites remained secret (which was not always the case), the publicly available imagery gave other governments and terrorist organizations useful clues as to how to hide their activities or achieve misdirection. Both India and Pakistan succeeded in concealing from the United States their preparations for the nuclear tests conducted in May 1998.

And it should be said that the changes also affected collectors of human intelligence in the CIA and the Defense Department, for imagery and especially signals intelligence often provide critical leads for officers in the field. This is so much the case that the NSA's General Hayden has hinted that human and signals intelligence ought perhaps to be combined within a single organization.[7]

The Challenge of Open Sources

The revolutionary character of technological changes obviously affected the ability of intelligence collectors to serve their various customers within the U.S. government. The volume of "take" by the NSA and the NRO became less and less manageable. The meaning of signals became less and less intelligible as information arrived in languages that few analysts commanded.

Worst of all, perhaps, the galloping information revolution strained the capacity of the intelligence community to perform its traditional function of providing policymakers with information and analysis not obtainable from open sources. Intelligence officers had long traded on their ability to give policymakers useful items of gossip not to be found in the morning newspapers. Elliott Richardson, undersecretary of state in the Nixon administration, once described to me the morning briefings he received from the department's Bureau of Intelligence and Research. He said that an analyst would usually put before him some juicy item of information, "like a cat depositing a mouse."

But these items tended to open doors for intelligence analysts, gaining them entrée to present their reflections on issues of the moment.

Satellite news collection, the proliferation of newscasts, the ferocity of competition among providers of spot news, and the extent to which post–cold war policy issues called for expertise not reserved to intelligence agencies—all these factors made it difficult for the intelligence community to muster any comparative advantage as information gatherers, on the one hand, or to devote time and talent to long-term analysis, as opposed to simple reportage, on the other. No single piece of evidence illustrates the plight of the intelligence community better than the fact that, as international terrorism came to figure among major security threats, most of the community's products concerning terrorism consisted of essentially unevaluated threat reportage. Before September 11, the most recent comprehensive analysis of the terrorist threat was a national intelligence estimate published in July 1995.[8]

Prospects

The challenge that this book addresses is thus formidable and becoming more serious almost by the day. But this introductory essay would be incomplete if it ended on what must seem an unhopeful note, for two other facts that readers need to bear in mind are, first, that the agencies making up the U.S. intelligence community have shown considerable resilience and adaptability in the past, and, second, that the United States has shown on more than one occasion capacity for rapidly reshaping its governmental institutions.

Indeed, adaptability has characterized modern U.S. intelligence institutions since their origin. Most of the U.S. intelligence community was *not* created for the cold war; its component agencies came into being to fight other wars or deal with other circumstances. The CIA had its origins in World War II. Until then, the United States had had no civilian intelligence agency. Some of President Franklin Roosevelt's friends pleaded with him to set up something resembling Britain's Secret Intelligence Service (MI-6). He turned to J. Edgar Hoover and asked Hoover to expand the Federal Bureau of Investigation (FBI), which Hoover did. The FBI first of all took on domestic security and counterespionage functions similar to those of Britain's Security Service (MI-5). Then Hoover established a U.S. Secret Intelligence Service, which fanned out across Latin America looking for Axis agents and links between Latin American governments and Germany, Italy, or Japan. But Roosevelt characteristically decided to create a new Office of Strategic Services (OSS) to be the U.S. MI-6 and to overlap with the FBI. Hoover, who never cooperated with anyone if he could help it, kept Latin America but left the rest of the world to the OSS, meanwhile guarding against OSS poaching on his internal security preserve.[9]

The OSS actually included not only a copy of MI-6 — in its Secret Intelligence Branch (SI) — but also, in its Secret Operations Branch (SO), a copy of Britain's new Special Operations Executive (SOE), created by Prime Minister Winston Churchill to "set Europe ablaze." The SI, like MI-6, recruited spies. The SO aided resistance groups, conducted sabotage operations, and sought actively to disrupt the enemy. In addition, the OSS had its own distinctive research and analysis branch (R&A), in which scholars, many of them refugees, pored over intelligence reports and information of all types in order to help the U.S. government select targets in enemy territory, analyze enemy vulnerabilities, and prepare for problems that would follow the termination of hostilities.[10]

President Truman disbanded the OSS in 1945. Two years later, as the cold war commenced, he began to bring it back into existence as the CIA. With the Korean conflict of the early 1950s, it came to be a large, well-funded, permanent part of the U.S. government. But it remained the OSS's recognizable child. Its directorate of plans (later renamed directorate of operations) combined the OSS's SI and SO branches. Its directorate of intelligence descended directly from OSS's R&A branch. The only part of the CIA created specifically for the cold war was a directorate of science and technology set up in 1963 primarily to exploit and build upon the U-2, the CORONA satellite program, and other breakthroughs in overhead reconnaissance.

Flexibility and the Capacity for Change

The CIA was not only derived from a World War II agency that reshaped itself to fight the cold war, it adapted fairly nimbly to changes in the cold war itself and in the government of which it was part. In the 1950s the CIA's analysis centered on the Soviet economy. Its chief assignment was to calculate whether the Soviets could actually produce and field the military hardware ascribed to it in threat analyses prepared by the intelligence services of the armed forces and of U.S. allies. Because of Soviet secrecy and deception, the data available on the Soviet economy were sparse and unreliable, and the CIA made some wrong guesses from which stemmed later gross misestimates of Soviet economic capabilities. Nonetheless, the CIA's economic models were innovative and imaginative and, for a time, yielded better figures about some aspects of the Soviet economy than those used by Soviet economic planners.[11]

At the end of the 1950s, President Dwight Eisenhower gave the CIA a new assignment as honest broker to sift competing estimates of the Soviet strategic threat produced by service intelligence agencies. Though the CIA initially produced simple split-the-difference estimates, it quickly and very successfully adapted to the new role. Though it was found in the 1960s to be overestimating, and in the 1970s to be underestimating, future Soviet force levels, its annual national intelligence estimates provided highly accurate data on the numbers and locations of Soviet intercontinental-range bombers and missiles.

In the 1970s the CIA began to broaden its portfolio. The U.S. abandonment of Vietnam, together with President Richard Nixon's pursuit of "détente" and West Germany's "Ostpolitik," seemed to signal stabilization in the cold war. At the same time, hearings by the Church and Pike committees, accompanied by energetic "investigative journalism," publicized failed and questionable covert operations of the cold war.[12] The CIA began to emphasize collection and analysis on new subjects such as energy and the environment. Operationally, it shifted from being risk-prone to being risk-averse.

These changes did not last. Soviet adventures in Africa, the Soviet invasion of Afghanistan in 1979, Soviet efforts to promote an antinuclear campaign in Europe, and the election of Ronald Reagan to the presidency in 1980 served to bring the cold war back in full force. Reagan's DCI, William Casey, was a veteran of the OSS's SO branch. He wanted the agency to fight Communists as SO and SOE had fought the Nazis. To some extent he succeeded, with the result that the end of the cold war found the CIA an organization that seemed fit for little more than contests with the Soviet Union and Communist China. But the fact is that the CIA was not only a creature of World War II but also an agency that had changed itself many times during the cold war. Its history suggests that it should be able to cope with the challenges of the twenty-first century, provided that it receives enough resources and managerial direction to overcome problems created by military demands for tactical intelligence, the continuing information and digital revolutions, and its own tendency to compete with news organizations rather than to stress its comparative advantage in longer-term and contextual analysis.

The NSA has roots deeper in history than the CIA does. It grew out of military and naval cryptological services that originated in the nineteenth century and that enjoyed a kind of golden age in the interwar years, when navy and army cryptographers *both* cracked Japan's most secret codes. After investigations of the Pearl Harbor attack revealed that the navy and army had failed to correlate their work, the cryptologists were put together in 1947 into an Armed Forces Security Agency, which then became the NSA in 1952. Though not without difficulty, the NSA adapted to changes in the cold war, collecting signals wherever the action of the moment happened to be and devising new methodologies as problems changed.

The State Department's Bureau of Intelligence and Research can be traced back to a group of OSS castoffs housed in the department during the interval between the abolition of the OSS and the creation of the CIA. The intelligence organization of the Department of Energy descends from a similar organization attached to the World War II Manhattan Project. And so on. Only the NRO and NGA were created for the cold war, but their capabilities were obviously not suited only to the contest with the Soviet Union. Hence it can be said generally that U.S. intelligence agencies were not designed exclusively for the cold war and that their histories indicate a healthy capacity to adapt to new circumstances.

Most of the balance of this book concerns the question of what it will take for the intelligence community as a whole to fit itself for the extraordinary conditions of the present. The point cannot be made too strongly or too often that the answer to this question will depend, in the end, not on the intelligence community but on Congress and the public —a subject discussed at greater length in a subsequent chapter. As just noted, most of the community exists because the nation created intelligence services as part of a massive response to the challenge from the Axis powers in World War II. These agencies were transformed—both in structure and practice—into cold war agencies as the nation responded to the challenge from Communism and the Soviet Union. The question now is whether the nation responds to the challenges symbolized by the September 11 attacks with comparable exertion and innovation.

Notes

1. See Douglas J. MacEachin, *CIA Assessments of the Soviet Union: The Record Versus the Charges—An Intelligence Monograph* (Washington, D.C.: Central Intelligence Agency, Center for the Study of Intelligence, 1996), available at www.cia.gov/csi/monograph/russia/3496toc.html.

2. See two other monographs by Douglas J. MacEachin, *Predicting the Soviet Invasion of Afghanistan: The Intelligence Community's Record* (Washington, D.C.: Center for the Study of Intelligence, Central Intelligence Agency, 2001), available at www.cia.gov/csi/monograph/afghanistan, and *U.S. Intelligence and the Polish Crisis, 1980–1981* (Washington, D.C.: Center for the Study of Intelligence, Central Intelligence Agency, 2001), available at www.cia.gov/csi/books/poland/index.htm. On misestimates regarding China's nuclear test, see Willis C. Armstrong, William Leonhart, William J. McCaffrey, and Herbert C. Rothenberg, "The Hazards of Single-Outcome Forecasting," *Studies in Intelligence* 28 (fall 1964): 57–70, reproduced in *Inside CIA's Private World: Declassified Articles from the Agency's Internal Journal, 1955–1992*, ed. H. Bradford Westerfield (New Haven: Yale University Press, 1995), 238–54.

3. See Gordon Nathaniel Lederman, *Reorganizing the Joint Chiefs of Staff: The Goldwater-Nichols Act of 1986* (Westport, Conn.: Greenwood Press, 1999).

4. See Philip Heymann, Howard Husock, Esther Scott, and Amy Tarr, "James Woolsey and the CIA: The Aldrich Ames Spy Case" (Harvard University, John F. Kennedy School of Government Case Program, Case No. 1339), available at www.ksgcase.harvard.edu/case.htm?PID=1339.

5. National Commission on Terrorist Attacks upon the United States, Hearing, April 13, 2004, 34–35, available at www.9/11commission.gov/hearings/hearing10.htm.

6. 107th Cong., 2d sess., S. Rep. 107-351, H. Rep. 107-792, *Joint Inquiry into Intelligence Community Activities before and after the Terrorist Attacks of September 11, 2001* (December 2002), 368–69, available at www.gpoaccess.gov/serialset/creports/911.html.

7. Ibid., 75–76.

8. National Commission on Terrorist Attacks upon the United States, *The 9/11 Commission Report: Final Report of the National Commission on Terrorist Attacks upon the United States* (New York: W. W. Norton, 2004), 341–42.

9. G. Gregg Webb, "The FBI and Foreign Intelligence: New Insights into J. Edgar Hoover's

Role," *Studies in Intelligence* 48, no. 1 (2004): 45–58, available at www.cia.gov/csi/studies/vol48no1/index.html.

10. Barry M. Katz, *Foreign Intelligence: Research and Analysis in the Office of Strategic Services, 1942–1945* (Cambridge: Harvard University Press, 1989).

11. Maurice C. Ernst, "Economic Intelligence in CIA," *Studies in Intelligence* 28 (winter 1984): 1–22, reproduced in Westerfield, *Inside CIA's Private World*, 305–29.

12. The Church and Pike special investigating committees were created by Congress in 1975, largely in response to revelations of CIA involvement in the overthrow of Chilean president Salvador Allende. After investigating allegations of intelligence agency wrongdoings, they recommended greater congressional oversight of the intelligence community and to this end created the Senate Select Committee on Intelligence in 1976 and the House Permanent Select Committee on Intelligence in 1977. See L. Britt Snider, *Sharing Secrets with Lawmakers: Congress as a User of Intelligence* (Washington, D.C.: Center for the Study of Intelligence, 1997), available at www.cia.gov/csi/monograph/lawmaker/toc.htm.

TWO   Understanding Friends and Enemies
The Context for American Intelligence Reform

Jennifer E. Sims

Throughout modern history, failures to identify adversaries and their strategems have handicapped states, contributed to miscalculations among statesmen, and heightened risks of war. In contrast, artful intelligence, including the capacity to distinguish friends from enemies and to design appropriate intelligence programs, has arguably proved stabilizing. During the cold war, each side's ability to develop effective collection and analytic programs to monitor the other helped clarify intent and discourage strategic war.

Distinguishing friends from enemies has, in turn, required good knowledge of technological, sociological, military, and political trends. Since the mid-nineteenth century, striking changes have occurred in these domains as the Industrial Revolution began to reshape warfare. The invention of the high-speed rotary press in 1819, which allowed the prolific production of written orders and the distribution of national newspapers, led to the creation of general staffs, including intelligence officers who could steal archived documents or learn enemy troop movements from civilian reporters. Mass production and standardized parts led to the equipping of large land armies. Monitoring factories and railways became useful for determining weapons production rates, military readiness, and belligerent intent.

Communications such as the telegraph and telephone expanded rapidly, increasing the capacity of senior civilians and generals to assert control over decisions relevant to the field. As technology put more power and control into the hands of governments, changing how they organized for war, intelligence services increasingly targeted private industry and national leaders to discern states' intentions in war and peace. By 1900 London had laid thousands of miles of communications cables and was, by the end of World War I, adept at listening in on them. By World War II, communications were mostly encrypted, wireless radios offered networking and mobility for spies and saboteurs, radar had been invented, and aerial photography had overcome its last technical hurdles.

Indeed, technology had changed so fast by 1945, and intelligence had played such a large role in Allied victory, that one participant, R. V. Jones, famously called World War II "the Wizard War."[1] Intelligence services that had mastered the challenges of such new technologies had distinct advantages. Those not paying attention were either deceived or vulnerable.

This chapter will discuss some of these broad technological, sociological, and political trends as context for U.S. intelligence policy in the twenty-first century. Its purpose, which is to explain the likely intelligence challenges ahead, will set the stage for the next chapter, which discusses the opportunities and limits built into the U.S. intelligence community's capacity to respond. Although the features of domestic context and international environment highlighted in these chapters are not the only ones that intelligence reform should address, they are arguably the most important. They are also controversial, because the underlying premises relate to definitions of hotly disputed terms, judgments regarding American culture, and a central paradox of U.S. intelligence policy few wish to acknowledge: that laws must be broken overseas if they are to be preserved at home. As democracies cope with the era of globalization, this intelligence paradox has become more confusing and painful. This chapter therefore offers a rather particular—some might say provocative—argument about the prospects for American intelligence reform.

Understanding the Playing Field: Toward a Theory of Intelligence

One fundamental premise is that intelligence cannot usefully be reformed without a good grasp of the theory behind what intelligence is or should be about. Good theory helps one understand causation and thus should, in the intelligence context, help identify the sources of success and failure before they occur. Unfortunately, intelligence theory is in its infancy—even definitions are contentious. Yet this chapter is built on the notion, argued elsewhere, that "intelligence" is best understood as the collection, analysis, and dissemination of information on behalf of national security decision makers. Decision makers are, by this and almost any other definition, integral to its function.[2]

In theory, decision makers may conduct their own intelligence or be deeply engaged in its management—as were Britain's Winston Churchill during World War II and General George Washington during the American Revolution. In practice, the wisest decision makers often distance themselves so as to gain efficiency and objectivity; they recognize that intelligence analysis should appropriately adjust, not reflect, their own predilections and prejudices. Such distancing may enhance the performance of an intelligence service but, taken too far, can also lead to mutual mistrust and failure between intelligence analyst and decision maker. Therefore, a high-quality intelligence process balances investment and direction from decision makers with unbiased collection and analysis.

A second premise is implied by the first: the most important immediate measure of success for any intelligence service is not the number of secrets it collects or the truth of the analyses it generates, but rather the timeliness, efficiency, and accuracy with which it supports national security decision making. Intelligence helps decision makers by acquiring and analyzing information that adversaries want to withhold in the interest of security—in other words, secrets. Yet, correctly designed, an intelligence service is not based on the assumption that competitors are protecting their most vital information, which may be leaked to the press or made publicly available out of ignorance or technological evolution, as was much of the information on the critical infrastructure of the United States before September 11.

Officials of an optimized intelligence service neither presume that the adversary's collection capabilities are limited to the functions of its publicly acknowledged intelligence institutions nor believe that an adversary's most precious secrets are, in fact, secret. These officials do not value information according to the difficulty with which it was acquired but according to its relevance and timeliness to the decision at hand.[3] Their purpose is to gain "decision advantages" for political leaders, diplomats, military commanders, and other U.S. government officials in order to secure the country's interests in both peace and war.

Given this definition of intelligence, diagnosing intelligence ills by examining only the interaction of those collectors and analysts carrying "intelligence" in their titles would be a mistake. One flaw of past commissions that have looked into U.S. intelligence problems has been the failure to examine what may be termed the "nonintelligence" sources of intelligence failure. Managers outside the intelligence community may be responsible for intelligence gaps arising from uncoordinated reductions in Foreign Service reporting or the purchasing of commercial imagery or underfunded research at the Department of Energy's national laboratories. In fact, the problems posed by the expanding pool of relevant information on matters of health, crime, and industry touch vital and sensitive matters of intelligence sharing, intelligence liaison, and counterintelligence policy that intelligence professionals alone cannot solve.

Third, intelligence fails when it does not improve—or, worse, degrades—the decision process it is supporting relative to that of its adversary. The retrospective measure of any intelligence service is its success in gaining insight into its adversaries' plans, intentions, and capabilities and providing advance warning of their intent to the appropriate officials. When an intelligence system fails to do this, it warrants review—even if that system has generally been accurate and timely in supporting decision makers' expressed needs. While this review may not, and perhaps should not, involve second-guessing of the policy choices made, it should make allowances for the limits of what intelligence can do if the decision-making process is flawed. If decision makers are unskilled as intelligence users, they will have difficulty gaining the advantage over U.S. adversaries no matter how good collection and analysis may be. Decision makers are part of the intelligence process; intelligence failures implicate them as well.

For example, decision makers often say they want warnings when they actually do not. Warnings usually imply a need to reorder priorities, including the allocation of resources.

Even good leaders dislike revisiting policy decisions, particularly those based on carefully derived judgments about an adversary's capabilities and intentions. An intelligence system unable to sustain collection against targets that would indicate that decision makers or their policies are wrong is an intelligence system unable to warn and therefore ripe for failure. That said, decision makers who receive warnings but do not shift course are themselves responsible for the failure to collect and analyze intelligence against emerging threats. A responsive, budgetarily constrained intelligence system cannot be very effective if it is not synchronized with the plans of the decision makers it supports.

The heart of intelligence, then, is not in the plumbing for getting raw data from the collector to the appropriate user. It is rather the enabling of appropriate action over time. Intelligence so defined includes support not just for today's decision maker but for tomorrow's. This point deserves emphasis. In support of complex democratic governments, successful intelligence must include a process for strategic collection against future threats and the analysis of macrotrends such that management choices can be made for the next several administrations. Thus a Democratic president successfully handled the Cuban missile crisis using an intelligence infrastructure designed and built in the early 1950s under a Republican president, Dwight Eisenhower. From this perspective the failures of September 11 were not so much failures of current intelligence but failures in long-standing strategic design.

Protecting the intelligence infrastructure for tomorrow's decision makers also means, however, that intelligence professionals must try to prevent the kind of blowback that occurs when the intelligence business goes awry—as a result of either substandard performance or overreach. This point is particularly important for democracies such as the United States during periods of high threat and aggressive intelligence reform. The need to preserve good capabilities while adjusting to new requirements raises several immediate questions about recent reforms. For example, if one of the most important requirements for future U.S. intelligence performance will be the delegation of decision making to networked intelligence professionals in the field, then how will the new intelligence chief empower these officials while providing expedited accountability for their actions?

All this leads to a fourth premise. Successful U.S. intelligence policy must conform to the requirements of American political culture and its requirements for legal restraint and accountability. If it does not, it will not work and cannot last.

Indeed, the analysis in this and the succeeding chapter will show that American national interest in the twenty-first century involves a paradox: to win against terrorists, transnational criminals, and proliferators of weapons of mass destruction (WMD), Washington will need to strengthen other states' democratic systems and the rule of law on which they are based, while at the same time undermining that system of laws wherever and whenever necessary to collect intelligence against those who would sponsor or harbor criminal elements and terrorists. Successful transformation of U.S. intelligence will require the creative ability to hold these two contradictory imperatives in mind—not only within the intelligence profession but within the broader American polity as well. The next chapter will show that U.S. political culture makes this task doable, though very risky.

To examine this challenge in depth, let us briefly review the international environment and its likely evolution over the next few decades. For the fifth and final premise is that, dramatic as the challenge of al-Qaeda's Islamist terrorism is, it would be wrong to reshape the intelligence system of the United States exclusively on the basis of what has been learned from the September 11 attacks.

The International Context

Only a brief discussion of the international context for intelligence is possible here. The trends selected are those most likely to affect how people will organize, cooperate, compete, and fight—in other words, where, when, and by whom important decisions will be made. They are, therefore, directly connected to the premises outlined above.

The essential point is that, for the first time since the creation, in 1947, of a standing U.S. intelligence establishment, U.S. national security policy has been pulled loose from the moorings of consensus on national security priorities. Containment of communism has given way to competing purposes that range from energy security to the promotion of democracy abroad, stability in the Middle and Far East, counterproliferation, and counterterrorism. While U.S. vital interests and the purposes of intelligence may be unchanging, the threats to those interests and thus national intelligence priorities are not.

Fluidity in national security policies poses special challenges for intelligence because intelligence must be focused on policymakers' priorities, geared to the right decision makers (perhaps a local police officer, a diplomat, or an F-16 pilot), and shaped to suit the types of decisions they are likely to make. Herein lies one of the U.S. government's greatest intelligence challenges, for the building of a sound intelligence capability will require that managers identify key decision makers and constantly calibrate and recalibrate support among them in response to rapidly changing needs over the next fifteen to twenty years. The priorities of a diverse and rapidly changing set of intelligence users must be not only discerned but anticipated.

Difficult as this task may be, it is not impossible. Although U.S. security policy may be fluid, the broad trends with which it will have to cope are clear: accelerated mobility of people, information, and capital; the growth of networked and transnational organizations; individuals' increased access to WMD; and the persistence of conflict and war among states. Future U.S. security strategies will have to deal with these trends; intelligence will need to understand and work with them.

NETWORKS, CLUSTERING, AND TRANSNATIONAL ACTORS

"Globalization" is a process arising from the combined effects of the communications revolution and the mobility of capital and technology and their effects on international politics.[4] These effects cut both ways. On the one hand, trade is flourishing; on the other hand, as industries extend themselves overseas, their national corporate identities fade and the provenance, security, and quality of their products become less well understood by those who purchase them. As Jim Gosler points out in chapter six, these changes present new opportunities for technology-based spying and information warfare, while at the same time complicating their inherent risks. As rich and poor countries profit from expanded trade, those in the middle, with neither cheap capital nor cheap labor, may lose out.[5] Preoccupied as we now are with failed states, we may be facing rising domestic and interstate conflict in what might be called the middle realm of the international system.

Yet perhaps of most interest from an intelligence standpoint has been the increased availability of information to the moderately affluent who have access to the Internet. This access has increased the potential power of politically motivated individuals by an order of magnitude. People can collect data, make decisions, broadcast their views, and find like-minded people relatively quickly using networks, weblogs, and websites. Furthermore, they can do so anywhere, any time, and in multimedia formats using cell phones and personal digital assistants. To grasp the significance of this change, consider ten days in the fall of 2004. On September 14 a blogger wrote that Bic pens could be used to pick Kryptonite Evolution 2000 U-locks; by September 19, 1.8 million people had seen the posting; by September 22 the Kryptonite Corporation had been forced to spend $10 million redressing the problem.[6] This vignette captures the point: transnational organizations involving traders, narcotics agents, smugglers, and spies have long existed; what is new is the capability of transnational groups rapidly to coalesce and expand by both serendipity and design. In the speed, scope, and fluidity of the decision making involved, this phenomenon is unprecedented.[7]

The nature of the groups that are forming in this way is somewhat surprising. Studies of Internet users have found that the propensity to network on the Web may start randomly but soon leads to the "clustering" of like-minded people.[8] Clustering may increase the total amount of information available to members through pooling of data. But because this information tends to be biased, it does not necessarily increase the rationality of members' decisions. In fact, clustering actually seems to cause people to harden in their views, as they seek and receive affirmation from the other members of the cluster, many of whom have even stronger views. When discouraged from exchanges with "outsiders" that might stabilize and moderate their thinking, clustered individuals are prone to networked groupthink and precipitous action. Whether organizing protests against the World Trade Organization, demonstrations against landmines, or an attack on the U.S.

electrical grid, interest groups now have the capability rapidly to become action groups capable of surgical interventions.[9] When employed with hostile intent, this new empowerment of individuals and nonstate networks, relative to large institutions and the state, is what is meant in part by the term "asymmetric threat."

The actions these groups pursue are, moreover, enabled by a commercial sector marketing technologies such as robotics, encryption, artificial intelligence, and personalized global communications. These cutting-edge industries are thriving in both civilian and military markets. For example, remote-controlled robots have been deployed by the U.S. government as fighters in Iraq, while commercially available robots are mowing lawns, sweeping floors, and taking out the trash—soon perhaps, given improvements in artificial intelligence, without being asked. Not surprisingly, the industry is expected to triple to $15 billion by 2010.[10]

Yet the most provocative technological changes from an intelligence standpoint may be those hardest to see. As Roy Want, a principal engineer at Intel Research/CTG, has written, "The most profound technologies are those that disappear. They weave themselves into the fabric of everyday life until they are indistinguishable from it."[11] A good example, cited by Want, is radio frequency identification technology (RFID), which is already being used to automate toll payments and track consumer purchases. Buildings modified to become environmentally efficient, to perform services for occupants and to adapt to their needs, are becoming smart enough to handle emergencies, provide status reports on their structural integrity after a terrorist attack, and direct first responders along the safest paths to victims.

Such sophisticated capabilities evolve from advances in the miniaturization of energy sources, sensors, and inferencing programs. These underlying technologies, once embedded in applications, are all susceptible to unauthorized use. Moreover, these advances may be connected as technologies evolve that permit electronic devices to talk to one another. Imagine a building that can sense its environment, the habits and needs of its occupants, and its own structural integrity, and then make complex decisions to optimize all of these—such as opening and closing air vents or adjusting the timing of elevators.[12] Then imagine you are a spy and consider what you could learn from this building—or what you could do if you controlled it.

Some critics worry that such commercial advances in miniaturized surveillance, personal communications, and robotics will significantly threaten privacy by radically increasing the power of governments to monitor individuals. Others argue that security surveillance within the private sector has long been tolerated, and that in the wake of September 11 public tolerance for government monitoring is rising. In any case, the government's need to counter domestic terrorism could become the path by which such technology, increasingly embedded in the civilian sector for inventory control, security, and domestic services, becomes available for the government's use. Whether this will be a good or a bad thing will depend in part on the development of protocols for the handoff of local and private information to the federal level.

The need for governments to cooperate with the private sector is also growing because of shifts in the locus and nature of innovation. In the 1940s and 1950s massive government-driven projects, such as building satellites or going to the moon, led to new commercial applications or spin-offs ranging from orange juice substitutes to non-stick surfaces. Now, the reverse seems true. Government agencies are increasingly spinning off national security applications from innovative commercial technologies. U.S. civilian agencies are particularly hard pressed to frame requirements for technologies they can barely anticipate; thus their missions often derive from, rather than determine, commercial successes. Given that adversaries have access to commercial products, good counterintelligence will need the cooperation of private enterprise more than ever before.

Indeed, the speed and quality of the private sector's innovation has prompted the Central Intelligence Agency (CIA) to launch In-Q-Tel, a venture capital firm sponsoring advanced technologies that meet CIA needs but that, destined to be sold commercially, are available at lower prices than typical government procurements. In-Q-Tel may not, however, help the intelligence community see what it does not yet know it needs, and this may be its greatest problem. On September 11 terrorists took embedded, commercially available technologies — aircraft and box cutters — and used them in surprising ways. Individuals can see applications for advanced technologies, hijack them, and act more quickly than any government agency can.

Several observers have noted that this shift in the relationship of government to industry and individuals has substantial implications for national security. Whereas a state's capacity for mobilizing its infrastructure and protecting its interior lines of communication used to be decisive for beating its foes on the battlefield, now foes can bring the battlefield to the state by using embedded commercial technologies and the Internet. In this new world, innovations in global communications and surveillance potentially augment the intelligence capabilities of networked adversaries operating in the private sector—often before government users have access to or see the application for the same technology.[13] With burgeoning threats to the national information infrastructure, systems administrators are part of the first line of domestic defense.[14]

Thus "information warfare," in which adversaries compete to degrade each other's communications and databases, comes with a peculiar twist for advanced industrial states: it involves recognizing the importance of dominating the adversary with surprise and omniscience, while understanding that the systems one may have to penetrate and compromise may be one's own.[15] The corollary is that any effort to bolster the security of those publicly accessible systems potentially improves the counterintelligence capabilities of adversaries as well. The powerful confluence of these trends — the government's need for surveillance, industry's increasing capacity to provide it, and the private sector's impetus to install it — poses one of the most significant conundrums for the advancement of U.S. domestic intelligence and the protection of civil liberties.

WEAPONS OF MASS DESTRUCTION

The threat posed by transnational groups and particularly by terrorists with grievances against the modern secular state is increased not just by the ability they have to hijack Western technology but also by their ability to arm themselves. Commerce in civilian technologies with weapons applications, such as genetically engineered organisms, chemicals, chemical precursors, and nuclear energy, when combined with the vulnerability of WMD storage sites in the former Soviet Union, have provided dangerous options for individuals and groups.[16]

Along with retaining collection against states that violate controls on these dual-use commodities, such as those limited by the Chemical Weapons Convention or the Nuclear Non-Proliferation Treaty, intelligence will need to continue to collect unilaterally against suspect states so it can map the networks that traffic in these materials with the tacit, if not the explicit, endorsement of their governments. Pakistan presents a good example of the complexities that arise when an ally in the global war on terror also harbors trafficking kingpins, ballistic missile enterprise, and a dual-purpose nuclear program.

In this regard, one of the worst trends from an intelligence standpoint may be the slow gathering and securing of "loose" fissile material in the international system. Since the collapse of the Soviet state and the growth of the Internet, the materials and knowledge needed for constructing WMD have become increasingly available. According to the U.S. National Intelligence Council (NIC), weapons-usable material was stolen from Russian facilities on at least four occasions between 1992 and 1999.[17] Graham Allison has noted that there are "more than two hundred addresses around the world from which terrorists could acquire a nuclear weapon or the fissile material from which one could be made."[18] Allison also cites a February 2002 NIC report to Congress that states: "Undetected smuggling has occurred, although we do not know the extent or magnitude."[19] While vigorous efforts are under way to secure these materials, the pace of action may not be sufficient to achieve competitive advantages over those attempting to steal them. Common criminals who assist saboteurs and terrorists with smuggling, financing, document forgery, and other logistics, are no less adversaries than the transnationally organized shooters and bombers themselves. Cybercriminals, the latest variant of this group, specialize in surreptitious acquisition of credit card information and the theft of personal identities. They organize quickly and hide in the open: according to published reports, one ring of Russian and Ukrainian criminals stole more than 1 million credit card numbers, then offered to sell computer security services to their victims before being caught by the Federal Bureau of Investigation in March 2001.[20]

Complicit criminals may not fit our profile of terrorists, may not know whom they aid, and thus may not see themselves as part of the transnational organizations they serve. Their connections may even run deep within elite circles in foreign governments — even friendly ones. The connections between espionage, official corruption, terrorism, and common crime suggest that diversified cover will be required to work clandestinely against complex transnational targets, including terrorist ones.

THE PERSISTENCE OF STATES AND THE DIVERSIFICATION OF THEIR INTERESTS

The desire of terrorist groups to gain access to nuclear technology and their improved ability to gather intelligence and plot attacks would be of little concern if states were competent in securing their sensitive assets and borders. The chief problem, of course, is that certain critical states are not, particularly Russia and many of its bordering countries. The question is whether this problem is actually systemic in character. The prominence of such recent failed states as the Taliban's Afghanistan, the Congo, Haiti, Somalia, and Sudan seems to suggest that the state system is coming apart—at least at the margins. In fact, although theorists and policymakers have noted the rise of transnational organizations and asymmetric threats, the implicit corollary to these trends, the decline of the state, is less often discussed. If transnational threats are rising, it seems logical to assume that states must be relatively weakened.

Yet such a downward trend in the power of states is far from clear. In fact, the emergence of transnational threats to security has already begun to encourage the strengthening of state structures, lending them renewed popular legitimacy after the hiatus that followed the end of the cold war and the dissolution of the Soviet empire. This trend is obvious in the United States, Britain, and Australia, countries that have significantly increased governmental prerogatives in matters of homeland security. But it is also evident in other states threatened with internal unrest and disorder. Russia's president, Vladimir Putin, used the September 2004 terrorist attack on innocent schoolchildren and their teachers in Beslan to legitimize the reassertion of state power for the sake of order and security. Ukraine, Georgia, and Belarus have also taken recent steps to strengthen, for better or worse, the hand of the state.

Indeed, the impetus for building strong defenses is not just terrorism; it is the continuing threats states pose to each other in the classic competitive sense. Japan budgeted $45 billion for defense for 2004, the biggest increase since 1997, with the majority of funds going to counterterrorism and ballistic missile defense.[21] Japan's motivation for the latter was, in part, the continuing steep rise in Chinese military capabilities, including the increased number, accuracy, and mobility of its nuclear delivery systems. China's decisions seem, in turn, to be motivated largely by decisions made in the United States, Japan, and Taiwan.

Even the evolution of the European Union, which has experimented with modest forfeitures of sovereignty for the larger purpose of gaining collective economic and political power, has in practice involved the reaffirmation of member-state prerogatives as much as it has their compromise. Europe arguably pursues an aggregation of power at the regional level, not the weakening of member states. And it does so as much to counter the economic and political weight of the United States as to protect itself from transnational threats.[22]

The rise of Europe as a regional partner and counterweight to the United States raises the possibility that, in the next century, friends may be intelligence "targets," too. In truth, they have always been this to some degree and will probably forever remain so. Even Britain, the closest ally of the United States in the twentieth century, has used secret intelligence and special access to sway U.S. government decision making in the past — particularly before both world wars and in the creation of the U.S. intelligence establishment. And while European decision making is hardly opaque, assumptions that friendly countries such as France, Germany, and Spain will continue to delegate strategic decision making to Washington or come to the support of American policies when asked have already been largely undermined. Britain opposed the United States on certain issues during the war in Bosnia; France and Germany opposed the U.S. invasion of Iraq; and Spain withdrew from the coalition of forces in Iraq when its citizens elected a new government.

As Europe increases its economic and political power, its member states' actions and intentions may increasingly diverge from those of the United States. Friends, having long followed the U.S. lead on key issues, can also face traumatic choices the United States must anticipate in its collection strategies. Should Japan choose to develop a nuclear weapons capability in the wake of a nuclearized Korean peninsula, the United States will face a crisis of major dimensions in its foreign and national security policies toward the region. These are the kinds of developments that trigger war of the old-fashioned variety, involving large conventional forces engaged on traditional battlefields. Such warfare has not gone away, and neither must intelligence capabilities, including, especially, Foreign Service reporting and open-source collection that can anticipate and prevent it.

Indeed, intelligence managers need not reflexively resort to clandestine means against such friendly "targets." The U.S. government could augment Foreign Service representation and open-source collection out of embassies.[23] Clandestine collection, reserved for the most critical and difficult targets, may be most important for collection against super-empowered individuals in friendly countries. Europe is, in fact, the destination of most worldwide travel, with 329.3 million arrivals in 2004—almost three times as many as the next largest tourist magnet, Japan.[24]

Though the challenges of collecting intelligence on friends are impressive, they are not necessarily more daunting than the more traditional challenges intelligence faced during the cold war and still faces today: collecting against hostile governments and particularly hard targets. The latter include those states that keep a stranglehold on both their citizens and the information available to them. Impenetrable states such as North Korea and Iran pose continuing challenges for intelligence collectors. Pyongyang's decisions on its nuclear program and its transfers of fissile material and ballistic missiles threaten to destabilize the Far East and metastasize these instabilities elsewhere.

Without listing all the threats that emanate from the traditional state system, such enduring problems as India-Pakistan, Iran, the Middle East conflict, and Armenia-Azerbaijan suggest that the decisions of states are likely to remain central to U.S. national security policy and therefore to U.S. intelligence requirements. This will put additional pressure on intelligence to discern options for rewarding as well as punishing them. In this regard, intelligence on the disposition of natural resources may become more crucial than ever to state decision making and therefore to the effectiveness of U.S. diplomacy.

RESOURCE SCARCITY

The highly respected environmental historian J. R. McNeill has observed that environmental stresses are rising, increasing the potential for interstate competition over scarce resources such as oil and water.[25] But he has also noted that the international, administrative, and technological abilities of states to keep pace and to cope with these changes are rising at least as fast, making such issues less important than the more traditional priorities shaping the security of states.

If policymakers and intelligence officials were only passive players in such coping strategies, McNeill's analysis would be prescriptive and intelligence managers might relax. However, as suggested above, intelligence is an integral player in support of the very diplomacy that results in such conflict prevention. These diplomatic operations require that we understand the incentive structures of foreign governments, factions, and insurgent populations. Resources may play an increasing part in the calculations of foreign officials and serve as useful carrots to gain cooperation on a host of issues of more direct import to U.S. national security. Understanding foreign incentive structures, particularly in states facing domestic unrest and the popularization of terrorism, may increasingly require an understanding of the critical energy and water problems with which they are dealing and which so strongly affect their domestic populations, whose tolerance, if not outright support, they require to govern.

Conclusion: The Evolving International System and Its Implications for Intelligence

The international system that unfolds over the next few decades is likely to be highly volatile, and to include both strengthened states and increasingly agile and empowered transnational actors. In such a context U.S. decision makers will want to preserve the country's security by anticipating and countering threats while promoting liberty, open markets, and stability overseas. Intelligence must penetrate foreign countries to learn the intentions of individuals and governments while preserving, to the extent possible, the stability and laws that keep states both predictable and democratic.

In fact, despite concern about the rise of major states as competitors, the United States has a strong interest in preserving and bolstering the state system—liberal or not—against the erosion of rules caused by rapid technological and economic change. This fundamentally conservative objective may on occasion require a radical capacity for the U.S. government unilaterally to preempt the actions of other states, whether or not it chooses to sustain the declaratory policy of preemption or not. The demands on intelligence for foreknowledge and for precision sufficient for interdiction—what is sometimes referred to as "actionable intelligence"—are likely to increase significantly over the next five years.

The ability of the U.S. government to protect its homeland will also depend critically on the ability of foreign governments to stop terrorists traveling or resting in theirs. The need for the United States to work with foreign governments, which has spiked in the post–September 11 years, has highlighted the importance and dangers of intelligence liaison. Such liaison relationships are perilous, as they offer the opportunity for foreign governments to shape U.S. perceptions through the proffering of biased or self-serving information. But this tension between collaboration and competition—a central conundrum of U.S. intelligence policy—has existed for many years. Despite occasional preferences for unilateral action, the United States has often found itself heavily involved in interstate persuasion and coercion of friends and competitors whose broader interests diverge significantly from Washington's—such as with China on North Korea or Pakistan on al-Qaeda.

Of course, the tighter and more complex the collaboration between states, the greater the risks associated with one party conducting "incompatible" operations against another. Indeed, as threats become more articulated and transnational adversaries more diverse, calculating the risks of collection against foreign governments—temporary allies, single-issue "friends," liaison partners, and threatening adversaries—will be much more complex than during the cold war. The need to moderate such risks makes the notion, expressed in some circles, that diplomatic access will be of decreasing relevance to intelligence collection both simplistic in theory and dangerous in its prospects.

Yet building and sustaining coalitions of the willing has always required some degree of risk. It takes good knowledge of prospective partners' intentions, superb counterintelligence capabilities, and an ability to discern or create the opportunities for collaboration that might not be present initially. Intelligence liaison, with all its promise and pitfalls, will continue to be of crucial importance in both collection and persuasion.[26]

Policymakers are also likely to pursue partnerships with international and nongov-

ernmental organizations as circumstances require. With global commitments to preserving international order, the U.S. government risks becoming a Gulliver—prostrate,
inattentive, and constrained by too many distractions—unless it delegates some threat
management and monitoring to others, including those it does not control directly.
Intelligence agencies must therefore become more sophisticated in finding ways to support the work of such organizations even as they seek to learn from them. The U.S.
government's ability to work with benign civil action groups when interests coincide
will be important in lowering the costs of such challenges while fostering better collection and the growth of modern civil societies overseas. These requirements again
highlight the importance of increasing the currency of exchange for such cooperation:
open-source intelligence.

In fact, both allies and adversaries are likely to rely increasingly on nongovernmental groups, cells, and international organizations for information and even operations.
Mobile nongovernmental or international teams can operate in areas where it is inap-
propriate or difficult for state representatives to act. The monitoring of compliance with
arms-control or ceasefire agreements could, for example, be facilitated by networks
of private citizens acting as contemporary versions of World War II port watchers. In
modern form they might behave as clusters on the World Wide Web. Such groups' effectiveness as collectors and collaborators will make them targets for U.S. collection as
well, particularly if employed by enemy groups or regimes. Indeed, the challenges of
collecting against cell-based organizations are likely to continue to exist even if terrorist
networks are utterly defeated.

Given the need for flexibility and resilience, the U.S. intelligence community will
need to behave as a transnational network itself, flushing transnational adversaries
from their sleeper status by stimulating them to act and thus reveal themselves. Such
techniques are already used in support of military operations in Iraq. The U.S. military's
"network" warfare—which involves highly mobile yet interconnected units—employs
ferreting techniques to stimulate enemy reactions and thus generate intelligence about
how the enemy thinks and behaves, quickly passing what is learned to other units operating nearby.

Such teamwork, tactical collection, and agility are also necessary for covert paramilitary operations, peacetime interdictions of destabilizing shipments of WMD, and the conduct of cross-border operations in pursuit of terrorist or criminal adversaries. Of course,
this kind of ferreting is a dangerous way to employ intelligence in peacetime, since it
may entail deception or provocation; but it may also be necessary. For such operations
to be adequately controlled and yet benefit operational decision makers, the information
collection, analysis (fusion and inferencing), transmission (to national, tactical, or operational levels), and validation will need to be as fast, secure, and automated as possible or it
will swamp their networks and degrade their ability to act. The processing and routing of

data, perhaps more than the collection of it, will be critical to gaining decision advantages in the future. So will the ability to decentralize the management of risk as intelligence is shared across the network.

As part of the "network" concept and in response to the new and demanding need for warning, U.S. intelligence might usefully employ roving U.S. penetration agents and sleeper cells for intelligence collection overseas. Such agents would differ from case officers in that they would collect intelligence principally themselves instead of recruiting spies. The latter approach is not likely to work against transnational groups with fanatical ideologies. Such threats as well as new opportunities can often best be discerned by those enmeshed in foreign countries. Sleeper cells, deeply embedded in foreign societies of concern, could be selectively turned on for reporting purposes, either at their own or at Washington's discretion. Operating under deep cover and with the aid of strategic intelligence, such agents could be empowered to collect intelligence for decisions not yet anticipated in Washington, thus significantly improving the warning function for the U.S. government. As operations move from peacetime to war, these agents would be in a position to help U.S. troops identify the enemy, rather than those who simply look like him.

Such penetration and sleeper agents, equipped with close-in technologies such as robotics, unmanned vehicles, and stealth drones, could work effectively against both terrorist groups and governments in whose territory these groups operate or who, quite independently, pose threats to the United States and its allies. The platforms used for measurement and signature intelligence (MASINT), which employs sensors designed to collect against chemical, biological, and nuclear threats by picking up the offending particulates in the air or ground, are best deployed close to their targets and using secure communications to exfiltrate data.[27] Commercially developed platforms and sensors are advantageous because they reveal little about sources — although, regrettably, something about techniques — if captured. Of course, to sustain necessary collection against hard targets, the United States will also need to retain stand-off technologies involving ships, high-altitude aircraft, and satellites.

In sum, the United States, with continued dominance in space technologies, robotics, and microelectronics, is positioned to take the offensive against both governmental and nongovernmental targets. Given the business-driven nature of the relevant technologies, intelligence managers will need to develop a relationship with the private sector that addresses the classified needs for *system* acquisition even if component parts remain unclassified. And for each step in offensive capability, the intelligence community must consider the defense — how these commercial technologies may be used to defeat the United States through reverse engineering and commercially developed countermeasures. Either the National Reconnaissance Office, with its capacity for large-system engineering, or the CIA's directorate of science and technology, with its understanding of the requirements for ground-based operations and platforms, could take the lead in developing systematic support for new operations.

Finally, it will be crucial to remember that, as transnational terrorist groups plan to make American cities their battlefield and foreign governments seek to anticipate and influence U.S. policies through their own intelligence operations, U.S. counterintelligence operatives, hospital workers, first responders, and local and state law enforcement will become ever more demanding intelligence users. They will also be among the first to acquire information on threats or attacks and will need to hand that information off even as they take actions to protect American citizens. They will need to make rapid decisions regarding quarantines, evacuations, and even requests for aid from the Defense Department. These decisions will involve judging whether local incidents are part of a deliberate attack by foreign agents. The Defense Department's decision to respond to these new requirements through the newly constituted Northern Command means that military intelligence must accurately assess domestic incidents and put them in national context.

A transformed U.S. intelligence service must be judged by its ability to warn of catastrophe, one that next time may involve weapons of mass destruction, and to give U.S. decision makers time to make the decisions they must to prevent it. If intelligence cannot hope to bat a thousand, it still must aim to win the World Series. Such a win doesn't require perfection; it just requires beating the other team — decision by decision.

With these considerations as a backdrop, it is useful now to consider the intelligence capacities the United States brings to this competition. For the United States to beat adversaries with box cutters, cyberviruses, a nuclear-packed suitcase, or ballistic missiles, it will need an intelligence community that can target its collection precisely and deliver timely information enabling preemptive diplomacy, coercion, or decisive strikes. That such an agile intelligence system can be reconciled with American-style democracy does not mean that it will be, or that it will necessarily be done right. Developing the capacity to combat the threats and take advantage of the opportunities of the modern era will require not only a thorough understanding of the challenges the United States faces but a deep understanding of the domestic politics of U.S. intelligence policy. Fitting what is needed with what the U.S. political system will be able to tolerate and execute is the subject of the next chapter.

Notes

1. R. V. Jones, *The Wizard War: British Scientific Intelligence, 1939–1945* (New York: Coward, McCann & Geoghegan, 1978).

2. Jennifer Sims, "What Is Intelligence? Information for Decision Makers," in *U.S. Intelligence at the Crossroads: Agendas for Reform*, ed. Roy Godson, Ernest R. May, and Gary Schmitt (Wash-

ington, D.C.: Brassey's, 1995), 3–16. More elaborate definitions exist, but they tend to move away from useful theory and to achieve descriptive results for those primarily interested in U.S. intelligence and how it works. See Mark M. Lowenthal, *Intelligence: From Secrets to Policy* (Washington, D.C.: CQ Press, 2003).

3. I do not mean to dismiss the importance of protecting sources and methods by which the intelligence was acquired. The "value" of a piece of intelligence can be understood as incorporating this attribute, which inheres in intelligence information to varying degrees. This value is felt most acutely in the case of loss, however, and is therefore a point beyond the scope of the present discussion.

4. The classic work on globalization is Thomas L. Friedman's *The Lexus and the Olive Tree: Understanding Globalization* (New York: Farrar, Straus and Giroux, 1999). For a more recent treatment, which details the specific effects on national security, see Michael E. Brown, ed., *Grave New World: Security Challenges in the Twenty-first Century* (Washington, D.C.: Georgetown University Press, 2003). For the debate on Internet governance, see Daniel W. Drezner, "The Global Governance of the Internet: Bringing the State Back In," in *Political Science Quarterly* 119 (fall 2004): 477–98.

5. Geoffrey Garrett, "Globalization's Missing Middle," *Foreign Affairs* 83 (November–December 2004): 84–96.

6. David Kirkpatrick and Daniel Roth, "Why There's No Escaping the Blog," *Fortune*, January 10, 2005, 47; Phillip Torrone, "Kryptonite Evolution 2000 U-lock Hacked by Bic Pen," posted on www.e~gadget.com, September 14, 2004.

7. For further discussion of this process as applied to a variety of contexts, see Ann M. Florini, ed., *The Third Force: The Rise of Transnational Civil Society* (Washington, D.C.: Carnegie Endowment for International Peace, 2000).

8. See Steven Johnson, *Emergence: The Connected Lives of Ants, Brains, Cities, and Software* (New York: Scribner, 2001); Albert-László Barabasi, *Linked: The New Science of Networks* (Cambridge, Mass.: Perseus Publishing, 2002), 35–117; Howard Rheingold, *Smart Mobs: The Next Social Revolution* (Cambridge, Mass.: Perseus Publishing, 2002), esp. 13–14.

9. For discussion of the benign forms this empowerment can take, see Rebecca Johnson, "Advocates and Activists: Conflicting Approaches on Non-Proliferation and the Test Ban Treaty," in Florini, *Third Force*, 49–81.

10. Peter H. Lewis, "Iraq's Robot Invasion," *Fortune*, January 10, 2005, 58.

11. Roy Want, "RFID—A Key to Automating Everything," *Scientific American*, January 2004, 58.

12. Ibid. Want uses the "get out of bed/start coffeemaker" scenario in a private home, but the idea is the same.

13. Martin Van Creveld, *The Transformation of War* (New York: Free Press, 1991); Philip Bobbitt, *The Shield of Achilles: War, Peace, and the Course of History* (New York: Knopf, 2002). For a provocative exploration of the problems accompanying globalization, see Amy Chua, *World on Fire: How Exporting Free Market Democracy Breeds Ethnic Hatred and Global Instability* (New York: Doubleday, 2003).

14. For one of the earliest and best-edited volumes on this topic, see Alan D. Campen, Douglas H. Dearth, and R. Thomas Goodden, eds., *Cyberwar: Security Strategy and Conflict in the Information Age* (Fairfax, Va.: AFCEA International Press, 1996). For an expanded discussion of this problem, see John Arquilla and David Ronfeldt, eds., *In Athena's Camp: Preparing for Conflict in the Information Age* (Washington, D.C.: RAND National Defense Research Institute, 1997).

15. For an interesting discussion of the implications of one particular category of public information on terrorist planning, see John C. Baker et al., *Mapping the Risks: Assessing the Homeland Security Implications of Publicly Available Geospatial Information* (Washington, D.C.: RAND National Defense Research Institute, 2004).

16. For a discussion of these threats and the varying perceptions of their likelihood before and after September 11, see Richard A. Falkenrath, Robert D. Newman, and Bradley A. Thayer, *America's Achilles' Heel: Nuclear, Biological, and Chemical Terrorism and Covert Attack* (Cambridge: MIT Press, 2001); Anthony Lake, *Six Nightmares: Real Threats in a Dangerous World and How America Can Meet Them* (New York: Little, Brown, 2000); and Bernard I. Finel, Brian D. Finlay, and Janne E. Nolan, "The Perils of Nuclear, Biological, and Chemical Weapons," in Brown, *Grave New World.*

17. Reported in Barton Gellman and Dafna Linzer, "Unprecedented Peril Forces Tough Calls," *Washington Post,* October 26, 2004, A1.

18. Graham Allison, *Nuclear Terrorism: The Ultimate Preventable Catastrophe* (New York: Times Books, 2004), 70.

19. Ibid., 73.

20. Dorothy Denning, "Information Technology and Security," in Brown, *Grave New World,* 93.

21. Economist Intelligence Unit, "The World in 2005," *The Economist: The World in 2005* (January 2005): 87–98.

22. For an excellent elaboration of this argument, see David P. Calleo, "The Broken West," *Survival* 46 (autumn 2004): 29–38.

23. Robert Steele has championed the cause of expanding intelligence capabilities to include open sources and diplomatic reporting longer and more vigorously than anyone else. See, for example, his book *On Intelligence: Spies and Secrecy in an Open World* (Oakton, Va.: OSS International Press, 2001) and his website, www.oss.net.

24. Economist Intelligence Unit, "The World in Figures: The Forecast for Fifteen Industries," *The Economist: The World in 2005* (January 2005): 99.

25. J. R. McNeill, "Environmental Change and Security," in Brown, *Grave New World,* 178–96.

26. See Michael A. Sheehan, "Diplomacy," in *Attacking Terrorism: Elements of a Grand Strategy,* ed. Audrey Kurth Cronin and James M. Ludes (Washington, D.C.: Georgetown University Press, 2004), 97–114.

27. For the growing importance of MASINT, see John D. Macartney, "John, How Should We Explain MASINT?" in *Intelligence and the National Security Strategist: Enduring Issues and Challenges,* ed. Roger Z. George and Robert D. Kline (Wasington, D.C.: Sherman Kent Center for Intelligence Studies, National War College, and National Defense University Press, 2004), 169–79.

THREE   Understanding Ourselves

JENNIFER E. SIMS

MOST AMERICANS would probably say that the business of intelligence sits uncomfortably with American political culture. Neither U.S. political institutions nor the values on which these are based easily accommodate clandestine operations, deception, secrecy, or law breaking. And yet the United States enters the twenty-first century as the greatest intelligence power on earth, with a global network of human and technical assets collecting and protecting an astonishingly vast number of secrets. In fact, the U.S. government dominates a worldwide trade in secrets that depends on reciprocal sharing of stolen information and the conduct of undercover operations. It has consistently run clandestine and covert operations for more than fifty years, even though such operations arguably have run counter to its policies of promoting openness, democracy, and the rule of law worldwide.

Although the end of the cold war allowed the United States to cut back its intelligence capabilities, the attacks of September 11 have prompted their revival. In fact, September 11 has led Americans to reconsider intelligence policies instituted in the 1970s that encouraged restraint through strengthened oversight and has inclined the public to tolerate increased domestic surveillance by law enforcement and intelligence agencies. The results, including the Patriot Act of 2002 and the revised approach to implementing the Foreign Intelligence Surveillance Act, have been widely criticized by an unlikely alliance of librarians, surfers, right-wing conservatives, and the American Civil Liberties Union.[1]

Such pendulum swings between aggressive collection and self-restraint have afflicted U.S. intelligence policy since its beginning.[2] They raise the question of whether U.S. intelligence transformation is a doomed enterprise—doomed to either overreach or excessive self-restraint. Even if in theory intelligence can coexist with democratic governance of the American kind, can it be engineered to do so in the world the United States now confronts?

The preceding chapter suggested that U.S. intelligence will need to operate in an ambiguous environment where intelligence "means" sometimes contrast sharply with desired policy "ends." This is nothing terribly new. U.S. strategy on a grander scale has long involved promoting democracy and civil liberties overseas while allying with dictatorial regimes when this was perceived to be necessary for a greater good. In doing this the U.S. has sometimes acted to strengthen military and security-related institutions at the expense of civil liberties. Intelligence operations have followed suit. Yet, at the level of operations and tactics, intelligence seems especially problematic when operations in the interest of current U.S. national security challenge those laws, treaties, and norms of behavior that overt policies specifically aim to protect and promote overseas in the interests of long-term stability and prosperity.

As U.S. intelligence is increasingly asked to improve its domestic collection and to work with dubiously governed states or transnational groups in the interests of national security, it will probably also face controversy should the arrangements go bad or be made public at times of reduced threat. Threats may pass, but the nation's sense of commitment to civil liberties and the rule of law endure—often peaking during times of peace and security. Thus, especially when they succeed, those acting to ensure the nation's safety may be held accountable for perceived compromises to its social and political fabric once an immediate threat has passed. It is essential that an expectation be built into the intelligence community that resilience will be required and that institutional accountability will be fair, if U.S. intelligence isn't to be driven to impotency and U.S. security put at risk. The key to resilience and accountability is a sophisticated understanding among the people and their governors of the domestic context for intelligence policy.

This domestic context involves three principal domains: the strategic political culture that shapes and limits national security policy, the character of the national security policy process in which intelligence must fit, and the distribution of resources among participants in the process. In all three domains, the cognitive biases of those involved, including the habits of thought reflected in the language of the intelligence profession, play major roles for better and for worse in the American way of intelligence.[3]

U.S. Strategic Culture and Its Relevance to Intelligence

Although bureaucratic politics is a well-researched subject with widely accepted insights for policy, the notion that strategic culture affects state policy is somewhat more controversial.[4] The issue is whether there is such a thing as an American strategic culture and, if so, whether it affects intelligence policy.[5]

Yet it seems indisputable that an American paradigm, derived from this country's history and laws, informs the way U.S. decision makers, analysts, and intelligence producers think about intelligence. If American culture is best understood as that soup of national ideals, norms, socioeconomic preferences, and intellectual and religious heritages that nurtures U.S. public life, strategic political culture is the subset of this mix that particularly influences the mindset of those involved in the intelligence process and those who evaluate it for the purposes of oversight and accountability.[6]

Although not all Americans think alike, it is arguable that they do share certain values and norms of behavior that transcend partisan politics. For example, the perceived right to privacy, while not actually set forth in the U.S. Constitution, is an enduring norm of American political life. When, in 1929, Secretary of State Henry Stimson shut down the Black Chamber, the U.S. government's first national cryptologic unit, with the explanation that "it was a highly unethical thing for this government to do," he revealed his sense that individual privacy not only matters to Americans but is to some extent a universal human right applicable even to foreign diplomats in peacetime.[7]

That Stimson, as secretary of war, later retracted his declaration and endorsed the growth and consolidation of national cryptologic capabilities after World War II reveals another feature of American political culture — pragmatism.[8] American values are deeply embedded and resonate strongly in the rhetoric of national policy; but when the nation is in jeopardy, one "gets done what needs to get done," even at the expense of a universal principle. Americans in jeopardy are nationalistic; at peace they are universalists; but they are always pragmatists.

In the nineteenth century, Alexis de Tocqueville recognized the pragmatic nature of American political culture and saw in it the seeds of greatness.[9] For Americans were not only pragmatic, they were industrious — a nation of tinkerers, peddlers, and inventors. The American entrepreneurial spirit embraces technology and, with a kind of liberal optimism, expects its application to solve more problems than it creates. For example, if innovations in cybersurveillance threaten privacy, Americans expect free enterprise and technology to invent a way around the problem — such as better encryption. According to cultural historian Jackson Lears, the two archetypes of the American experience are "the self-made man . . . who believes he will get rich through his own hard work . . . [and] the gambler, who believes that with the next turn of the cards, providence will deliver the Main Chance."[10] But in the contest between luck and hard work, hard work wins out, shaping Americans' sense of their own destiny.

Americans' hard work, fueled by their historical optimism, has engendered a culture of respect for those who prosper by their own devices. According to a Pew Center poll cited in an article in the *New York Times*, roughly 65 percent of Americans believe success is up to them, compared to roughly 5 percent of people in Bangladesh, or 30 percent in Italy and Germany.[11] Like a large magnet, American society has historically drawn the optimists from these other countries in its immigrant pool, fueling and sustaining the myth with each new wave of immigration. Thus Americans invent and reinvent themselves. They are not so much isolationist, aloof, or reclusive in spirit as they are busy. Americans want to be left alone to get things done.

Of course, the number of great American inventors is probably matched by the number of inventive scam artists who have bilked their fellow optimists. That such snake-oil salesmen and con artists are romanticized in popular American culture is a symptom less of the nation's suspect character than of its short memory and grudging respect for profitable artistry of all kinds.[12] As discussed in Donald Daniel's chapter in this book, the issue of deception illustrates the tension in American culture between the value placed on open political discourse and the value placed on pragmatic artistry and the importance of keeping family secrets. Secrecy and even deceit can be tolerable when they are welded to an honorable enterprise. In the absence of the latter, both of the former are reviled.

Americans have a deep suspicion of governmental secrecy and worry about its connection to governmental overreach.[13] The McCarthy era, in which federal power was used to impugn suspected Communists, and the Vietnam and Watergate era, in which federal agencies and the White House ran clandestine operations against perceived internal threats, left their marks on American political identity.[14] References to these episodes in American history have become iconic and trigger public wariness of Washington's national security establishment. While Communists had infiltrated the government before and during World War II and insurgents had professed intent to combat civil authorities in the 1960s, what was politically salient and now best remembered in national folklore were the state's excesses in countering these threats.[15]

As searing to the national psyche as these episodes were, they did not involve the military directly in significant domestic operations.[16] Of all the constraints on federal action, the American tradition of keeping federal troops out of bedrooms, bars, and schools has the longest history. As Robert W. Croakley has written in *The Role of Federal Military Forces in Domestic Disorders, 1789–1878*:

> Opposition to the use of military force in the enforcement of civil law is deeply imbedded in American tradition. It derives both from British precedents and from the experiences of the American Revolution, the ostensible cause of which was the use of British troops to enforce oppressive measures. The image of hated Redcoats shooting down innocent citizens in the Boston Massacre of 1771 was a vivid one, easily transferable to any soldier employed as an instrument of internal control by a central government.[17]

This opposition to a domestic role for federal troops developed into opposition to any standing peacetime military force that might threaten the domestic population. In the American view, "a standing army . . . could be the instrument only of a monarchy, not of a democratic state."[18] Thus the termination of wars, including the cold war, has usually been accompanied by a reflexive domestic drive to demobilize.[19] If one adds the abiding suspicion of a standing military to the deeply felt need to keep police and espionage powers separate, one can appreciate the ease with which walls have been constructed between intelligence and law enforcement functions during peacetime — both in American law and in the habits attending their execution and enforcement.

Although the 9/11 Commission and others have criticized this divide for inhibiting the flow of information between law enforcement and intelligence, respect for the divide is arguably deeply embedded in American tradition and culture. President Truman, for example, was inspired to reassure the American people that his creation of a standing intelligence establishment would not lead to a Gestapo-like culture in which unchecked national security prerogatives and intrusive investigations in the name of state security would override due process of law.

Indeed, Americans have always considered the United States a nation of laws, not of men, to paraphrase John Adams. When tensions arise over the competing norms that inform U.S. strategic policy, Americans look to the law for guidance. The essential link between American law and the U.S. approach to international politics became very clear at the end of the cold war, when Federal Bureau of Investigation (FBI) Director Louis Freeh was deployed on a mission in support of democracy in the former states of the Soviet Union. President Bill Clinton and Director Freeh agreed that the best guise under which to pursue a policy of democratic enlargement would be law enforcement. When pressed by the Central Intelligence Agency (CIA) to coordinate activities to ensure that one hand of the U.S. government knew what the other was doing, law enforcement agencies balked. Faced with demands by the State Department for assurances that cooperation with foreign law enforcement agencies would not compromise foreign policy priorities, the FBI was not initially compliant. To the minds of law enforcement officials and many of the Americans whom they serve, democracies are built on the concept that nothing is above the law.

For Americans, deep respect for the law and recognition of its relationship to democratic process are joined to the supposition that most political actors are rational and therefore susceptible to reason and deterrence — a contentious yet widely held lesson of the cold war. Although often ascribed to liberal internationalists and arms controllers, such optimistic assumptions were broadly evident in the bipartisan political support for intervention in Iraq in 2003. Leaving aside the question of the accuracy of the intelligence underlying the intervention, the basis for war entailed an assumption that Iraqis wanted democracy and order and that American victory and right reasoning among the Iraqis would somehow cause these things to come about.

Thus, to the extent that intelligence is perceived by Americans and democratic allies as undermining law, it is seen as risky at best and dirty and un-American at worst.[20] And yet Americans have demonstrated that they will make exceptions for intelligence when national security is at stake. Not only does the use of extraordinary intelligence capabilities become justified in the public mind when the state is at risk, but the rule of law, including treaty obligations, may be jettisoned in favor of the security of the state and unilateralist initiatives.

The potent mix of ideals and self-interest that characterize American strategic culture helps to explain some of the special features of what has been called the American intelligence identity.[21] Although intelligence experts have assembled a rather long list of the key traits that make up this identity, five effects seem especially important for a consideration of intelligence transformation: a tendency to equate intelligence with secrets, which has led to neglect of open-source intelligence; a tendency to think of intelligence as intended primarily to counter threats rather than to discern opportunities; the persistence of decentralized intelligence institutions and in particular resistance to embedding command over intelligence within the military or command over law enforcement within the intelligence community; a technological emphasis on intelligence collection methodologies; and a schizophrenic approach to intelligence oversight.

Each of these is covered to some degree in other chapters in this volume. However, one of them will be discussed here because of its deep and pervasive effects on the capacity of the U.S. government to respond to the challenges outlined in the preceding chapter.

INTELLIGENCE AS SECRETS

Of all the influences of strategic culture on intelligence, the first, relating to neglect of open sources, may be the most insidious.[22] As a moth is attracted to flame, so American intelligence since the mid-twentieth century has been fixated on the secret affairs of state. This dangerous propensity is all the more remarkable in that history has demonstrated the enormous value of open-source information, such as the data collected by the White Lady network, which tracked the movement of German railcars across the continent during World War I; the intelligence amassed by port watchers in the Pacific during World War II; and the information gleaned from German tradeshows on encryption technology during the interwar period.[23] Even the dangers posed by newspaper reports on U.S. intelligence successes, such as the famous leak by the *Chicago Tribune* on the importance played by code breaking in the U.S. victory over the Japanese at Midway, suggest that information need not be kept secret to be of great intelligence value — for better or for worse — to the adversary. Perhaps the modern American failure to grasp the value of open sources, reflected in the public's deep ambivalence about leaks (which amount to open sources for the adversary), is attributable in part to the experience of the cold war. For most of their existence, U.S. intelligence agencies worked against the Soviet Union, a particularly secretive state, as their highest priority. It is therefore perhaps not surprising that secret sources are now, almost instinctively, the most prized.

But regardless of how it originated — culturally or pragmatically — a fixation on secret sources now amounts to a debilitating cognitive bias. A number of U.S. adversaries are less secretive than the Soviet Union was, and they do not necessarily know how to keep their actions out of the public eye. Many choose, because they can, to hide in plain sight by living, organizing, and working among us. Others may not hide the truth but instead manipulate it on the not unreasonable expectation that Americans look principally for secrets and stubbornly believe in them. Whether Saddam Hussein was this clever is doubtful and as yet unknown. But he could have been.

The problem is not simply diminished collection; neglect of open sources also affects management and reform. Agencies, such as the Departments of State, Commerce, and Energy, that collect information for national security purposes need to be supported and reconciled with the missions of other agencies. Instead, senior U.S. intelligence managers and their critics persist in thinking about U.S. intelligence largely in terms of functions performed by National Foreign Intelligence Program (NFIP) agencies, the Joint Military Intelligence Program, and the Tactical Intelligence and Related Activities programs within the Department of Defense. Intelligence functions are consequently and tautologically defined as those functions performed by these agencies. When reconciling budgets, only the State Department's small NFIP element, the Bureau of Intelligence and Research (INR), is recognized as intelligence-related, while the larger managerial stakeholders, such as the bureaus of human resources, diplomatic security, and consular affairs have been left out. As a result, budgets for interrelated missions involving the State Department and the intelligence community are developed and submitted to Congress with insufficient coordination at best and usually none at all. And the Office of Management and Budget (OMB), divided functionally to reflect categories understood by comptrollers and appropriators, regularly fails to reconcile them.

Similarly, a common flaw of U.S. intelligence oversight and past U.S. commissions on reform has been their failure to take into account what might be termed the "non-intelligence" sources of intelligence failure. Congressional intelligence oversight committees seem institutionally hampered in solving functional problems in intelligence as a result of their jurisdictional limitations. While they may see the need to grapple with the intelligence problems caused by the underfunding of the Department of State, for example, they do not want the responsibility to help fix them. As Britt Snider's chapter in this volume points out, with multiple congressional committees already engaged in the intelligence appropriations and authorization process, lawmakers are not interested in further complicating an already complicated process. They are also turf-conscious. While defining intelligence as "that which intelligence agencies do" helps simplify the messy problem of oversight, it sacrifices function for form.[24]

The propensity to equate intelligence with secrets is a cognitive block that afflicts Americans far more than it does their terrorist adversaries. The disparity is particularly worrisome in that much of what should be protected information within the United States is not. Until recently sensitive blueprints on the vulnerabilities of critical infrastructures were available on the Internet. Recognizing the importance of open sources to the intelligence process does not, of course, mean that sound intelligence practice should neglect to secure one's own information — quite the opposite. And yet the process of deciding what should be classified, which should be a crucial issue in an open democracy, is still unclear. To take just one example, the detailed budget of INR in the State Department's budget is unclassified within the congressional appropriations process. In the intelligence budget, however, it is secret. Both the CIA and the State Department are aware of the discrepancy but are unsure how to resolve it since there are equities and history on both sides.

Sloppiness in classification management and disregard of open sources have other serious repercussions. For example, consumers of intelligence tend to value highly classified information more than information culled from the unclassified domain. This confusion of the sensitivity of the source or method with the quality or importance of the information is subtly reinforced by the intelligence community's inclination to prioritize the dissemination of its most highly classified information according to the recipients' respective ranks and prior clearances rather than on the basis of their respective needs — a practice senior policymakers routinely endorse for fear of leaks. Yet, denied the information, low-ranking intelligence analysts and "action officers" cannot do their jobs, which causes policy, intelligence products, and morale to suffer over the long term.

Unfortunately, reform-minded intelligence officials may continue to underestimate the critical importance of the flow of gray or open-source intelligence from the state and local levels to Washington. The first information on a bioterror attack may come from hospitals; information on suspicious surveillance of high-rises may come from their security services and first responders. The stigma U.S. political culture attaches to intelligence should not cause U.S. intelligence and public officials to shy away from the crucial task of figuring out how to build suitable alliances with U.S. citizens and the private sector for crisis identification and management.

A problem related to the neglect of open and private sources is the prejudice against new or uncleared customers for intelligence. Officials who do not receive intelligence but think they should must often press to get it. There is no effective system for determining new "need to know"; what we essentially have is a club in which membership must be sponsored by someone higher up with clearances and influence. If this defensive approach is restrictive to those within the traditional security establishment, it is far worse for newer domestic parties. How does the CIA know whether to give a new institution or decision maker intelligence? Should it be able to do so without White House approval if this would change who the players are on a given matter of policy? In the new, fluid international environment, warnings of impending attack may require alerting someone who has never received intelligence before. Unfortunately, as of this writing, no one is designing a process that selectively and dynamically integrates hospitals, police, firemen, CIA officers, FBI agents, border security officials, and Foreign Service officers into a coherent system for warning, crisis management, and intelligence sharing.[25] Cognitive models, patterns of thought, and political preferences — preferences that find their most frequent expression in bureaucratic politics — stand in the way.

Bureaucracies and the Politics of the U.S. Intelligence Cycle

The influence of American political culture on U.S. intelligence activity is pervasive, and the result is a distinctively American paradigm for intelligence. Once recognized, the conceptual, theoretical, and cognitive blocks inherent in this paradigm can be reduced to some degree. While not, in other words, immutable aspects of the American system, they are nonetheless embedded in the national psyche and thus difficult to change.

Less difficult to change and easier to identify is the institutional setting in which the intelligence process must work—such features as bureaucratic structures and systems for policymaking in the executive branch. The national security policy process provides the playing field on which intelligence functions. Changing it for the sake of making intelligence support easier is arguably to put the cart before the horse. Nevertheless, its nature shapes intelligence performance and therefore must be well understood by those seeking to revitalize the business.

This is not to say that the policymaking process is somehow immune to the cultural influences discussed above. For example, suspicion of federal power has contributed to the persistence of divided intelligence functions among federal agencies, despite recurrent proposals to centralize them. Although the Department of Defense has sought increased control over intelligence, backed by cogent arguments about the critical importance of support to the warfighter, Congress has never agreed to consolidate secret power in the hands of the military, and indeed the Intelligence Reform Act has done the opposite. The divided intelligence authorities that involved the director of central intelligence (DCI) in budgeting and long-range planning and the secretary of defense in budget execution have now, with the creation of the position of director of national intelligence, reduced further any concerns about excessive power in the Pentagon while sharpening the battle lines over resources. Thus institutional arrangements continue to reflect preferences embedded in American political culture that seem to persist even in a time of war.

But the point here is that, regardless of the derivation of the bureaucratic system in place for national security decision making, the nature of the national security bureaucracies—their cultures and mandates—and the policy process themselves influence how intelligence is done in the United States. Reviewing these dynamics, while keeping the influences of national strategic culture in mind, reveals some of the most difficult aspects of any plan for intelligence transformation. Although it is beyond the scope of this essay to run through this bureaucratic backdrop in its entirety, a discussion of its most important aspects will suffice.

THE INTELLIGENCE CYCLE AND ITS AMERICAN VARIANT

The theoretically ideal intelligence process is a simple intelligence cycle beginning with customer requirements and then progressing to collection, processing, analysis, and dissemination to the relevant decision maker. What makes this model useful is not that it is an accurate depiction of the American intelligence system, or even of most systems, but that it allows us to develop simple metrics for performance and to compare the intelligence system in any government to what is perhaps ideal. If the definition of intelligence offered in the previous chapter holds, then ideally decision makers tell intelligence officials what they will be deciding and in what priority, receive timely information needed for their decisions, have confidence that what they are receiving improves rather than degrades their decision making relative to the adversary, and give feedback on whether their needs are being met. Overall secrecy is required for the protection of sources but also to ensure the integrity of the system so that decision advantages can be secured. Intelligence fails utterly if poor security allows the adversary to gain competitive advantages by compromising or even hijacking the system for hostile purposes.

In comparing the American system to the theoretical ideal, four features of the U.S. process stand out: the complex, bureaucratic, iterative, and competitive nature of national security decision making; the disconnect between intelligence providers and users, on the one hand, and process managers or administrators, on the other; the rigidity of the intelligence-related budget process and its impact on the flexibility of intelligence; and the weakness of institutional arrangements for joint strategic planning among national security decision makers and intelligence providers.

The following discussion suggests that the best features of U.S. intelligence may be its decentralized nature, which ensures that collection and analysis are competitive and thus validated. Its worst features may be the absence of both integrated collection management and a certain stickiness in providing intelligence support to new customers — reinforcing the cultural predilections discussed above.

BUREAUCRATIC COMPETITION, POLITICIZATION, AND CONSERVATIVE BIAS

As explained above, the intelligence process begins and ends with the decision maker who needs its support. Successful performance requires a locus in the government for deciding who needs to be getting intelligence on threats and opportunities at any given time—in other words, whose requirements must be met. Without getting this right, an intelligence system is doomed to fail, since it can be neither relevant nor timely for the decision makers concerned.

In the U.S. system, managing what might be called the customer set is difficult because of bureaucratic politics. Policymakers compete for influence, seek to use intelligence to gain leverage, and have an interest in keeping competitors in the policy process from using intelligence to eclipse their own roles. This incentive system runs directly counter to the intelligence officer's interest in providing unbiased intelligence to all those who are likely to have an impact on the policy in question. As Mark Lowenthal has shown in his article "Tribal Tongues: Intelligence Consumers, Intelligence Producers," natural, profession-based objectives drive analysts and policymakers apart.[26]

However, a second aspect of the competitive U.S. policy process drives intelligence and policymakers together and is arguably the greater force. Competitive and iterative policy formulation encourages policymakers singly and as a group to limit those who have access to the best information. The decision maker's interest in maximizing influence and control over the decision-making process is entirely compatible with the intelligence manager's interest in limiting access to sources and methods to only a few customers.[27] This dynamic reinforces the cultural trends, thus biasing the system against new intelligence users or those policymakers low down in the bureaucratic hierarchy. At its worst, it increases the risks that intelligence will be politicized as analysts seek to hitch their stars to a particular bureaucratic high-flyer and his favored policy outcome.

In any case, without a built-in advocate for their access or knowledge of the intelligence to motivate them, new customers find that support is often slow in coming or nonexistent. The system tends to be conservative and biased against them. This problem has clearly plagued U.S. intelligence since Pearl Harbor, when key military commanders were kept outside regular channels of intelligence dissemination even though their bases or missions were clearly at risk. Neither the army commander, General Walter Short, nor the commander in chief of the Pacific Fleet at Pearl Harbor, Admiral Husband Kimmel, regularly received the high-level Japanese signals intercepts known as "Magic." What is worse, responsible officials back in Washington didn't know it at the time.[28] Similar problems affected U.S. intelligence prior to the tragedy of September 11, when information did not flow to irregular customers in the FBI.

Interestingly, intelligence is also needed for decisions within the U.S. intelligence community to manage collection platforms such as buildings and planes or to recruit personnel with unusual language skills. When those responsible for making such decisions find themselves excluded from this flow of critical information, they may become uncooperative, engendering further restrictions on the dissemination of intelligence and causing interagency friction. Of course, this friction only makes matters worse. The net result is that the U.S. system tends to be biased in favor of legacy users and involves occasional bartering among them for access to information or collection resources. This characteristic of U.S. intelligence, manifested as poor interagency intelligence sharing, was also among the causes of intelligence failure prior to September 11.

The question remains how this conservative bias originally came about in a society that would seem to reward innovation, pragmatism, and change. One explanation, useful for understanding Pearl Harbor, is that concern over the security of intelligence information tends to bias its owners from releasing it, particularly to untested users. But perhaps the most important systemic explanation is that the cold war rigidified

U.S. intelligence. For decades the Soviet target was consistently dominant and relatively impenetrable. Information flowed largely in one direction—from intelligence agencies to policymakers. Collection agencies needed relatively little guidance and sought it only on the most pro forma basis. Intelligence agencies had substantial resources and a clearly articulated strategy—containing communism and deterring strategic nuclear attack—against which to array them.

In other words, while top policymakers needed intelligence, the intelligence process did not appear to need them, except perhaps, in the realm of arms control. Given the peculiarly static nature of international politics during this period, U.S. policymakers rarely had to press new requirements on intelligence agencies or make a case for the salience of the issues with which they were dealing. Intelligence requirements for large technical collectors were generated in a standing "deck" that was massaged at the margins each year. Sensors arrayed on satellites, buildings, or ships posed few management problems for policy agencies and were easily accommodated in a defense budget with upward growth curves.

In sum, during the cold war, the customer set for intelligence varied hardly at all from one year to the next, its members were largely satisfied, and concerns about resource constraints were few. Washington-based users were at the top of the hierarchy and the National Security Council (NSC) staff held particularly strong sway. The most senior staffs had positions and portfolios that were relatively fixed and mostly based in large bureaucracies in Washington, which, when personnel turnover occurred, secured access to intelligence for the newcomer that matched the access institutionalized earlier. With the machinery of intelligence support to decision making thus locked in place, few on the policy side questioned who held the keys or the competence of the drivers.

When the international system broke free of its rigid bipolarity in the 1990s, policymakers still needed intelligence—perhaps more than ever—but now intelligence agencies also needed *them*. They needed to know the thrust of national security strategies and policy priorities. They needed support for budgets that Congress was eager to cut. In the typical atmosphere of postwar American retrenchment, they began to worry about failure.

As a result, intelligence agencies were quick to adapt to new requirements for networked military operations overseas, particularly after Desert Storm, the first war against Iraq, revealed that imagery was superb but that poor capacity for sharing among the military services courted disaster. As the intelligence community adapted to rising demands for support to military operations, a conceptual divide emerged between "national" customers (those based in the Pentagon, State Department, and NSC) and "warfighters" (military units deployed overseas). In the aftermath of the war, this bifurcation became cemented in the mindset and lexicon of the intelligence community. The admirable responsiveness of the military to the intelligence community's need for guidance regarding operational-level customers and their needs, combined with bud-getary incentives (discussed below), led the intelligence community to increase support to military operations at the expense of civilian users at the operational level or broader national needs.

Civilian operators may be the least well known of these customers, falling as they do outside the traditional set of national users and the new priority of military operators in the field. These civilians were the nonmilitary decision makers outside Washington, such as FBI field officers, legal and commercial attachés, chiefs of mission, deployed Foreign Service officers, including consular and diplomatic security officers, and em-bassy platform managers (communications teams, building managers, construction planners, etc.). As the nature of warfare was changing and low-intensity conflict, nation building, and peacekeeping problems grew in the Middle East, Bosnia, Haiti, Congo, Somalia, and other hotspots, so did the deficiencies in intelligence support to diplo-matic operations.

Washington's anemic response to the need for more flexibility and intelligence sup-port to civilians in the field is hard to explain. It has partly been a result of prejudices ingrained by long-standing bureaucratic practices. For example, the State Department's Bureau of Intelligence and Research (INR) has rarely regarded its mission as providing analytic support to deployed officers overseas and, at least early in the post–cold war period, had neither the funds nor the bureaucratic mandate to help. The CIA, faced with declining budgets, made choices about where to cut staff and narrow its overseas missions based on top-down requirements coming from Washington that, in the after-math of Desert Storm, emphasized the military. As a result of these other priorities as well as of declining budgets, and without consulting INR or the affected ambassadors, the CIA cut the number of stations overseas, narrowed their missions, and curtailed support to country teams, including some dealing with the hotspots mentioned above. As field requirements were increasing, intelligence support to diplomatic operations was declining.

Although the root of the problem in lagging support to deployed civilians may be traced to the complacency of an intelligence system that had worked for years on au-tomatic pilot, the disconnect was exacerbated by other, more bureaucratic problems. Policymakers' personal interest in intelligence support but lack of interest in getting involved in its management had evolved into disconnects not just between bureaucra-cies but within them as well, leading to poor internal coordination.

A good example of the failures that can result occurred in the 1990s, when State De-partment budget officials cut embassies and staffing in one volatile overseas region, even though the countries involved were becoming a looming priority for senior policy officials and the White House. Unfortunately, these cuts occurred at the same time that the decline in intelligence budgets was causing CIA program managers to cut personnel overseas in the same region. Because intelligence managers saw no need for it and policymakers had never demanded it, there was no process for reconciling these plans in a serious way. When reporting on developments in this region dropped precipitously, policymakers were surprised and incredulously sought answers for why information was so scant. What remains perplexing is why this incident brought no major top-down push for better sharing among civilian decision makers at the operational level, the way it had among military operators after Desert Storm. The sole remedial effort, to be discussed further below, was instead effectively squashed.

Although this case involved routine budgeting, the same disconnect has been apparent during crises, though classification requirements prevent detailed discussion of the circumstances. It can be said, however, that civilian management officials decided in the 1990s to evacuate U.S. government facilities overseas before intelligence arrangements had been made to preserve related collection capabilities. In one instance the gap in timing was only a matter of hours, yet the gap in collection that emerged as a result was so great that it caught the attention of members of the Cabinet. In fairness to the officials at the time, they had no idea that their simple decisions on the timing of an evacuation — considered largely an internal administrative matter, albeit with significant political consequences — would be so damaging to the intelligence process. No institutionalized process was in place to tell them so.

Of course, as mentioned above, not all decision makers are oblivious to the intelligence system of which they are a part and which also supports them. Decision makers who have direct operational need for the intelligence, such as those in the military services and arms control community, often do much better than most. For example, at the end of the cold war, policymakers in the Arms Control and Disarmament Agency fought for more direct intelligence support and in particular better knowledge of the budgets for intelligence collection and dissemination systems. When the agency was folded into the Department of State and came to rely on INR for its support, the contrast with other policy bureaus on these issues was striking. Arms controllers organized a working group under the newly formed Intelligence Resources Board to wrest greater information from the Defense Department about funding for sensors and platforms crucial to the maintenance and negotiation of important treaties.

Such engaged and operationally oriented customers aside, most civilian policymakers do not know which intelligence collectors support them or the potential implications of their loss, such as the failure of a satellite, budget cuts for a major collection program, or the health of the communications systems that support reporting from the field. Most probably these issues are believed to belong either to other bureaucracies about which these officials know little, or to management hierarchies over which they have little control and less interest. Management cones in civilian agencies are often regarded as important to the policy process only if they protect or augment program-related budgets — that is, the currency needed for policy initiatives. And civilian management specialists, buying into that paradigm, exercise large discretion in communications, facility construction, and management of other agencies' U.S. presence overseas, with little understanding of the impact on policy. In the U.S. civilian system the analyst is the face of intelligence for most national policymakers, yet neither the analyst nor the user at the national level considers in much depth, or spends much political capital preserving, the security or sustainability of the system that supports him.

Apart from cold war habits, other reasons for this disconnect between U.S. civilian intelligence users and managers of intelligence platforms and information systems are not hard to discern. The cultures of engineers or budget officials and policymakers or analysts are vastly different. Career paths, with some exceptions, tend to isolate those responsible for keeping the machinery for information gathering and dissemination running smoothly from those responsible for informing and driving policy.

Divided career paths are accompanied by divided fortunes. Policymakers in civilian agencies tend to have higher status than the systems managers and often escape professional accountability for failing to help managers do their jobs well. Perhaps the most striking example has been within the White House itself, where the power and authority wielded by the NSC staff has been exercised without line knowledge of the operational constraints of the executive-branch agencies or military services that have had to carry these policies out. What has looked like insubordination in the eyes of senior civilian NSC staff has looked like ignorance and arrogance in the eyes of military operators more aware of logistical constraints.

As the NSC staff has become increasingly directive and operational, this gap has led to more frequent problems with implementation among civilian agencies. The development of secret plans to step up U.S. operations in Colombia, the Congo, or Iraq can emerge from the White House "fully coordinated" with policymakers from State, Defense, and senior levels of the CIA, and still blindside those who are responsible for augmenting the communications, platform security, personnel, and transport involved in carrying out the operations. The supplemental budgets for these activities—especially the budgets not directly tied to the defense appropriations process, such as for embassy communications, operations, and security—are usually late and inadequate as a result.

BUDGETS AND PROGRAMS

Perhaps nowhere does the stress, finger pointing, and recriminations that result from these failures of coordination and communication more greatly exacerbate bureaucratic conflicts than in relations between the CIA and State Department—in part because their programs are so intertwined and their appropriations so rarely reconciled in OMB or in Congress.

Although this point has been made earlier, one example in particular serves to illustrate how difficult a problem this will be to fix—even when both agencies, backed by their most senior leadership, see merit in doing so. In the mid-1990s, inadequate support to overseas ambassadors led to unprecedented joint requests by senior intelligence and State Department officials for augmentation of State's budget on national security grounds. This reallocation of resources within the pot of money appropriated to the "Commerce, State, and Justice" account was necessary to match initiatives in the "Defense" account that directly and seriously impinged on State's operations. In effect, one could not undertake the defense-related initiatives without upgrading State Department operations that were not otherwise a priority for funding in an extremely tight budgetary environment.

The Office of Management and Budget, which has long had entirely separate vetting processes for national security and foreign policy accounts, was initially unresponsive, then confusing: it authorized money to be put in the intelligence budget, where, unmatched by a separate appropriation for State, it could not be spent for State Department operations. When officials sought to resolve the matter with congressional staff responsible for State Department appropriations, the staff members balked, not, apparently, because the proposed funding increase for State threatened appropriators' competing priorities, but because committee staff strongly objected to the association of the State Department's mission of open diplomacy with what, for them, were the far less appealing intelligence functions the proposal highlighted.

In this context, it is not hard to see why the Defense Department evolved into the dominant force in intelligence management, processing, and requirement-setting, even in peacetime; it has institutionalized, if Byzantine, procedures for joint program planning with other national security agencies, including the intelligence agencies and supportive appropriators in Congress who understand the requirements for coordination. It is also easy to see why the CIA Directorate of Operations would increasingly and willingly give lower priority to support for State Department operations than to the deployed military unless specifically instructed otherwise. That is the incentive structure the budget, resources, and management infrastructure created.

If the OMB, the central agency for reconciling interagency disconnects through the budget process, has been so deeply divided, how can the agencies that it manages do any better? Can it really be surprising that State Department managers, responsible for such vital intelligence-related functions as security and communications, tend to see intelligence plans springing forth from the intelligence community as Athena was launched from the head of Zeus: unilaterally, willfully, and, to a certain extent, awesomely? National security has been, at least for civilian managers, a bureaucratic trump card that is played too often and too inadvertently by surprise.

THE QUESTION OF STOVEPIPES

While the nature of bureaucratic politics is thought to be well understood by Washington's insiders, evidence suggests that the hidden implications of bureaucratic maneuvering are both profound and poorly understood even among policy elites.

For example, it is possible that "stovepiped" intelligence collection, a commonly bemoaned bureaucratic problem in which hierarchies control the intelligence process they "own," is not the source of the U.S. problem with intelligence sharing among agencies. In fact, since the end of the cold war perhaps the greatest weakness in the U.S. intelligence system has been the bureaucratic divide between those responsible for the performance of intelligence sensors (radar or signals, imagery and human collectors, etc.) and those who fund and manage the platforms on which these sensors ride (airplanes, satellites, U.S. government buildings overseas, ships, etc.). Bureaucratic practices have created this divide, and U.S. strategic culture and cold war habits perpetuate it. Controlling the intelligence community's access to platforms has been one of the most effective and yet unintentionally destructive ways that other national security agencies that are also customers for intelligence have exercised influence over intelligence collectors and their missions.

One deleterious side effect of the *absence* of collection stovepiping has been distortion of collection "tasking"—an issue explored in depth in Jim Simon's chapter in this volume. Here it is worth noting only that the formal system for setting intelligence requirements overlays the collection agencies' preferential approach to customers. These preferences have been based on customers' power over budgets, programs, and access to targets. In other words, without adequate vertical mission management of sensors and platforms, a hidden bureaucratic bias has evolved. It is expressed in the form of customized support for favored bureaucratic customers through, for example, the CIA's operating directives, which allocate resources outside the formal requirements process. This is why, despite budgetary authorities' having been formally divided between the DCI and the secretary of defense, the intelligence community has for years strongly preferred the biggest budget executor and platform manager of all, the Defense Department. As budgets have shrunk, this preference has grown.

The intelligence reform bill passed in 2004 could correct some of these problems. In light of the evolving threats and likely U.S. strategies outlined in the previous chapter, the matter is urgent. Civilian agencies, including especially their deployed law enforcement personnel, defense attachés, and diplomatic officials, will be more heavily engaged than ever in shaping the overseas security environment. While the interagency dynamics involved were and continue to be understandable, the disposition of collection assets against targets should be a matter of policy, not budget pressures related to hosting agencies such as the Department of State.

Although it would make eminent sense for the White House to compel interagency cooperation, history suggests that this will be difficult. If we consider the complex of agencies involved in the mission of homeland defense, the bureaucratic hurdles to rational budgetary and management decisions become overwhelming. Fortunately, in the homeland security case, first responders in some cities and states are moving ahead with the acquisition of information technologies that will allow them to network with each other as potential threats build and to hand off appropriate information automatically if these threats are realized.

The FBI, with its network of field offices, is seeking ways to link up with these systems and in come cases already has. Unfortunately, the Department of Homeland Security (DHS), concerned not to extend its hand too obviously into the domain of domestic collection, is largely disconnected from these initiatives and has no systematic way of learning about the commercial innovations, technologies, and applications being developed at the local level. This is unfortunate; for a modest outlay, these local initiatives could be rationalized into a nationwide network for crisis management at the local level, a network that would preserve the American preference for local control while allowing an embedded, automated capability for handoff of data to the federal level if a nationwide crisis were to occur.

The Role of the Director of National Intelligence

The director of national intelligence (DNI) may be able to overcome some of these problems of bureaucratic rigidity. He could also make them much worse if a new, large bureaucratic staff tries to impose changes with a heavy hand. Agencies are, after all, likely to develop strategies to counter what they fear will become additional debilitating bureaucratic processes and regulations.

The new office will be most effective if it can take on some of the problems outlined in this chapter without demanding credit for solving them. It should avoid replicating chains of command, especially to chiefs of station in the field, and focus on making the budget process work so that those chiefs have the resources, communications, and platforms they need to get their jobs done. In the process, agencies concerned with intelligence, platform management, and policy will need to be encouraged to develop internally coherent approaches to their missions and be more transparent about their intentions.

It would be a mistake, however, to presume that the new DNI, now given managerial authority over all intelligence agencies, thus has all the authority needed to run U.S. intelligence. The position will always require cooperation from other agencies managing or controlling information needed for national security decision making. In the future these agencies may include the Center for Disease Control, state police, public utilities, and even private hospitals, all of which are generating and storing digital data.

In the information age, the reach of any intelligence system — whether here in the United States or overseas — is potentially very broad. As the previous chapter showed, the problems posed by this expanded pool of intelligence-relevant information on matters of health, crime, and industry touch vital and sensitive matters of intelligence sharing, intelligence liaison, and counterintelligence policy.

The creation of the new position of the DNI will not in itself end the bias against open, unclassified, or nonintelligence sources. But the DNI is likely to find bias an obstacle to moderating the risks and costs of overseas collection operations, because it prevents intelligence managers from delegating collection to nonintelligence agencies and frustrates the timely processing of all-source intelligence. Creating this kind of cultural change will be among the DNI's greatest challenges and most important jobs.

The office should also avoid insisting on uniformity across the intelligence community. Bureaucratic cultures are good if they evolve out of sound recruitment, training, and teamwork, and when they work successfully they need less sublimation than support. Indeed, instead of rewarding "likeness" among senior intelligence officers, the intelligence community may need to promote those who embody their missions best and reward those who demonstrate great tolerance for cultural disparities among national security bureaucracies.

Finally, serious efforts must be made to increase the U.S. government's agility in the field. It would be naïve to suppose that the creation of the office of the DNI and a new national counterterrorism center at the top will do anything in this respect. These new offices could slow down decision making overseas if they turn out to be additional places that harried chiefs of station, ambassadors, and regional commanders must consult before acting. One reason why the DCI always remained dual-hatted — overseeing both human intelligence collection and intelligence community operations writ large — was that chiefs of station, who perform both these missions in the field as counterparts to ambassadors, did not need or want two separate bosses. They should not see their authority reduced or complicated, especially at a time when the tempo of overseas operations is increasing.

Given the volatile and fluid nature of international politics, the DNI should act swiftly to clarify command relationships. He should empower these officials by showing restraint when considering interventions in the field. Swift action should also be taken to acknowledge that the powers of the office, which are and should be substantial, will be restrained by other authorities. The DNI will want, with White House backing, to play an active role in striking this balance so that it optimizes both intelligence performance and oversight.

In accomplishing this mission, the DNI will ideally recognize that bureaucracies do not mean that stovepipes are inevitable. Bureaucracies can be good in so far as they clarify command relationships, ensure accountability, and augment efficiency through the regularization of procedures. They cause problems when they exert too much hierarchical control when networking is needed. The production of intelligence in the United States is a mission to which networking is crucial, because no single stovepiped bureaucracy is responsible for getting the job done. Even within a single collection discipline, many agencies play a part, and if they don't, other "mission partners" logroll to get the results they need. When they do play their parts well, the results can not only be spectacular but can disprove the belief that bureaucracies, networking, and agility are mutually exclusive.

DISPROVING THE STOVEPIPE PREMISE:
THE DISC EXPERIMENT AS A "LESSON LEARNED"

To put both bureaucratic politics and cultural obstacles to reform in context, it is useful to consider the diplomatic intelligence support center (DISC), an interagency effort at innovation and reform from the 1990s. It is a story well worth telling because it illustrates the points made in this chapter and some of the remaining opportunities and difficulties facing the new DNI in the volatile networked intelligence environment of the future.

The DISC initiative occurred in the mid-1990s, when intelligence budgets were being cut and the intelligence needs of policymakers were on the rise. The NSC staff had noticed the urgent need to sort intelligence priorities. Presidential Decision Directive 35 (PDD-35), which established these priorities during the first Clinton administration, emphasized support to military operations while overlooking diplomatic operations of rapidly increasing importance, such as consular affairs (visa processing), diplomatic security, peacekeeping, crisis negotiation, and diplomatic liaison.[29] As a result, PDD-35 triggered the disengagement of routine intelligence support to U.S. government embassies and consulates at a number of posts overseas. Notably, both intelligence community officials and policymakers at the Department of State omitted what was later termed intelligence support to diplomatic operations or "SDO" from PDD-35.

The Bureau of Intelligence and Research, which was itself constrained by the State Department's declining budget, felt it could not sacrifice its core analytic support to headquarters by expanding support to overseas embassies in critical need. INR's solution to the need for support to diplomatic operations was to innovate. Its signature effort to do so during the war in the Balkans involved the coordination of a diplomatic intelligence support center for the ambassador in Sarajevo.[30] INR's brief effort to reverse the loss of intelligence support to embassies and bridge the divide between management and policy illustrates how mindsets and turf wars can be overcome, on the one hand, and reinforced in their inhibition of innovation and adaptability, on the other.

The DISC was an interagency, all-source, dedicated analytical unit, modeled on the Defense Department's innovative concept of the national intelligence support team

(NIST), which had powerfully augmented the intelligence support available to field commanders during the first Iraq War (1991). Indeed, the strongest initial support for the State Department's idea of creating a DISC came from the Defense Department, whose intelligence managers recognized the ambassador's stark need in this case. The embassy in Sarajevo was, after all, the size of a shoebox; it had been equipped to perform only as a sleepy outpost. Suddenly it was under sniper fire and hosting VIPs engaged in shuttle diplomacy. Within months it had become a focal point for implementing the Dayton Peace Accords. Yet in early 1996 it was operating with unarmed civilians in a war zone without intelligence support for its mission. The CIA had been told to concentrate on the mission of force protection. As a result, timely intelligence on developing threats and Serbian violations of ceasefire agreements around Sarajevo was getting to the secretary of state but not to the local ambassador or chief U.S. negotiators. Support to military operations (SMO) had trumped protection of civilian and diplomatic operations.

Faced with intelligence priorities carved in stone, INR sought to innovate. The DISC was conceived by INR and cooperatively designed by an interagency team. All involved recognized the urgent need for close-up tactical intelligence support to the embassy-based country team — support that was intimately connected to national collection systems. Intelligence agencies donated special secure equipment; an INR officer drove the equipment through blizzards and over mountain passes to get it to the embassy; State Department communicators and security officers assisted with the setup, and a representative of the DCI was put in administrative charge of all the DISC's functions.

The interagency group of analysts that worked in the DISC eventually received a presidential award. Then, despite the ambassador's protests, INR steadfastly dismantled the DISC once the spike in intelligence requirements had ended. The idea had been to fill a gap, not to enlarge the bureaucracy overseas permanently. Thus reassured, State Department managers positioned themselves to support future initiatives of the same kind when needed. Even the appropriate congressional committees, once briefed, agreed to provide funding for future DISCs as the need might arise.

Despite the DISC's success and the demonstrated ability to dismantle the unit once its purpose had been served, the CIA blocked subsequent efforts to perform similar services for nonmilitary field operations. The CIA's judgment, accepted by senior policy officials at State, seemed to be that intelligence support to ambassadors should remain uniquely the province of the CIA — despite the fact that serious gaps in support had emerged as a result of the CIA's limited resources and preferential service to military requirements in a high-threat zone.

Whether or not the decision to prevent future DISCs was correct, the ramifications were serious for the underlying process that the DISC represented. By preventing future DISCs, and indeed by objecting to the entire initiative after the fact, the CIA effectively discouraged similar problem solving by INR and the intelligence community at large. Not only was the DISC concept lost, but so was the capability to innovate in an intelligence component.[31]

THE QUESTION OF STOVEPIPES REVISITED AND EXTENDED

The case of the DISC illustrates a controversial point made earlier: although most observers of U.S. intelligence criticize the intelligence community for being excessively stovepiped in its collection disciplines, the opposite is actually the case.

To recall the earlier discussion, if stovepiped collection means vertical control over the command of sensors, platforms, and communications systems involved in getting data from its source to the user, the U.S. system is hardly stovepiped. Sensors are arrayed on a variety of platforms that are not under the control of the collection agency that depends on them. This holds true for the CIA, which uses both official and nonofficial cover, and for the National Security Agency, which uses National Reconnaissance Office satellites, as well as ships, aircraft, and other ground-based platforms funded and managed by others in the U.S. government.

What most critics mean when they refer to "stovepipes" is actually the tendency of collection managers to logroll—that is, to use access to their "take" from their sensors to leverage access to budgets, policy, or the product of other sensors. And logrolling, as already discussed, may reflect the lack of a process for identifying new or needy intelligence customers. Far from reflecting stovepipes, this behavior may actually demonstrate bureaucratic weaknesses, not strength. Collection agencies, unable to manage their enterprises vertically, seek leverage over mission partners by manipulating the currency they do control: raw data. In this case, breaking down or further weakening bureaucracies will solve nothing. What is needed is enterprise management—a function that the Defense Department has long performed, albeit poorly.

Indeed, the existence of logrolling explains the Defense Department's insistence on retaining some budgetary control over the major technical collection agencies; it can't afford to let logrolling of this kind, brokered by civilian players, interfere with intelligence support either in the buildup to war or in war itself. Defense Department officials do not want to find themselves in the position the State Department found itself in Sarajevo: under fire, ill equipped, and dependent on others. Keeping command and control of sensors, assets, and platforms assures a binding of collection to requirements that in turn ensures the degree of agility so necessary for overseas operations.

The DISC illustrates both the demands of the new international environment and its central management issue. The issue may be less the problem of stovepipes than the problem of their absence; the issue is less how to loosen the Pentagon's hold over collection than how to strengthen the Department of State's, the FBI's, and the Department of Homeland Security's so that agility can be sustained during both peacetime and war.

If we cannot solve this problem for traditional overseas operations, solving a similar set of issues for law enforcement and intelligence at the state and local levels will be next to impossible. In both cases, collection stovepipes and the distortions they introduce are far less problematic than the failure to manage collection effectively across the sensor-platform divide and to engage managers and analysts in creative solutions that go outside existing arrangements.

THE PREVIOUS CHAPTER suggested that the international system has become much more fluid since the end of the cold war. Laced with opportunities as well as threats from traditional state adversaries and transnational groups, this environment demands far greater agility and assertiveness from intelligence than the U.S. national security establishment has demonstrated in the past. But it also requires exemplary strategic vision—a willingness to resist the tyranny of current intelligence and to align resources against both today's needs and tomorrow's.

Unfortunately, the Intelligence Reform Act of 2004 may, in at least one way, make it harder to achieve this agility and get intelligence managers to focus on the next "worst threat." Preoccupation with mission-oriented centers, so comfortable to the American pragmatist, may make it difficult for managers to focus on the kind of mission-free strategic analysis that allows U.S. intelligence to identify new threats, new opportunities, and new decision makers and then make the necessary adjustments. Work will need to be done to ensure that the stovepipes many thought they were eradicating do not actually appear in the form of mission-conscious centers with tight holds on requirements, operations, and budgets.

Apart from clarifying command chains and brokering bureaucratic arrangements and budgets, the new DNI could usefully prevent this worrisome outcome by sustaining both a strategic estimative process untethered to the fortunes of any mission "center," and a commitment to balanced and creative resource distribution based in part on the results. Such an office could also provide the appropriate context for planning operations designed to lure terrorist adversaries into traps or strategic errors as opposed to simply killing them, which may not bring lasting results against hydra-headed networks.

A cursory reading of American strategic culture suggests that the public is not likely to oppose the more aggressive collection and even the proactive deception this might entail, so long as the rationale for operations remains tightly aligned with America's strategic purpose and appropriate oversight is in place. Intelligence managers can innovate, tinker with, and adjust to these new demands if encouraged to do so, but they require leadership at the top that can ensure that the strategic plans of one agency do not conflict with another or with broader U.S. policy purposes.

There are areas, however, in which intelligence responsiveness is likely to prove sticky. The operating style of American intelligence is plagued by cognitive biases, institutional rigidity, and bureaucratic roadblocks that hamper communications among those responsible for cross-agency planning, programming, budgeting, and execution, including senior managers and policy officials not formally within the intelligence community. Oversight mechanisms have failed to pick this up because the divides crippling the national security agencies are reflected precisely in the Office of Management and Budget and in the committee structure on Capitol Hill.

The DNI may be able to minimize this long-standing friction among agencies without resorting to the creation of new centers. Conventional wisdom holds that the fundamental problem in achieving teamwork lies in the political cultures of the intelligence agencies concerned. Yet, as this analysis has shown, at least anecdotal evidence suggests otherwise. The DISC was created and executed by interagency collaboration, and it succeeded because of, not in spite of, the differing outlooks, ideas, and expertise of the agencies involved. Bureaucratic cultures, as with the broader American strategic culture from which they grow, provide a model for success and an esprit de corps that help recruitment, loyalty, retention, and a sense of mission. The mixing of many of these cultures has led and can continue to lead to innovation. Much as diversity adds to the workplace, so diversity in bureaucratic cultures can be a net plus, helping managers to see problems from different angles: law enforcement, clandestine operations, diplomacy, and budget.

On the other hand, if day-to-day operations poison teamwork through blindsiding, miscommunication, and turf mentality, the sum of the parts will be less, not more, than it ought to be. In these circumstances, bureaucratic cultures will be defined more in opposition to others than by mission requirements. The new DNI, by exercising leadership, can inhibit such tendencies. It is time for the user community—especially senior civilian policymakers and political appointees—to learn the intelligence business, treat it as life's blood, and view managers as collaborators, not service providers. The claim that there is no time to understand or "manage" the infrastructure of intelligence will no longer wash. Decision makers remain ignorant of it at their peril.

The gravest problems for intelligence may nonetheless lie not where intelligence bureaucracies are most deeply dug in but on the domestic front, where they barely have established their footing—largely because of constitutional and cultural blocks to assertive federal roles in domestic monitoring and operations. In some cases, innovation might best be left to the state and local levels as authorities grapple, for example, with the need to develop methods for distinguishing naturally occurring epidemics from biological attack and to develop information-processing tools to map the likely evolution of epidemics against available resources.

In other cases, such as monitoring critical infrastructure, protecting sensitive federal installations, and dissemination of intelligence before, during, and after terrorist attacks, the federal government will have to take a larger role in domestic intelligence gathering and handoff. This sensitive subject will be discussed in greater detail in Henry Crumpton's chapter on homeland security. Here it will only be noted again that Americans are skeptics on domestic intelligence because of their suspicions about federal intentions. That the private sector conducts surveillance for commercial or private security purposes does not mean that those same cameras are welcome in the hands of federal authorities.

The FBI's recent efforts to collect information derived from law enforcement activities seems to be a useful first step in improving collection, so long as it does not overstep the bureau's traditional role. But, for just this reason, it may not fix the problem of domestic collection entirely. The accumulation of raw intelligence data as a corollary to ongoing investigations that might be relevant to national security officials is different from active collection on those officials' behalf or in response to intelligence leads gleaned from overseas operations. Given U.S. cultural preferences, the latter role might best be played by the CIA, which has no authority to arrest or incarcerate. With the FBI still dedicated to the law but mandated to share, and the CIA needing law enforcement data to adequately collect domestically, bureaucratic friction is likely to develop over the question of civil liberties and public protection. In such circumstances, bureaucracies help rather than hurt U.S. objectives and keep operations balanced with respect to the requirements of U.S. strategic culture—albeit now with domestic security a strengthened mission.

In fact, it may be best to consider how the federal government, and DHS in particular, can distance itself by assisting or subsidizing local and private initiatives to manage information, such as that relating to hospital traffic, bridge use, and dam and reservoir protection, in exchange for protocols that allow federal participation in these networks once certain thresholds for threat have been breached. Such protocols, which would need to be openly arrived at, could serve as a mechanism for public discussion of the modalities for federal intervention in the cause of domestic intelligence, whether by the CIA, the FBI, the DHS, or Northern Command. That this process will be controversial and difficult makes it all the more important for the United States to revitalize overseas intelligence operations as its first line of defense.

Finally, this chapter has suggested that strengthening U.S. intelligence can be achieved not despite American preferences for openness and restraint but because of them. In this respect this chapter has elaborated on Ernest May's arguments in chapter one about the resiliency of U.S. intelligence institutions and, more important, the adaptability of their policies and practices. American talents for technological progress, entrepreneurship, and even creative deception are vital to successful collection against modern threats.

At the same time, the U.S. government's experiences with intelligence overreach and the corresponding development of intelligence law render the American political system uniquely positioned among modern democratic states for conducting an intelligence war against terrorists. The U.S. system has institutionalized a capacity for careful yet aggressive action that rests less on faith in leadership than on experience, law, and the U.S. constitutional system of checks and balances. Institutional changes that disrupt this inherent capacity would be dangerous indeed. Insofar as the United States has only begun the intelligence transformation process it needs, this caution is worth keeping well in mind.

Notes

1. See Michael Moss and Ford Fessendun, "New Tools for Domestic Spying and Qualms," *New York Times*, December 10, 2002.

2. For an excellent history of U.S. intelligence, see Christopher Andrew, *For the President's Eyes Only: Secret Intelligence and the American Presidency from Washington to Bush* (New York: Harper Collins, 1995).

3. While cognitive biases are important to understanding the American approach to intelligence and will be mentioned throughout this chapter, a good general overview of the problem can be found in Richards J. Heuer Jr., *Psychology of Intelligence Analysis* (Washington, D.C.: Center for the Study of Intelligence, CIA, 1999).

4. The literature on strategic culture is wide-ranging. See, for example, Peter J. Katzenstein, ed., *The Culture of National Security: Norms and Identity in World Politics* (New York: Columbia University Press, 1996). For its application to the intelligence problem, see Michael A. Turner, "A Distinctive U.S. Intelligence Identity," *International Journal of Intelligence and Counterintelligence* 17 (January–March 2004): 42–61. See also Wesley K. Wark, "Introduction: Learning to Live with Intelligence," *Intelligence and National Security* 18 (winter 2003): 1–14.

5. For a thorough discussion of the role of strategic culture in American intelligence policy, see Turner, "Distinctive U.S. Intelligence Identity." Turner cites the work of Donald Snow, *National Security* (New York: St. Martin's Press, 1995), 42–64.

6. I have discussed these points in "Domestic Factors in Arms Control: The U.S. Case," in *Arms Control: Cooperative Security in a Changing Environment*, ed. Jeffrey A Larson (Boulder: Lynne Rienner Publishers, 2002).

7. Andrew, *For the President's Eyes Only*, 72.

8. For Stimson's role during this period, see ibid., 122–25.

9. Alexis de Tocqueville, *Democracy in America*, trans. Henry Reeve (London: Longman, Green, Long, and Roberts, 1862).

10. Quoted in John Leland, "Why America Sees the Silver Lining," *New York Times*, June 13, 2004, sec. 4, Week in Review, 1.

11. Ibid.

12. The American author of *The Wizard of Oz* was also known for creating the first window displays in New York City's department stores in the early 1900s. The American public knew these fantastical displays were designed to manipulate them into purchases and were thus motivated by the desire to make a profit, but they loved them anyway. Christmas window displays are still a beloved New York City tradition. These windows, along with Disney, Hollywood, and Las Vegas are the entrepreneurial expression of American creativity and the public's taste and talent

for fantasy. Integral to fantasy, of course, is the art of deception. See Christina Rosenberger, "The Mail: Fantasy for Sale," letter to the editor, *New Yorker,* October 27, 2003.

13. See Kate Martin, "Civil Liberties and Domestic Intelligence," *SAIS Review of International Affairs* 24 (winter–spring 2004): 7–22.

14. See Loch Johnson, *America's Secret Power: The CIA in a Democratic Society* (New York: Oxford University Press, 1989), 3–38 and 133–82.

15. Ibid.

16. Some might argue with this assertion. Loch Johnson has noted that investigative commissions in the 1970s found that army intelligence participated in investigations against thousands of American citizens during the Vietnam War era. Ibid., 5.

17. Robert W. Croakley, *The Role of Federal Military Forces in Domestic Disorders, 1789–1878* (Washington, D.C.: Center of Military History, U.S. Army, 1988), 3. The same suspicion fueled opposition in the South to efforts by federal troops to stop the atrocities of the Ku Klux Klan during Reconstruction—another example of a fleeting attempt to use the combined powers of arrest, force, and intelligence in a domestic context. The further point about the American public's long-standing aversion to combining the federal powers to use force, to arrest, and to spy has been forcefully made by James Simon, former associate director of national intelligence for administration, who lectured at Georgetown University on October 3, 2003.

18. Croakley, *Federal Military Forces in Domestic Disorders,* 3.

19. Turner, "Distinctive U.S. Intelligence Identity," 47. See also Jo Anna Ensum, "Domestic Security in the United Kingdom: An Overview," in *Protecting America's Freedom in the Information Age, a Report of the Marble Foundation Task Force* (October 2002), 102–3.

20. For an excellent in-depth discussion of this issue, see Frederick P. Hitz and Brian J. Weiss, "Helping the CIA and FBI Connect the Dots in the War on Terror," *International Journal of Intelligence and Counterintelligence* 17 (January–March 2004): 1–41.

21. Turner, "Distinctive U.S. Intelligence Identity," 42.

22. The earliest and most persistent advocate of this view has been Robert Steele, founder and CEO of Open Source Solutions. His website and books include extensive evidence of the importance of open-source information to the modern intelligence enterprise. See *The New Craft of Intelligence: Personal, Public, and Political* (Oakton, Va.: OSS International Press, 2002); and *On Intelligence: Spies and Secrecy in an Open World* (Oakton, Va.: OSS International Press, 2001).

23. For an interesting overview of these cases, see Jeffrey T. Richelson, *A Century of Spies* (New York: Oxford University Press, 1995), passim.

24. Not everyone in the intelligence community is afflicted by this blind spot. The exceptions have included certain members of the intelligence community management staff, the associate director for collection, Charlie Allen, and the leadership of the National Reconnaissance Office, especially Keith Hall, its director, who established a special liaison relationship with the Department of State's management bureaus in recognition of the department's importance as a "platform manager."

25. See Bruce Berkowitz, "Intelligence for the Homeland," *SAIS Review of International Affairs* 24 (winter–spring 2004): 1–6.

26. Mark Lowenthal, "Tribal Tongues: Intelligence Consumers, Intelligence Producers," in *Strategic Intelligence: Windows into a Secret World,* ed. Loch K. Johnson and James J. Wirtz (Los Angeles: Roxbury Publishing, 2004), 234–41.

27. See Jack Davis, "A Policymaker's Perspective on Intelligence Analysis," *Studies in Intelligence* 38, no. 5 (1995).

28. Andrew, *For the President's Eyes Only,* 119.

29. For more on PDD-35, see Mark Lowenthal, *Intelligence: From Secrets to Policy* (Washington, D.C.: CQ Press, 2000), 170–81.

30. Mention of the DISC was first made in *State* magazine. Marjorie Niehaus, "Bureau of the Month: INR," *State Magazine,* U.S. Department of State (November–December 1996).

31. INR later significantly reduced its efforts to coordinate with management bureaus in favor of its core mission of all-source analysis. The department subsequently established an office for intelligence resources and planning and an intelligence resources board to perform the functions of innovation and resource oversight in cooperation with INR—an effort that has struggled to survive and may no longer exist.

PART TWO New Capabilities

FOUR

Integrating Open Sources into Transnational Threat Assessments

AMY SANDS

AS THE THREAT that was central to the cold war national security paradigm has changed, the traditional reliance on classified information must also change. Throughout the cold war era, intelligence relied heavily on data collected either by human spies or by technical collection activities. All these data were classified and their use was usually controlled, and thus limited, by the agencies and groups collecting the information. Analysts came to rely excessively on classified information, which many believed was the only type of information that could be trusted and valued. Insufficient effort was made to exploit the knowledge of the academic community, whose area experts often had years of regional travel, residence in foreign countries of concern, language training, and personal and professional foreign contacts. While nonclassified materials may have been used, they were often seen as marginal sources.

As discussed in the previous chapters, today's security environment differs from previous ones in some very basic ways. First, there are more players, more issues, and thus more complexity; second, more destructive technologies are available; and third, societies are more accessible and therefore more vulnerable. As the facts in the AQ Khan case demonstrate, linkages between transnational actors are more easily accomplished given the transportation and mobility of individuals today. This multiplicity of concerns and threats presents the intelligence efforts of any state with enormous challenges.

In this context, using open-source information is central to developing high-quality, relevant intelligence assessments. Several years ago, during a United Nations Special Commission (UNSCOM) inspection in Iraq, an American inspector realized that he needed more information about Iraq's missile programs for an interrogation the next day. Recognizing that there was no way for him to obtain this information through intelligence channels in time, he contacted colleagues at the Center for Nonproliferation Studies at the Monterey Institute of International Studies, which has several databases that track these sorts of activities using only open sources. He was able to acquire the necessary information from this source within a few hours of his request, share it immediately with his international team of inspectors, and use it during the discussions the next day.[1] This story provides a powerful example of how critical access to open-source materials and a knowledgeable analyst may be to achieving a desired national security outcome.

The intelligence community has had a hard time recognizing the value of open sources and then using them. Part of the problem lies in the reason why most states create and sustain intelligence organizations — namely, the collection of and assessment of "secrets" relevant to protecting the national security interests of their state. Since open sources, by definition, do not provide secrets, the task of collecting and assessing this type of data would appear at first glance not to fit within the understood purpose of an intelligence community.[2]

To think about open sources this way, however, is to miss their value. As Joseph Nye said during his tenure as chair of the National Intelligence Council, "open source intelligence is the outer pieces of the jigsaw puzzle, without which one can neither begin nor complete the puzzle . . . open source intelligence is the critical foundation for the all-source intelligence product, but it cannot ever replace the totality of the all-source effort."[3]

Open-source information can complement, supplement, clarify, and frame the "secrets" uncovered via human and technical means. In some cases it may help target a source of classified data, or it may provide information that, while repetitive of classified materials, can more readily be used in international or public contexts. In other situations, open sources may eliminate the need for certain types of collection activities, permitting resources to be redirected toward efforts where acquiring classified data is most critical.

The current set of transnational threats requires that analysts use and integrate all the available sources. Local newspapers, journals, speeches, and academic papers provide rich insights into a society's way of thinking and acting, insights that may make a difference in how to assess a threat and thus how to handle it. The executive summary of the Aspin-Brown Commission on the Roles and Capabilities of the U.S. Intelligence Community recommended that "greater use be made of substantive experts outside the intelligence community. A greater effort also should be made to harness the vast universe of information now available from open sources."[4] Without increasing significantly the use of open-source materials in every facet of the intelligence assessment process, efforts to prevent and counter today's security threats will not succeed.

Defining Open Sources

The first step to doing a better job of collecting and using open sources must include a better understanding of what open sources are. Traditionally, the term "open source" has been defined negatively; that is, as information that is not classified. But what does "classified" mean, especially in an international context?

Classified information includes materials collected or developed using some type of secret, hidden, or covert activity or method. The materials and data that an agency such as the International Atomic Energy Agency (IAEA) or the Organization for the Prohibition of Chemical Weapons (OPCW) collects from formal state declarations and inspections might also be considered classified, having been collected with the understanding that such data will have limited access and use. On the other hand, proprietary company-owned or personal information is rarely considered classified, even if it might include financially sensitive, legally protected, and personally damaging data. Open-source materials may become classified if the process used to obtain them reveals sensitive sources and methods, intelligence community requirements, or policy concerns.

It is important to note that the same critical information obtained from a "closed" society, such as North Korea or Cuba, may be classified or not, depending on the collection methods involved or its sensitivity. For example, if a British academic during the Cuban missile crisis had mentioned to friends seeing an unusual number of Soviet military personnel while traveling on the island, he would have been providing open-source or unclassified corroboration of intelligence photos taken by an American U-2 plane showing unusual military buildings and facilities under construction. If that professor had worked for an intelligence organization, his comments would have been handled as highly sensitive intelligence. In either case, the revelations could have put him at significant risk, thus meriting a U.S. decision to classify them.

Framing open sources by what they are *not* provides a vague and not very satisfying definition. Open sources can be viewed more constructively and positively as:

> Any and all information that can be derived from overt collection: all types of media, government reports and other documents, scientific research and reports, commercial vendors of information, the Internet, etc. The main qualifiers to open source information are that it does not require any type of clandestine collection techniques to obtain it and that it must be obtained through means that entirely meet the copyright and commercial requirements of vendors where applicable.[5]

Open sources can be organized into four categories: general, widely available data and information; "gray" literature; targeted commercial data; and individual experts.

A comprehensive open-source collection system would try to obtain the following types of materials: global, multilingual coverage from general media (newspapers, wire services); regional media and reports (English and non-English); data from websites; electronic databases (free and subscription); interviews; company reports (such as annual reports); surveys and questionnaire responses; government documents (testimony, reports, commission studies); scientific literature; commercial satellite imagery; and declassified or leaked information.

The use of what has become known as "gray" literature can provide unique information that bolsters the intelligence community's depth of understanding of an issue, person, region, or program. The U.S. interagency gray literature working group defines gray literature as including but not limited to "research reports, technical reports, economic reports, trip reports, working papers, discussion papers, unofficial government documents, proceedings, preprints, research reports, studies, dissertations and theses, trade literature, market surveys, and newsletters. This material cuts across scientific, political, socio-economic, and military disciplines."[6] Gray literature is characterized by its limited availability, either because few copies are produced, existence of the material is largely unknown, or access to information is constrained.[7]

Today, open-source information is widely available in part because of the fall of numerous closed societies and in part because of the globalization of communications. Large areas of the globe, previously closed off to the outside world, are now accessible. At the same time, rapid advances in information technology have made it much easier to move information around the world quickly, allowing it to be disseminated to a global audience. The quantity and variety of open-source materials available electronically have increased exponentially. Nightly news reporters provide live feed from places halfway around the world. Advances in several types of technologies have allowed new kinds of information to be delivered via commercial imagery, videotapes, satellite-linked instant reporting, chat rooms, webcasts, and bulletin boards.

In addition, primary sources such as government documents, websites, or interviews with key individuals may be available in their original languages but without the need to travel very far. With the advent of advanced information technologies, analysts can now use sophisticated search engines, multiple language search-and-translation tools, visualization packages for trend analysis and data manipulation, and high-resolution commercial satellite imagery. The revolution in information technology opens up the possibility of getting diverse open-source data from all over the world at a constant and rapid pace. Open sources are now easily accessible to intelligence analysts — literally, they are at their fingertips — if these analysts are properly trained to exploit them.

Of course, having an extensive amount of open-source information does not translate directly into having an equivalent amount of open-source intelligence (OSINT). OSINT is open-source material that has been evaluated for its utility to decision makers and validated. This filtering and assessment process is critical to the effective exploitation of open sources, given the magnitude of the data stream and the lack of control over their production and availability. Unfortunately, it is also a step that is often forgotten. When it is, the value of open-source materials may be missed or analysts may be overwhelmed by too many open sources. When Senator Daniel Patrick Moynihan commented after the 1998 Indian nuclear tests, "It didn't take spies or spymasters simply to read what Indian leaders said and to take it seriously," he was pointing to the intelligence community's failure to adequately validate openly available information relating to India's nuclear intentions.[8]

Effective Use of Open Sources

As indicated above, open sources should never be seen as replacing classified information. Nor is it likely that they will provide a "smoking gun" about some issue or threat, since, like other types of intelligence sources, open-source materials will probably be fragmentary, providing only pieces of a larger puzzle. They may be indirect or circumstantial data that require additional information and analysis to place them properly in any threat assessment. There may also be so many available open sources that analysts will be unable to see the "forest for the trees," or, for that matter, even to see that there are trees.

Another characteristic of open-source information is that it is rarely the result of tasking by an analyst or policymaker. Open sources are produced for purposes other than intelligence assessments; accordingly, an analyst has to rely on what exists, understand why it was produced, and be sensitive to the potential for errors, bias, and misinformation. While much the same can be true for classified and even technical data, open sources may not get the same level of validation and quality control as these other sources. One reason to collect and cull large quantities of open-source materials from a broad and diverse set of sources is to find multiple sources that confirm relevant data. While having so much information readily available is a boon, it can also become a nightmare to an intelligence analyst who is already facing piles of classified information to evaluate.

The magnitude of open-source intelligence is so substantial that analysts have to develop means to wade through it and find the worthwhile data. Effective exploitation of open-source information requires, in addition to advanced information technologies, human experts in the topics or regions from which the materials are emerging. Years ago Richard Pipes, a well-known Soviet expert, made this point when testifying before the House Permanent Select Committee on Intelligence:

> It [open-source material] is a very immense body of literature but a trained person can scan it quite rapidly. . . . When the volume is extremely large, you can develop analysts who go through it quickly, and then if they are well trained, their eyes will alight on what are the critical things . . . in the political field you have an enormous volume of material available which, if intelligently used, gives you a very good idea of their [Soviet] intentions, and then if you superimpose or add it to the military information you have from intelligence sources, you obtain a very good picture of what the Russians are up to.[9]

Trained analysts can do much more than just sift through large amounts of open-source materials efficiently. During the cold war, intelligence analysts in both the United States and the Soviet Union recognized the value of tracking the published scientific papers of key individuals in various military technology development programs.

When a recognized Soviet scientific expert would stop publishing for a period of time, an American analyst would use that change in behavior as an indicator of possible new technologies being developed, with implications for national security. Using such open-source indicators, the analyst would then turn to other sources to determine exactly what those new technologies might be, how far along a country might be in their development, and the possible implications of such developments.

It is unlikely that pinpointing the activities of foreign scientists through their publications, or lack of them, will be as useful in the future as it was during certain times of the cold war. However, using open sources to develop a more thorough understanding of scientists' professional portfolio, including what research and training they are currently pursuing, where they got their education, what international conferences they attend, what international research institutes they may have visited or worked at, could provide critical information relating to a group's choice of weapons, its ability to develop certain capabilities, or its network of connections.

Intelligence analysts will need to be able to do more than "surf the net." They will not only have to possess a good understanding of the substantive issues but also be familiar with those working outside the intelligence community on these issues, where relevant open-source materials might be located, and know how to use technology to assess, collect, and store the information. For example, during the immediate postconflict situation in Iraq, it might have been very helpful for intelligence analysts in the field supporting military operations to have had online access to the histories of various Iraqi tribes. With this type of background information, coalition troops in Iraq and the Iraqi survey group might have had better insight into local relationships and been able to better exploit them. Intelligence analysts will have to develop a broader vision of their roles, resulting in their being "able to identify, task, and interact with subject matter experts outside of the Intelligence Community, most of whom do not hold traditional clearances."[10]

In addition to needing analysts with the necessary language, education, and cultural exposure, modern technologies can facilitate the collection, sorting, prioritizing, and even translating of the mountains of open-source information available. Finding that one critical piece of information in all these data will require more than just an expert analyst. It is now possible to use sophisticated data-mining programs and robust search engines to collect and organize electronically available open sources. To make these programs reliable, however, they may need to be finely tuned and fully tested by the analysts and experts expected to use them. Without such direct engagement, the analysts will not trust that these programs are actually gathering all the relevant information. They will continue to do their own searches even if this is a much slower process that may not get done.

To keep pace with the fast-moving transnational character of events as well as local contexts, the intelligence community must do a better job of integrating OSINT with classified data for analysts. New information technology capabilities may offer analysts the necessary tools to exploit fully such an all-source information flow. Linking technology to relevant experts will diminish the sense of "looking for a needle in a haystack" or the "signal-to-noise" problem that today's communication revolution has exacerbated. For example, advances in visualization technologies allow for better trend analysis and pattern recognition of extensive amounts of data. With such capabilities, analysts may be able to "see" more quickly and thus identify critical illicit trading nodes, a commonality in operational methodology, or even a person at the center of certain activities. Without technologies to sort, note repetitions, prioritize, and search intelligently through diverse types of data streams, it will be difficult to transform open sources into OSINT that might provide critical information about intentions, actions, networks, and trends, and thus detect significant security threats.

Open-source materials are most effective if the analyst understands their relevance to specific types of questions. Although the location of a country's covert biological weapons (BW) laboratory is not likely to be found by combing through reams of unclassified information, an analyst could potentially learn from annual reports of companies and research institutes which scientists or groups in that country are working on research related to BW. Using this information as a catalytic clue, analysts could then focus other covert efforts on identifying and locating hidden facilities or programs.

This example underscores the growing importance of open-source information in the identification and tracking of threats related to weapons of mass destruction (WMD). These threats involve dual-use technology. Understanding the technology, the manufacturers, and the supply network demands the use of open sources. Numerous websites with detailed information on manufacturing processes or images of equipment could provide critical information to analysts about exports, items discussed in classified materials, or industrial capabilities.

As the number of states with "virtual" chemical, biological, and even nuclear arsenals—that is, nonweaponized WMD capability—grows, the intelligence community will also need to improve its understanding of a state's or nonstate actor's motives, goals, and intentions. A profile of the "strategic personality" of such actors will be important when assessing when, how, and why they might break out of commercial activities and cross the WMD threshold. To do this type of assessment well requires a diverse, multidisciplinary team with access to cultural anthropologists, historians, economists, political scientists, business consultants, scientists, and psychologists.

Open sources can also be critical in evaluating social, political, and economic trends. As Gregory F. Treverton notes in *Reshaping National Intelligence in an Age of Information*, the U.S. national intelligence officer for warning in 1994 developed her assessments of a potential financial problem looming in Mexico based on work with some

Wall Street analysts who were pessimistic about the Mexican situation. In doing so, she "broke out of the isolation that was—and is—all too characteristic of American intelligence."[11] But, because her negative assessments were not linked to a better understanding of the domestic political dynamic facing the ruling Mexican political party and were not aggressively outlined or briefed, the United States missed an opportunity to be proactive as this financial crisis unfolded.

In the aftermath of the crisis, it became apparent that the assessments from all sides concerned with this event were not based on secrets; open sources provided the core information. In this case analysts, even those with a pessimistic interpretation of the financial realities of Mexico at the time, framed their assessments around their confidence that the Mexican government would take action to devalue the peso. The little-known fact that such a move was extremely problematic for Mexican politicians was not given much weight in the U.S. government's assessments of this situation. If, in fact, some additional classified information had become available about Mexican reserves and integrated into these assessments, a more thoroughly informed discussion could have taken place and perhaps would have tilted the assessments and policies in a different direction.[12] Therefore, it is important that analysts using open-source information have realistic expectations and a solid understanding of how best to leverage the knowledge gleaned from such materials.

When to Use Open Sources

Open sources can play a critical role in several situations, either as an integral part of an intelligence assessment, as a means to protect sources and methods, or as a way to facilitate international and operational activities. The key to effective use of open sources is understanding when they can be of value, how to obtain them, and how to evaluate their accuracy. First, they can provide the foundation or frame of reference for an intelligence assessment without which analysts might miss the purpose of some event. The analysts could end up misinterpreting the available classified information or making other errors in judgment. Michael Barletta made this point in his discussion of the U.S. strikes against the al-Shifa pharmaceutical plant in Sudan following the 1998 bombing of the embassies in Africa.

> Senior U.S. officials were shown to have been ignorant of key facts at the time of their decision to bomb the plant. U.S. political authorities and intelligence officials were not aware that: 1) Shifa was an important producer of pharmaceuticals in the Sudan and its products were widely available in Khartoum pharmacies; 2) U.S. officials at the United Nations had approved Shifa's proposed export of veterinary medicine to Iraq under the U.N. oil-for-food program; 3) Shifa was not under heavy military guard but quite open to Sudanese and foreign visitors; 4) the plant was not owned by the government but by a Saudi banking consultant with some ties to the Sudanese anti-Islamist opposition.[13]

Whether the U.S. retaliatory attack on the al-Shifa facility in Sudan was warranted or not, the intelligence community might have been better prepared to deal with skeptics if it had studied available unclassified information about the plant.

Second, open-source information can be used instead of classified materials to protect sources and methods. In these situations the open-source information permits the sharing of information with the public, foreign officials, inspectors, or military personnel without endangering people or assets in the field. Whenever open and classified sources are linked, special gains may be attainable. For example, something a journalist reports might provide a missing piece of data that allows the intelligence community to better target its collection effort. If open-source information acts as a catalyst to other activities, however, or helps to facilitate public discussions, the intelligence analyst must be careful to protect his classified sources. The intelligence community's "footprint" cannot be so obvious as to lead back to a classified source or provide insight about a classified collection method.

Third, open sources can in some cases provide critical information from sources that are more acceptable than the U.S. government. For example, the exposé by a group of Iranian expatriates and dissidents about specific nuclear facilities in Iran, including commercially available photos and other details, forced the IAEA to confront Iran. Eventually, Iran had to admit to having undeclared activities and agreed to allow several inspections of these previously undeclared nuclear sites.

Fourth, during any operation, regardless of whether it is a military activity or an onsite inspection, having ready access to open-source materials can be critical. Now that high-quality commercial satellite imagery is available online, it can be used in real time to help situate a team in the field. Although imagery from the intelligence community may be difficult to downgrade, open sources provide material that can easily be shared in an international context with non-American colleagues, even with adversaries if appropriate. Numerous examples in Iraq, Iran, and the former Soviet Union have demonstrated that OSINT is critical to American officials' ability to accomplish their tasks without endangering classified information.

Finally, open sources can provide information on methodology and theory that will help an analyst develop a rigorous assessment. This type of "ivory tower" open-source information provides paradigms, concepts, and theories that a good analyst will integrate into his approach to evaluating the various data available.[14]

Obstacles to Effective Use of Open Sources

The obstacles to using open sources effectively are extensive and include conceptual limitations, language barriers, and weak technical infrastructures. Some of these problems are not unique to the exploitation of open sources but reflect organizational issues, turf rivalries, and inadequate human analytical capabilities.[15] U.S. analytic tradecraft is generally hurt by limitations in critical foreign-area expertise and languages, insufficient technical expertise, and poor intra- as well as interorganizational (including international) coordination and collaboration.

Overcoming institutional and analytical prejudices against open sources, coping with the magnitude of open-source information, and developing means to ensure quality control represent the most important challenges to the OSINT discipline. Initiatives have been under way for some time to address all these barriers, but progress has been slow and limited in scope. To overcome these challenges, OSINT will require higher priority and thus more resources and persistent attention from senior intelligence managers. This commitment will be difficult to secure. The culture of the intelligence community tends to devalue the use of open sources except in marginal ways. In part because open sources are by definition available to the public, they remove one of the psychological benefits of being an insider with special information. Relying on classified information immediately limits those with whom an analyst can discuss issues and creates a wall between those with access and those without it. Intelligence analysts must, by law, exclude outsiders without clearance from access to classified information; but in this way they create an exclusive club that inhibits the use of relevant and potentially significant expertise. Also, as noted earlier, many intelligence analysts trust only classified information. They may put excessive confidence in such materials, perhaps in the belief that they have been closely vetted and validated during the collection process. This stamp of approval for classified information, and the bias favoring it over other sources, can cause analysts to be closed off to data emerging from researchers who use open sources.

Intelligence analysts have often been skeptical that open sources can add anything of value to an investigation.[16] A favorite example in the intelligence community concerns the prelude to India's nuclear tests in 1998. Despite the Bharatiya Janata Party's clear statements of intent in this regard during its election campaign, the U.S. intelligence community neither heightened its monitoring of the nuclear test site nor increased its collection of relevant open-source literature after this party won the election. Rather than recognize the significance of the change in Indian domestic politics and the potential implications for its nuclear weapons program, much of the intelligence community (and policy community) remained static in its approach to India, choosing to downplay the warning indicators from open-source materials. The result was that the United States, along with many other countries, was caught unprepared when India performed a series of nuclear tests in the spring of 1998.

The institutional mindset that devalues open-source intelligence and limits the ongoing engagement of nongovernmental experts must be challenged and changed. While in recent years parts of the intelligence community have initiated several new outreach efforts, these relationships cannot easily be fully collaborative and are difficult to sustain beyond a specific conference or workshop. During a crisis the policy community is more likely than the intelligence community to call upon such external networks. The intelligence community needs to foster and strengthen initiatives aimed at increasing the analysts' ongoing access to open sources and outside experts.

Another obstacle to the effective use of open sources concerns a set of information technology issues. First, computer security experts are still grappling with how to provide analysts access to both classified and unclassified systems at their desktops. One approach has been to obtain unclassified databases and dump them into classified systems, which often causes the open-source materials to become classified. Another approach has been to have unclassified systems available in certain central points, where analysts can then access the Internet to search for additional data. But analysts then have to download the materials to CDs or floppy disks and physically walk the data to their computers. This use of the "sneaker net" to move the open-source data from one system to the other is cumbersome and unlikely to be widely practiced, especially during crises. Since the Wen Ho Lee incident, in which questionable materials were downloaded from Lee's classified system to an unclassified one, the "sneaker net" approach has been discouraged and in some cases prohibited.

Moreover, even as the U.S. government spends tens of millions of dollars to improve information retrieval, sorting, and dissemination systems, the magnitude of available open-source material seems to grow daily as the pace of the information revolution accelerates. Yet these phenomenal capabilities are not part of the daily intelligence scene. Analysts within the various agencies that make up the intelligence community continue for the most part to pursue their research and assessments as they always have, jockeying for position in the interagency process of vetting, where there is little time or incentive to use open-source materials.

Some of these obstacles will diminish as technology evolves in a way that facilitates easier integration of all sources of information. The next generation of analysts will probably demand easy and ongoing access to at least electronic open sources because of their own comfort level with using the Internet for research, analysis, communications, and dissemination. Thus the mere passage of time will eventually cause the intelligence community to overcome some of these mindset and institutional barriers. But can the United States afford to wait for these generational changes to occur, given our security environment?

A final issue about open-source materials relates to their quality. How accurate is most open-source information? How does one determine the veracity of information that is generated for reasons that usually have little to do with intelligence requirements? As Judy Miller, a well-known *New York Times* reporter, commented in February 2004 on the NPR talk show "The Connection," "My job was not to collect information and analyze it independently as an intelligence agency [analyst]; my job was to tell readers of the *New York Times*, as best as I could figure out, what people inside the governments, who had very high security clearances, who were not supposed to talk to me, were saying to one another."[17] Like most mainstream journalists, Miller saw her job as reporting what people were saying, not as investigating whether or not it was true. Thus her articles would not have significantly advanced intelligence analysts' knowledge of a given issue. The Mexican financial crisis, mentioned above, is a clear case in which the objectivity of the data emerging from Wall Street should have been questioned. Given the rush to exploit opportunities in Mexico, researchers for Wall Street firms were not trying to protect U.S. security concerns but to support their groups' marketing activities.[18]

This lack of control over all aspects of open-source material development means that users of the information must find ways to validate its accuracy. Collectors and analysts of any type of information can become politicized and subjective in their work, as demonstrated by the erroneous reports, from those inside and outside the government, of Iraq's WMD in the months leading up to the March 2003 U.S. attack on that country.

The Internet presents its own type of validation challenge. Unlike newspapers or television news reporters, whose bias is well known or whose accuracy is often questioned, information on the Internet can appear authoritative even when its author is unknown. Given the magnitude of information retrieved via the Internet, it is often hard to determine the accuracy of each piece of data or be familiar with the hundreds of thousands of websites from which open-source intelligence might come. Analysts must become familiar with those websites whose information can generally be trusted, but at the same time develop criteria for determining the veracity of any information obtained from them if they are to exploit the richness of the Internet rather than be exploited by it.

Future Considerations and Recommendations

New information capabilities, which reflect the transnational and multifaceted nature of the current environment, provide both opportunities and potential pitfalls for the intelligence community. First, as the intelligence community works to make more effective use of open sources, it must recognize that these same sources will also be available to groups outside the government. This aspect of the open-source revolution — fast, universal access to a stream of information from around the world — has a downside. The intelligence community may be pressed to produce its own assessments ever more quickly and without sufficient verification and critiques.

The intelligence community has already found itself competing with nongovernmental and media groups for accurate assessments of rapidly unfolding events. During the summer of 1997, an event was detected at or near a Russian test site near the Arctic Circle. The initial assessment was developed very quickly by the U.S. intelligence community and indicated that the event might be a low-yield nuclear test by the Russians in violation of the Threshold Test Ban Treaty and the Comprehensive Test Ban Treaty (CTBT). The problem was that the event was detected not only by the U.S. intelligence community but also by the new CTBT monitoring center and by academic researchers worldwide. Very diverse technical interpretations of the data were provided quickly, which led to conflicting assessments. This incident put U.S. intelligence on notice that other groups, with similar information, might be able to present immediate technical analysis that caused its own assessments to be suspect. This type of situation may erode the credibility of the intelligence community's assessments in the eyes of the public, policymakers, and the international community.[19] The question of whether Iraq had WMD provides another example of how open sources can muddy the waters. The intelligence community was both a source for many reporters (leaked information and unclassified versions of classified estimates) as well as a user of materials that reporters and area experts were gleaning with their own capabilities.

Second, the effort to retrieve, translate, and exploit open sources will require significant resources. The Foreign Broadcast Information Service (FBIS), which acts as the primary source of foreign open-source materials for the U.S. intelligence community, survives on a minimal budget when compared to other intelligence collection efforts. Strengthening the FBIS by building on what it calls its "smart front end—dedicated human beings with cultural ties to the countries of interest and continuity with the issues,"[20] would not be anywhere as costly as developing, launching, and exploiting data obtained from satellites; yet it could have the potential for providing a wealth of new information.

Third, in the long run, the question is whether intelligence organizations in the United States (and elsewhere) will be able to develop technical and human resources to facilitate the manipulation of all these materials. Specifically, will the network of diverse human resources be cultivated and sustained, and will there be organizational support for the effective use of open sources? Transnational threats require that the intelligence community develop analysts with transnational competence, which means relying more extensively on open-source materials and expertise.[21]

The very nature of the transnational threat demands that we have analysts with language capabilities and area knowledge to understand local situations in relationship to global, transnational, and international trends and impacts. Analysts need a professional network that transcends territorial borders, and they need to be comfortable turning to local as well as global information. Most important, they have to be open to the diversity of cultural paradigms, which may have different rules, communication patterns, and norms. The intelligence research professional of the future will also need to have good multicultural communication and language skills, as the U.S. intelligence community works more consistently and collaboratively with its foreign counterparts. American analysts will also have to use experts and materials generated in other languages and communities outside the United States. All these activities are designed to improve the analysts' abilities to get inside the heads of potential adversaries. To defeat the transnational networks of actors such as Osama bin Laden or AQ Khan will require a dynamic, interactive transnational effort that relies on all relevant information, regardless of its classification.

One way to gain access to the expertise needed is to collect as much open-source information as possible, and to use advanced information technologies to facilitate collection, sorting, and prioritizing of the gigabytes of information. Another approach would be to establish focus groups. The members of these groups could have security clearances, act as sounding boards, and come from outside the government, with recognized foreign-area, economic, or linguistic expertise. By engaging with such groups over time, intelligence analysts could develop a rapport and trust with their members. The intelligence community would improve its access to open-source information and the unclassified perspectives necessary to improve its capabilities to deal with the new complexities and diversities of current international relations, not only on a daily basis but also during a crisis. An extension of this idea would be to establish special national reserve units that would consist of area or issue experts. These reservists could have limited obligations in terms of military training, be preapproved for appropriate security clearances, and be available during any crisis that required their expertise.[22] Such an approach would give the United States the flexibility to surge its resources to fit specific situations.

Open sources must become a routine part of the intelligence community's information flows. While the suggestions made in this chapter are not as flashy as satellite imagery or human spy stories, they may pay off in equally significant ways. Providing intelligence analysts with insights into the way others think and act, as well as unique data, reports, and comments, will address some of the major gaps and blind spots for which the intelligence community has long been criticized. For open sources to become an integral aspect of intelligence assessments, an investment in developing the relevant human resources inside and outside the intelligence community will be needed. Equally important will be having organizational leadership that monitors the use of open sources and works to eradicate the current bias against open sources. Only then will assessments be truly all-source.

Notes

I am grateful to my research assistant Jennifer Machado for all her assistance in the production of this chapter.

1. Timothy V. McCarthy, senior analyst at the Center for Nonproliferation Studies and former UNSCOM inspector, personal discussion with the author, Monterey, Calif., June 2004.

2. Mark Lowenthal, *Intelligence: From Secrets to Policy* (Washington, D.C.: CQ Press, 2000), 5.

3. Joseph Nye, speaking to members of the Security Affairs Support Association, Fort Meade, Md., April 24, 1993.

4. Commission on the Roles and Capabilities of the U.S. Intelligence Community (Aspin-Brown Commission), *Preparing for the 21st Century: An Appraisal of U.S. Intelligence, Executive Summary* (Washington, D.C.: U.S. Government Printing Office, 1996).

5. Mark Lowenthal, "Open Source Intelligence: New Myths, New Realities," *Defense Daily Network: Special Reports*, June 24, 2004, available at www.defensedaily.com/reports/osintmyths.htm.

6. Bruce Fiene, executive secretary, science and technology intelligence committee, open source subcommittee, memo, October 15, 1994. Quoted in *NATO Open Source Intelligence Reader* (staff of supreme allied commander, Atlantic, General W. F. Kernan, and supreme allied commander, Europe, Rear Admiral F. M. P.'t Hart, and Open Source Solutions, Inc., February 2002), 4, available at http://www.au.af.mil/awc/awcgate/nato/osint_reader.pdf.

7. Robert David Steele, "Open Source Intelligence and Strategic Generalizations," Open Source Solutions, Inc., August 25, 2003, http://www.oss.net.

8. Gregory F. Treverton, *Reshaping National Intelligence in an Age of Information* (New York: Cambridge University Press), 108.

9. Excerpt republished in Jeffrey T. Richelson, *The U.S. Intelligence Community* (Cambridge, Mass.: Ballinger Publishing, 1985), 175–76.

10. *NATO Open Source Intelligence Reader*, 4; McCarthy, personal discussion with the author.

11. Treverton, *Reshaping National Intelligence*, 97–98.

12. Ibid.

13. Michael Barletta, "Report: Chemical Weapons in the Sudan," *Nonproliferation Review* 6 (fall 1998): 130.

14. McCarthy, personal discussion with the author; various discussions with intelligence analysts from 2002 through 2004.

15. Prominent reviews and commissions relating to the U.S. intelligence community include the 1995–96 Commission on the Roles and Capabilities of the U.S. Intelligence Community (Aspin-Brown Commission); IC21: "The Intelligence Community in the 21st Century" (House Permanent Select Committee on Intelligence Staff study, 1996); "Modernizing Intelligence: Structure and Change for the 21st Century" (Odom study, 1997); "Intelligence Community Performance on the Indian Nuclear Test" (Jeremiah report, 1998); Rumsfeld Commission on the Ballistic Missile Threat (1999); "Countering the Changing Threat of International Terrorism," a report from the National Commission on Terrorism (Bremer Commission, 2000); Advisory Panel to Assess Domestic Response Capabilities to Terrorism Involving Weapons of Mass Destruction (Gilmore Commission, third annual report, 2001); Deutch Commission on Weapons of Mass Destruction (2001); "A Review of Federal Bureau of Investigation Security Programs" (Webster Commission, 2002).

16. In 2002 I was told by an analyst at the Defense Threat Reduction Agency that a proposed study on Iraq's security services could not be done without classified information. Using open-source gray literature, an analyst at the Center for Nonproliferation Studies in Monterey put together one of the most detailed studies of this key Iraqi organization. It was so good that the

British government plagiarized it heavily in one of its key reports. See Mike Lewis, "Government 'Intelligence' Report on Iraq Revealed as Plagiarism," *Federation of American Scientists,* February 6, 2003, available at www.fas.org/irp/news/2003/02/uk020603.html.

17. Quoted in Franklin Foer, "The Source of the Trouble," *New York Metro,* June 7, 2004, available at www.newyorkmetro.com/nymetro/news/media/features/9226/index.html.

18. Treverton, *Reshaping National Intelligence,* 97–98.

19. This assessment was leaked and used to justify critical comments about Russian behavior and the CTBT. Eventually a revised assessment, which reflected the likelihood that this was a seismic event located offshore near the Russian test site, was quietly released.

20. *NATO Open Source Intelligence Reader,* 13.

21. Peter H. Koehn and James N. Rosenau, "Transnational Competence in an Emergent Epoch," *International Studies Perspectives* 34 (2002): 105–27.

22. McCarthy, personal discussion with the author.

FIVE

Clandestine Human Intelligence
Spies, Counterspies, and Covert Action

JOHN MACGAFFIN

OUR NATION'S clandestine service—the heart of the Central Intelligence Agency (CIA) and its Directorate of Operations (DO)—is at a critical crossroads. The road signs here should read "Success" and "Failure," but of course they do not. The future of clandestine HUMINT,[1] however, depends entirely on which road is taken. Simply put, the twin disasters of the September 11 attacks and the analytic conclusion that Iraq had weapons of mass destruction (WMD) represent systemic weaknesses and failures whose roots of responsibility go far beyond the traditional intelligence community and include policymakers, Congress, and many others. Weaknesses of both offense and defense will certainly lead to similar or even worse tragedies in the future unless these deep-seated problems are corrected. The need for real transformation in clandestine HUMINT—as well as in other elements of the intelligence community—seems absolutely inescapable. The inevitability of even greater damage to our core economic and national security interests should this warning go unheeded constitutes an irresistible imperative for change.

The World of Clandestine HUMINT

No matter what changes in structures or authorities lie ahead, clandestine HUMINT will nonetheless remain the indispensable element of national intelligence collection. While overhead reconnaissance systems were critical and irreplaceable for monitoring possible Soviet troop movements through the Fulda Gap in central Europe during the cold war or for attempting to overhear Soviet Politburo members' conversations around Moscow, the essential secrets we need to uncover today in the face of terrorist and other threats are no longer as susceptible to technical attack as they were in the past. Osama bin Laden stopped using his Inmarsat[2] communications system to send instructions to his al-Qaeda operatives around the world shortly after an unknown government official revealed— perhaps on background—that those conversations were being monitored by U.S. intelligence.[3] Another nail was put into this particular coffin when Justice Department officials discussed this capability in the course of the east Africa bombing trials in the southern district of New York in 2000–2001. Other foes have long been able, figuratively, to pull up the sheets — that is, to conceal evidence of hostile activities — just before regular over-flights of our spy satellites would have brought it into view. For these and other reasons, unfortunately, it falls almost exclusively on clandestine HUMINT, supported by expert analysis and integrated into wise, enlightened policymaking, to give us insight into the secret plans and intentions of those adversaries who would do us "unthinkable" harm in the decade ahead.

Certain characteristics of clandestine HUMINT separate this collection discipline from others: its potential for extraordinarily high gains matched by high risks; its integral relationship to covert action and counterintelligence; its inherent vulnerability to abuse and to errant, opportunistic tasking; and its heavy dependence on forms of cover and collection that are not owned or controlled by the intelligence community.[4] The failure of both policymakers and HUMINT managers adequately to acknowledge and deal with the advantages as well as the problems of HUMINT lie at the heart of the U.S. government's current intelligence weaknesses.

Indeed, this chapter argues that transforming clandestine HUMINT is not only urgently necessary but must entail a return to first principles, including recognition of the nature of the discipline that makes it unique. Otherwise, simply changing bureaucratic structures, increasing personnel, and even diversifying HUMINT cadres will not solve HUMINT's current weakness. After discussing the terrain of HUMINT and its most important features, this chapter offers rules to follow if clandestine HUMINT is to be reestablished as an effective instrument of U.S. statecraft.

First Principles

The *ne plus ultra* of first principles, which should be understood by collector, analyst, and policymaker alike, is that clandestine HUMINT should only be employed when it is clear that no other option is available or has a real possibility to succeed. Clandestine HUMINT — to properly distinguish it from those aspects of overt, nonsecret intelligence collection involving human players — is not simply one of a number of options available. It should be the final and critical option. Some of the country's greatest intelligence failures, as well as its most embarrassing intelligence "flaps," have occurred because people ignored this simple principle. The expulsion of U.S. government personnel from Paris in 1995, which will be discussed below, is a case in point. The skilled human resources required to penetrate the enemy's most secret councils are too scarce, and the risks of disproportionate "collateral" damage to other national interests too great, to employ clandestine HUMINT for anything but pursuit of the truly indispensable secret. Two examples: a single clandestine HUMINT asset reporting from within the Iraqi army's suspended WMD program might have changed the nature of the U.S.

reaction to Saddam Hussein; and one clandestine HUMINT source among Muhammad Atta's co-plotters in Hamburg, or among the would-be hijackers assembled in San Diego, could have disrupted and perhaps prevented the September 11 attacks. But our nation's clandestine HUMINT apparatus did not produce these critical assets when we most needed them.

To further complicate matters, clandestine HUMINT itself includes a diverse range of activities. In addition to foreign intelligence (FI), both counterintelligence (CI) and covert action (CA) are, to a significant degree, integral parts of clandestine HUMINT. Put another way, FI, CI, and CA are impossible without the capabilities provided by clandestine HUMINT. FI is that secret or open information needed to uncover the plans and intentions of prospective adversaries and foreign powers in general. The clandestine portion of foreign intelligence is acquired by U.S.-government-controlled secret activities (unilateral operations) and by secret activities controlled in part or whole by a foreign, usually governmental, partner (liaison operations). FI slides into CI and vice versa, depending on whether a foreign country's intentions are or are not aimed against the United States. Especially when those intentions are hostile, the most aggressive aspects of CI include deep human source penetration of enemy intelligence services as well as the use of double agents and deception to misinform an adversary's intelligence services and policymakers, while at the same time informing our side of those hostile intentions.

Counterintelligence is not, as the Congress and much of the executive branch apparently believe, an activity apart from HUMINT. It *is* HUMINT, and it is separated from HUMINT at the peril of collector and consumer alike. Spies in other nations' intelligence services must be recruited, not only to enable us to unmask and neutralize spies in our own government and military, but, perhaps more important, to enable policymakers to understand the most secret intentions of adversaries and to calibrate our offense and defense accordingly.

Finally, covert action can be understood only if, and can never be successful unless, it too is recognized as an integral element of clandestine human intelligence capabilities. The clandestine human intelligence capabilities required to understand an adversary's secret intentions (FI and CI) are the same as those needed to implement secret activities to thwart or modify those plans (CA and CI) and then to determine whether one's efforts are actually having the desired impact (FI and CI again). Since the 1974 Hughes-Ryan amendment, the U.S. government has attempted to establish mechanisms to ensure that policymakers not only authorize CA operations but are directly involved in CA planning and evaluation. Yet the American public still labors under the impression that if one could just get rid of the "Department of Dirty Tricks" in the CIA, the U.S. could return to an "honorable" foreign policy. Both in design and in practice, FI, CI, and CA are elements of U.S. foreign policy, not something apart.

The fact is that foreign intelligence, counterintelligence, and covert action are all conducted within the CIA's Directorate of Operations, often by the same people and often interchangeably, in their minds, because these activities are threads in a common fabric. For this reason all three activities have significant oversight by both the president and Congress. In the case of covert action, congressional oversight is often extraordinarily detailed. Fastidiousness in observing the distinctions among these three activities is not risk aversion but political savvy in a town where a problem in one area, such as a CA activity gone awry, can have a devastating impact on important FI and CI activities as well. Indeed, the importance of understanding the interrelatedness of these constituent parts of clandestine HUMINT, and the risks entailed in failing to distinguish among them, suggests the need to consider each in greater detail, to underscore both their unique requirements and their essential synergies.

Counterintelligence Is HUMINT

There is a world of misunderstanding swirling around the relationship of counterintelligence to clandestine HUMINT. A great deal of it is caused and exacerbated by bureaucratic structures and practices across the intelligence community.

Properly understood, the universe of counterintelligence embraces that range of threats that would cause "unthinkable" harm to our core national and economic security interests. This has been referred to as "big CI" and is contrasted with the lower-level tasks of uncovering spies (counterespionage) and learning the capabilities and strength of the world's intelligence services. The latter purpose has been called "little CI" and is the stuff of which spy novels are made. Aldrich Ames, who spied for the Soviets from within the CIA for nine years, was operating in the world of "little CI." Although what Ames gave over did not destroy the United States' core security interests, it destroyed the lives of some extraordinarily valuable Soviet agents operating on behalf of the CIA within the Soviet intelligence system and denied their critical insights to U.S. policymakers.

Presidential Decision Directive 75 (PDD-75), originated by the Clinton administration (and one of the few national security PDDs actually retained by the Bush administration), attempted to put counterintelligence in its proper perspective. Elaborating the concept of "big CI," PDD-75 drew the important conclusion that we could no longer proceed as though there were a finite number of opponents (the USSR, North Korea, China) against whom we needed to maintain vigilance. That had been a successful strategy during the cold war, but since the collapse of the Soviet Union a very large number of players had developed numerous ways to cause us grievous harm. Consequently, instead of monitoring only specified opponents, the key strategy would now be to focus on those interests that policymakers designated the "crown jewels" of our core national and economic security. The intention of this new approach was to recognize that the threats themselves are strategic and that the response therefore must be strategic as well. Obviously such a response can only be conceived and driven at the national policy level.

While the concept and intellectual core of PDD-75 found almost universal, enthusiastic reception in the intelligence community and in Congress, the specific organizational structures and practices, notably the new national counterintelligence executive (NCIX) that it spawned, have so far been successfully resisted by turf warriors within the bureaucracy. Although executive orders of two administrations assigned to the NCIX a centralizing responsibility for both defense and related offense within the realm of CI, little or no progress has been made. The Clinton administration appointed as its head a relatively inexperienced Federal Bureau of Investigation (FBI) field office chief who had neither the background nor the stature to bring the new regime into being. As a result, the NCIX has had no real directing power over the various agencies engaged in counterintelligence — a sad commentary on the actual authority and impact of an executive order.

The FBI in particular has been single-minded in trying to block implementation — first of the PDD and then of the Counterintelligence Enhancement Act of 2002, which put the NCIX into law. Determined to keep all of CI — both big and little — within its traditional and exclusive realm, the FBI has refused to provide either the personnel or the information required to support this presidentially mandated effort. Instead it continues to suggest that this new national structure with strategic purposes be integrated into the FBI's national security division. In March 2005 President Bush signed a new "National Counterintelligence Strategy for the 21st Century," which further emphasized the role of the NCIX in leading an aggressive CI program for the nation. The FBI was not quick to endorse this enhanced role.

Covert Action Is Also HUMINT

Next in the list of misunderstood and misused elements of HUMINT comes covert action, traditionally and simplistically described as that option of U.S. foreign policy that lies between military action and diplomatic activity. Covert action rests on a foundation built through clandestine human intelligence capabilities.

Because it seems at first glance to be a deceptively simple way to cut through intractable foreign policy problems, whether of our own making or born abroad, covert action has been a magnet for policymakers. The Clinton administration requested a remarkable number of CA proposals to deal with the increasingly troublesome array of problems it faced in the early 1990s, only to conclude that covert action could not save the United States from overt military intervention. But even when covert action appears to be an appropriate tool of foreign policy, as in the initial covert supply of weapons and other support to the Afghan mujahadeen after the Soviet invasion in 1979, it often brings with it unexpected consequences, such as the rise in Islamic fundamentalist power and influence in Afghanistan following the Soviet defeat and withdrawal.

Covert action employs all the tools of HUMINT — spies, counterspies, liaison services, radios, newspapers, armies, special operations personnel, and more — in support of a policy-driven effort to influence events and views in foreign lands without disclosing the hand of the U.S. government. Because CA has been employed to one extent or another by every president, Democrat or Republican, since the CIA's establishment, the agency has a responsibility to develop and maintain the skills and logistical capacities required to carry out such programs on short notice. In unhappy fact, however, some of the crucial capabilities for covert action are dismantled or allowed to atrophy when a specific threat recedes. For example, when the Soviets withdrew from Afghanistan, U.S. covert operatives and their attendant HUMINT support structure ended, only to be reconstructed in haste and at great expense when they were needed to combat the Taliban and bin Laden in that same country years later. Still, even when skills and capabilities for covert action exist, it is not always an easy or clear decision for an administration to employ them. The case of the war against terror is a good example.

For several years before September 11, 2001, the United States had the capability to remove Osama bin Laden from Afghanistan or to kill him. The CIA knew bin Laden's location almost every day — sometimes within fifty miles, sometimes within fifty feet. This was known from information provided by foreign governments, from the CIA's own human sources, and from technical sources like the Predator unmanned aerial drone. Special Forces capabilities had been developed over the previous fifteen years as a result of the legislative reforms that followed the abortive hostage rescue attempt in Iran in 1980. The irony, and indeed the tragedy, is that somewhere between fifteen and thirty Special Forces personnel died or were injured preparing for just that mission that would have removed bin Laden.

Through this period of the late 1990s, the CIA and the military were repeatedly told by policymakers that not enough was known to take paramilitary action against bin Laden. The advice was, "Go back and try again. Collect more information. We need to know well in advance exactly when bin Laden will be in such-and-such a house or on such-and-such a convoy trail." But the fact is that in peacetime intelligence will never deliver the kind of certainty the policymakers said they required. At some point policymakers could have taken a political gamble and moved forward with such an attempt. They did not. In retrospect, with almost three thousand Americans killed in the September 11 attacks, that decision seems remarkably wrong.

Instead, in retaliation for the bombings in east Africa, the U.S. military, on August 20, 1998, launched what were thought to be politically less risky cruise missile attacks on six bin Laden training camps in Afghanistan and on a pharmaceutical plant in Khartoum that had formerly been used by bin Laden and was thought to be involved in producing precursor chemicals. "We only missed him by half an hour," remarked a White House aide ruefully. The uproar over the Khartoum target, whose validity could not be clarified one way or another, was such that no further attacks were carried out by the United States until the shock of September 11 prompted more. Thus the seventy-five cruise missiles that were launched, at a cost of $1 million apiece, were for naught, and the intelligence community was castigated for poor support in targeting the pharmaceutical plant.

But, as indicated earlier, intelligence did have precision against relevant targets. On at least two occasions, in December 1998 and in February 1999, the opportunity arose to launch air attacks in the Qandahar area with the objective of killing bin Laden. Key CIA personnel, both in the field and in Washington, thought this was feasible, but the director of central intelligence (DCI) held back from giving the go-ahead. Larger political considerations seem to have influenced the DCI's hesitation, notably the possibility that innocent civilians might be killed, and in particular, in the case of the second attack, that visiting diplomatic officials from the United Arab Emirates might become targets.[5] Though opinions in Washington differed at the time, there is no doubt in retrospect that there was (and is) no higher-value target than bin Laden, and that the February 1999 opportunity should have been seized, particularly because in that case the target complex was not in an urban area. Ironically, the prospect of political embarrassment, which apparently contributed to the Clinton administration's reluctance to act more decisively in this case, can be just as likely a result if an administration chooses not to act.

For these reasons and others, since the era of more or less untrammeled covert operations in the 1950s and 1960s, successive U.S. administrations and congressional oversight committees have decreed a formidable array of steps for approving, coordinating, and monitoring covert action programs. Although these will not be reviewed in detail here, one informal step is worth special mention. Former DCI William H. Webster once outlined the most sensible of "rules" for considering covert action. He said that the CIA should put forward to the president and the National Security Council only those covert action proposals that could withstand public scrutiny if disclosed. Webster said that "if a normal American would not say, in such a circumstance, 'Oh, now I understand. Of course my government is taking these secret actions. It makes great sense in the world as I know it and is consistent with U.S. policy as I know it,'" then he would not send such a proposal forward to the president for signature. In brief, if disclosed inadvertently, covert action should meet the Webster test.[6]

Most important, presidents must make the broad purposes underlying the covert actions they authorize more widely acceptable to the public so that tactical opportunities, when at last optimized at considerable risk to sources and methods, are politically tolerable and thus can be taken advantage of in peacetime. While the greatest possible precision may be necessary for covert action, presidents act wisely when they build the public consensus necessary to make the inevitable limits of this precision politically tolerable. They carry this burden in the knowledge both that past presidents preserved the integrity of intelligence so that covert options would continue to exist and that they must do the same for future presidents, who may face equally grave or even graver threats to the nation's security.

The Rule for Clandestine HUMINT

Having described the terrain, let us now return to the two-part rule suggested earlier. Clandestine collection of HUMINT must be employed only in pursuit of information that is truly essential to the most critical tasks of civilian and military national security affairs and only when that information cannot be acquired in any other way.

When either of these two conditions is missing, the outcome almost always suffers. If clandestine human source collection is driven by any lesser standard—that is, if it is driven simply by analysts or others in order to satisfy more diffuse needs—the precious resources available will be wasted, while broader national interests will be put at risk unnecessarily. Likewise, if the secret sought does not rise to the "absolutely indispensable" level, then again scarce resources will be squandered and national interests put unnecessarily at risk of "collateral damage." Put another way, the secret sought must be one that an ambassador cannot get by asking a foreign government official, something that a defense attaché cannot count while watching a military parade, or that the Foreign Broadcast Information Service cannot transcribe from Radio Kabul and put on the president's desk each morning.

If a clandestine collection operation had been compromised while trying to obtain Soviet nuclear codes during the cold war, the reaction of policymakers and the public would have been that this was an acceptable risk and should be tried again. Such was apparently not the reaction in 1995, however, when a U.S. clandestine collection operation in Paris was alleged to have been compromised, American personnel were expelled from the embassy there, and all manner of sensational charges were passed back and forth between capitals and recounted in the press. It seems that neither of the two elements of the rule was in place, because the information sought was not absolutely critical and it could have been acquired in some other way. The reactions of policymakers and the public were therefore understandably harsh.

Most fundamentally, the raison d'etre of clandestine HUMINT should be the understanding of the truly secret aspects of those threats posing the most serious challenge to our core national and economic security interests. During the cold war most of those threats were associated with the USSR in one way or another. Clandestine HUMINT was at its best when it addressed only that small subset of secrets that were both critical to national security and otherwise unavailable. And so it is today. Clandestine HUMINT has to focus, laser-like, on those crucial secrets we must have but cannot otherwise obtain. And today most of them reside not in Moscow but on a mountaintop with bin Laden in Pakistan's northwest frontier province; in Iraq with a colonel who had or had not overseen the destruction of Iraqi WMD in the 1990s; in Europe and the United States in the secret meetings of al-Qaeda hijackers as they secretly planned their attacks for almost a decade, both in the shadow of a Hamburg mosque and in the parking lot of a Florida flight school; in a Chinese weapons development lab; in a discussion between the North Korean leader and his closest associates; or even in Jerusalem in the small "special group" that meets after Israeli cabinet sessions to discuss next steps in Gaza and the West Bank.

Transforming Clandestine HUMINT

If the case is so clear, then why cannot the United States do better? If the core mission of clandestine HUMINT has not changed, but only its specific, contemporary applications, then why cannot one get back to basics, get it right, and get the job done?

The good news is that we can and must do exactly that. The bad news is that, once again, turf wars and professional jealousies interfere and frustrate this goal. Walt Kelly and Pogo had it right: "We have met the enemy and he is us."

Revolutionary change, for all practical purposes, has eluded us over the past five decades, despite the almost unbroken string of committees and commissions that have documented the significant need for it. Yet it is certainly possible that the momentum now established by the 9/11 Commission, proposals by the president, recent legislation, and the WMD Commission may produce real change. It is the belief of the contributors to this volume that the proposals for change in policies and practices can, if earnestly pursued, deliver truly significant improvement in performance with less disruption, pain, and cost than major structural change would bring. With regard to clandestine HUMINT, in any event, the three critical steps presented below will be essential.

Three steps, apparently simple but actually quite challenging in a real-world context, could move the U.S. national clandestine HUMINT capacity from what it is now—inadequate and unsatisfactory—to one that can meet the challenges of terrorism, proliferation, and yet unknown threats ahead of us. Rapid and decisive steps are critical to providing necessary authority to senior managers of clandestine HUMINT, particularly the DCI; enforcing lanes among collectors; and staying the course in tradecraft through improved training and operational consistency.

PROVIDE AUTHORITY

The apparently endless debate over the adequacy of the DCI's authority has been disingenuous at best, and, given the tragic costs of recent intelligence failures, has actually bordered on the obscene. The 9/11 Commission "uncovered" no major issue that had not been known for years to government officials and a succession of commissions and congressional committees. This was particularly true of the now "common knowledge" that the DCI lacked sufficient authority to do his job and that this contributed to the September 11 disaster. In fact, this issue had been repeatedly discussed since shortly after the National Security Act of 1947 became law. No serious practitioner successfully made the case that the authority provided to him was adequate to his statutory responsibilities. There were those (especially in the Defense Department and, sometimes, the State Department) who argued that the DCI's limited control over budgets and personnel was not a real problem because they (Defense and State) would exercise appropriate authority over their departmental interests and prerogatives. Clearly, this position had not stood the test of time.

Over time, the DCI attempted to compensate for his lack of real community-wide authority and substituted a process that at best attempted only to distribute pain (and pleasure) equitably. Instead of a "straight line" between important collection requirements at one end and collectors at the other, an impenetrable community management organization headed by an associate DCI and ranks of deputies emerged. On paper it had the inarguably important mission of rationalizing priorities and resources across intelligence disciplines and entities. In practice, however, few operational program managers at any intelligence agency either understood or could influence this crucial process.

As a result of this disjuncture between operations and management, intelligence community management functioned in a nether world where officials with little practical experience in collection or analysis made decisions in which execution year funding failed to meet the needs of the case officer, technical collector, or analyst. An Iranian analyst in the directorate of intelligence lacked funds for foreign travel or Farsi training; a DO station chief had insufficient staff to cover priority tasking or funds for operational travel; a technical collection program had its funding levels changed partway into a system's multiyear development schedule; a Foreign Service officer was unable to travel to parts of his country of assignment; and the FBI spent significant effort monitoring intelligence activities of countries of little national security interest to the United States while failing to devote sufficient coverage to subjects of greater interest.

In reality the intelligence community was a chimera at best, and many of its parts, especially in the Department of Defense (DoD), would have it no other way. Because it is the $400 billion gorilla of the U.S. government, DoD has no interest in making its intelligence priorities or expenditures conform to the whims of its puny $20 billion second cousins.[7]

Now, of course, more robust and inclusive authorities under the new director of national intelligence (DNI) have the possibility of bringing at least the intelligence agencies into better alignment and reducing this historical impediment to acceptable performance by our national intelligence system. Unfortunately, and despite a fairly wide misunderstanding of this point by government officials and public alike, the 2004 intelligence reform legislation does not guarantee that anything at all will actually change. The legislation is only a starting point. The bureaucratic mattress mice of the various intelligence departments have successfully resisted reform since at least 1947 and there is nothing in the legislation to ensure that this will change. While the vulnerabilities that contributed to September 11 and the misreading of Iraqi WMD capabilities are now exposed for all to see, the creation of the new DNI superstructure is no guarantee that the job will get done or the necessary authority executed.

Consider, for example, the arguments advanced by the Defense Department to counter General Brent Scowcroft's proposals to distinguish between "national" and "departmental" intelligence entities and capabilities. DoD has argued that the National Security Agency (NSA), which intercepts communications and other signals, is first and foremost a tool to serve the warfighter (down to the lowest possible level) and not, as others would argue, a resource that serves intelligence collection requirements across the full range of government departments and interests. DoD wants the NSA to remain under some degree of direct day-to-day supervision by the Pentagon. Indeed, it is hard to imagine how the DNI will establish line control of such a large agency given the Pentagon's stake in maintaining its own control.

But if, for the next five years, the technical collection agencies the Pentagon wishes to control—NSA, the National Geospatial-Intelligence Agency (NGA), and the National Reconnaissance Office (NRO)—are largely managed by the DoD and focused on serving the interests of the warfighter down to the lowest possible level, how far will the U.S. government be able to improve its day-to-day ability to exploit the world's diplomatic communications, to map global narcotics production in Latin America, or to develop space platforms for collection of civilian-sector information?

Former DCI George Tenet, like his predecessors, lost the national versus departmental contest to Team DoD at almost every outing. Prior to the report of the 9/11 Commission, the Pentagon was intent on extending the DoD HUMINT reach well beyond traditional support to military personnel and on moving toward a DoD ("departmental") HUMINT capability that would permit it to target its own clandestine human collection assets against nonmilitary "secrets" of state and of nonstate actors, friend and foe. Ironically, the effect of the *9/11 Commission Report* and the subsequent intelligence reform legislation has been to embolden the DoD to establish a stand-alone departmental HUMINT capability that targets many of the same areas and issues as do other members of the intelligence community, especially the CIA.

"Preparation of the battlefield," the new mantra and justification for DoD intelligence collection anywhere in the world, would become the watchword of a new military intelligence tied neither to imminent hostilities nor to the political sensitivities of our relationships with other states. In fact, this mantra has recently morphed even further and is now "preparation of the environment," which (almost certainly intentionally) conjures up images of psychological warfare and a peacetime "battle for men's minds." Activities that in the past have been treated as covert action (and have therefore come under close presidential and congressional scrutiny and oversight), could also be carried out as battlefield (or "environment") preparation without the special safeguards of traditional covert action. If the DoD continues on this path, we could soon have two entities—CIA and DoD—conducting the same intelligence collection activities in the same space, without a clear, authoritative controlling mechanism apart from a centralized staff, with no line authority, under the DNI. Even more troublesome, we could also have the CIA and DoD conducting CA-like activities in the same space, with the CIA working under the traditional executive and congressional oversight and the DoD working under "special activity program" (SAP) rules. This would be worse than what existed before the 2004 reforms.

Without the ability to direct and ultimately remove, if necessary, the officials at the FBI or DoD responsible for implementing key elements of national intelligence strategy when their performance is unsatisfactory, there can be no real national focus to intelligence and no meaningful director of it. The FBI's domestic intelligence collection must respond to national intelligence priorities, not to the attorney general's law enforcement priorities. The DoD's contribution to national intelligence must not be impeded by its tactical collection efforts — or vice versa. Most important, the DNI must have the authority to determine whether the collection efforts of all elements of the U.S. government — FBI, DoD, NSA, CIA, Coast Guard — are satisfactory. To its great shame, the intelligence community has never had a real system of keeping score; it has never been able to distinguish between those collection programs that have been truly effective and those that are more form than substance. The individual components of the intelligence community never wanted such a system. The DNI must bring scorekeeping to the table as a first order of business.

Only a clear and complete assignment of authority and responsibility for "national clandestine HUMINT" will end such a needless — and dangerous — waste of scarce human resources and enable the country to develop HUMINT capabilities to overcome the weaknesses responsible for the tragic intelligence failures of the recent past. Whether that authority resides in the new DNI or in an enhanced and empowered head of CIA is not, in the final analysis, as important as simply ending the present dangerous and dysfunctional impasse.

ENFORCE LANES

With unambiguous assignment of authority for clandestine intelligence collection, counterintelligence and covert action reposing in the DNI (or strengthened for the

head of CIA), a quantum improvement in capability, as well as significant savings in resources, could be quickly achieved simply by enforcing "lanes" across the entire enterprise. This is particularly true for HUMINT. Practically no element of the intelligence
enterprise seems to be disciplined by an understanding of appropriate, efficient, and
effective lanes. Overall, the clearest example of this failure can be seen in our counterterrorism efforts. Sadly, the national counterterrorism effort more closely resembles
kids' soccer than it does professional football. It has no discipline, no lanes, and appall-
ingly inadequate results.

FBI and CIA officials abroad contact the same foreign intelligence and security services on the very same issues. The FBI says it is doing law enforcement tasks. The CIA
says it is collecting foreign intelligence from the same folks on the same subjects. Then
the Defense HUMINT service comes along and deals with the same people as well. The
uncoordinated efforts of these agencies often cause more harm than good and, most
important, deprive us of the advantage over terrorists that we should have. And so we
fall further behind.

Just as the overall national structure requires that someone be in charge, so the interaction with foreign governments on intelligence matters requires a common, controlled
approach lest we find ourselves exploited in one way or another by our friends and foes
alike. This need has become even more apparent and more critical as law enforcement
activities and intelligence collection activities begin to occupy the same foreign space
at the same time.

The FBI distinguishes between law enforcement and intelligence in matters such
as terrorism and maintains that it (as law enforcement) should be free to share information, carry out investigative and operational activities, and undertake an extraordinarily broad range of joint activity with foreign law enforcement counterparts without
coordination or integration with the rest of the national effort. In fact, the FBI's transfer
of information to a foreign law enforcement or security organization about the plans of
al-Qaeda is comparable in every meaningful respect to the president's picking up the
phone to convey the same information. The DNI must have authority, on behalf of
the president, to integrate this aspect of intelligence into foreign policy overall. And as
the head of CIA's and DNI's representative overseas, the CIA station chief must have
clear authority to moderate and coordinate these increasingly complex foreign intelligence relationships.

While the FBI risks complicating rather than advancing U.S. intelligence interests
abroad, it has yet been unable significantly to improve its own performance in intelligence gathering against terrorism and other threats here in the United States. As was
the unhappy case before September 11, the FBI still does not understand the scope of
al-Qaeda's presence within the United States, does not know whether there really are
"sleeper cells" at large in the land or what terrorist groups really intend to accomplish

in the United States. The FBI must acquire significant human source penetrations of al-Qaeda's U.S.-based apparatus, if one exists. It has none, and it cannot answer these questions. Yet the FBI sends hundreds of special agents overseas each month to investigate terrorism and terrorist groups. If it remained in its lane, the FBI would be required first to focus on home, and stay at home, until each of its fifty-six field offices was on top of the threat posed by terrorist organizations. Prior to September 11, the FBI itself evaluated all fifty-six field offices as "red," signifying that none had the infrastructure in place to truly understand the terrorist threat in its territory. The objective was that each field office earn a rating of "green" relative to the terrorist threats for which it is responsible. Unfortunately, they would all still be rated red today, except that the metric is no longer employed.

Likewise, the CIA's Directorate of Operations should abandon, or hand over to others, those aspects of clandestine collection that do not point directly to the second element of the rule—those key secrets that policymakers cannot obtain in any other way. While debriefings and interrogations of captured terrorists can yield important information, this information certainly can be obtained by others. There are thousands of military personnel who, if properly supervised, could do this and other work, which now overwhelms the small case officer cadre of the CIA's Directorate of Operations. Likewise, military intelligence personnel could assume the tactical support to the warfighter's tasks (how wide is the road? how strong is the bridge?) that have occupied more than several hundred CIA personnel, first in Bosnia and now in Iraq. This is not clandestine HUMINT, and precious specialized resources should not be diverted to such tasks.

The same imbalance of personnel versus mission can be found even closer to home. It is not generally known, but there are more FBI special agents assigned to the FBI's New York field office than there are CIA case officers worldwide. (There are approximately twelve hundred FBI special agents in New York alone and more than twelve thousand worldwide.) A more effective application of FBI personnel to domestic intelligence collection would go a long way toward fixing the systemic weaknesses that contributed to September 11.

The comparatively small number of case officers available to the CIA's clandestine service is not, in itself, cause for alarm. Certainly the case officer cadre could profitably be increased significantly, but that is not the real issue. Precious case officer and analytic expertise, even if increased 100 percent, must keep unwavering focus on the most important targets. Instead of judging performance by the number of interrogation reports disseminated or of tactical reports provided to the military, the directorate's metric ought to be focused almost exclusively on acquiring those few indispensable human source penetrations of groups that would attack our core national and economic security interests.

It may strain belief, but a world-class clandestine capability against this standard can actually be measured in single digits. One high-level, authoritative HUMINT penetration of Saddam Hussein's WMD program would have had more impact than all of Ahmad Chalabi's refugee debriefing, interrogation reports, and dubious secret reports combined.[8] One high-level, authoritative penetration of bin Laden's inner circle five years ago might have enabled us to prevent September 11 altogether. The clandestine service has penetrated difficult targets like these in the past, and policymakers know from experience how powerful and important this knowledge can be.

STAY THE COURSE

Even if we solve the problems of authority and mission, there remains one last piece critical to success: consistency. The U.S. government's HUMINT effort must stay the course over time, through fiscal years and through changes of administration. While this clearly applies to all aspects of intelligence, it is especially important for clandestine HUMINT. The CIA's Directorate of Operations, as the presumptive center of HUMINT excellence in our government, deserves a measure of criticism for its own shortcomings in this area.

The clandestine service must stick to its task—not when the going gets tough or dangerous (it has a well-deserved history of that), but rather when the going gets boring or expensive or even less sexy than usual, and when the policymaker is less taken with the immediate importance of a target or activity. Lack of staying power afflicts almost every aspect of the service, from investment in language training, to building expertise in personnel, to developing long-run operations with uncertain payoffs, to searching out new cover and access innovations.

The problem is compounded by factors external to the CIA. The agency's senior leadership, the National Security Council, other government departments—not only State and DoD, but others as well—and the Congress deserve a substantial portion of responsibility for our chronic inability to stay the course in developing those capabilities and assets, the absence of which has contributed to the current critical HUMINT shortfall.

External factors aside, however, the Directorate of Operations has lacked the will to stick to the most difficult task when other targets, other interests, or other approaches have been available. The directorate has not always had the will to insist that case officers leave the comfortable confines of official cover and strike off into new territory where they must gain direct access to those who would cause grave harm to our national interests. The directorate has not always had the will to keep training, career development, and reward focused on this core mission. Since at least the directorship of John Deutch and his big-military-systems orientation, the directorate has been seduced—sometimes willingly, sometimes unwittingly—by the softer trappings of modern management. HUMINT today is very difficult, and it can be very dangerous. Ironically, there is wide agreement within the clandestine service that consistency is key, but the requisite organizational will has not yet emerged.

Organizational will is required to train many more clandestine service officers in Arabic, Farsi, Dari, and other languages. Organizational will is required to keep these students in language training until they are fluent, rather than pull them out prematurely when some other inevitable "priority" tempts management to reassign them. Organizational will is required to commit individuals and funding over the long term to the most important targets, without being diverted by old notions of "career diversity" or budgetary pressures. And most of all, organizational will is required to make "risky" calls, not so much those that threaten physical danger but those in troubling areas where no textbook solution is obvious and no outcome predictable. This cannot happen without cooperation from other agencies and oversight committees.

Clearly, the CIA's Directorate of Operations is not solely responsible for the malaise that has befallen it and clandestine HUMINT overall. Many others have failed to muster sufficient will to overcome extraordinary obstacles. Despite assurances to the contrary, CIA and intelligence community management has not always put its authority and resources on the line when required to advance HUMINT. The National Security Council has not put the necessary force behind the need for HUMINT improvement, and other government agencies have often tended to compete rather than lend support and leverage.

Ultimately, this lack of will reflects a failure of leadership. Recruiting the right people and giving them the right training are critical to the resurgence of "will" and consistency in HUMINT practices and programs. To have the right impact, such leadership needs support from those responsible for rewarding right practice with consistent funding. This means that Congress must accept the challenge of sustaining best practices through careful and just programmatic review—and this requires that Congress acknowledge its own failures in intelligence oversight. Busy playing "gotcha" rather than "helpya" with the intelligence community, the two oversight committees nonetheless were aware of the shortcomings in HUMINT that played a major role in the failures of September 11 and Iraqi WMD. They certainly bear significant responsibility for these failures.

The last of the three areas for change is undoubtedly the most difficult. Providing the necessary authority to the DNI and using that authority to ensure that all stay in their own lanes—these things can set the scene for success. Without consistency and the will to stay the course, however, prospects for real progress are not very bright.

We will never be able to acquire the secrets policymakers absolutely must have, or to understand the threat that individuals, organizations, and nations pose to our core security interests, or secretly to manipulate people and events in support of our critical interests, unless we can significantly improve clandestine HUMINT. The intelligence community has never before been able to put aside the parochial interests of its component parts and truly organize itself for the "national good." Can it happen now? Is failure an option?

Notes

This chapter was prepared with the participation of Charles Cogan.

1. Literally, "human intelligence," that is, intelligence collected by people, not machines. In this chapter the term HUMINT will be used to refer only to clandestine HUMINT, in which the collector operates in secret. This is in contrast to overt HUMINT, which includes the open acquisition of intelligence by defense attachés, Foreign Service officers, other U.S. government officials, and others.

2. Inmarsat is a global corporation that operates a constellation of geostationary satellites that extend mobile phone, fax, and data communications to every part of the world except the poles. End users can dial into the international telephone network and send data over the Internet at any time simply by connecting to an Inmarsat satellite.

3. Ari Fleischer discussed the harm caused by this leak in a White House press statement, June 20, 2002.

4. Clandestine HUMINT is not an isolated collection capability because the sensors, platforms, and dissemination systems are not owned or controlled by a single agency. In fact, one of HUMINT's greatest problems is that no entity is responsible for ensuring that surges in HUMINT collection efforts are accompanied by adequate infrastructure. Policymakers may agree to fund increases in the numbers of case officers for a particular mission but fail to provide the resources necessary to provide cover, platforms, and communications, especially when those logistical supports are provided by agencies or entities outside the intelligence community. The failure to address this problem stems from flaws in management within the intelligence community, the national security system, and oversight agencies.

5. National Commission on Terrorist Attacks upon the United States, *The 9/11 Commission Report: Final Report of the National Commission on Terrorist Attacks upon the United States* (New York: W. W. Norton, 2004), 130–31 and 137–38.

6. Conversation with former DCI William Webster.

7. The DoD's budget in FY 2005 is $399.6 billion.

8. In the run-up to the Iraq invasion, the Pentagon valued the reports coming from Chalabi's exile group, the Iraqi National Congress. State and the CIA did not.

SIX   The Digital Dimension

JAMES R. GOSLER

SINCE THE END of the cold war the conduct of espionage has been irreversibly altered, owing in large part to the rapid expansion of global reliance on information technology (IT). Clandestine photography of secret documents stored in the filing cabinets of a senior official has been relegated to a minor role. Intelligence targets are increasingly using computer networks as the repositories for their secrets. As a result, clandestine photography is rapidly yielding to sophisticated technical operations that exploit these networks. A spy with authorized access to these networks — an insider — can exfiltrate more than a million pages of sensitive material within a microelectronic memory device easily concealed within a watch, an ink pen, or even a hearing aid.

Ten years ago the technology associated with such an operation would have been available to only a few intelligence organizations. Today this technology is available to anyone, and such a device could be built and concealed for less than $10,000.[1] Furthermore, thanks to the pervasive nature of the Internet, clandestine technical collection no longer requires physical proximity to the target. U.S. information systems can be remotely targeted and their secrets collected and exfiltrated to any part of the world.[2] The Internet has the additional advantage to the adversary that his clandestine communications infrastructure is free.

This operational transformation is fueled by the global availability of affordable and highly sophisticated technology. Advances in microelectronics, microsensors, computers, software, networks, and telecommunications have made it practically impossible for any business, including those of intelligence and defense, to succeed without taking advantage of the efficiency and performance gains afforded by modern IT. This technology has transformed the way information is created, stored, processed, viewed, shared, and transmitted. Consequently, unimaginable volumes of information, including the secrets of businesses and nations, are available to both authorized and unauthorized viewers. The same technology that has enabled this global shift in business practices also provides the tools to exploit and attack intelligence and military systems.

Unfortunately, the contest between the offense and the defense is dreadfully mismatched, with the advantage strongly in the offensive corner. The inherent complexity of current software and hardware components defies comprehensive security evaluations, and despite the claims of some vendors, there is no "holy grail" of information assurance, nor is there likely to be in the future. Complexity not only makes evaluation extremely challenging, it also provides abundant opportunity for inherent vulnerabilities to be deeply embedded within a target system. Additionally, the global nature of IT makes it virtually impossible to determine a system's pedigree. The design, fabrication, testing, logistics, maintenance, and operation of these systems provide intimate access opportunities to an adversary intent on subtle modifications that will compromise confidentiality, integrity, or availability.[3] While progress is being made in reducing inherent vulnerabilities, an adversary's opportunities to introduce a vulnerability into a system through a life-cycle approach is ever increasing.

The technology used by the U.S. public and private sectors is virtually identical to that of our allies and our enemies. Global use of the same commercial technology, which significantly accelerated during the 1990s, greatly complicates our ability to manage risks.[4] While we must protect our critical systems from exploitation by an enemy, we must also guarantee the ability to maintain our influence over the adversary's systems. Astonishing as it may be, the requirement to simultaneously defend and attack a common technological infrastructure forms the conceptual underpinning of the U.S. information dominance strategy and encapsulates the National Security Agency's (NSA) strategic plan. While these requirements appear to be mutually exclusive and competing, they are in fact critically interdependent activities.[5]

Critics claim that the U.S. intelligence community is becoming blind and deaf. This is patently untrue. The volume of information available from both open- and special-source collection is by any definition overwhelming. Countless reports convey useful metrics to help comprehend the enormous volume of information available today. Once again, the impressive advances of technology, combined with associated innovative applications, enable this explosion of information.

According to a computer industry almanac press release,[6] the worldwide Internet population in 2005 will exceed 1 billion people with access to some 300 billion web pages.[7] The NSA has estimated that "in 2001 our species spent some 187 billion minutes on the phone — in international calls alone."[8] While the intelligence community is not deaf, it is drowning! The challenge of transforming mountains of often unrelated multimedia and noisy information into credible, validated, and actionable intelligence will prove to be one of the most demanding technical problems facing the intelligence community over the next five to ten years. Fortunately, several promising approaches are emerging to address various aspects of the "big-data problem."

If successful in achieving the proper balance in exploitation and defense and by securely solving the big-data problem, the intelligence community can gain a tremendous advantage in leveraging the vast amounts of available intelligence-relevant information. If we fail to solve the big-data problem, we will miss opportunities to find, thwart, and in some cases eliminate our enemies. If we fail to achieve the appropriate balance of offense and defense, our adversaries could deeply and secretly embed themselves in our critical systems. Then, at a time of their choosing, they could shift the balance of power. The potential effect of this asymmetric approach could be devastating. There is clear evidence that many of our opponents understand the advantages of this form of "unconventional warfare."

Difficulty of Cultural Transformation

The remarkable advances in technology have had a profound impact on our way of life. The rate at which these changes have occurred has outpaced the ability of the intelligence community to adjust culturally and fully embrace this new paradigm. While impressive progress has been made in some sectors of the community, in many ways we are still operating and thinking like battleship commanders in an aircraft carrier world, or as Bill Black, deputy director of the NSA, frequently says, "We still want to build carburetors."[9] There are many military and industrial examples of the magnitude of the social and cultural challenges that must be overcome if we are to survive the consequences of a massive paradigm shift caused by one or more disruptive technologies.[10] A few examples will help to clarify aspects of this challenge.

Historians have provided perspective and analysis of the U.S. Navy's reluctance to understand and adopt the tremendous tactical and strategic advantages of air power during World War II. While an in-depth study of this failure would provide useful insight into our current struggles with culture and disruptive technology, we must content ourselves here with an illustration of the "battleship think" embedded in the judgment of many senior naval officers. On November 29, 1941, Navy and Army met on a football field in Philadelphia. The football program displayed a majestic picture of the USS *Arizona* above the caption, "It is significant that despite the claims of air enthusiasts no battleship has yet been sunk by bombs." How could so many intelligent and dedicated leaders have missed the obvious?

In *Only the Paranoid Survive,* Andrew Grove provides us with a glimpse into the psychology that informed such a statement. During the 1980s the Intel Corporation was faced with significant competition from the Japanese in the design, fabrication, and marketing of memory devices. Grove's book graphically conveys the agonizing struggles within the company to adapt its failing business strategy and transform Intel into the world leader in microprocessor technology. "When a strategic inflection point sweeps through the industry," Grove writes, "the more successful a participant was in the old industry structure, the more threatened it is by change and the more reluctant it is to adapt to it. . . . But when the structure of the industry changes, all of these elements change too. The mental map that you have been carrying with you all these years and relied upon in charting your company's course of action suddenly loses its validity.

However, you haven't had a chance to replace it with a new mental map. You haven't made the explicit substitutions about how things are done now versus how they were done before, or who matters now versus who mattered then."[11]

Louis Gerstner Jr.'s account of the recovery of International Business Machines Corporation amplifies the Intel case. Prior to Gerstner's arrival in April 1993, IBM was in serious decline. Under his leadership, not only did the company reverse its downward spiral, it once again became a dominant force in the international computer business. This case study clarifies many of the cultural factors inhibiting IBM from effectively adjusting to the environment of the new global market.[12] Both the Intel and IBM stories illustrate that large complex organizations can adjust to a changing world and accomplish the transformation without falling prey to business competitors.

In *Men, Machines, and Modern Times,* Elting Morison describes the efforts of a navy lieutenant, in the early 1900s, to persuade senior naval officers to adopt new technology that would dramatically increase the effectiveness of naval gunfire.[13] The frustration experienced by Lieutenant Sims, coupled with his contempt for the stonewalling and blacklisting of his seniors, compelled him to bypass the chain of command and communicate directly with the president of the United States.[14]

While not advocating the bloodletting of political opponents, it is essential to understand that the game has changed and that we have yet to sufficiently adapt to either the new intelligence collection opportunities or the new corresponding threats. Adapting to these new realities will be exceedingly difficult, but it must be done. Men and women must be identified who understand and will work to nurture the relationship between technical operations and human operations such that they become mutually supportive. Likewise, they must foster the relationship between the offensive and defensive elements, as well as encourage the creation of analysis techniques needed to take advantage of the abundant information available for collection today.

It is primarily through the leadership of a new cadre of professionals that critical changes will take root and become the norm. Only then will a new environment be developed to encourage and protect the level of risk taking and innovation necessary to address these problems. And only then will the bonds of ownership and devotion to the comforts of the past be broken. In tandem with the leadership and environment adjustment, a new vision and associated roadmap will naturally develop. This process will identify policy obstacles to be negotiated, legal gaps and obsolescence to address, and modern business practices to adopt.

Clandestine Collection Challenges

Specific current offensive capabilities and limitations are necessarily classified and cannot be addressed here. There are, however, a sufficient number of examples in the public domain that are either less sensitive in nature or dated, but still exemplify the offensive approach and highlight some of the challenges faced by the clandestine collection community.

Are there observable symptoms, relative to technical collection and information assurance issues, that the intelligence community is approaching Grove's strategic inflection point? Absolutely. In *A Secret Life,* Benjamin Weiser relates the story of Ryszard Kuklinski, a colonel on the Polish General Staff whose principal duty involved preparing Poland to prevail in a potential confrontation with the North Atlantic Treaty Organization (NATO). His reputation and position provided him legitimate and regular access to the Soviet Union's "crown jewels," including Soviet war plans. For nine years, beginning in 1972, he clandestinely supported Central Intelligence Agency (CIA) efforts to discover the details of Polish/Soviet plans. Colonel Kuklinski secretly photographed approximately forty thousand pages of sensitive documents.[15] As depicted in Weiser's book, the skills required to conduct this operation were well aligned with the strengths of the CIA's Directorate of Operations (DO). The DO's culture, hiring criteria, training, tools, and relationships had evolved to manage such traditional operations effectively.

Weiser explains that the role of technology was to support human operations. Disguise, concealment devices, photographic equipment, suicide pills, and covert communications are examples of technology used to support these activities. Today these secret documents are developed, edited, published, shared, searched, and transmitted by IT. While printed copies still exist within filing cabinets and safes, these documents are also available in IT networks, and it is there that their full utility can be realized. The technology used to clandestinely exploit or attack these systems is markedly different from the tools used to support Kuklinski's mission.

Clandestine tradecraft also takes on new meaning in the information age. In the classical world of espionage, the agent and case officer require cover for action. Prior to a clandestine rendezvous, they must ensure that they have not been followed. The case officer may need documents to convince the local authorities that he is someone else. He will use concealment devices to hide stolen secrets. While clandestine cyber-tradecraft has analogous characteristics, its expression is very different. Today a case officer will execute a surveillance detection route (SDR) prior to meeting an asset to ensure that the spy is not being introduced to the local counterintelligence service. The cyberversion of a case officer must also conduct an SDR to ensure that the local firewall and intrusion detection system does not detect him.

As Grove pointed out, "who matters" has also changed. Not only do we have access to documents, images, sound files, video, and programs; the technology itself has access to the same information. Thus the operating system, word processor, test equipment, communications hardware, microprocessor, or even the security firewall can function as the access agent. The programmer, test engineer, quality assurance engineer, shipper, microelectronic fabrication process engineer, salesman, system engineer, and literally dozens of other people can influence the technology that is intimate with the information of intelligence interest and can recruit "the technology" to be his spy. Arguably this augments the role of human intelligence (HUMINT) from one supported by a technical operation to one supporting the technical operation. Today the relationship between human operations and technical operations must continue to evolve from "master/slave" to strategic partnership.

The objectives of intelligence and military power have not changed, but the manner in which we achieve those objectives has been marked by gradual evolution and occasionally disruptive or revolutionary modification. Those who do not adapt quickly enough to these strategic inflection points find themselves at a significant disadvantage. This is true in business, intelligence, and defense.

Willie Sutton was once asked why he robbed banks. He responded, "Because that's where the money is." While there is still money in our brick-and-mortar banks, the "mother lode" is located within the cyberworld. The skills, tools, and tradecraft possessed by a Sutton would be of little value in robbing a cyberbank. For intelligence collection, the same is true. Over time the location and form of the information have changed. Correspondingly, the skills, tools, tradecraft, partnerships, and culture have been forced to evolve.

For most people this cyberworld is distant and mostly fictional. Some, even within the intelligence community, doubt the magnitude of resources, time, and risk a motivated intelligence organization will expend to achieve its operational objectives. The reality is that many formidable intelligence services are willing to commit the necessary resources and to take bold actions to achieve their operational objectives. Unfortunately, the price of admission into this offensive endeavor has been significantly reduced. While it is still very expensive to build and operate a world-class global offensive capability, effective participation is affordable not only to many nation-states but also to terrorists.

Once again the principal enabler for this reduced cost of entry is the affordability and global availability of sophisticated technology. Today's terrorist organization can communicate and coordinate activities through the Internet for a nominal cost. Terrorists benefit from the ability to hide their communications within billions of other transactions. From the terrorist's perspective, this is a weak signal in a high-noise environment, providing him both cost-effective and high-impact operations.

On October 25, 1990, Congressman Henry Hyde introduced testimony into the congressional record conveying his concern with the Soviet intelligence penetration of the U.S. embassy in Moscow still under construction. In testimony, he revealed the highlights of another cleverly conceived and conducted Soviet technical operation. This Soviet operation was known within the intelligence community by the codename "GUNMAN."[16] In 1984 the United States discovered that a number of IBM Selectric typewriters within the U.S. Embassy had been intentionally modified (bugged) by the Soviets. Evidently, the Soviets knew these typewriters were the embassy's preferred choice and developed an operation to provide sufficient private, unobserved access to the typewriters. In parallel with operational access development, a team of engineers designed and produced a hardware implant requiring both deep concealment within the typewriter and quick installation during the initial close-access opportunity. The Soviets were successful in their efforts. Access was achieved during part of the logistics phase prior to delivery to the embassy when the typewriters were unsecured. Evidently, the Soviet implant secretly captured all keystrokes typed on the machine and transmitted the information to a nearby listening post. According to Congressman Hyde, this Soviet operation produced intelligence for years.

Additional examples of successful intelligence collection are provided in *Tower of Secrets*, by Victor Sheymov. A member of the highly secretive Soviet Eighth Chief Directorate, Sheymov was responsible for ensuring secure Soviet worldwide cipher communications. Apparently the Soviet leadership found significant advantage in allowing those responsible for the defensive mission to be cognizant of the KGB's offensive approaches.[17] Sheymov provides a wealth of useful insight into Soviet clandestine tradecraft and innovative uses of technology.

The Soviets unmistakably understood the importance of keeping cryptology secure. They used the customary HUMINT approach, recruitment of those with legitimate and routine access to the cryptographic key, such as John Walker's team, to an exceptionally successful degree. The technical approaches are less obvious but equally powerful. Sheymov explains, "There were three main technical aspects of cipher-communications security: the mathematical basis of the cipher; the electromagnetic 'leakage'; and the acoustic 'leakage.'"[18] Evidently the Soviets used a broad spectrum of approaches to exploit U.S. cryptography. The full extent of their operational success is known only to them.

While dated, these examples illustrate the value of collecting intelligence close to its source. They also convey the real and aggressive nature of serious intelligence organizations. Whether it be a human operative supported by covert communications, video surveillance, telephone taps, room audio, or a technical operation supported by a clandestine human source providing life-cycle access to key technology, having secret access to high-impact end points is vital.

A sophisticated and effective intelligence organization intent on conducting aggressive and modern espionage operations against its opponent's end points will possess many of the following capabilities/characteristics:

- Worldwide presence (in the target's back yard);
- Mature operational tradecraft (allows for full and nonalerting integration of case officers, assets, and technology into the target environment);

- Diverse network of trusted foreign and domestic partners;
- Worldwide secure communications and logistics;
- Integration of human and technical operations (mutually supportive);
- Effective security and counterintelligence program (keeps its operations and assets secret);
- Mature midpoint collection;
- Integration of offensive and defensive missions (mutually supportive);
- Comprehensive training program for all aspects of business.

Intelligence organizations that possess these characteristics are able to conduct operations yielding immense advantage to the collector or attacker. These aggregated capabilities make those used in the Eligible Receiver 97 (ER97) exercise look trivial by comparison. While the defense has achieved some noticeable progress in preventing and detecting the ER97 level of attack, it has lost ground to the more sophisticated approach.[19]

The world-class capabilities described are not obtained easily. They are extremely resource-intensive to develop and require decades to mature. By prudently increasing offensive investments and by better integrating human and technical collection elements, we can increase the price of admission into the top level of intelligence collection. By augmenting our offensive capabilities, we can operationally afford to eliminate vulnerabilities that can be exploited with less sophisticated techniques. This requires significant new investment in our defensive approach and a tight coupling of our defensive and offensive elements. Thus, if an adversary is to successfully exploit our systems, it must invest the resources required to operate at the world-class level.[20]

Information Assurance and Computer Network Defense Challenges

The defensive challenges are daunting! Today there is no clear approach to effectively offsetting the advantages of the offensive adversary. What are the intrinsic characteristics and environmental factors of the defensive situation that have resulted in a growing gap between offense and defense? They include technology complexity; impracticality of comprehensive evaluation; design, production, and maintenance functions performed globally; imbalance of focus and competing aspects among confidentiality, integrity, and availability; insufficient insight into the offensive investments, approaches, and organization of opponents; lack of coordination and cooperation between offensive and defensive elements; no national-level ownership; and the absence of a national research-investment strategy.

The complexity of the technology and the evaluation challenges are intertwined. In the early 1980s advances in microprocessor technology were just being introduced into some of our most security-critical applications. Because of the critical nature of these applications, expectations were that a comprehensive security evaluation would be performed. Yet even the technology of the early 1980s presented formidable challenges to performing credible vulnerability assessments and provided tremendous opportunities to an adversary.

To place these evaluation challenges in perspective, it is useful to compare a few of the IT advances of the past twenty years. In the early 1980s IBM chose to use the Intel 8088 in its debut of the IBM personal computer. The processor had 29,000 transistors, ran at 4.77 MHZ, and utilized 3,000-nanometer technology. By comparison, the current Intel Pentium 4 has 125 million transistors, runs at 3,600 MHZ, and utilizes 90-nanometer technology. The disk drive sector has produced even greater performance increases, with the capacity of the drives increasing from 10 megabytes to more than 800,000 megabytes.[21] While authoritative comparisons of software have been difficult to obtain, increases in this area have been equally impressive. The early Microsoft disk operating system (DOS) had about 100 kilobytes of code, whereas the current Windows-based operating systems are estimated to contain about 1 million kilobytes of code.

To perform a comprehensive security evaluation of these systems, it is not enough to understand the software and hardware completely. The evaluator must also have a comprehensive understanding of subtle interactions between the two. With the complexity of IT-based systems having increased by roughly a factor of one thousand while our evaluation capability has progressed nominally at best, the task of the security evaluator has grown to impracticable levels. Today these evaluations are performed, but they are of questionable value. In general, the insecurity of a system cannot be eliminated through a security evaluation.

The Defense Science Board (DSB)'s "2003 Summer Study on (DoD) Roles and Missions in Homeland Security" report supports this conclusion. The report states: "With both the capability and complexity of hardware and software-based components increasing at the rate of Moore's Law, the ability to detect anomalies, control configuration, and evaluate and assure the trustworthiness of these systems is markedly diminished. A classified experiment conducted in the mid-1980s demonstrated the overwhelming challenges of discovering subversive constructs in microcontroller-based systems of the time. The complexity and dynamics of today's technology makes the ability to perform credible vulnerability assessments even more challenging now, if not impossible."[22]

The adversary can recruit technology to be its spy. Technology development and production are a global endeavor today. As dozens of countries typically participate in the production of a system, it is impossible to determine system provenance. Opportunities to clandestinely influence a component during its global path to birth are simply endless.

This view was succinctly conveyed in 1984 by Ken Thompson, a Bell Laboratories computer science researcher, in his Turing award paper, "Reflections on Trusting Trust." "The moral is obvious," Thompson wrote. "You can't trust code that you did not totally create yourself. (Especially code from companies that employ people like me.) No amount of source-level verification of scrutiny will protect you from using untrusted code."[23]

Thompson's insight was progressive, and the situation he described is even worse today, for today you may not even be able to trust code that you created entirely yourself! There is abundant evidence of well-intentioned expert programmers inadvertently designing software that behaves unpredictably under unusual circumstances. The security challenge here is a system challenge. While Thompson might have had complete confidence in his software design and implementation, including its binary representation, he would probably have no confidence in the fidelity of the hardware platform on which the software was executed.

The undersecretary of defense for acquisition, technology and logistics recently requested that the chairman of the Defense Science Board form a task force on the national security implications of microelectronic fabrication and design's migrating offshore. Michael Wynne's tasking letter states, "the offshore movement of manufacturing and design capability could lead to inability to assure design function. The failure to assure design function could result in the intentional insertion of unknown vulnerabilities into vital pieces of equipment and result in the exploitation by a foreign government."[24]

Protecting the confidentiality of information has been the defensive team's focus for decades. This imbalanced perspective has minimized the research conducted to protect the integrity and availability of service in an intelligent, deliberate, and hostile environment. While significant research has been conducted to assure the availability of service in a natural disaster, the challenges of ensuring availability in an adversarial environment are much more daunting. Within the confidentiality domain, there has been tremendous reliance on the mathematical properties of cryptography. It is important to note, as Sheymov suggests, that cryptography is more than just mathematics. It is also about implementation and procedure. The recruitment of a John Walker or the conduct of a close-access operation, as detailed in *Tower of Secrets,* illustrate that an effective offensive strategy must be rooted in a sound systems approach.

The DSB 2003 summer study concludes that collection, analysis, and reporting on foreign information operations (IO) capabilities are inadequate. The defense will never be able to stop or deter all possible attacks. Insight into the opponent's offensive capabilities and limitations is crucial to developing an optimum defensive architecture. The DSB report acknowledges the NSA as unique in its IO responsibilities. It is responsible for the DoD's computer network exploitation mission and vital to the nation's computer network defense mission. In particular, the DSB report asserts that NSA's information assurance directorate (IAD) "has the largest and most experienced group of information-assurance experts in the country."[25] The relationship between IAD and the offensive elements of the NSA and CIA must be formally established and meaningfully strengthened.

In addition, there is no clear indication of a national investment strategy for information assurance. *Trust in Cyberspace,* a 1999 publication of the Computer Science and Telecommunications Board (CSTB) and National Research Council concludes that there is inadequate funding for research in the information security arena.[26] The statement of work for a current CSTB project, "Improving Cybersecurity Research in the United States," will attempt to identify revolutionary new approaches in support of the information assurance discipline. The project's statement of work asserts that no one organization has ownership for cyberresearch and that the government has been "sporadic" in its approach to funding research in this area.[27]

In conjunction with a more disciplined strategy of investment in information assurance research, we must stimulate interest within the United States for students capable of acquiring security clearances to study computer security, and we must provide career opportunities for the best of class. Today's defensive culture consists of rules, specifications, and theory. The defender unnecessarily constrains himself to operate within this artificially bounded environment. On the other hand, the attacker observes no such rules. He does not allow himself to be constrained and frequently works outside the bounded environment of the defender. He attacks you where you are weak.[28] If we are to be effective in defending the nation's critical infrastructure against computer network exploitation and attack, we must enhance the attacker mentality within our defensive culture.

In summary, we have lost considerable ground in the defensive arena. The search for "security by specification"—i.e., by adhering to a comprehensive set of security checklists—has led the nation down many dead-end alleys. The hope that we could solve the security challenge by creating a perfect set of checklists has weakened our defensive cadre.[29] An absence of effective metrics to determine the impact of any given defensive investment on the opponent has resulted, in many cases, in no return on that investment. Lack of cooperation and information exchange between offensive and defensive elements, coupled with insufficient insight into our opponent's offensive capabilities and strategy, have caused the defensive elements to be overly myopic. This limitation has resulted in an imbalanced focus on addressing the prevention and detection of an adversary remotely attacking one of our systems utilizing an inherent vulnerability.

Consequently, any successful defensive strategy must effectively address the following:
- Decreasing the inherent vulnerabilities within our hardware and software;
- Increasing the difficulty of an adversary introducing vulnerabilities into our systems through life-cycle approaches;

- Increasing our ability to deeply evaluate critical components — design for evaluation;
- Increasing the cost and uncertainty to an adversary attempting to exploit our vulnerabilities;
- Increasing the probability of detecting a component (hardware or software) behaving badly (violating a security requirement);
- Increasing the probability of attributing the bad behavior to the adversary;
- Increasing the consequences to the attacker for its bad behavior.

Opinion is deeply divided about both the impact of a defensive failure and the health of our defensive capabilities. A number of knowledgeable seniors within the intelligence community and external computer security experts believe that more defensive progress has been made than this chapter would imply. Debate, both public and private, should be strongly encouraged. The resulting insights should be used to develop the first national strategy in this area.

Big-Data Challenges

The challenge of transforming mountains of heterogeneous, noisy, and incomplete information into actionable intelligence must be met if we are to realize our national security goals. Typical intelligence analysis tasks associated with counterterrorism or counterproliferation illustrate the challenges. The counterterrorism question foremost in the minds of policymakers and the public today is the "warning" question: when and where will the next terrorist attack occur? In counterproliferation an important task involves assessing the likelihood that a biomedical institute is involved in covert bioweapons research in addition to its overt medical research. These tasks illustrate many of the characteristics of typical analysis questions. In each case the target is a large, complex, dynamic "network" of interdependent elements (e.g., people, technology, facilities, information, etc.) that seeks to obscure its activities. A principal consequence of this complexity is that any "signatures" associated with a target's activities that may have been collected by the intelligence community are likely to be faint, subtle, and transient, and may be embedded in a myriad of databases maintained by separate agencies. Each of these databases contains massive amounts of heterogeneous, incomplete, inaccurate, and even contradictory information, the overwhelming majority of which has no relevance to the task at hand.

Indeed, except in the fortuitous situation in which a communication is intercepted, a spy uncovers plans, or a clandestine technical operation acquires information that details the time and place of a planned terrorist attack, assessments of terrorist activities are intentionally obscured. In the absence of direct insight, questions must be answered by discovering and exploiting complex, subtle relationships among various pieces of noisy, incomplete information. In fact, even evidence as seemingly compelling as an intercepted communication or human intelligence must be interpreted from the perspective that terrorists may employ "denial and deception" methods. Thus it is critical that analysts work to discover a broad range of potentially relevant information, integrate and assess this information, and then use it to develop a comprehensive picture of their target through careful, quantitative, and rigorous analysis. Although there are other aspects of the big-data challenge that do not translate well to standard data-mining methods, it is this requirement to extract "deep" information from massive yet incomplete data that appears to be most critical.[30]

Consider the problem of anticipating an attack by a covert terrorist network if the identities of only a few members of the network are known. The target is a complex, dynamic network of people and technology, and there is considerable uncertainty in the parameters that define the target. The terrorists are attempting to realize an objective while masking their activities. The data sets that may contain terrorist signatures are truly massive, heterogeneous, incomplete, and possibly full of errors and contradictions. Moreover, the signatures themselves are likely to be faint, transient, and buried in a sea of irrelevant information. Yet, notwithstanding these technical challenges, new approaches show promise in extracting useful hidden information from the networks to support the warning function.

By examining the communication data for signatures associated with the activities of the terrorist network, by characterizing the communication patterns that correspond to collaboration in covert networks, and by initially focusing on communication externals, knowledge of the identities of a few network members can lead to the discovery and identification of other members. In addition, because only the externals are analyzed, this approach is expandable (scalable) to extremely large data sets and is robust to significant incompleteness and errors in the data and a very high ratio of nonrelevant to relevant data. Interestingly, it has been demonstrated that the extent to which covert networks can operate clandestinely is fundamentally limited, and that by adopting increasingly sophisticated communication and operation security procedures the terrorist network potentially increases its profile.[31] While the specific details are beyond the scope of this chapter, it is worth noting that properly exploiting the temporal information of externals is a powerful tool for both target discovery (identifying additional members of the network) and warning (detecting trends in behavior that warrant additional scrutiny).

As detailed in the DSB 2003 summer study report, if we are to significantly reduce our chances of another high-impact surprise attack, we must shift from a culture of "need to know" to "need to share." Analysts must be connected to distributed databases and, consistent with security policy, must be permitted to apply a chosen suite of approved analytic tools to the data to satisfy their queries. However, this aggregation of information will increasingly become an attractive target itself. Our adversaries will acquire significant strategic advantages if they are able to penetrate these systems in order to compromise our collection sources and methods, corrupt the integrity of the information, or deny our use of these warehouses of information during a time of crisis.

In addition to the cultural shift and the IT foundation necessary for collaboration, mechanisms must be developed to ensure that legal requirements are strictly followed. Advanced analytic tools should be developed as well to reveal the deeply hidden insight contained within the system. To address key information voids, the analysts need to interact with the collection architecture. Finally, the system must be protected from a sophisticated adversary intent on compromising the confidentiality, integrity, or availability of this national resource. Success for this new enterprise requires that the offense, defense, and the analytic cadre work together as a seamless team. If we are to solve many of the national security problems facing the country within this decade, each of these principal activities must be healthy, appropriately resourced, and in balance such that we do not create bottlenecks. Since this is an overall systems challenge, doubling our investment in one area alone does not guarantee improvement in system capability.

Winning the war on terrorism requires aggressive development of a secure architecture that makes the information within the intelligence community available to analysts. These analysts must be equipped with a full spectrum of tools that allow them to "connect the dots" and mitigate the threat of terrorism. Realizing this vision will mean enacting the following reforms:

- Transitioning the culture from "need to know" to "need to share;"
- Developing the IT infrastructure that enables this level of collaboration;
- Protecting the network from both internal and external threats;
- Establishing the nature of these threats through aggressive collection, analysis, and reporting;
- Effectively coupling the defensive and offensive components of the intelligence community;
- Establishing a threat-based investment strategy for information assurance;
- Convincing the owners (collectors) of the data to include their information in the network and make it available to the analysts;
- Increasing investment in end-point collection in order to penetrate high-value targets and compensate for the global reduction of IT vulnerabilities resulting from our increased information assurance posture;
- Increasing the investment and utilization of advanced mathematical techniques to discover the subtle intelligence insights buried within the vast store of the intelligence community databases.

Summary

By examining organizations that have undergone significant cultural transformation, one can begin to find a few common elements that help to explain the reluctance of seniors to reform their institutions. Even in the face of organizational obsolescence, seniors are unwilling to adapt the business strategy to the changed operating environment. As Gerstner comments aptly, "Successful institutions almost always develop strong cultures that reinforce those elements that make the institution great. They reflect the environment from which they emerged. When that environment shifts, it is very hard for the culture to change. In fact, it becomes an enormous impediment to the institution's ability to adapt."[32] This is an astute assessment of the intelligence community today.

A recurring theme of this chapter has been the accumulated impact of technological advances made over the past decade. In many cases these advances have been a double-edged sword. The tools available to support human operations have increased in sophistication and dropped significantly in cost. At the same time, however, breakthroughs in biometrics greatly complicate a case officer's ability to operate safely under an alias. The more apparent dichotomy involves the promise of end-point exploitation and the difficulty of end-point defense.

The global availability and affordability of advanced technology have forced both business and government to fully incorporate these capabilities into the conduct of operations. While business can no longer compete otherwise, at the same time business makes itself extremely vulnerable to a failure (whether of confidentiality, integrity, or availability) of the information that the technology is processing, storing, or communicating. It is this irreversible dependency, the desire and need to network these systems, and the intelligence value of the information, that have radically increased the attractiveness and utility of clandestine technical end-point collection. As a result, an increasing percentage of resources needs to be provided to these techniques, and the relationship between human and technical operations must be adjusted accordingly. When human and technical operations work together as effective partners, mutually supporting each other, problems that have been intractable in either domain will potentially be solved.

Those responsible for ensuring that our IT-based infrastructure is adequately protected must have increased insight into how both the United States' and our opponents' offensive capabilities are applied to exploit and attack systems. Today our adversaries develop our software, fabricate our microelectronics, assemble the components on our printed circuit boards, and remotely maintain our systems. These adversarial opportunities, coupled with our inability to effectively evaluate these systems, our total dependence on these systems, and the impact of a failure in these systems, have exposed our striking defensive deficiencies.

Unless the agencies of the U.S. government responsible for defending the IT-based elements of our infrastructure take into account these foreign strategies, our IT-based systems will eventually be compromised, perhaps catastrophically. A threat-based investment strategy for information assurance must be developed. These value-added defensive investments, in conjunction with appropriate increases in our offensive capacities, will allow us to proceed aggressively with the systematic elimination of many system vulnerabilities that are exploitable by less competent adversaries. But this is only the first step in a long journey to address the imbalance between offensive capabilities and our defensive response.

As the intelligence community makes the transition to a need-to-share culture and the sharing of very diverse types of information becomes commonplace, new analysis tools and approaches will be needed to highlight the diminishing signal in a growing background of noise. While countless technical obstacles must be resolved to develop and integrate a fully functional architecture that will satisfy the big-data-problem requirements, two are key. First, to protect this system from exploitation and attack, we must make breakthroughs within the discipline of information assurance. If the intelligence community cannot prevent an adversary from compromising our sources and methods, it will potentially be counterproductive for us to aggregate this body of sensitive information. Second, the practice of applying mathematically rigorous techniques to examine the deep properties of complex networks, such as the social network of a terrorist organization, shows great promise and should be encouraged. As these activities progress in both the open and classified communities, terrorists will find it increasingly difficult to communicate safely. By denying them the safe use of modern technology, we could force them to operate in isolation in the caves of Afghanistan and thus greatly reduce their overall operational effectiveness.

If the United States is to better position the intelligence community to address the challenges of the new-world-order threats, then at a minimum considerable cultural reform is required. Congress and seniors within the intelligence community must provide sufficient incentive to systemically modify the behavior within and among its various elements. Only through this level of cultural transformation will the community be positioned to continue its exemplary service in protecting the nation.

The intelligence community at large knows that revolutionary change is required. In some cases, suggestions are being made in frustration that, if implemented, could significantly put at risk the current capability of our intelligence community, which is significant. Even a temporary disruption of this value to national security could have dire consequences. Unfortunately, the status quo within the intelligence community will eventually be unable to sustain its current value because of the inefficiencies resulting, in part, from insufficient innovation and unproductive internal competition. Therefore, with the intelligence train moving at maximum speed, we need to be able to transform the environment of risk taking, technical and operational innovation, and partnerships without slowing down.

While much progress is still required, promising movement is taking place. Some community seniors have recognized the need for change not only in the technical areas addressed in this chapter but in the many other technical and operational components of the community. Emerging technical operational activities have been embedded within the DO. Significant change has already occurred within the NSA and additional architectural studies are being conducted by independent groups to provide recommendations for further change. The DSB and the new Intelligence Science Board are commissioning studies to examine obstacles to progress. In the end, we should carefully examine and appropriately adopt elements of the Intel and IBM transformation strategies. There is no easy path, and every path has abundant associated risks. If the Intel or IBM journeys had failed, we could have lost valuable companies. If intelligence community transformation fails, we place the country at great risk.

As Price Pritchett put it in his book on "new work habits for a radically changing world," "Organizations can't stop the world from changing. The best they can do is adapt. The smart ones change before they have to. The lucky ones manage to scramble and adjust when push comes to shove. The rest are losers, and they become history."[33]

Notes

The views expressed in this chapter are solely my own and are not intended to represent the views of any organization with which I am associated, including Sandia National Laboratories, the DOE, the NSA, the CIA, or the DoD. I would like to acknowledge the contributions to this chapter of Richard Colbaugh, Trudy Blake, Rick Wilson, and Walter Jack.

1. In general, today's technological advances greatly favor offense over defense. The innovative application of this modern technology coupled with a worldwide clandestine service represents a formidable adversary.

2. John Hamre, interviewed on *Frontline* ("Cyberwar!"), February 18, 2003, available at www.pbs.org/wgbh/pages/frontline/shows/cyberwar/interviews/hamre.html.

3. The development of system access during the various stages of system life (design, fabrication, testing) in conjunction with the subversive modification of the system is often referred to as the life-cycle approach.

4. In this context, risk management means balancing the advantages of our offensive capabilities with the potential consequences of our defensive shortfalls.

5. J. M. McConnell (vice admiral, retired), "The Future of SIGINT: Opportunities and Challenges in the Information Age," unpublished paper, 2001.

6. "USA Tops 160M Internet Users," *Computer Industry Almanac Inc.*, December 16, 2002, available at www.c-i-a.com/pr1202.htm.

7. "Global Internet Statistics," Global Reach (2004), available at www.glreach.com/globstats/index.php3.

8. Lieutenant General Michael Hayden, "Transformation 2.0: Cryptology as a Team Sport."

9. William Black, private communication, Fort Meade, Md., August 5, 2004 (internal NSA document).

10. Clayton M. Christensen, *The Innovator's Dilemma: When New Technologies Cause Great Firms to Fail* (Boston: Harvard Business School, 1997).

11. Andrew S. Grove, *Only the Paranoid Survive: How to Exploit the Crisis Points That Challenge Every Company* (New York: Doubleday, 1996), 50, 134.

12. Louis V. Gerstner Jr., *Who Says Elephants Can't Dance?* (New York: HarperCollins, 2002).

13. Morison illustrates the magnitude of Lieutenant Sims's proposed change. "In 1899 five ships of the North Atlantic Squadron fired five minutes each at a lightship hulk at the conventional range of 1600 yards. After 25 minutes of banging away, two hits had been made on the sails of the elderly vessel. Six years later one naval gunner made fifteen hits in one minute at a target 75 by 25 feet at the same range—1600 yards: half of them hit in a bull's eye 50 inches square." Elting E. Morison, *Men, Machines, and Modern Times* (Cambridge: MIT Press, 1966), 22.

14. Ibid., 17–34.

15. Benjamin Weiser, *A Secret Life: The Polish Officer, His Covert Mission, and the Price He Paid to Save His Country* (New York: Public Affairs, 2004).

16. U.S. House of Representatives, Rep. Henry J. Hyde, Introduction to "Embassy Moscow: Attitudes and Errors," *Congressional Record*, October 25, 1990, E3489.

17. Victor Sheymov, *Tower of Secrets: A Real Life Spy Thriller* (Annapolis: Naval Institute Press, 1993), 141.

18. Ibid.

19. Colin Robinson, "Military and Cyber-Defense: Reactions to the Threat," Center for Defense Information, November 8, 2002.

20. It should be noted that other strategies would be possible if the United States and its adversaries did not use the same IT and consequently share many of the same vulnerabilities. For example, a reversal of the dependence on commercial technology for our critical systems would be another viable strategy.

21. Christensen, *Innovator's Dilemma*.

22. DoD, Defense Science Board, *DoD Roles and Missions in Homeland Security, Final Report* (summer report to the acting undersecretary of defense, acquisition, technology, and logistics) (Washington, D.C.: U.S. Government Printing Office, 2003).

23. Ken Thompson, "Reflections on Trusting Trust," *Communication of the Association for Computer Machinery* 27 (August 1984): 761–63.

24. Michael Wynne, acting undersecretary of defense for acquisition, technology and logistics, "Memorandum for the Chairman, Defense Science Board, Terms of Reference," Defense Science Board task force on high performance microchip supply, December 18, 2003.

25. DoD, Defense Science Board, *DoD Roles and Missions*.

26. Fred B. Schneider, *Trust in Cyberspace*, Computer Science and Telecommunications Board, Committee on Information Systems Trustworthiness (Washington, D.C.: National Academy Press, 1999).

27. Computer Science and Telecommunications Board, "Improving Cybersecurity Research in the United States: Statement of Work," available at www.nationalacademies.org/cstb/project_cybersecurity_sow.html.

28. Alfred Price, *The History of U.S. Electronics Warfare: Rolling Thunder through Allied Force, 1964 to 2000,* vol. 3 (Arlington: Association of Old Crows, 2000), 498–502.

29. Richard Proto, conversation with author, Fort Meade, Md., July 7, 2004.

30. There are numerous research and development activities underway within both the public and private sectors intended to improve our ability to better manage and exploit the data we are collecting. This section is not intended to be a comprehensive survey of these activities.

31. Richard Colbaugh and Kristin Glass, "Identifying Facility Function Using Complex Systems Analysis," *Journal of Intelligence Community Research and Development* (forthcoming).

32. Gerstner, *Who Says Elephants Can't Dance?* 182.

33. Price Pritchett, *The Employee Handbook of New Work Habits for a Radically Changing World: 13 Ground Rules for Job Success in the Information Age* (Atlanta: Pritchett & Hull Associates, 1994).

SEVEN   # Analysis and Estimates
Professional Practices in Intelligence Production

Douglas MacEachin

THE INVESTIGATIONS of intelligence performance on the terrorist threat prior to September 11 and on the question of Iraq's weapons of mass destruction (WMD) have convinced the U.S. body politic that change is needed in U.S. intelligence components and practices. The issues of debate have not been whether to change but what to change and how to do it.

The debates have focused mainly on issues of large scope, such as whether to establish the position of a director of national intelligence separate from that of the director of the Central Intelligence Agency (CIA) and, if so, how to define its authority. Organizational restructuring, such as creation of new issue-targeted national intelligence centers, has already become law with the passage of the National Intelligence Reform Act of 2004. This act is in turn likely to prompt further changes as the structures it has created cause ripple effects and thus further adjustments—whether by direction or reaction—in subordinate components of the intelligence community.

It is this ripple effect that ultimately will determine whether and how whatever changes are made to the overall structure and organizational components actually affect the shortfalls that have been identified in the intelligence product delivered to users. The outcome will at the end be shaped by the way in which changes in authorities, organizational components, and interrelationships affect not just the capabilities of the intelligence community but its professional practices — how those new authorities and capabilities are employed.

This momentum creates a valuable opportunity. It generates the force that can finally break through the barricades that have blocked numerous earlier efforts to bring about needed changes. Multiple studies and reports submitted to the legislative and executive branches over the past few decades have singled out many of the same problems identified in the post–September 11 studies, and have proposed similar changes that did not make it through the barricades.

At the same time, this momentum for change carries certain risks. The challenge is to direct its force to ensure that the results address the specific problems that led to critical failures in the intelligence mission. The risk is that a series of organizational changes will permit the same problems to live in new residences.

Dealing with this risk requires identifying the specific factors that have caused or contributed to the shortfalls in the performance of the intelligence mission. This provides a "target agenda" for change. The changes need to be designed for the dual purpose of eliminating (to the extent possible) the specific factors that have caused or permitted the shortfalls and developing new capabilities and professional practices to strengthen overall mission performance. This chapter seeks to make a contribution to this end by outlining reforms to analytic tradecraft within the U.S. intelligence community.

Implementing changes in professional practices, however, requires overcoming the Washington axiom that constructive criticism is an oxymoron. The first and most formidable obstacle to reform is reluctance to acknowledge that there have indeed been failings, and that there are indeed flaws in practice. One cannot design treatment without identifying what needs to be treated. And this cannot happen without acknowledging that something needs to be treated. Identifying flawed practice requires, of course, examination of the performance of the intelligence mission to identify where it failed to meet mission requirements.

The common, almost reflexive initial reaction to intelligence failures is to see them as a result of deficiencies in collection—a failure to acquire the vital information. Much of the rhetoric on the recent failings appeals to this conventional wisdom and beats the familiar drum that we need more spies. It is certainly true that the recent investigations demonstrate that significant improvements are needed in intelligence collection. There is little disagreement on the judgment that this is not simply a matter of more resources but of different resources. There is also consensus that it is *not* just a matter of resources but equally a matter of practices—the employment and coordination of the resources. Much of the problem arises from a need to adjust to new challenges in a new intelligence collection topography. The collection architecture constructed over the decades of the cold war needs to be reshaped if it is to deal with what now constitute the principal national security threats.

Information shortfalls notwithstanding, however, numerous studies of many if not most of the cases defined as intelligence failures in recent decades have demonstrated that they resulted as much if not more from what was or was not done with information that *had* been acquired—that is, how it was collated, interpreted, and communicated.

It is this segment of the intelligence chain—the use of information obtained—to which this chapter seeks to provide a contribution. With due respect for the dangers of oversimplification, the chapter compares key shortfalls in the use of intelligence information leading up to the terrorist attacks of September 11 with a sampling of what has been revealed in examinations of other adjudged intelligence failings over the past decades. What do they have—or appear to have—in common with regard to the use of intelligence information? What are the fundamental differences? The chapter does not presume to provide final solutions but rather to offer a framework for identifying factors that permitted the shortfalls to occur and for designing practices to counter them.

Two fundamental problem areas stand out — one relatively new, or at least relatively newly revived, and one timeless. The first is a decline in the U.S. intelligence community's commitment to strategic analysis and the crafting of strategic intelligence products. This has been singled out not only in the reviews of intelligence performance on the terrorist threat leading up to September 11 but also in studies of intelligence performance on other contentious issues in the past decade.[1]

The second problem is the enduring trap described variously as "cognitive bias" or "cognitive disassociation" or, in more derogatory terms, "mindset," "preconception," and "groupthink." Taking on this issue entails treading on the sensitive terrain of inherent human weaknesses. A common response to critiques of "cognitive bias" or "mindset" is that they are "unhelpful." The science of "cognition" is too often regarded as academic theory. And while intelligence managers periodically attempt to make analysts aware of cognitive pitfalls, these efforts have been most commonly relegated to classrooms and have rarely made it into line practices of intelligence analysis or the evaluation of finished products.

But intelligence is a profession of cognition. This is what the job is all about — how we absorb and mentally process information coming to us, and how the receivers of our product absorb and mentally process what we give them. That is the chemistry that ultimately determines the impact of the information collected. Shortfalls in strategic analysis and problems of cognitive bias are often entwined in dangerous combinations; the art and practice of intelligence must include a conscious and deliberate effort to disentangle and correct them.

The Measuring Stick: Mission Performance

Before exploring the problems of cognitive bias and strategic deficiency in greater depth, it will be useful to consider the role that both have played in past intelligence failures — with failure defined as deficient support to the decision-making process that resulted in a significant setback for U.S. policy. Performance metrics are thus directly related to the decision-making process that an intelligence establishment has been designed to support, and cannot be understood apart from this process.

Indeed, likening September 11 to Pearl Harbor has become part of the public and political lexicon and has reenergized the long-standing emphasis on "warning of attack" as the prime metric for evaluating intelligence success and failure. This warning role, however, is not distinct from but rather inseparable from the basic metric for assessing intelligence performance across the board — its effectiveness in providing policymakers with the information necessary for making decisions, starting with the judgment on whether a policy decision is needed. If so, what needs to be decided? If action is needed, what kind of action, and how will it be carried out? What are the choices? In U.S. experience, the failure to understand options, transcend bias, and temper optimism has infected intelligence and the decision-making process it serves.

The policy-decision process requires intelligence that can be used for assessing alternative courses — including the alternative of taking no action — in terms of potential results, feasibility, and cost-benefit tradeoffs. The dimensions of the decision framework extend from the strategic — revising or forming new long-term strategies — to ongoing operational-tactical decisions and planning how and with what resources to attempt to carry out the actions decided upon. This fundamental decision and action framework applies across the board, from military planning and operations to foreign and international economic policies.

The intelligence impact on this decision process in turn depends on the combination of content, presentation, interpretation, and timeliness. In effect, what is known, what is communicated and how, and when. The strength of each of these elements draws on the others. Depending on the way these factors are combined, the impact of the whole can be greater or less than the sum of the parts.

For example, many historical studies have described a failure to share communications intercepted in the weeks prior to December 7, 1941, as having permitted U.S. forces to be caught in a "surprise attack." Similarly, one of the factors that the post–September 11 investigations have highlighted is the sharing and distribution of information, particularly between components of the U.S. foreign and domestic intelligence communities and law enforcement agencies. Many of the proposals now being considered are motivated by the perceived need to eliminate obstacles that impeded the sharing of information that might have enabled the September 11 attacks to be derailed.

These obstacles are frequently characterized as the result of the intelligence community's failure or reluctance or bureaucratic inability to drop practices designed for the cold war that are unsuited to today's challenges. To a large extent, however, the "walls" between the intelligence and law enforcement communities that have previously impeded information sharing are not products "designed" for the cold war as much as they are the survivors of it. They arose from the competing objectives in the use of intelligence — domestic law enforcement had a need to avoid contamination of evidence for court prosecution, while foreign intelligence had a need to prevent exposure of sources and methods. During the cold war the costs of these walls — with the notable exception of counterintelligence cases — were not perceived to be high enough to overcome perceived needs.

In other areas of information sharing, many observers have noted that the end of the cold war actually resulted in a degree of atrophy. During the cold war era, the push and pull for critical intelligence from both analysts and policymakers were for the most part strong enough to overcome bureaucratic divides and ensure that intelligence usually got to where it needed to go. When the Soviet Union disappeared as a major threat and nothing clearly moved up to replace it, the push and pull among and between collectors and analysts and the principal customers they served subsided. Bureaucratic walls became salient factors in dissemination, particularly of intelligence on newly emerging threats such as terrorism.

The costs of these various barriers are now painfully evident, and many self-initiated steps to eliminate them have already been implemented by the agencies that make up the intelligence, law enforcement, and homeland security complex. These actions have been directed both at eliminating the obstacles to information sharing and promoting incentives for it—in effect, fueling the "push-pull" forces by establishing requirements and setting up organizational components specifically tasked with this function.

Lessons from History

Though information-sharing issues have prompted comparisons of September 11 to Pearl Harbor, some historical studies have also concluded that the more fundamental shortfall that led to the surprise attack on Pearl Harbor was in the strategic intelligence produced in the preceding year. They cite information going back well before the summer of 1941 that revealed that Japanese imperial aspirations in the Pacific region were already in conflict with U.S. interests there, and that these were taking Japan on a path that could result in a military confrontation. According to this interpretation, it was the U.S. failure to absorb this strategic risk fully that resulted in military forces' and intelligence resources' unpreparedness, their failure to give priority attention to intercepted communications that suggested that some significant action by Japan was imminent.[2]

The United States knew it was at war with Japan once Pearl Harbor was attacked. But when did Japanese leaders know they were going to war with the United States? Were there any signs that this possibility was sufficient to warrant a strategic review of its implications? Were there any signs that additional decisions should be made, such as putting forces on alert or expanding the list of those receiving intelligence? The focus of this line of examination is not on the warning of an attack at a specific time on a specific target, but rather on the determination that there was a plausible risk that some attack might take place.

With due respect for the dangers of oversimplifying historical comparisons, similar questions can be raised about intelligence performance prior to September 11. In both cases the U.S. government failed to absorb the strategic dimensions of a threat and therefore failed to correct operational shortfalls in intelligence posture; the resulting gap arguably impeded national policy discourse on preemptive options.[3]

Years before September 2001—indeed, well over a year before the August 1998 attacks on the U.S. embassies in east Africa—U.S. intelligence had substantial detailed information showing that Osama bin Laden had declared war on the United States and was heading an organization dedicated to this purpose. He had in fact publicly issued his "declaration of war" in August 1996, and U.S. intelligence had learned shortly afterward that it was a repetition of a declaration he had been preaching to his organization since the early 1990s.

Information acquired by that time had also revealed that bin Laden's organization had already been involved to varying degrees in a number of deadly attacks on Americans in the preceding years, including assisting the Somalis in attacks on U.S. troops that culminated in the October 1993 downing of two U.S. helicopters, the deaths of eighteen Americans, and the wounding of seventy-three others. Among the many indications of his desire to cause mass casualties was information revealing that he had attempted to procure weapons-grade nuclear material. In February 1998 bin Laden had again publicly issued a declaration of war on the United States, this one also signed by the heads of four other terrorist groups, explicitly calling on Muslims worldwide to fulfill their "individual duty" to kill Americans—whether military or civilian—"in any country it is possible to do it." And he made similar statements in press interviews in the following months.[4]

The virtually simultaneous truck bombings of two U.S. embassies in east Africa in August 1998 fully conformed to what the previous information had indicated was the threat posed by bin Laden's organization, and U.S. intelligence immediately learned that these attacks had in fact been carried out under bin Laden's direction. An indication of his organization's commitment to such operations was revealed in information obtained in the ensuing months that the planning for this attack had begun well over four years earlier, when bin Laden chaired a meeting at which the U.S. embassy in Nairobi was selected as a target. The operation had been carried out by a cell he had established in the early 1990s to manage the weapons and training support for Somalis attacking U.S. forces there. A voluminous body of information obtained in the ensuing months further expanded the intelligence community's knowledge of his organization, its collaboration with globally dispersed terrorist groups, and its intent to kill large numbers of Americans.[5]

Soon after the attack on the USS *Cole* in a Yemen port in October 2000, U.S. intelligence confirmed that the top two commanders of the attack were key operators of bin Laden's organization. Both had already been identified as having been involved in the 1998 attacks on the U.S. embassies.

Even with due respect to the benefits of hindsight, one could reasonably have read this accumulation of information as indicating that as long as bin Laden's organization remained at large, it would continue to pursue its goal of killing large numbers of Americans. And unless each and every attempt bin Laden made was detected and preempted, Americans would continue to be killed as a result of his efforts.

But, as described in the *9/11 Commission Report,* the intelligence community's acquisition of this information did not result, before September 11, in the policy establishment's recognition of the threat as sufficiently compelling to warrant an attempt to "rally the American people to a warlike effort . . . to eliminate it." This issue was not "joined as a collective debate by the U.S. government, including the Congress."[6]

Whether such efforts would have led to actions that preempted September 11 is a question that now must be left to the counterfactual. But defensive assertions that such efforts would not have worked anyway sidestep the more pertinent point that no effort was made and raise the question, "why not?" And even leaving aside the issue of whether the September 11 attacks might have been prevented in this way, might such efforts have at least increased the chances of an alert posture that could have minimized the obstacles to information sharing and prevented the loss of clues about the attacks described in the post–September 11 reports?[7]

Problems Old and New

To a certain extent, what the 9/11 Commission has described as a failure of "imagination" in the absorption of information accumulated on the al-Qaeda threat reflects a common problem identified in numerous studies of intelligence failures in past decades. The intelligence record is replete with cases in which a sizable body of information pointed to the strong possibility that something would occur, yet U.S. policy officials were taken by surprise when it did occur.

In the summer of 1968, for example, the Soviet Union and its Warsaw Pact allies were observed mobilizing a military force of some three hundred thousand troops surrounding Czechoslovakia. This mobilization included the call-up of tens of thousands of reservists. The units had their full complement of combat equipment, including tanks and armored personnel carriers, and by late July they were receiving large numbers of trucks drawn from reserve depots, trucks also used to support the annual fall crop harvests. Several combat aircraft regiments had been deployed to bases near the borders. This was at the time when a new Czechoslovak government was leading an aggressive reform movement that threatened to create a major fissure in the USSR's control over Eastern Europe. All of this had been seen and reported by the U.S. intelligence community. Yet, according to official records of a meeting in the White House on the evening of August 20, convened shortly after these forces launched their invasion of Czechoslovakia, the president and all of his top national security cabinet officials expressed surprise that this invasion had taken place.[8]

In September 1973 U.S. intelligence collectors learned and reported that Egypt was calling up military reservists and conducting major exercises, and that Syria was moving military forces to the Golan Heights bordering Israel. The U.S. government shared this information with the Israeli government. On October 4–5, information was obtained that Soviet personnel were being evacuated from Egypt and Syria on Soviet military air transports. Yet when Egypt and Syria simultaneously launched an invasion of Israel on

October 6 — setting off what is now commonly referred to as the Yom Kippur War — both U.S. and Israeli officials expressed their surprise.[9]

In November 1979 U.S. intelligence observed two Soviet combat divisions being mobilized near the Soviet border with Afghanistan. These divisions comprised some twenty-five thousand troops and were fully equipped with combat equipment such as tanks, armored personnel carriers, field artillery, and even anti-aircraft artillery. These same divisions and two others had been seen in what were, for the units in that area, highly unusual exercises in the preceding months, involving the call-up and training of large numbers of reservists. An airborne division in the same area was seen preparing for deployment. In the preceding months, U.S. intelligence had learned that several thousand Soviet troops had already been deployed to Afghanistan, and that the bulk of them were at an operational base that had been set up at an airfield north of the Afghan capital of Kabul. In the first week of December the number of Soviet troops at this airfield was doubled, and Soviet combat aircraft were seen being deployed to USSR airfields in the regions bordering Afghanistan.[10]

This activity was occurring at a time when the Soviet-sponsored Afghan regime's hold on power was becoming increasingly tenuous, and when Moscow's political leverage had been seriously eroded. Yet after the Soviets launched their invasion on December 24, senior policy officials — including President Jimmy Carter — said they had not received adequate warning.[11]

In mid-1981 the confrontation between the Polish regime and the Solidarity opposition movement had reached the point where Solidarity was directly challenging the Communist Party's authority. U.S. intelligence was aware, from the time the movement had begun to surge two years earlier, that the Polish regime had begun preparing contingency plans for imposing martial law to crush it. The intelligence information also revealed that the Polish leaders had been under intense pressure from Moscow for more than a year to carry out this military crackdown. This information was being provided to U.S. intelligence officers by a military officer of the Polish General Staff who had been assigned to the task force developing the plans to impose martial law and who had for much of the preceding decade been one of the most important U.S. human intelligence sources in the Soviet military alliance.

By September Solidarity had raised the intensity of confrontation to a new order of magnitude. A month later a major shake-up occurred in the leadership of the Polish Communist Party and the top position of party secretary was taken over by the man who already held the top positions in the military and the civilian government and who was in charge of the martial law plans. In early November the U.S. intelligence source escaped from Poland and was flown to the United States. He told his U.S. interlocutors that he had been informed before he escaped that the Polish regime had already decided to implement the martial law plans to crush Solidarity.[12]

Yet when the Polish regime, on December 13, 1981, imposed martial law, U.S. policy officials were surprised and made public statements to this effect. One told the media that there had been a failure of "intelligence gathering and assessment." Another was somewhat kinder in acknowledging that the administration had considerable information on the fact that plans for a military suppression had been prepared, but had been "caught off guard" when they were actually carried out.[13]

Intelligence leading up to the September 11 attacks shared a problem in common with these cases. In each of them a sizable body of information pointed to a potential event that nonetheless caught U.S. policy officials off guard. But the problem shared with the intelligence failures of September 11 was not a strategic one. To the contrary, each of the previous failures involved specific, known, and in most instances observable preparations for the use of military force in a specific state or states, arising from a self-identifying crisis situation. None of the critiques of these intelligence failures has claimed that the strategic picture was not fully fleshed out, or that there was no detailed reporting of the preparatory measures.

In all of these cases a base of in-depth, detailed intelligence products had already drawn a "tapestry" of the strategic environment even before the indications of a specific crisis situation began to emerge. These products ranged from encyclopedic-style informational "surveys" to individual agency "assessments" to interagency forecasting "estimates" (national intelligence estimates, or NIEs). This was the output of the standing practice of maintaining a strategic military and political survey of a cold war world divided, in intelligence terms, into allies, opponents, and nonaligned entities. As the crises in each of the cited cases began to emerge, the initial daily intelligence reporting was disseminated against this background. In each case, the overall strategic picture was updated at periodic intervals, with analytic products collating and providing interpretations of all the information that had been acquired up to that point.[14] Sound strategic analysis itself cannot, however, prevent failures resulting from cognitive bias. In each of these cases and many others as well, studies have found that failures resulted not from deficient strategic analysis but from cognitive bias.

In 1968, for example, the key question was whether the military forces being marshaled around Czechoslovakia's borders and the major military exercises being conducted — some inside Czechoslovakia — were contingency preparations for a Soviet invasion or merely a bluff designed to coerce the new Czechoslovak leaders into toeing the party line in Moscow. The dominant conclusion was that it was the latter. This rested heavily on the premise that Moscow would not view the consequences of developments in Czechoslovakia as worth the price of a military intervention. It was assumed that Moscow believed such action would snuff out the growing momentum of "détente" in Europe.[15]

Similarly, in 1973 U.S. officials could not believe that Egypt and Syria would be so foolish as to invade Israel, given Israel's demonstrated military superiority (a superiority demonstrated again, when the October invasion did in fact take place).[16]

Likewise, the underlying premise of the assessment of the prospect of a Soviet military intervention in Afghanistan in 1979 was that Moscow would realize that this held the possibility for their own Vietnam; and that even in the unlikely event that the Soviets did resort to military intervention, they would prepare a "massive" force that far exceeded what was available from the units garrisoned in the region. The forces readied in the latter half of 1979 did not come close to this model, and therefore the U.S. government did not believe that invasion was imminent. (It is now known from Soviet archives that, contrary to the assumption of the intelligence analysts, the plan that was carried out was exactly the one that Moscow had been preparing in the preceding seven months.)[17] Another plank supporting the judgment that invasion was not coming was the continuing premise that the Soviets would not risk losing the benefits of détente.[18]

In the case of Poland and Solidarity, the fundamental premise in assessing the intelligence information was that, absent a massive insertion of Soviet military force, the Polish regime would not be able to impose the military crackdown even if it wanted to, because the Polish army — at least the rank and file — would not use force against its own populace.

None of these unfortunately erroneous premises was completely without merit. In virtually every instance, moreover, they were explicitly shared by U.S. policymakers.[19] The record of the August 20, 1968, meeting at the White House documents the view that Moscow's interest in détente would deter the Soviets from invading Czechoslovakia. The element of hope also was almost certainly a factor; President Johnson was already slated to appear on television within the next few days to announce the beginning of U.S.-Soviet negotiations on strategic arms limitation (SALT). Egypt's and Syria's military preparations in late September 1973 occurred at a time when the U.S. government was preparing for Middle East peace negotiations scheduled to begin at the end of October. The Soviet military preparations on the Afghan borders took place as Congress was deliberating on whether to support the arms control treaty (SALT-II) that President Carter had signed with Soviet leader Leonid Brezhnev in Vienna several months earlier. The view that only the Soviets could or would implement a military crackdown in Poland was held even more intensely by some policy officials.[20]

From the perspective of analytic tradecraft, the flaw was not in figuring these key premises into the assessments and forecast. The flaw was in not confronting the fact that in each case the premise was the decisive factor. The premise should have been examined for what it was. It should have been assessed on the basis of how heavily it rested on direct evidence and how heavily on assumption. And each scenario should have been reexamined on the basis of what an alternative picture would look like if the premise were removed from the equation.

The lesson to be drawn is that however successful the efforts at correcting identified shortfalls in strategic intelligence may be, the "cognitive bias" or "mindset" trap will survive unless and until practices specifically designed to counteract it are embedded as standard procedures in line units responsible for intelligence analysis and production.

The Basics: The Strategic Foundation of Analysis and Estimates

Pre–September 11 deficiencies in intelligence analysis relative to the threat posed by the new terrorist phenomenon were not the result of an intelligence community wedded to cold war production practices. Rather, they appear to have been the result of failure to adapt proven practices to a threat that did not conform to the model against which the use of those practices originally evolved. A decline in the practice of strategic intelligence, when combined with long-standing cognitive blocks, created a dangerous blind spot. In other words, the "preconception" trap was a contributing factor in the strategic intelligence shortfall. Until September 11 the concept of a "strategic threat" had been wedded to state actors and military forces. Insofar as this concept had been applied to the hierarchy of nonstate threats, it had focused mainly on those that were — or were believed to be — state-supported quasi surrogates.

But by the 1990s independent nonstate actors were becoming strategic threats. Information acquired by 1997 made a prima facie case that as long as bin Laden's organization continued to operate it would continue to launch deadly attacks on Americans. Bin Laden's intentions were confirmed by the subsequent attacks on the U.S. embassies in August 1998 and the attack on the USS *Cole* in October 2000. Historians will debate for decades why, given the knowledge of bin Laden's intentions and demonstrated commitment to carrying them out, the United States did not adopt a more warlike posture for dealing with his organization.

The good news is that the practice of strategic analysis is readily applicable to the new intelligence challenges once the need is recognized. The director of central intelligence (DCI), George Tenet, had already begun to initiate steps in this direction before September 11, although the intended measures were still in the formative stage at the time of the attacks.[21] Recognition of the need for better strategic analysis in the intelligence community writ large is reflected in a number of measures taken since September 11, including the creation of the Terrorist Threat Integration Center and, most recently, the establishment of the National Counter Terrorism Center. Although the main obstacle to these needed changes prior to September 11, and to some extent since then, has the classic turf mentality, anyone manning a defense tower on a bureaucratic wall today is in a precarious position indeed.

As in all enterprises, adapting established analytic practices to new challenges requires breaking some locked-in processes geared to specific targets. As reform efforts loosen the old models or ways of doing business, efforts also need to be made to avoid becoming locked in to a new model and target set. There is always the risk that the focus on bin Laden's al-Qaeda organization will drive all analytic practices, and this risk must be guarded against. Analytic fads are dangerous—for example, a number of intelligence officials have lamented that the practice of strategic intelligence has eroded as the result of an almost Darwinian evolution; increasing demands for current intelligence in a post–cold war climate have caused analysis to conform to an emerging information age of instant news bites. And today's intelligence audience has become accustomed to receiving much of its global picture from such sources.[22]

The weaving together of a large body of evidence into a comprehensive, detailed intelligence tapestry should not, however, be treated as part of an "either-or" tradeoff with the more concise products delivered to top policy officials, but rather as capital investment for the overall intelligence production process. This point was made some forty years ago by Sherman Kent, who described the "intelligence surveys" and "research products" as the foundation of the intelligence "pyramid."[23] They can and should be disseminated in their full, detailed form to a wide spectrum of other intelligence officials at the "desk-officer" level in policy agencies and departments. They also can and should be used to craft additional products tailored to specific officials at various levels. The "slam-bang" quality of the tailored products is a direct function of the strength of the foundation product. The stronger the base of the pyramid, the more power it can generate to the peak.

This intelligence production process needs to be carried out with attention to the content of information flow to the receivers—what one former intelligence practitioner calls "the consumption process."[24] A policy official, like anyone else, receives and absorbs ongoing intelligence reporting in a "cognitive sphere." Cognitive studies are replete with test cases illustrating that the impact of new information is affected by the "information tapestry" possessed by the user. Within organizational structures this information tapestry includes the information possessed by the broad groups that interact within their organizations after the new information is received. Broad dissemination of in-depth studies may generate additional insights, as analysts in related disciplines add threads at the margins or tighten the weave; it certainly allows more analysts to see missing threads or identify critical new ones that appear. In this way strategic surveys directly and critically enable warning and the production of useful current intelligence.

Another factor that should reinvigorate the production of detailed in-depth products is the increasing role they can play in supporting the gathering of intelligence information. A basic principle of the intelligence cycle is that collating what is known or reported tells what we do not know, and this is a guide to what we need to learn. This is not a new idea. But the needle-in-a-haystack nature of the search required against the threats we face today places an even greater demand for honing the collection efforts from broad-area coverage down to high-resolution targeting. And this makes the "information in–requirements out" cycle ever more tightly bound. The more precisely the needed information can be identified, the more effectively it can be obtained.

The Strategic Intelligence Mission: A Summary of the Escalating Challenge

While much of the current discourse on analytic tradecraft revolves around terrorism and the September 11 experience, this experience should be considered mainly as a lesson learned. Terrorism is a weapon and a weapons-employment tactic. The first objective of strategic intelligence is to identify potential opponents who might use this weapon and might ultimately do so against the United States. To resort again to the analogy of September 11 and Pearl Harbor, in both cases the United States learned only after suffering a devastating attack that it was at war with an enemy who had decided much earlier that it was at war with the United States. That said, identifying the potential enemies who could resort to terrorism against the United States is a vastly different challenge from identifying a nation-state employing traditional armed forces.

Bin Laden's organization came together in the holy war in Afghanistan in the 1980s and matriculated in the first half of the 1990s in Sudan. Its goals and global reach reflected the outlook that its founders and key operatives brought from long experience with underground insurrectionist movements spawned by the conditions in their homelands, mainly but not only in the Middle East and North Africa. They identified the United States as the main enemy—the "head of the snake"—largely because of the U.S. government's perceived relationship to their original enemies, the regimes in their home countries.[25]

This enemy did not fit the model of what had been perceived until then as the main terrorist threat. Until the dimensions of bin Laden's organization and goals began to be fully absorbed in the late 1990s (and then by only a limited number of experts), the intelligence community mainly saw terrorists—not incorrectly, given historical background—as consisting primarily of nationalist groups driven by local agendas and state-sponsored groups whose agenda conformed to their state sponsors'. The threat to the United States from the nationalist groups was viewed as mainly to U.S. citizens and facilities in their home countries, where the United States was seen as the supporter of the regime that was the terrorist groups' enemy. The greatest threat to the United States was usually described as coming from state-sponsored groups whose sponsor treated the United States as its enemy.[26]

Because bin Laden's organization and motivations did not conform to any of the threat models that preceded it—whether groups or states—the intelligence community did not recognize it as a strategic enemy early enough. Now that bin Laden's organization is recognized as such, the old model's constraints are broken. The challenge for U.S. intelligence now and in the future is to spot the emergence, and preferably the preemergence, of new potential enemies who might choose to use terrorism against the United States and its allies, and not to get locked into the current model. This basic lesson is easily forgotten as interaction with old enemies becomes more sophisticated and complex.

This need to retain cognitive agility presents a daunting challenge. An intelligence map formerly defined mainly in terms of states and their borders and alliances is increasingly becoming a maze of groups and transnational affiliations. Conditions similar to what spawned the emergence of al-Qaeda can be found across a vast global stretch encompassing the Middle East and much of Africa and stretching through the Caucasus and ancient Kurdistan, and central, south, and southeast Asia. Major terrorist groups are already engaged in local conflicts in these areas, and—as was the case with Middle Eastern groups that were critical to the emergence and evolution of al-Qaeda—they or their offspring have the potential to become declared enemies of the United States. Cells from many of these groups are already embedded in many Western states.

The complexities of this twenty-first-century threat topography make it essential to institutionalize a system of strategic research, surveys, and analytic assessments produced and updated on a rolling basis by analytic teams assigned to cover various areas. Such a system is essential for spotting and tracking emerging threats from this morass, and will provide the base for the variety of intelligence products for diverse policy recipients. These areas of analytic focus need to be defined less by national boundaries than by sociopolitical composition and connections, with mandatory consultation and joint efforts among the analytic groups, to avoid these areas' becoming "bureaucratic turf."

Ideally, these analytic teams or task groups should be made up of experts drawn from across the intelligence community. And all of their products should be community products, with the same kind of interagency imprimatur as NIEs have now. They would be the drafters of periodic NIEs submitted for community coordination at the highest level. Obviously, the research compilations and analytic assessments of existing and evolving situations could be coordinated at the line management level. Disagreements need not and should not be resolved through compromise, but instead should be spelled out in the product. To the extent that these disagreements reflect competing cognitive biases, laying them out may offer unexpected insights.

Confronting Ourselves

Whatever successes may be achieved in dealing with the strategic intelligence practices, the ultimate age-old analytic vulnerability to single premises demonstrated in the earlier cases described above will persist until it is directly confronted and measures specifically designed to deal with it are embedded as standard practices. It has done no good and will do no good to dismiss as "unhelpful" efforts to root out cognitive bias, by whatever name it is called. Review after review of adjudged intelligence failures has found cognitive bias to have been a—if not the—principal factor.

The difficulty in confronting this analytic vulnerability is that such terms as "mindset" have derogatory connotations. Developing practices to help reduce the risks cognitive bias poses to analytic products simply requires recognizing that it is an inherent human frailty. It is worth noting in this regard that former Secretary of State Henry Kissinger, in his look back on the events of 1973, has asserted that our erroneous assumptions regarding Egyptian and Syrian views of Israeli military superiority, in his words, resulted in "an intelligence failure" that grew out of "our mindset." (He clearly includes himself among the guilty).[27] The potentially catastrophic costs of failing to make necessary changes require that the question of blame be put aside.

Of course, it is much easier to make changes through redistribution of resources than to correct problems stemming from fundamental human vulnerabilities. As mentioned above, some critics still tend to brush aside such efforts as a useless academic exercise. One can hope that at least some of the current momentum for intelligence reform will be directed at bolstering the study of the science and tools of this field. Some of this effort should be devoted to reexamining the effectiveness of some of the practices that have already been established. A common, almost reflexive response to charges of "mindset" and "groupthink" is to establish separate, offline components specifically charged with thinking "out of the box," or "red-team alternative analysis." These are well-intentioned and potentially valuable measures. But an evaluation needs to be made as to whether their effectiveness is at risk of being undermined by a fundamental cognitive bias of its own.

For example, experience has demonstrated that assigning someone a "warning" function can free up that person's thinking but impede the impact of that thinking. Because the job is to warn, the product that warns is greeted with a "what else?" reaction. Because the job is to produce "out-of-the-box" ideas, the product is too often received with a predisposition to see it as the product of an assignment to "come up with crazy ideas that have little to do with the real world." Too often, as soon as they hit someone's inbox with the label of "alternative," the receiver puts them on the back burner.

A more effective way to enhance the impact of these efforts would be to embed them in the line analysis and production components. This has in fact been done in several places and, depending on management's openness to such approaches, the impact of alternative analyses has been enhanced. They are most effective when the construction of alternatives begins by testing the alternative mixings of the factors known, identifying the premises that make up the planks carrying the most weight in the analysis of potential outcomes, and testing what happens to the existing interpretations if those premises are removed or altered. This testing should be juxtaposed with testing of the information on which the premise is based. Equally important to the process is the consideration of unknowns that could have a major impact and the testing of these unknowns by inserting alternative values into the existing information mix.

Such reforms should be transparently incorporated into the finished intelligence products. This is of critical importance. The receiver needs to know the factors shaping the potential outcomes, and alternatives that could have a significant effect — not only for absorbing the implications but perhaps also for policy decisions. This does not mean that every product needs to go through this process. But there should be an institutionalized practice for periodic "step-back" efforts.

The same questions about changes or new factors that could critically affect outcomes need to be fed back into the information-collection requirements. The needs for advances in this area have long been recognized by at least some students of intelligence tradecraft. In a world of growing new "emergences" that do not fit any existing models, the needs for developing practices to offset cognitive bias are all the more important. Again, once the need to deal with inherent intellectual vulnerabilities is accepted, there are many tools and methods that can be tested, adapted, and institutionalized in the standard practices. One can only hope that the initiatives already undertaken in this arena will be reinforced rather than overrun by the momentum for revitalizing the intelligence community.

Notes

1. Regarding the terrorist threat, see National Commission on Terrorist Attacks upon the United States, *The 9/11 Commission Report: Final Report of the National Commission on Terrorist Attacks upon the United States* (New York: W. W. Norton, 2004) (hereafter *9/11 Commission Report*), 90–91 and 340–44. Other studies that have made the same judgment are the June 1998 report from the panel commissioned by DCI George Tenet to examine intelligence community performance on the nuclear tests by India and Pakistan, and the July 1998 report from the Congressional Commission to Assess the Ballistic Missile Threats to the United States (PL201). However much one might quarrel with some of the final conclusions of these studies, they all identify specific examples of the erosion of strategic intelligence products in the post–cold war era.

2. One of the earliest such studies was Roberta Wohlstetter's *Pearl Harbor: Warning and Decision* (Stanford: Stanford University Press, 1962).

3. See *9/11 Commission Report*, 118–19 and 341–43.

4. This information and that in the following paragraphs on what was known of bin Laden's organization, objectives, and involvement in earlier attacks on the United States is summarized in the *9/11 Commission Report*, chapter 2. A more detailed description of what was known in the 1997–98 timeframe is in "9/11 Commission Staff Statement No. 15," June 17, 2004, available at www.msnbc.msn.com/id/5224036/. The text of bin Laden's August 1996 public "Declaration of War against the Americans Occupying the Land of the Two Holy Places" is available at www. terrorismfiles.org/individuals/declaration_of_jihad1.html. The February 1998 "Text of World

Islamic Front's Statement Urging Jihad against Jews and Crusaders" (trans. Foreign Broadcast Information Service) appeared in the London-based Arabic publication *Al-Quds al-Arabi*, February 23, 1998. A sample of his subsequent public statements can be seen in "Hunting Bin Laden," PBS *Frontline* broadcast, May 1998, available online at www.pbs.org/wgbh/pages/front-line/shows/binladen/who/interview.html.

5. The sources of this new information are described in the *9/11 Commission Report*, 127.

6. Ibid., 341–43.

7. Among the more prominent instances of opportunity long before the 2001 "summer of threat chatter" is the case of the trail of two of the hijackers, who attended a January 2000 meeting in Kuala Lumpur known at the time to have been set up through channels previously identified in connection with al-Qaeda and the African embassy bombings. Their trail was dropped just after the gathering broke up, as they were about to depart for the United States. They went on to be part of the crew that hijacked the plane that crashed into the Pentagon. This was initially cited in the congressional joint inquiry and in some detail in the *9/11 Commission Report*, 181–82, and was widely reported in the media.

8. I served on a task force following the military buildup at the time. The complete invasion force and the invasion deployment are shown in the translation of a map obtained from Soviet archives after the end of the cold war, presented inside the cover of a compilation of archival materials that appear in Jaromir Navratil, *The Prague Spring '68* (Budapest: Central European Press, 1998), produced as a joint effort with the National Security Archive in Washington. Document 109 of this collection (pp. 445–48 of the book) is a copy of the minutes of the White House meeting of August 20, 1968, in which various participants, including the president, secretary of state, and deputy secretary of defense, express surprise at the event.

9. I participated in the reporting on the movement of Egyptian and Syrian forces and was present when the decision was made to contact Tel Aviv. Regarding the level of surprise, see former Secretary of State Kissinger's account in his book *Years of Upheaval* (Boston: Little, Brown, 1982), 450–67. Kissinger's account includes the information on the air evacuation of Soviet dependents.

10. From April 1979 through the Soviet invasion at the end of the year I was assigned to an interagency group at the Pentagon and was engaged full-time in tracking the Soviet military preparations in Soviet regions north of Afghanistan. Much of this information has now been declassified and is described in a CIA/CIS monograph, *The Soviet Invasion of Afghanistan* (interagency intelligence memorandum, October 1980), located at the National Security Archive, Washington, D.C.

11. See the account by former Secretary of State Cyrus Vance in his book *Hard Choices: Critical Years in American Foreign Policy* (New York: Simon & Schuster, 1983), 283–85. A notable exception was the president's national security advisor, Zbigniew Brzezinski, who had been prodding senior intelligence officials to reexamine what he considered too complacent a view.

12. Much of the information from the source and from other reporting at the time has now been declassified. For a full detailed account, see Douglas MacEachin, *U.S. Intelligence and the Confrontation in Poland, 1980–81* (University Park: Pennsylvania State University Press, 2002).

13. On the "failure of gathering," see comments by Assistant Secretary of Defense Perle, "Pentagon Aide Says U.S. Failed to Anticipate Moves," *Washington Post*, December 14, 1981, A1. Expressions of surprise by other officials are in "Polish Situation Sets Up Complex Choices for U.S.," ibid., December 15, 1981, A16; "Caught off Guard," ibid., December 15, 1981, A23; and

"High Officials Make No Secret They Were Caught Off Guard," *New York Times,* December 18, 1981, A17. For statements about "considerable information," see comments by former Secretary of State Alexander Haig in "U.S. Informs Poland, USSR of 'Serious Concern,'" *Washington Post,* December 14, 1981, A1; "U.S. Acts Warily," *Washington Post,* December 15, 1981, A1; and Haig's memoir, *Caveat: Realism, Reagan, and Foreign Policy* (New York: Macmillan, 1984), 242.

14. In the case of the 1968 invasion of Czechoslovakia this included a comprehensive assessment disseminated two months before the invasion, laying out the political dynamics as the burgeoning crisis appeared headed for critical juncture. It was followed a month later by a detailed compilation of information on the forces deployed around the borders of Czechoslovakia and the recent steps taken to raise their readiness for a sudden attack. In the case of Afghanistan a string of similar analytic products was disseminated throughout the national security establishment three months prior to the invasion, integrating the information on military and political developments as Moscow's control there appeared to be eroding significantly. While the specific signs of the preparations for the invasion of Israel in 1973 were more sudden, the reporting of the preparations was delivered to a policy audience that had already received several comprehensive assessments, beginning five months earlier, describing Egyptian and Syrian efforts to improve the posture of their military forces. These were accompanied by reports of political dynamics in play in an already tense situation. An even larger number of similar intelligence products were distributed on the evolving situation in Poland in the two years preceding the imposition of martial law in 1981. I co-drafted the July 1968 report on the status of the military buildup. The intelligence assessment of the crisis disseminated a month earlier has been declassified. See "'Czechoslovakia: The Dubcek Pause,' U.S. Intelligence Assessment of the Crisis, June 1968," in Navratil, *Prague Spring,* 166–71. Regarding sources on the 1973 invasion of Israel and the reporting on Afghanistan, see notes 89 and 910.

15. This analysis is based on my participation in the debates at the time. Lest I be accused of overlooking differences in capabilities, it should be noted that a significant enhancement in collection capabilities took place well after the invasion of Czechoslovakia that, had it been available at the time, could have provided about twenty-four to forty-eight hours' advance "tactical warning." But even that would have been a case of learning that the trains had left the station.

16. Again, this assessment is based on my participation in the debates at the time, but former Secretary of State Kissinger has expressed the same view in *Years of Upheaval,* 459–62.

17. When it became clear a few months after the invasion that Moscow had indeed gotten itself into a quagmire, the joke in the halls of the CIA was that the agency's analysts had gotten it right and the Soviets had gotten it wrong.

18. Declassified paper from CIA archives, interagency intelligence memorandum, "Soviet Options in Afghanistan," September 1979, available on request from the CIA.

19. As noted above, Zbigniew Brzezinski was a notable exception (see note 11).

20. Regarding policy officials' outlook on the prospects for invasion of Czechoslovakia as reflected in the White House meeting on August 20, 1968, see Navratil, *Prague Spring,* 166ff. These minutes also include allusions to the arms control talks being planned. For an insightful policy official view on the assumptions that led to the miscalculation of Egyptian and Syrian military preparations, including the scheduled peace talks, see Kissinger, *Years of Upheaval,* 453 and 459–67. Regarding fixation on the Soviets as the threat to Solidarity, see "Allies Said to Agree with U.S. On Poland," *New York Times,* March 28, 1981; "Haig Is Troubled by Soviet Moves on Polish Border," *New York Times,* March 30, 1981; "Weinberger Sees Poles Threatened with Inva-

sion by Osmosis," *New York Times,* March 8, 1981, A1; "Weinberger Warns of Repression," *New York Times,* October 23, 1981, A1. I was directly involved in administration preparations for the Senate hearings on the SALT-II treaty in the second half of 1979.

21. *9/11 Commission Report,* 342.

22. Many intelligence managers have described this problem. See, e.g., ibid., 91.

23. Sherman Kent, "Estimates and Influence," in *Sherman Kent and the Board of National Estimates: Collected Essays,* ed. Donald Steury (Washington, D.C.: CIA Center for the Study of Intelligence, 1994), 33–42.

24. Hal Ford, "The Pearl Harbor NIE," in *Estimative Intelligence: The Purpose and Problems of National Intelligence Estimates,* rev. ed. (Lanham, Md.: University Press of America, 1993), 8.

25. *9/11 Commission Report,* 59. In addition to the intelligence materials provided to the commission, this "head-of-the-snake" metaphor was described in testimony by former members of bin Laden's organization in the African embassy bombing trials, the transcripts of which are now available to the public. See *United States v. bin Laden,* No. 5 (7) 98 Cr. 1028 (SDNY), testimony of Jemal Fadl, February 6, 2001, transcript pp. 265–66, and testimony of L'Houssaine Kherchtou, February 21, 2001, transcript p. 1163. The transcripts are available at www.findlaw.com.

26. Some intelligence officials may well contest this description of the dominant perception models of the terrorist threat. But these are the models portrayed in virtually all of the strategic terrorist reviews prepared through the mid-1990s that have been made available to the public.

27. Kissinger, *Years of Upheaval,* 465. Lest it appear that I think I am immune to this frailty, I should note that I too have fallen into the same trap more than once. One of the more memorable instances concerned the Soviet agreement in April 1988 to withdraw all troops from Afghanistan within the next nine months (in fact the last troops were withdrawn seventeen months later). My "mindset" on this issue cost me $100 in wagers with two State Department officials.

EIGHT   Denial and Deception

DONALD C. F. DANIEL

ALL NATIONAL GOVERNMENTS have intentions, capabilities, and activities that they wish to hide from other nations and adversaries. To protect these official secrets, they engage in denial, practices that suppress indicators of the truth from reaching prying eyes and ears. They can also engage in deception, activities that deflect prying eyes and ears from the truth and fasten them instead on false alternatives. The more significant the secret to the state's welfare, the more the associated denial and deception can be characterized as strategic in nature.

With much attention now being given to transforming the U.S. intelligence community, it is appropriate to address the contemporary relevance of the United States' employment of strategic denial and deception and to suggest implications for the community's transformation. I argue in this chapter that

- Though denial and deception are often referred to as if they were a unit, they are distinct but complementary endeavors performed for a variety of specific purposes; of the two, deception is the more demanding.
- The United States practices strategic denial as a matter of course. Its resort to strategic deception seems a matter of exception.
- Notwithstanding the complications that circumscribe strategic deception, it remains highly attractive for use against state adversaries.
- It remains an open question whether engaging in strategic denial or deception against terrorist groups would be of sustained significant value.
- Timely and reliable intelligence is necessary for successfully conducting strategic denial and deception. This requirement underscores the importance of what is already an objective of all transformation plans: upgrading the intelligence community's ability to provide information about an adversary's capabilities, intentions, predispositions, and actions.
- Technical virtuosity and acumen are also important to the success of strategic denial and deception. The U.S. intelligence community already has considerable experience with denial. It is also well positioned institutionally to undertake or assist in deception, and it will be better positioned operationally if a transformed intelligence community recruits "plotters" and provides them with a tradecraft niche where they can hone their skills.

The first part of this chapter outlines basic terms, specific motives for resort to denial and deception, national proclivities toward them, factors that condition operational success, and the relation of denial and deception to a state's intelligence apparatus. The second part particularizes the generalizations offered in the first part to the United States and its intelligence community. The third part offers some conclusions and recommendations.

A Primer on Denial and Deception

Concepts and basic features. Denial and deception are complementary activities with the same basic aim: protecting a secret.[1] Denial, the simpler concept, is negative in nature since it involves limiting access to information, saying nothing about it in public, concealing its physical manifestations, and ensuring that otherwise revealing activities remain "under the radar." Paradoxically, when a government *denies* publicly the existence of a program that it actually has in hand, it has already crossed over into deception. This is a more complex and positive endeavor because the deceiver wants the adversary to pick up false signals that will draw him away from the truth.

Strategic deceptions can go on for years and usually involve more than perpetuating lies as generally understood. Lying means making a statement the content of which is untrue, but in a broader sense it can also involve manipulating or taking advantage of the context—true information and real events—in order to enhance the seeming veracity of a falsehood. This is artifice. Winston Churchill once described deception as providing truth with a bodyguard of lies; artifice is the protection of lies with a bodyguard of truth.

The most elegant deceptions are the misleading variant in which the deceiver causes his target to fasten on one false alternative to the truth. The aim is to have the target reject all alternatives except the one that suits the deceiver. Misleading deceptions are particularly attractive when the deceiver can keep indicators of the truth from ever reaching the target, but when he cannot do so, the deceiver might exploit ambiguity as a way of increasing his deception. Here he confronts the target with at least two choices as to what the truth may be, one of which could be a truth whose indicators cannot be completely hidden. The greater the number of compelling alternatives, the smaller the possibility (*ceteris paribus*) that the target will settle on the truth as the basis for his actions. The more plausible and consequential an alternative, the more the target probably will give it the benefit of his doubts. He cannot risk doing otherwise.

Although both variants are conceptually distinct, their effects can shade into each other as a deception evolves. A deception intended to mislead may degenerate and increase uncertainty when it becomes increasingly difficult for the deceiver to hide its indicators. The end result, however, still serves his interests.

In sum, denial and deception are separate but overlapping and mutually supportive endeavors that governments employ to protect their secrets. Deception requires denial if it is to succeed, and denial may sometimes require deception if it is not to fail. Because of this symbiosis, they are usually referred to as a unit, but they are more like fraternal twins, deception being the more complex and demanding.

Motivations. States undertake strategic denial and deceptions for a variety of reasons. The truism that knowledge is power is a primary motivator. Keeping an adversary in the dark, getting him to chase shadows, lulling him into a false sense of security or insecurity, stealing his secrets without his knowledge — all such measures provide a competitor with an advantage or can help offset his opponent's politico-diplomatic, military, and/or economic superiority. In particular, weaker adversaries are driven to seek ways — including denial and deception — to redress the power balance. Saddam Hussein may not have come clean about Iraq's lack of weapons of mass destruction (WMD) because he hoped the United States would be deterred from attacking him out of fear that he would use his presumed weapons to repel the attack.

A second motive, one as relevant to a strong power as to a weak one, is to reduce costs. This is obvious in military campaigns when a projected victor still works to minimize his casualties by camouflaging his moves and attacking where the enemy does not expect. No one doubted that the United States and its coalition would drive the Iraqis out of Kuwait in 1991, but this did not stop General Norman Schwarzkopf from resorting to an amphibious feint and executing the "Hail Mary" operation.

A third motive is fear of embarrassment or of having to explain oneself. This is especially relevant when a government's practices violate a norm, a treaty commitment, its own stated policy, or the trust of its friends and allies. The Iran-Contra affair of the 1980s directly contradicted vociferous and repeated White House declarations that it would not negotiate for hostages. This duplicity dismayed U.S. partners who had believed that the United States would never waver on the issue.

A fourth motive combines elements of the first three. Governments determined to achieve a strategic goal often see value in preventing premature disclosure of what they are about. They implement denial and deception to ensure that no one stops them while their strategic program is still in development. Once *le fait est accompli*, they might happily go public to garner political advantage and, as a bonus, win the plaudits of friends who praise them for their cleverness. Clandestine nuclear development programs (especially by nations that signed the Nuclear Non-Proliferation Treaty) are a classic example. Iran's development of a nuclear capability would reshape the power balance in the greater Middle East and earn it the appreciation of those who await an Islamic counter to Israel's nuclear weapons.

National proclivities. While all nations are motivated to engage in denial, if not outright deception, they nevertheless may differ in their proclivity to do so. One reason may be the nature of the government.[2] Many observers argue that authoritarian governments have a built-in bias toward denial and deception because they are accustomed to keeping secrets from and lying to their people. They also have confidence that tight control of their governments will allow them to keep a lid on their activities. While the leaders of democracies also turn to strategic denial and deception when circumstances warrant, they seem more willing to be circumscribed by laws, oversight committees, and the conviction that some activities — such as disseminating internal propaganda or lying to domestic legislators — are beyond the democratic pale. A second reason is the circumstances in which states find themselves. For example, democratic "restrictions" on denial and deception usually loosen when the nation is at war or under grave threat. A third reason is culture. Asian cultures, for instance, assume that interpersonal deception will and should occur between individuals as a means of protecting face by deflecting threatening truths.

Factors that condition success. Six factors condition the success of strategic denial and deception. First, competitors can usually be counted on to seek out information about each other. Denial plays against an adversary's eagerness while deception plays to it. That is, while the denier conceals information from the opponent, the deceiver happily provides him with false clues.

A second factor is that intelligence is an inherently difficult business against a skillful adversary determined to hide the truth, and this is especially true when an adversary employs deception because of its potential to provide the deceiver with an "unfair" advantage. The significance of this factor is best understood by considering that a denier's inadvertent release of indicators of the truth need not be detrimental to his cause even if picked up by his opponent's intelligence system. Rather, the indicators may fall into a gray zone and compete with other signals for attention.[3] What in hindsight is seen as a critical piece of information may be treated at the time as one of too many ambiguous "dots" that remained unappreciated and unconnected, not because the intelligence analysts are dim-witted but because of inherent limits in the capacities of humans and organizations to give valid meaning to confusing and imprecise data under the pressure of time.[4]

While a denier can only benefit from any limits on his opponent's intelligence service, the consequences for the deceiver can be mixed. He too benefits when leaks of his deception go unnoticed or unappreciated, but he does not want his false signals to suffer the same fate. Hence the astute deceiver transmits his signals "loudly" and frequently enough to ensure that a target trolling for data cannot help but pick them up.

In this regard the deceiver has an "unfair" advantage: he knows the truth while the target must explore its alternatives against a backdrop of lies and artifice. Studies of strategic deceptions analyzing a large number of instances are rare, suffer from replicability shortcomings, and are limited to military cases. Barton Whaley assembled what is probably the most widely used database. An initial version covered sixty-eight cases of strategic encounters (from 1914 to 1968) and a later version, ninety-three cases (1914 to 1973). Separate analyses of the different sets indicate remarkable success—slightly above .9 for both analyses—when deception is attempted. Not surprisingly, the latter study concludes that "ignoring the potential usefulness of . . . deception . . . would be imprudent in a strategic encounter."[5] Indeed, a target who suspects deception but cannot prove it is worse off, because his suspicions will lead him to distrust his own intelligence, including accurate information.

A third factor in the success of denial and deception is that deniers and deceivers need detailed knowledge of how their opponents gather intelligence. They must account for all of their adversary's sensors lest he possess a "looking glass" that makes him privy to their efforts and puts them at risk of being strung along or ambushed. In addition, the more they know about how an opponent gathers and processes intelligence, the more precisely they can tailor their own activities. An opponent's imaging satellites, for example, may provide a few minutes' coverage of an area twice a day. Knowing the periods of coverage, a denier would schedule his activities outside them. A deceiver, however, would schedule his inside. If a deceiver understands, furthermore, that an opponent places high confidence in specific channels, he will attempt to place his false signals in them.

A fourth factor is that a denier or deceiver must understand his adversary's perspectives, i.e., his expectations, biases, beliefs, desires, and fears. It is well known that these features of cognition and emotion influence how individuals and groups perceive, process, and evaluate new information. Psychology and everyday experience affirm that most people tend to see what they expect or want to see, believe what they are predisposed to believe, and dismiss or color information that goes against the grain of their biases and current beliefs. They also readily attend to information of significance to their interests, with perceived threats being given special attention.[6]

Specific knowledge of these features is generally more important to the deceiver than to the denier. A denier's ability to keep something hidden can be independent of what his opponent expects or is predisposed to believe. A denier can benefit, of course, by hiding indicators of the truth where the opponent might not be predisposed to look or to realize their significance, but if he can shield the indicators from his opponent's data-gathering sensors altogether, then, by definition, he has achieved a technical success independent of his opponent's predispositions.

Also, a technically successful denier may still not be politically successful if the opponent, notwithstanding a lack of evidence, continues to attribute to the denier the very intentions, capabilities, or activities that the latter is effectively hiding. In that case, the denier may find it expedient to engage as well in deception, and if he does so, psychology and case analyses suggest that a deceiver who tailors his activities to reinforce a target's preconceptions has a huge advantage, for his target has already gone far down the road that the deceiver intends.[7] Similarly, a deceiver who understands that his activities run counter to the target's predispositions can focus his campaign on the target's sensitivities, especially his fears. The astute deceiver aims to have his false indicators shake up the target and force him to reconsider his biases and beliefs. This can be done, for instance, by confronting the target with a "large" and compelling "fact" that is reinforced over time with additional phony indicators and artifice. If the "fact" causes the target to believe that he now has an opportunity to make a major gain or, even better, if it exploits his most profound anxieties, he will consider it seriously.

A fifth factor important to the denier/deceiver is steadily flowing, current, and reliable information about the adversary's actions, intentions, and reactions. This information can help a denier or deceiver decide what secrets to keep and how he should do so. In addition, feedback on how and why the target is reacting is absolutely critical, because strategic campaigns usually take place over an extended period. The denier/ deceiver must know how he is doing and what adjustments to make. Without reliable feedback he risks not only failure but, even worse, entrapment, should his opponent suspect that denial or deception is afoot.

A sixth factor is having in hand a well-organized cadre of astute practitioners of denial and deception. Astuteness has broader dimensions and complexity when applied to a deceiver than when applied to a denier. One dimension is technical virtuosity. For the denier this may mean little beyond knowing how the opponent gathers intelligence and making sure his collectors are prevented from picking up indicators of the truth. This aim involves time-honored activities such as restricting access to programs and documents, communicating only on secure circuits, and keeping objects out of sight. For the strategic deceiver, technical virtuosity can be far more complex. For example, it may seem paradoxical, but when trying to get a target to do what he is not inclined to do, it can be useful to make him vigilant, even though that very vigilance could be instrumental in his rejecting the deceiver's seductions. An individual who is either relaxed or under great stress is likely to follow his predispositions, but when in the in-between state of moderate tension or vigilance, he is likely to be more open-minded as he searches for information with which to make a rational decision.

Particularly for a deceiver, astuteness also implies flair, pluck, artistry, a keen interest in "playing the game," an ability to place oneself in the opponent's shoes, and a supple and narrative frame of mind. Theodore Sarbin, a psychiatrist, expanded on the last two dimensions and labeled them "acumen."[8] He began by analyzing the characteristics of strategic deceptions and saw them as complex, dynamic, and high-stakes endeavors grounded in the circumstances of the day. Best fitted to operating in such circumstances, he argued, are "plotters"—people possessing narrative as opposed to scientific skills. They have active imaginations and are particularly well suited to constructing and amending scripts in real time. Their minds focus not so much on patterns and generalizations as on the uniqueness of events and their contextual complexities. They are comfortable "moving with the experiential flow, and responding flexibly to change and novelty as the target . . . enacts his roles."[9]

In sum, the same basic factors condition the success of denial and deception, but deception is the more complicated to undertake and requires more effort. It is also the more attractive because of the "unfair" advantage it can accord the deceiver.

The roles of intelligence services. Embedded throughout the discussion of conditioning factors is the importance of good information. The denier/deceiver should obtain it from an intelligence community possessing covert and highly reliable windows into the opponent's policy and intelligence domains. Without this level of covert support, he is open to failure and, where deception is concerned, he would be well advised to stand down so as to avoid ambush.

When an intelligence service is providing information about opponents, it is doing what it does every day outside the context of denial and deception. There are, however, three specialized roles open to an intelligence service to help policymakers undertake denial and deception. One is that, in the normal course of tracking what opponents are doing, intelligence analysts might engage in "action analysis," i.e., looking for opponents who seem ripe for deception and bringing them to the attention of policymakers. Other, more active roles are those of tradecraft advisor and executive agent. When employing denial and deception, policymakers can do so on their own, rely on their own in-house denial-and-deception group, if it exists, or fall back on the intelligence community, with its depth of knowledge about an opponent, its stress on keeping secrets, its "internal" employment of denial and deception to protect intelligence sources and methods, and its experience in covert operations. Because of these qualities, intelligence organizations may be best suited to nurturing a government's dedicated denial-and-deception cadre, one that stays in place as policymakers come and go.[10]

American Employment of Strategic Denial and Deception

Motivation and proclivity. America is no different from any other state: it too is motivated to protect secrets whose exposure could reduce its leverage, increase its costs, subject it to public embarrassment, or jeopardize its achievement of a strategic objective. Notwithstanding that the United States is one of the world's foremost democracies, its legislators and citizens generally give the executive branch considerable leeway in foreign policy,[11] and they are particularly reluctant to rein in leaders when the country is in the midst of war or confronted with a worrisome peacetime threat. Some leaders are well aware of this disinclination and have operated accordingly. The American public, for instance, was just as surprised as the rest of the world by Nixon's opening to China, a secret that was heavily guarded (even from William Rogers, the secretary of state) over the months that Henry Kissinger laid the groundwork with Chinese officials. Whatever Americans thought of the policy, there was no outcry about how Kissinger brought it about. Similarly, some U.S. military leaders during the cold war were aware that American military pronouncements, deployments, and exercises could shape Soviet thinking and deployments in ways that could strategically benefit the United States in a hot war. Evidence suggests that elements of the Soviet military took the bait, and should the full story be told, Americans almost certainly would applaud what was done.

Nevertheless, there are limits to what the public and Congress will accept. When it was learned in February 2002 that the Pentagon was establishing the Office of Strategic Influence (OSI), the public reaction forced Secretary of Defense Rumsfeld to announce its closure seven days later. The OSI's mission was to build up foreign support for U.S. efforts against terrorism and Saddam Hussein, and its methods included the planting of false news in foreign media. Among the objections were that OSI was incompatible with the United States as a democracy; that it would undermine the credibility of the U.S. government and the Pentagon in particular; that allies would strongly object to their media, people, and governments being deception targets; and that information planted abroad would find its way into U.S. media, misleading the American public and violating laws against U.S. government propaganda being disseminated domestically.[12]

That this example deals with deception is not accidental. U.S. efforts to deny adversaries access to secrets rarely generate internal controversy except when they fail. As illustrated by the Robert Hanssen and Aldrich Ames cases, the American people and their representatives want their vital secrets protected and become angry only when foreign powers succeed in stealing them. In contrast, strategic deception generates more disquiet and, according to one informed observer, it is rarely practiced in peacetime. The State Department, this observer writes, sees deception as incompatible with its mission, and the Central Intelligence Agency (CIA) avoids it so as not to violate laws intended to keep it out of the domestic arena. No less important is that "orchestrating public actions to add verisimilitude . . . in Congress or the Fourth Estate is," as he puts it, "unthinkable with the former and impossible with the latter."[13]

In sum, it would seem that while America's democratic traditions, open society, and bureaucratic sensitivities may not always predispose its leaders to engage in strategic denial and deception, they nevertheless have considerable leeway to do so in foreign affairs. There is no inherent objection in American society to employing strategic denial and deception, but there are restrictions when it comes to deception. These would seem to include the following rules: do not jeopardize the nation's moral integrity and democratic ideals; do not break the law; do not lie or otherwise violate the trust of the people and their representatives in Congress; keep your messages out of the domestic press and stay out of domestic affairs generally; and do not tarnish America's international image or unduly anger its friends.

Factors conditioning success: some implications for U.S. intelligence. In the first part of this chapter, I identified six factors as affecting success. One was the nature of competition. Though it may be decades before the United States again faces an interstate competitor comparable to the Soviet Union, it must now contend with regional powers such as Russia, China, and India; worrisome WMD powers or aspirants such as Iran, North Korea, and Pakistan; and nettlesome states such as Cuba and Syria. While their intelligence capabilities may not match those of the former USSR, they still pose a challenge to U.S. denial, though probably not an overwhelming one. Granted, some features of any denial campaign would have to be specialized to deal with each of these and other countries, but most of what is done to deny the best of them probably would suffice for the rest. Not so, however, for deception, since campaigns would have to be tailored to the perspectives, actions, and intelligence capabilities of each target. A one-size-fits-all approach will not suffice.

The United States now also competes strategically with terrorist groups that cannot be deterred, and while no tool must be ignored that could counter them, the relevance of strategic denial and deception is not at all clear. Groups like al-Qaeda often seem guided by their own peculiar ideologies and by "abstract and apocalyptic notions of a global war between good and evil." [14] Single-minded in their determination, they patiently march to their own beat. Unlike the Soviet Union during the cold war, they probably are relatively indifferent to most U.S. official pronouncements, military exercise plans, and the like. Their "intelligence" activities are probably limited in scope and heavily oriented to gathering the tactical and publicly available information necessary to stage attacks. The United States undoubtedly should deny terrorists information about its intelligence capabilities and its antiterror plans, but terrorists generally protect themselves not so much by discovering what the U.S. is actually about as by remaining flexible, keeping below the "radar," and avoiding obvious activities (such as the imprudent use of cell phones) that can give them away, even when this cautious approach slows the pace of their activities. They understand that the United States is working to insinuate itself into terror groups and to entrap the members, but they seem to address this threat mainly in "local" ways, such as working within insular "cliques" made up of relatives and trusted friends. Groups like al-Qaeda have amorphous infrastructures and lack a centralized intelligence apparatus such as states possess; they are generally not trolling for and systematically analyzing a deceiver's signals to begin with.

The second factor identified above as conditioning success is that intelligence seems an inherently difficult task when confronting skillful deniers and deceivers. The significance for U.S. denial is underscored by the limited intelligence capabilities possessed by many U.S. adversaries. Some, for example, may not have satellites or sophisticated signals-intercept capabilities to uncover U.S. secrets. Their having fewer intelligence channels may make it more difficult for the United States to transmit deceptive signals, but if it does so "loudly" and frequently enough, they should get through to those with the capability and willingness to capture and analyze them.

The next three factors all revolve around the importance of reliable and continuing information about a target if deception and denial against it are to succeed. This requirement goes directly to the quality of American intelligence. The United States has the best-financed and most technologically sophisticated of intelligence services, but we are nevertheless finding it more rather than less difficult to gather intelligence against priority targets and to understand what makes them "tick." Adversaries are now more sensitive to what it takes to thwart U.S. collection. A turning point in heightening their awareness came in the mid-1970s, when Britain's "thirty-year rule" allowed the intelligence story of World War II to be told.[15] Since then books, science or technology journals, intelligence journals (hardly any of which existed three decades ago), news magazines, and Internet sites have become awash in information about intelligence gathering. Their content (even when inaccurate) is a constant reminder that "Big Brother" is out there. Those who wish to keep secrets from the United States now avoid cell phones or discard them after limited use. They also use signals encryption or hard-to-intercept digital or fiber-optic transmission systems. Even agent-based operations are becoming more hazardous; countermeasures and detection devices are making it harder to maintain a false identification. An article looking ahead to 2015 predicted that "this trend toward denying and deceiving U.S. intelligence will be on a global scale."[16]

The intelligence community, of course, is not standing still. It has identified promising technologies and their potential application, and it is moving forward.[17] The issue is whether it is moving at a rate that exceeds what adversaries are doing to frustrate the upgrades. Again, terrorists may be particularly difficult to contend with in any case owing to their ability to remain under the radar no matter how much the radar is improved.

Technical improvements, furthermore, are only part of the solution when it comes to comprehending a target's perspectives, intentions, and potential reactions. Saddam Hussein, Kim Jong Il, and Osama bin Laden illustrate the depth of problems here. Notwithstanding the priority assigned Saddam, American intelligence evidently never penetrated his inner sanctum and seemingly had no way to check the inaccuracies of the reports channeled through Ahmed Chalabi. Kim's nuclear weapons programs and his seeming willingness to sell arms to any buyer with cash make him more dangerous than Saddam ever was, but he seems well insulated against the prying eyes of American intelligence. As for bin Laden, "a senior intelligence official" has said that the CIA does have Pakistani, Afghan, Uzbek, and other agents inside his network "but . . . not . . . where key information about any future attack would be discussed."[18] To succeed at denial against these and similar targets may not necessarily require a looking glass into their decision domain, but strategic deceptions against them could not succeed without one.

The sixth factor identified in the first part of this chapter is the availability of a cadre of professionals adept at denial and deception. U.S. intelligence personnel are awash in secrets, and protecting them through denial is second nature to them. In addition, the intelligence community is well staffed with highly experienced personnel dedicated to maintaining the confidentiality of sources and to countering foreign intelligence services. Counterespionage specialists aim to prevent penetrations by outsiders and the turning of insiders such as Ames and Hanssen.

Technical specialists bear the brunt of maintaining the security of collection and communication systems in an environment where, as noted earlier, it has become more difficult to do so. Some specialists also assist in or are directly responsible for the security of policymaker communications. It is impossible to present here an assessment of the overall astuteness of the intelligence community in denial, since its successes by definition go unheralded. One can write about the failures (such as not stopping Hanssen earlier), but only insiders can make a valid assessment of successes. The good news is that denial is part of the intelligence community's culture, and it constitutes a tradecraft resident in various, albeit scattered, portions of the community.

In contrast, deception is probably not second nature to intelligence personnel, except to those who employ it tactically in covert operations, and it does not seem to be a tradecraft nurtured in any part of the executive branch. Walter Jajko, a well-informed former U.S. official, calls for the institutionalization of a strategic deception capability and the recruitment of career personnel in this craft.[19] The standards for recruitment cannot be those of the ideal intelligence analyst if Sarbin is right about the characteristics of the astute deceiver. As noted earlier, he contrasted scientific versus narrative frames of mind. The scientific mind is detached, deliberate, pattern-seeking, bound by evidence, and methodologically careful. It is the appropriate template for recruiting and training analysts.[20] In contrast, Sarbin's acute plotters are intuitive, imaginative, attentive to the unique context-specific elements of a situation, quickly responsive, and undetached. Unlike intelligence analysts, they do not aim to inform U.S. decision makers but rather to ensure that the target's decision makers are misinformed.

If deception plotters are given an institutional home within the intelligence community, they would probably work alongside personnel experienced in conducting covert operations within the bounds of legal regulation and congressional oversight. This is important considering the democratic nature of the American polity, and it is a major reason why the intelligence community seems a particularly appropriate place for housing such a group, if one is formed.

Denial, Deception, and the Transformation of the Intelligence Community

Like all other states, the United States engages in strategic denial as a matter of course in order to protect its official secrets. This practice generates internal controversy only when the American public and legislators become aware of a failure such as the Hanssen and Ames cases. In contrast, U.S. employment of strategic deception seems more the exception than the rule. One reason is that it is subject to many rules. The OSI case illustrates that being seen to violate these rules can raise considerable controversy. Depending on point of view, such is the price or the glory of living in a democracy that guards against excesses and wants to be assured that the ends justify the means.

The information requirements for denial and particularly for deception underscore the importance of what is already an objective of all transformation plans: upgrading the intelligence community's ability to provide information about adversary capabilities, intentions, predispositions, and actions. Denial and deception aside, this is what policymakers expect of the community every day, and upgrading it brings the intelligence community full circle in that it involves "self-denial," i.e., instituting measures to protect its own sources and methods.

Though strategic deception is not user-friendly, intelligence community transformation should nevertheless capitalize on the "unfair" advantage that strategic deception can provide the United States when confronting state-based adversaries. Transformation should include encouraging intelligence analysts to engage in "action analysis." It should also include recruiting a cadre of "plotters" and providing them with an institutional home within which they can sharpen their skills. Placing the cadre within the intelligence community (as opposed to the policy side of the government) will help prevent any violation of the rules that circumscribe deception. This is because the community is well used to legal regulation and congressional oversight.

Finally, no concern for intelligence community transformation can ignore its impact on U.S. counterterrorist efforts. It would be satisfying to end this analysis by arguing that engaging in strategic denial and deception against terror groups such as al-Qaeda and its affiliates will consistently pay big dividends. It is not at all clear, however, that this will be the case. The mindset of terrorists, what they attend to, how they operate, how they are (not) structured, the difficulties of penetrating their decision circles, their ability to operate under the radar — all put into doubt the sustained value of engaging in strategic denial and deception against them.

Notes

1. This section draws heavily on a two-year study I directed. See Donald C. F. Daniel and Katherine L. Herbig, "Propositions on Military Deception," in *Strategic Military Deception*, ed. Donald C. F. Daniel and Katherine L. Herbig (New York: Pergamon Press, 1982), 3–30.

2. Barton Whaley, "Conditions Making for Success and Failure of Denial and Deception: Authoritarian and Transition Regimes," in *Strategic Denial and Deception*, ed. Roy Godson and James Wirtz (New Brunswick, N.J.: Transaction Books, 2002), 41–94; M. R. D. Foot, "Conditions Making for Success and Failure of Denial and Deception: Democratic Regimes," ibid., 95–114; and J. Bowyer Bell, "Conditions Making for Success and Failure of Denial and Deception: Non-state and Illicit Actors," ibid., 129–62.

3. Jack Davis, "Strategic Warning: If Surprise Is Inevitable, What Role for Analysis?" *Sherman Kent Center for Intelligence Analysis Occasional Papers* 2, no. 1 (2003): 8, 11, available at www.cia.gov/cia/publications/Kent_Papers/pdf/OPV2No1.pdf.

4. Rob Johnston, "Integrating Methodologists into Teams of Substantive Experts," *Studies in Intelligence* 47, no. 1 (2003), available at www.cia.gov/csi/studies/vol47no1/article06.html.

5. On the study of sixty-eight cases, see Richards J. Heuer Jr., "Cognitive Factors in Deception and Counterdeception," in Daniel and Herbig, *Strategic Military Deception,* 60. The study of ninety-three cases is in Ronald G. Sherwin and Barton Whaley, "Understanding Strategic Deception: An Analysis of 93 Cases," ibid., 177–94 (quotation at 192).

6. Heuer, "Cognitive Factors in Deception," 31–69.

7. Intelligence community subject-matter experts are particularly prone to searching out supporting evidence and filling gaps with data from previous experiences. Johnston refers to this as "the paradox of expertise." Johnston, "Integrating Methodologists into Teams."

8. Theodore Sarbin, "Prolegomenon to a Theory of Counter-Deception," in Daniel and Herbig, *Strategic Military Deception,* 151–76.

9. Ibid., 162; see also Walter Jajko, "Commentary," in Godson and Wirtz, *Strategic Denial and Deception,* 115–22.

10. Some observers are leery of giving intelligence agencies too much responsibility for deception at the expense of policymakers. This is a management issue. See, e.g., Foot, "Conditions Making for Success and Failure."

11. See Louis Klarevas, "The 'Essential Domino' of Military Operations: American Public Opinion and the Use of Force," *International Studies Perspectives* 3, no. 2 (2002): 413–37.

12. See James Dao and Eric Schmitt, "A Nation Challenged: Hearts and Minds; Pentagon Readies Efforts to Sway Sentiment Abroad," *New York Times,* February 19, 2002, A1; and Eric Schmitt, "Pentagon and Bogus News," ibid., December 5, 2003, A6.

13. Jajko, "Commentary," 119.

14. For the information contained in this paragraph, see Marc Sageman, *Understanding Terror Networks* (Philadelphia: University of Pennsylvania Press, 2004), 151; and Lawrence Wright, "The Terror Web," *New Yorker,* August 2, 2004, 40–53.

15. The general public, for example, finally learned about the role of the decoding operation at Bletchley Park in winning the war.

16. Aris A. Pappas and James Simon Jr., "The Intelligence Community: 2001–2015," *Studies in Intelligence* 46, no. 1 (2002), available at www.cia.gov/csi/studies/vol46no1/article05.html.

17. Ibid., 5–7, and A. Denis Clift, "Intelligence in the Internet Era," *Studies in Intelligence* 47, no. 3 (2003), available at www.cia.gov/csi/studies/vol47no3/article06.html.

18. Walter Pincus, "Bin Laden's Inner Circle Eludes CIA," *Washington Post,* July 24, 2004, A10.

19. Jajko, "Commentary," 115–22.

20. See Carmen Medina, "What to Do When Traditional Models Fail," *Studies in Intelligence* 46, no. 3 (2002), available at www.cia.gov/csi/studies/vol46no3/article03.html; and Steven R. Ward, "Evolution Beats Revolution in Analysis," *Studies in Intelligence* 46, no. 3 (2003), available at www.cia.gov/csi/studies/vol46no3/article04.html.

PART THREE Management Challenges

NINE

Managing Domestic, Military, and Foreign Policy Requirements
Correcting Frankenstein's Blunder

James Monnier Simon Jr.

THE MODERN U.S. intelligence community resembles Frankenstein's creature: an impressive achievement in its parts, but flawed as a whole. Pieced together over many decades, it is an elaboration of legacies; an amalgamation of ill-fitting pieces put together at differing times by different, and sometimes indifferent, workmen. While Mary Shelley's creation had a defective brain, many believe that today's intelligence community has a defective nervous system that cripples its coordination and balance.

The image of a crippled giant is made worse by the context. The twenty-first century is, in some respects, more dangerous than the cold war. As the first chapters of this volume have made clear, terrorists and others wishing us ill do not have the communications need, the volume of activity, or the mass of secrets that made the Soviet Union such a lucrative target. Terrorists are much smaller, more agile, more mobile, and more time-sensitive targets. The ability to acquire and process information quickly is essential to the success of fast-tempo operations against fast-tempo targets and equally necessary to counter modern terrorists. Such agility can be achieved only if management and requirements systems help, not hinder.

Nowhere is this more evident than in the system customers use to request intelligence. Intelligence must be on-line, all the time, and instantly responsive to the needs of policy officials, law enforcement officers, and commanders. It is and ought to be a servant. A servant requires a master, and in our system this master is the government's national security community, including those charged with operational activities—predominantly the military and the clandestine service, but often diplomats, law enforcement, and aid officials.[1]

Of course, customers have many other things to do, so they in turn need a routine and effective way to tell intelligence what they want, or, in the language of the bureaucracy, a "requirements system." As the interests of the United States have grown, our definition of national security as focused on victory in war has expanded to include nearly every aspect of the human condition, and the need to direct the necessarily limited resources of United States intelligence has become paramount. Unfortunately, left largely to their own devices, intelligence collection agencies have built a complex and opaque system for doing this. All too frequently customers describe the intelligence-requirements process as a black hole that occasionally seems to produce results, if in an unpredictable and sometimes surprising fashion. The master's need for a thinking servant has produced a difficult and unruly one.

This chapter offers suggestions for taming the monster. It begins with a review of the U.S. requirements system and the causes of its inefficiencies, then discusses what ought to be changed. It concludes with a specific program of governance that the new director of national intelligence (DNI) might usefully implement.

The U.S. Collectors and Their Requirements System

Most nations, and specifically the United States, organize their intelligence structures around the means of collection. History has a lot to do with why this is so, but so does the desire to protect hard-won secrets and to concentrate adequate expertise in order to succeed in a fundamentally complex business. The consequence is that our system is dominated by the agencies that perform the actual task of collecting the data, processing it for the use of others, and disseminating their findings to customers. Each has its own terminology, unique routines, and differing expectations of what a customer can ask for.

Arguably the most successful collection-management system was once employed by the Foreign Broadcast Information Service (FBIS). Timely high-quality support was provided without any formal requirements system. Expert field collectors essentially applied consistent common sense. For its part, the FBIS's substantively expert head-quarters staff devoted considerable time and effort to maintaining expertise, overseeing field operations, and remaining in close contact with its customers. The combination of these factors justified unusually high confidence in the FBIS's operations. Significantly and uniquely, the FBIS had an extraordinary customer network consisting almost exclusively of experts within and outside government. Less knowledgeable customers were able to rely on this expertise for quality control and to presume that what ought to be done was being done. Unfortunately, as the need for new resources to keep abreast of technology became more acute, and as the volume of information on the Internet increased exponentially, the FBIS lacked a way to measure its value-added contributions beyond the anecdotal and so lost much-needed resources and time.

The imagery community remains the most open and therefore the most micro-managed of collectors. Because of the stochastic character of imagery collection and its computerized collection-management system, every requirement and detail of every imaging operation can all be tracked by customers anywhere in the world. All of this openness has a high cost. Its complexity requires that the National Geospatial-Intelligence Agency (NGA) and every customer organization devote years of training and large numbers of imagery-collection managers in order to use its systems effectively. This cost is so high that it is beyond the means of all but the largest agencies. When images were a scarce resource, this may have made sense. Now that the time imagery analysts have is scarcer than the images themselves, it is futile for customers to task collection without the certainty that someone will look at it. (This is not to suggest that imagery should not be collected and stored for future use—it should—only that this sort of collection is best handled by NGA, not by primary customers.) The fascination with the minutiae of imagery tasking has also tended to shift customers' focus to the technological marvel of imagery collection from space and away from the frustrating complexities of exploitation and reporting. To some degree, we task imagery so intensively simply because we can.

The National Security Agency (NSA)'s signals-intelligence (SIGINT) system provides another successful model of high-volume collection and reporting. It is prized for its marriage of substantive expertise with operations that ensure that U.S. SIGINT has high quality as well as high volume. The NSA is the opposite of the NGA in that the controlled serendipity of its collection-management processes is hidden not only from those beyond the "green door" but from many intelligence community insiders as well. For both the NSA and its customers, a nearly exclusive focus on collection has helped create a serious disconnect between resources devoted to the collection effort and those available for processing and reporting. This gap is compounded by the inherent difficulty of linking requirements to resources, making it nearly impossible for anyone, even within the NSA, to measure the value of specific programs and platforms. In a time of profound change in the target set, rapid technological change, and an increasingly obsolescent SIGINT architecture, the NSA needs both increased funding and serious help from U.S. industry to remain at the top of its game.

The strengths of the clandestine human intelligence system are the operational flexibility of its case officers and its ability to provide substantive support for exploiting lucrative sources. In theory, as practiced by the Central Intelligence Agency and the Defense Intelligence Agency (DIA), the requirements process is one in which collectors take on or decline tasking; thus customers get a degree of predictability, whether or not an issue will be worked. Well-founded security concerns and the rational fear that customers would intrude into operational decision making has resulted in the unintended consequence that the formal requirements mechanism has become so cumbersome that customers resort to informal means whenever possible. Intelligent tasking of specific assets is even less satisfactory because of security concerns and, in the too-frequent absence of collector initiative, usually puts the onus on the customer to develop a good working relationship with the collector. This requires considerable, and sometimes excessive, effort on the part of customers to produce a response, leaves too much to individual initiative, and too often leaves the case officer without the support needed to gain the most from collection opportunities.

Overt human intelligence is predominantly collected by the Department of State. In terms of bang for the buck, this is the best deal in town. The State Department has a large body of competent professional officers whose insight into foreign events is much prized by customers. But the State Department is more resistant to direct tasking than to any other collection activity, and, although it rightly fears repercussions from the occasional leak, it also seems to consider collection on behalf of anyone outside the department a breach of etiquette. More serious is that whenever the State Department is short of resources, an apparently chronic condition, the first thing cut back is reporting activities.

The measurement-and-signatures-intelligence (MASINT) system is unique in that it owns no collection systems and no production components. Its major role is to push technology and ensure that processing is provided and data disseminated to customers. In this sense it resembles a customer association more than a collector's stovepipe. Its weaknesses are mostly a consequence of the nascent state of the MASINT discipline, but also a function of the intelligence community's general incoherence in using collection requirements to address all-source questions.

So What Is Wrong?

Like Frankenstein's monster, the U.S. requirements system works, but it is a crude simulacrum of the system we need. Defenders argue that we are well served by the existing structure and highlight its undeniable ability to bring resources and expertise to bear. They point with pride to its contributions to victory in the cold war. History is on their side, but even the strongest supporters question whether the requirements system remains adequate to meet the changed nature of new threats to the United States and its allies.

Recently the intelligence community completed yet another effort to identify key issues and set priorities. Such efforts are familiar. They begin modestly enough with firm intentions to exercise self-discipline, but in a few short years the expansion of the number of issues creates an undifferentiated mass of little worth.

In fact, the "requirements" system has few friends. It is untidy, encumbered by process, and generally unaccountable. Some insist that we would be better off without it altogether. Supporters of a "requirements-less" intelligence system tend to cluster around two poles. Some argue that collectors are hamstrung by the formality of the requirements system. This formality has an inherent rigidity that inhibits initiative and forces collectors, who tend to be closer to the target than customers are, to put the less-informed customer's idea of what is needed above the informed judgment of the proximate collection agent. Others argue that how we collect has become more important than what we collect. A "requirements-less" system is a form of naïve inductivism—a belief that if we can gather enough facts, explanatory and predictive theories will emerge spontaneously.

A second cluster of opponents argue that the collection-requirements process is a charade maintained by the collection agencies to steer customers toward the doable, the "low-hanging fruit," and away from difficult but necessary work. Their solution is to make intelligence directly responsive to those in positions of authority. Setting aside the question of whether those in authority are qualified to perform this service to the nation, being responsive to only the highest levels of government ignores Orwell's maxim that "some pigs are more equal than other pigs." The argument about which pig counts the most on a given day already consumes much time and effort. After the president, there is an extensive list of aspirants to the title of second pig. Stripped of its emotional context, what is being urged is the displacement of expertise by ignorant authority.

No complex organization can depend on consistently wise direction from customers, collectors, or analysts. All organizations that succeed over time find ways to account for the variance in the quality of their personnel. This is especially true of a constitutional republic that uses law and the routine of bureaucracy to protect the nation against the occasional incompetence of those in charge. Since the future is unknowable and the limitations of human imagination well understood, the goal is not to create a perfect system but one that, despite occasional failure, can safeguard the nation. Absent a coherent requirements system responsibly managed, experience reveals a consistent failure to focus collection, systematically identify gaps, and take action to ameliorate the effect of missing pieces of the puzzle.

The Consequences of a Collector-Centered System

Because collectors and many of their components accept requirements only at the time and in the manner of their choosing, customers must submit requirements in a serial fashion, using many separate and unique formats and means of communications. The inherent complexity of this process means that each customer needs specialists to deal individually with each collector. These specialists, in turn, feed a larger superstructure that attempts to bundle and adjudicate requirements in a collector-specific fashion, and, above it, another superstructure that tries to integrate requirements strategically across the collector spectrum. These superstructures give the impression that the customers are in charge and that their requirements matter, but in reality the primary collectors, given the variables of their unique situations, collect what they can, and then find a requirement in which to cloak the hard-won prize.[2]

This may be a rational process for collectors, but it has unintended consequences for customers. Unfortunately for the best-laid plans, customers think and act in space and time, not by intelligence source. Geographic and functional matters, not the bureaucratic structure of the intelligence community, are the issues of national policy.

Because the intelligence community is organized into discipline-specific hierarchies, it is nearly impossible for customers to impose coherence and internal rigor on the requirements process. With few exceptions, customers exert little effort to enable collection and, discouraged by the tasking process, have adopted the philosophy of "more, better, faster." The inevitable consequence is that the current process necessarily disaggregates intelligence requirements by collection discipline—an efficient solution, perhaps, but not an effective one, especially against complex targets such as terrorist networks, which require the integrated application of all possible resources.

When all is said and done, the collection system conforms to collectors' business processes rather than those of its customers, leading to untoward costs and inefficiencies. Even large policy departments can no longer afford the cost associated with dealing with each collection agency on its own terms. A system that requires everyone to submit detailed collection requirements necessitates a series of elaborate and expensive collection-management bureaucracies to do the paperwork—much of it meaningless. Not only do customers have to create such bureaucracies, but each collector has one or more as well. Some years ago the estimated number of collection managers in the U.S. government was in the thousands. That number has grown and continues to grow. This entire marching army is recruited, and sometimes conscripted, at the expense of primary needs.

To make matters worse, the very size of these armies affects requirements. As Napoleon observed, God is on the side of the big battalions. This is especially evident on the demand, or requirements, side of intelligence, because customers deal individually with collectors and lack the means to pursue unified strategies. Although users of intelligence range from diplomats to law enforcement officers, the big battalions in this case belong to the Department of Defense (DoD) and especially to the combatant commanders. Historically, this has seriously disadvantaged smaller users, like the Departments of State, Treasury, and Energy, that lack the sheer number and diversity of requirements as well as formulaic intensity of the DoD customer. This situation, which tends to focus resources on the here and now to the disadvantage of strategic interests, will only grow more confused with the maturation of the Department of Homeland Security and the inevitable assertion of its national security interests.

Today's system has become a morass of rules and procedures the complexity of which elevates wasteful process to the status of an objective. The process has become an end in itself—an arena of bureaucratic gamesmanship that absorbs valuable resources. Beyond adding frustration to government service, its most tangible effect has been the creation of powerful incentives to use informal systems. Customers increasingly seek to circumvent the formal system by requesting the intervention of senior officials. These officials, importuned under the most pressing of circumstances to make decisions outlined imperfectly at best, can only take "their best shot." It should be no surprise that senior officials have become convinced that it is only by their efforts that the system responds. In fact, we lurch from near disaster to near disaster, often squandering collection opportunities and occasionally doing irreparable harm to sources and methods.

No successful complex system can be managed by the consistent use of exceptional means. Certainly one of the symptoms of a dysfunctional system is the need to use unusual means to achieve routine ends. Ultimately this approach wastes the time and energy of senior officials, who are required to devote effort to assuring an obvious outcome. At the individual customer level, the use of informal methods can be desirable, efficient, and effective, if there is a productive analyst-to-collector network. If there is not, the inherent inefficiency of the informal system overwhelms customers, who must devote time and energy to finding idiosyncratic points of influence. The problem is that serial idiosyncratic behavior lacks coherence, strategic purpose, and accountability.

Finally, this inherent discord is multiplied by the added layer of collector-controlled compartmentalization, which makes it nearly impossible for a customer organization to comprehend the potential range and interrelationships of sources. The preoccupation of the security bureaucracies with our theoretically infinite vulnerability has led to a series of antediluvian security regimes across the community that are robbing us of the promise of modern information and communications technology. Simply put, there appears to be a common premise that if we do not know what we are doing, no one else can find out either. We pay an enormous price in efficiency and occasional failure because each collector establishes its own communications and security regimes that serve only parochial interests.

Cleaning up this mess will take more than good intentions; it requires deliberate policy decisions. Some argue that the creation of the office of the DNI at last gives someone the requisite authority to do something useful; others, including this writer, are far less optimistic. Regardless of who is right, the issues facing the DNI (and the rest of us) are urgent. The United States cannot continue to invest increasing resources in collection management or to live with the current system. Each new collection program brings with it new tasking systems with their attendant manpower, training, and operations and maintenance costs. Whenever money is tight (and it always is for this type of activity), these are the first funds to be sacrificed. The consequence is a progressive dumbing down of our ability to task intelligently as we become more reliant on checklists and appeals *ex cathedra*.

The DNI's objectives should be clear. The U.S. government can no longer afford to have customers spend so much of their intellectual capital ensuring that forms are filled out correctly and trying to exploit the collector's resource-allocation calculus. Increasingly our organizations are falling victim to Tenner's "law of diminishing specialization," as more and more highly paid people are spending significant time performing clerical functions.[3] The U.S. government can no longer afford to let each collection discipline have its own requirements system but must have a single system to contain costs as well as to ensure that the smaller civil customers are not disenfranchised by the expense and complexity of the current collector-centered process.

What Ought to Be

A requirements system, as a first principle, must engender confidence. Customers not only want intelligence, they want to be assured that the system is at least trying to respond and that if something useful is found they will get it in a timely fashion. It is in our common interest to create a system whose routine operation naturally generates this confidence — an open system. The challenge is to create an open system that is both secure and does not encourage our national predilection for micromanagement.

We must start by recognizing that the considerable differences among the business lines of the various collectors make it unwise and probably impossible to construct a rigid system that would subject all collectors to the same process. There is a natural tendency for outside observers to overgeneralize and see simple solutions. But hard experience tells us that we must also recognize that things are the way they are not because everyone involved is an idiot but because many, if not most, of our current practices have some merit.

What, then, are some of the imperatives for a transformed requirements process? First, the management system must have a dual character. Most of the time the U.S. government is best served by a loose collection-requirements system that relies on an intelligent, aggressive collector as the central actor. In this scheme, customers provide priorities and guidance on what subjects are of interest, evaluate collector effectiveness, and provide expert support to collectors as required. In some circumstances, however — usually operational support and crisis response — the reformed collection-management system must allow the assumption of greater control by senior officials and operators.

Having the flexibility to adapt to both routine and crisis is crucial to an effective collection-management system. Most collection is routine and serves the analytic community. It contributes to the patient, long-term aggregation of data that allow us to answer complex questions and prepare for the unforeseen. The implicit premise of the routine system, that experts in the analytic and collection communities know best, must be modified when intelligence collection is in direct support of operations, whether clandestine, military, or diplomatic. In these circumstances, collection as well as analytic priorities have to be driven by the direct customer or decision maker, assisted by intelligence experts. The customer's questions tend to be simple and have factual or binary answers and a short time-horizon, but they are time-critical. In these instances, experts can help, but collection, processing, exploitation, and analysis must respond to the customer's operational tempo.

Second, the United States needs an on-line, round-the-clock system that conforms to the demands of modern decision making and not the convenience of intelligence bureaucracies. The current system uses a control model designed to limit official corruption that has been in service since the presidency of Chester A. Arthur.[4] It is slow and cumbersome in today's computer-oriented world. In a world where the ability to acquire and process information quickly is essential to the success of high-tempo operations, today's requirements system proceeds at a stately pace indeed.

Policymakers and commanders need direct two-way access to the primary providers of both data and, ultimately, finished analyses. Customers need tools and sufficient visibility to allow visualization of the entire picture across intelligence disciplines. In short, they need to know what is known and what has been estimated. Armed with this knowledge, customers would be able to affect collection and task analysis to meet their specific needs, a significant improvement over the current system, which is defined by generic requirements derived at a distance and executed at the initiative of the collector. Because competition for scarce resources is inevitable, the government needs adjudication authorities at the task-force level, the White House, and all points in between.

This concept, joined with modern technology, would allow the government to alter the fundamental relationship between national customers and collectors: the former would no longer simply send requirements to each collector; the latter would be charged with pulling the customers' requirements from a single system. Each authorized customer would create a coherent, prioritized set of requirements for information—not collection—in common info-space.

Such a model would permit urgent tasking analogous to the military's system for requesting fire support by combat commanders who go directly to whomever can provide help. Time is not wasted by requests moving up and down superfluous chains of command. The power of initiative and direction is derived from the customer, not controlled by those providing the support. This type of system is quick, agile, and accountable. If applied within the intelligence community, it also has the unique attraction of being driven by the customer instead of the collectors' bureaucracies.

There are two important caveats. In the fire-support case, higher-ups monitor all activity and intervene and adjudicate as necessary because there is usually a limit on the resources available. This would be no less true for intelligence, but the need for timely oversight may be even more critical. Another important difference between providing fire support to combat units and intelligence support is that the former responds to a larger plan that anticipates and accounts for calls for support within planned operations of defined scope. Intelligence community players can plan and anticipate, but they cannot predict with precision what will be needed or where it will be needed.

All too often the current process fails to provide the kind of tailored and rapid response required by the new threats that face us. Even if processes, practices, and procedures now in place are well intentioned, they tend to widen the distance between collector, analyst, and customer through the use of management mechanisms that center around the collector's bureaucratic interests rather than the customer's needs. Today's system was not the result of neglect. It was developed in response to the massive amounts of material being sought from the various disciplines in support of the equally massive statistical-sampling effort we used to ensure our plans and to warn us of danger. Its inherent inefficiency was subsumed by its scale.

Third, modern intelligence requires the entire tasking process to move not only with great speed but with an unprecedented degree of integration among collectors, analysts, and customers. Bringing the government's enormous collection and analytic capacities to bear against terrorists and other nonstate threats demands a process for managing those capacities in a hands-on and participatory fashion that is distinct from the intentionally anonymous, formatted architectures that served us so well in the past. We can never again allow the pre–September 11 situation of having significant information in our grasp, but in a system that was designed, essentially, to segregate that information rather than integrate it.

Fourth, the collectors need more freedom of action and more support from those whom they serve. The collection-management system should be driven by experts, but it should not be designed to expend all the collectors' resources. A meaningful percentage of collection resources should be reserved, with policymakers' acquiescence, for the collectors' own use. Such freedom of action will ensure flexibility as well as creativity of response. Collectors should be encouraged to exceed expectations, demonstrate creativity, invest in long-term collection efforts, and work hard problems.

Specifically, policymakers and analysts ought to stop tasking the details of collection. Except for specific circumstances related to crises and operations, these experts should resist their inclination to tell collectors how to do their job. Instead, a reformed system must make explicit the responsibility of the customer to enable collection through responsive guidance. No one has enough experts any more, so the larger collection community must be able to draw upon talent wherever it can be found. In return, collection, especially precisely targeted close-access programs, must become more responsive to customers' direction.

For too long customers have not seen it as their duty to support collectors by providing adequate targeting support. Collectors are given either lengthy, detailed tomes based on the assumption that they are uninformed, or nothing at all. Because customers have other duties, they should not provide detailed guidance except as needed by the collectors to further their operational endeavors. Analysts have successfully supported targeting activities, proving their worth in enabling collection. Physical space limitations and legitimate security concerns, however, make it necessary to improve connectivity between these analysts and primary collectors. This connectivity must exist throughout the national security community to promote timely and effective cooperation and to improve the primary collectors' ability to get direct support from analytic components.

While we want to eliminate redundant collection, effective tradeoff decisions may best be made by analytic customers. Analysts can judge what degree of multiple-source confirmation is required to allow them to advance or disprove a hypothesis. A coherent requirements system allows the analyst to see the breadth of potential coverage and identify unnecessary redundancy.

One key to inspiring the confidence customers will need before they can stop trying to micromanage collectors is rigorous and fair customer evaluation of the substantive contribution of individual programs and platforms coupled with improved management information. Collectors welcome feedback on the value of collection because it helps them make better decisions about allocating resources, but what they need are objective data. Without effective evaluation, we are left with dueling anecdotes and lack the means to inform increasingly difficult programmatic decisions. As we construct a new system, a guiding objective should be that it gathers data nonintrusively to support both evaluation and management information. We would want it to help collectors and analytic components allocate resources, identify requirements for new or expanded collection programs, identify which programs could be closed or cut back, and provide management with information about the relative efficiency and effectiveness of the intelligence cycle and its components.

The Role of the Director of National Intelligence

A common priority and security structure, along with rules of the road, should be promulgated by the DNI. As simple as this may seem, the complexity of the American system means that many must agree — notably the secretaries of state, defense, and homeland security, the attorney general, and the Congress; this is a serious problem, as most of the recent feeble effort at intelligence reform makes evident.

With little more than a bully pulpit at his disposal, the DNI nonetheless must try to create a system that allows each customer to specify his own priority, understanding that the final determination many not please him, as all requirements are placed in context. Case-by-case determinations of relative tactical priority should be made by the collector, the customer having the right of appeal to a structure governed by the DNI. To discourage the proliferation of requirements and to assist smaller agencies that lack the resources of larger ones, all customers would be able to agree to requirements posted by others and yet specify their own priority. Collector subelements would be required to review requirements for their usefulness.

DNI policy should mandate that collector reporting be linked to specific requirements in order to create the basis for a modern dissemination system. Once established, changes in a customer's requirements should prompt an "automatic alert" message to collectors. Collectors should be able to identify customers, know who to ask for help when necessary, see the range of customers' requirements, and identify which other collectors had contracted to provide intelligence. Customers should be able to track what programs and platforms do and do not contribute to satisfying their requirements.

Requirements more specific than the high-level set discussed above, however, should arise only as a direct result of collector initiative, with the exception of those where the proximate customer has urgent operational needs. If more detail is needed, collectors are better suited to focusing and refining their own work than customers are. A system for effective evaluation should provide the customer with the leverage needed to ensure that collectors respond to requirements.

The requirements system ought to provide a common ground where customers for specific types of intelligence are matched with providers. The true collection managers — the primary collectors — are in the best position to know what their collection, processing, and reporting resources can do. If provided with an easy but consequential mechanism by which to survey customers' requirements and find matches for capabilities, collectors would be better positioned to manage both resources and risks.

For customers, an essential characteristic of this common ground is the means of calibrating and influencing collector performance. This requires considerable insight into collector processes now only commonly available from NGA. Oversight ensures that the system responds to the policies set by the DNI on behalf of the national command authority. Common policies and rules must be established and the performance of both customers and collectors must be evaluated. The DNI should sponsor studies and programs to address more intractable problems, especially those posed by the critical need for computer security. Finally, someone in the intelligence community should be formally charged with the task of advancing cross-disciplinary collection strategies, identifying gaps, and proposing ways to close them.

In the transition phase, or when genuine security considerations demand it, each intelligence discipline process could be overseen by a virtual subcommittee composed of a subset of involved agencies. Their role would be restricted to resolving conflicts in collection priorities and initiating appropriate action when the collector certifies that a specific requirement cannot be satisfactorily collected. Specific tasking authority should be delegated from the DNI to the most effective operational level in a discipline-specific manner. It would be presumptuous to detail how this should be done, but a single individual ought to be accountable for the end-to-end collector process (collection, processing, reporting, dissemination) for each major subset of geographic and topical requirements.

One hopes that this would lead to devolution of authority from the massive central processing bureaucracies in each of the collection agencies and, in time, to the ability to recapture these positions and funds for more productive work. It is a common complaint among primary collectors that they could be far more productive and innovative without being micromanaged by headquarters. This argument is usually dismissed as self-serving, but its widespread currency gives it a measure of validity and makes it worth examining.

Real change can be achieved only through perseverance and determination. Congress continues to support the basic need for reform but is unable to understand how to make it work. For their part, the agencies have been all too willing to cut their own funding for reform initiatives because someone else will benefit, and the gains are not reflected in a zero-sum budget designed to protect stovepiped missions and programs. The U.S. intelligence community stands at a crossroads, beset with new problems and saddled with an amortized and practically irreplaceable architecture and physical plant. How it adjusts to new realities will affect the nation's security for decades. We must choose wisely.

Notes

1. In exceptional situations, the customer may be a proximate one, that is, a specific official who needs the information to inform a decision that is to be made. Unfortunately, the specificity of customer need and the self-evident clarity of the information to be collected come together only on rare occasions. Nearly all intelligence is either collected in response to a general need or requires substantial analytic intervention to guard against deception, place into context, or determine the validity of the information acquired. In a real sense, proximate customers are served by intermediate customers who are, in fact, analysts. Analysts may be those serving formally as such in the intelligence agencies or members of staffs and senior officials of the policy departments of the government.

2. The term "primary collector" is used throughout this chapter to distinguish that part of an intelligence organization that provides collection, processing, discipline-specific analysis, exploitation, dissemination, and reporting.

3. See Edward Tenner, *Why Things Bite Back: Technology and the Revenge of Unintended Consequences* (New York: Vintage Books, 1997).

4. President Arthur championed civil service reform and died in 1886.

Intelligence and War

Afghanistan, 2001–2002

HENRY A. CRUMPTON

IN THE WEEK after the September 11, 2001, terrorist attacks on the United States, the president ordered the director of central intelligence (DCI) to launch a covert war against al-Qaeda and its Taliban supporters in Afghanistan. This campaign, wedded to covert and overt U.S. military operations, depended upon all-source intelligence. The Central Intelligence Agency (CIA), therefore, collected and analyzed intelligence for policymakers, diplomats, warfighters, its own covert-action operators, allied forces, and Afghan covert-action partners. Human intelligence (HUMINT) served as the foundation for the plan outlined by the CIA's counterterrorist center (CTC) chief, Cofer Black, to the DCI and president. Moreover, the CIA's operations officers and assets provided not only the HUMINT for the covert-action plan and military campaign, but also the means for its execution. This interdependence of intelligence, covert action, and war folded into a broader policy strategy offers lessons for future counterterrorism conflicts. So do the examples of leadership and partnership, which grew from understanding the passions of men, the fundamentals of conflict as taught by strategists throughout the ages.

By the second week of December 2001, three months after the president's directive, all major Afghan cities had fallen to U.S. and coalition forces and allied tribal militias. Several teams of CIA and U.S. Army Special Forces personnel, scores of clandestine U.S. military raiders, and U.S. airpower had destroyed the Taliban regime and disrupted al-Qaeda, killing or capturing approximately 25 percent of the enemy's leaders. More than twenty al-Qaeda training camps had been secured, providing hundreds of documents, videos, phone and e-mail accounts, and other global operational leads. Exploitation of al-Qaeda weapons of mass destruction (WMD) testing sites had begun. Five to ten thousand enemy troops had been killed, while U.S. casualties remained extremely low. More than five thousand prisoners had been captured, some of intelligence value. Surviving enemy forces were on the run. The collapse of the Taliban denied al-Qaeda a pseudo-nation-state partner and reduced al-Qaeda's sanctuary to ragged pockets along the Pakistani border, pushing other members into Pakistani cities, where many were captured. The Afghan people began reclaiming their country, and the United States began constructing a partnership with an emerging legitimate government.

History

The CIA did not start from scratch in Afghanistan. On the contrary, HUMINT networks with roots in covert action against the USSR and its puppet Afghan government from 1980 to 1992 provided continuity in intelligence collection. Although the networks deteriorated as the U.S. government lost interest in Afghanistan and the CIA lost funding and support in the 1990s, CIA officers maintained sufficient links for regeneration. In 1999 the CIA, with the approval and support of the National Security Council (NSC), renewed its collection efforts in Afghanistan as a sanctuary for al-Qaeda, the group responsible for the August 1998 bombings of U.S. embassies in Kenya and Tanzania. Specifically, the CTC pushed hard to deploy intelligence officers into Afghanistan, knowing there is no substitute for direct HUMINT collection. From February 1999 to March 2001, the CIA sequentially deployed five teams into the Panjshir Valley of Afghanistan to rebuild an intelligence liaison relationship with the Northern Alliance. The Northern Alliance was a loose coalition of various militias, including Tajik, Uzbek, and a few Pashtun tribal groups, generally located in the northern part of the country. The alliance between the Taliban and al-Qaeda pushed anti-Taliban elements and the CIA together. The budding partnership between the Northern Alliance and the CIA included information sharing, funding, training, and joint operations. Joint operations also included the deployment of reconnaissance teams and the recruitment of intelligence sources.

Starting in 1999 the CIA redoubled its recruitment efforts throughout Afghanistan, especially in the Pashtun tribal areas in the south and east. This was part of the CTC's broader strategic plan to penetrate al-Qaeda and its sanctuaries; local sources could report on al-Qaeda and its host environment. The CIA acquired sources that provided useful intelligence and initiated modest covert-action campaigns. These HUMINT assets formed complex webs that stretched across tribal strata and included powerful warlords, Taliban functionaries, al-Qaeda support staff, soldiers, businessmen, and self-proclaimed criminals. This network ranged from fully vetted, reliable, well-trained, courageous foreign nationals to transient, unscrupulous mercenaries. Some of the sources served as singletons who answered directly to CIA officers via covert communications, while others were part of clan-based networks, some not knowing their ultimate employer. Significantly, the assets covered most of Afghanistan and various levels of society. Their reporting supported U.S. diplomatic, military, and covert-action initiatives.[1] Diplomatic efforts focused on pressing Pakistan and other Islamic state partners to influence the Taliban and on constructing counterterrorist coalitions in the region. By September 10, 2001, the CIA had more than one hundred sources and subsources operating throughout the country.

Strategy

This intelligence allowed the crafting of a strategy that relied upon a center of gravity not found in a single geographic point, a specific enemy battalion, or the Taliban command, control, and communications. Rather, the center of gravity rested in the minds of those widespread tribal militia leaders, who were allied with the Taliban and al-Qaeda out of political convenience or necessity. The CIA understood this political dynamic and could therefore define the enemy in the narrowest terms — for example, as al-Qaeda and intransigent Taliban leaders — while viewing all other Taliban or Taliban-allied militia as potential allies. In other words, the enemy was not Afghanistan, not the Afghan people, not the Afghan army, not even the Taliban per se. The enemy was al-Qaeda, foreign invaders who had hijacked the Afghan government from the Afghan people. The CIA strategy depended upon persuading militia forces allied with the Taliban of this view, and convincing potential allies that their future rested with the small CIA and U.S. military teams, although they were heavily outnumbered and sometimes surrounded. In short, the CIA and the U.S. military, with the help of Afghan tribal allies, would recruit tribal armies among erstwhile enemy forces.

Executing this strategy required superior intelligence and superior intelligence officers on the ground, which would in turn be used to support superior U.S. military force. There were three levels of application. First, the United States needed a demonstration of force enhanced by speed, stealth, and precision. On October 7, 2001, the U.S. Air Force and U.S. Navy launched the air campaign. Thanks to the professionalism of the U.S. military and its advanced technology, these bombs hit their targets with unprecedented accuracy. Moreover, munitions arrived with no warning, and target markers shifted at the turn of a laser-designator manned by Special Forces on the ground. CIA officers and Afghan assets, armed with global positioning systems (GPS) and covert communication, specified many other targets, especially those deep behind enemy lines. These assets were especially effective in targeting urban sites, then verified through other HUMINT, signals intelligence (SIGINT), or imagery sources. Enemy concentrations throughout Afghanistan were obliterated, and survivors were confused and afraid. Within days, stationary enemy air defenses were destroyed. The success of this attack also affected the morale of U.S. allies and of Taliban allies not yet under fire. The former were encouraged and the latter began to reconsider the viability of their alliance with the Taliban.

The formula for the application of power depended upon binary elements, CIA officers, and U.S. Special Forces, which together created the glue that held the operation together. The CIA's paramilitary officers, with their deep knowledge of special operations and intelligence, provided the most adhesive element of this mixture. This was especially critical because there was no previous joint planning or training; the blended glue emerged from professionalism rooted in a sense of collective mission and personal relationships built on mutual respect. The result was a war of supreme coordination between Afghan tribal allies and U.S. airpower. The CIA delivered the HUMINT and the Afghan tribal armies. The Special Forces brought tactical skills and linked the ground to the air. Sensor and shooter merged, producing teams that delivered uniquely accurate and awesome force. The weapons and delivery systems included joint direct-attack munitions, Afghan cavalry, long-range snipers, AC-130 gunships, individual saboteurs, Afghan artillery, and thermobaric munitions. Intelligence provided the aim point for this force, concentrating its impact and enhancing its efficacy. Power, as defined by Prussian strategist Carl von Clausewitz and English historian John Keegan, is the ultimate arbiter of war.[2] The United States is the world's undisputed military leader, which is reflected in its kinetic power; in Afghanistan, intelligence afforded speed, stealth, and precision that enhanced the power exponentially. But power alone did not win the war.

The second level of the application of military force, more complex and less appreciated than raw power, was the attack on the enemy's strategy. The ancient Chinese military strategist Sun Tzu stressed this in his classic text, *The Art of War*. Unlike Clausewitz and Keegan, Sun Tzu viewed espionage as essential to war, because victory rests upon knowing the enemy and thereby gaining "strategic advantage" (*shih*).[3] Intelligence informed the CIA of the enemy's plans and intentions and also about the Afghan allies' preferences and capabilities. Al-Qaeda expected either a tepid response, such as cruise missiles scattered around Afghanistan, or a slow concentration of U.S. military forces followed by an invasion. The first option would pose little real threat. The second, while a greater challenge, also offered the enemy greater opportunity, given that a heavy invading army would provide clear targets in an environment well suited to insurgent warfare. Al-Qaeda's assumptions were not unreasonable given the precedents of U.S. disengagement from Somalia and the Soviet retreat from Afghanistan. In this reasoning al-Qaeda made one of the most common mistakes of military reasoning: they were "prepared to fight the last battle." Al-Qaeda incorrectly assumed that the United States would not learn and not adapt, and it was therefore prepared for a battle similar to the one in Mogadishu.

Between September and December 2001 Western pundits held up the Soviet defeat in the 1980s and the British rout in the 1840s as warnings to U.S. military planners. These experts, however, like al-Qaeda, considered only the possibility of a conventional U.S. response. The notion of inserting small teams of clandestine collectors and warriors into various sectors of Afghanistan, subverting the enemy, rallying local militia, supplementing this with bold air and commando strikes, and integrating all of this into an overarching policy goal of establishing a viable Afghan government never entered their calculus. The element of surprise enhances power geometrically.

Speed was essential, not only because it can reinforce surprise but also because of the al-Qaeda threat. Given the terrorist group's global network, demonstrated capabilities, confirmed efforts to acquire WMD, and preference for multiple attacks, the U.S. intelligence community and policymakers feared more attacks in the immediate wake of September 11. The United States had to strike rapidly, to disrupt the al-Qaeda command structure and perhaps prevent the next attack. There was no time to plan and execute a conventional military response. Again we quote Sun Tzu, who wrote, "War is such that the supreme consideration is speed."[4] This was true in Afghanistan and will be the case in future counterterrorist wars.

Learning the right lessons from history, especially local history, is important, in a war dependent more on local political dynamics than conventional Western perceptions. In the summer of 1997 elements of the Northern Alliance controlled Mazar-e-sharif and established a land bridge to Uzbekistan. They cut Highway 1, which runs from Kabul through the Salang tunnel north to Konduz. Northern Alliance forces, under the overall command of the brilliant Ahmed Shah Masood, trapped the Taliban in a pocket around Konduz; but Taliban air resupply and the eventual subversion of Uzbek militia subcommanders in Mazar-e-sharif saved the Taliban from potential disaster.[5] Learning from this lesson and listening closely to HUMINT sources and Afghan allies, the CIA outlined a similar military plan to U.S. Central Command (CENTCOM) on October 3, 2001. CENTCOM commander General Tommy Franks, innovative and bold, recognized the potential and assigned navy SEAL Admiral Bert Calland to partner with the CIA. Shortly thereafter, Franks, accompanied by Calland and CIA officers, met with Northern Alliance commanders and intelligence officials to forge an agreement for attack. Later, Calland and more CIA operatives were deployed into Afghanistan to work with Northern Alliance intelligence officials and generals to listen, learn, refine, and execute.

By late September 2001 Uzbek tribal leader Dostam, part of the loosely structured Northern Alliance, aimed to recapture Mazar-e-sharif and eventually expand his small patch of turf to the borders of Uzbekistan. Tajik Panjshiri Northern Alliance commander Fahim hoped to attack from his northeast mountain strongholds to the west, toward Talaqan and Konduz, and to the south, toward Kabul. Ismail Khan wanted to attack from his base in central Afghanistan to the west, cutting the ring road and eventually taking the western city of Herat. Hazara Shia leader Kalili focused on the capture of Bamian and the surrounding area, to the west of Kabul. Pashtun tribal leader Karzai thought he could establish an enclave near his home village of Torin Kowt, and then move south to capture Qandahar. Pashtun tribal leader Shirzai also wanted to capture Qandahar but preferred to attack from the Pakistan border area and drive westward toward this urban enclave of Taliban leaders. Because the CIA had links of trust and confidence with these tribal allies, knew their strengths and weakness, and understood the expectations of the enemy, CIA leaders crafted a plan that reinforced the Afghan allies' own inclinations. The CIA and the U.S. military worked to pull these autonomous

Afghan allies into a single, coordinated, offensive effort. Within seventy-two hours Mazar-e-sharif and Kabul had both fallen, to be quickly followed by Bamian and Herat. With the land bridge established to Uzbekistan in the west, Highway 1 cut between Kabul and Konduz in the south, Northern Alliance Tajik-dominated mountains in the west, the Amur Darya River blocking escape to the north, and with allied forces attacking from all sides and U.S. air strikes from above, the enemy suffered a catastrophic defeat in the Konduz pocket. Bands of allied tribal militia cut other sections of the ring road and trapped enemy forces in smaller pockets throughout northern Afghanistan. This was 1997 all over again, but this time the enemy had no means of escape.

In the south and east, a more ambivalent local population of Pashtun tribals provided less geographic advantage. There was no secure territory from which to launch ground attacks against Qandahar. Yet again history and HUMINT illuminated the possibilities. Internal Pashtun rivalries and growing disenchantment with the Taliban presented opportunities. CIA assets had already launched sabotage operations against Taliban forces, especially around Qandahar, and intelligence revealed the fear and confusion among Taliban leaders. Moreover, Hamid Karzai represented a rare national hope. Highly respected by various tribal leaders, including the Panjshiri-dominated Northern Alliance, Karzai believed that he could raise an armed militia in his home region and carve out a small area in which to begin offensive ground operations. In one of the most heroic acts of the war, the future president of Afghanistan infiltrated enemy lines in Torin Kowt and rallied his tribesmen into a ragtag fighting force. A small team of CIA and U.S. military forces were deployed at night via CH-47 helicopters under enemy fire; they landed on a lily pad in an enemy pond. They joined Karzai's forces and rallied more militia, calling in U.S. airpower for protection, then launched an offensive to the south. Taliban and al-Qaeda forces in Qandahar drove north to meet them. The November 17–18 U.S. and Afghan victory over al-Qaeda and Taliban forces south of Torin Kowt was critical, because it opened the way to Qandahar and provided a victory for Karzai, perhaps the only Afghan political leader who could pull together the north and the south. Otherwise, southern Pashtuns fighting northern Tajiks, in particular, could turn a Taliban defeat into a broad civil war and deny the United States the military and political victory it sought.

In addition to these joint U.S.-Afghan efforts, U.S. Special Operations Forces operated with brazen unilateral impunity throughout southern Afghanistan, destroying enemy infrastructure, capturing prisoners, killing Taliban operatives, and raiding the residence of Taliban leader Mullah Omar. U.S. Marines also played a key role in the Qandahar area. Intelligence guided and supported these unilateral missions and, in the aftermath of raids, provided assessments such as the devastating psychological impact on enemy leadership. On December 7 U.S. and allied Afghan forces captured Qandahar.

By taking advantage of local military-political objectives, the United States harnessed the tribal forces already in motion and provided massive reinforcement via intelligence, communication, coordination, and firepower. And, when necessary, unilateral action complemented and encouraged natural tribal political tendencies. In other words, the CIA strategy, accepted and expanded by CENTCOM, reflected much of the Afghan allies' own geographical aims.

The third level of application, deeper than raw power or geographic strategy, required understanding why the Afghans waged war. Why men fight often determines who they fight and defines how they fight. Thucydides, in *The Peloponnesian War*, explored the motivations of societies and warriors; this ancient historian's lessons are still important today.[6] The Afghans fought for more than mere survival; thus force alone was insufficient (contrary to Clausewitz and Keegan). The Afghans fought not only for conventional geopolitical gain. They fought as much for prestige and honor, defined in their tribal terms, as for anything else, often more. Understanding these motivations and providing them with the opportunity to earn greater honor was the path to U.S. victory. This required intelligence beyond conventional HUMINT or SIGINT. It required images far deeper and more complex than satellite systems could provide. It required a cultural understanding based on trust and confidence, even bonds of empathy, with Afghan allies. It also required a special brand of intelligence officer who could map the human terrain and lead a multilateral collection of tribal elements to fulfill their own unrealized objectives.

Granted, those Afghan tribal leaders allied with the Taliban and al-Qaeda wanted to live, and they grew increasingly concerned about the application of U.S. power. They become more worried when confounded by a strategy that placed small, mobile U.S. teams behind their lines and saboteurs within their ranks. They needed options. The CIA, working with Afghan partners, offered them a series of choices. First, if they cooperated with the United States, they improved their chances of survival. In concert with CIA intelligence and covert action, U.S. air power reinforced this by quickly attacking some of the enemy Afghans who rejected the offer of partnership, which inclined survivors and others to reconsider U.S. overtures in a different light. Lethal coercion, although it has limitations, is a clear and fundamental baseline in war; in fact, it defines war. Clausewitz got that part right. The second, deeper benefit focused on caring for the families, the clans of these potential allies. In October 2001, especially in the high central mountains, winter was fast approaching. These impoverished Afghans needed tents, clothes, medicine, food, Korans, toys, and much more. The CIA and the U.S. Air Force responded. Within sixty days, from mid-October to mid-December 2001, U.S. aircraft delivered 1.69 million pounds of goods in 108 airdrops to forty-one locations throughout Afghanistan. Each drop was tailored to the specific requests of teams on the ground. Imagine the power conferred upon the Afghan tribal leader who sided with the United States, whose clan's needs fell from the sky within seventy-two hours of his request. Their desperation was addressed, and their leader won honor and prestige among his people. Tons of other supplies arrived from clandestine overland networks. More were delivered by overt means, to highlight the U.S. response in humanitarian terms. The deliveries even sparked competition among tribal leaders for CIA benefits; others offered their services once they learned of the potential rewards.

These airdrops, of course, also included weapons and munitions. Now the Afghans had the means to kill their real enemies — those Arab, Chechen, Pakistani, and Uighur invaders. With CIA intelligence, U.S. firepower, and their own weapons, these Afghans had an unprecedented opportunity to enhance their warrior status among their tribes. The CIA's covert action reinforced the Afghan warrior's identity. He could fight and win, rightfully claiming victory as his own. Moreover, the Afghan fighters began to view the handful of U.S. warriors as comrades-in-arms. After all, these fellow fighters had demonstrated courage by placing themselves at such risk; these teams were at the mercy of their Afghan hosts. They shared the Afghans' hardships and danger. Finally, they talked about a new Afghanistan. They provided hope.

Another benefit, of course, was material self-interest. The CIA handed out millions of dollars. This bought influence and helped induce the defection of thousands of Taliban-aligned militia. Some Afghan partners provided for their clans and tribes with this money. Some pocketed the funds. All understood the origin of the largess and the reciprocity it required.

U.S. power is usually measured in terms of kinetic strength, but the power of empathy, honor, prestige, hope, and material self-interest can complement raw strength and produce a more effective, more enduring victory. This is the lesson of Thucydides. And, the power of thermobaric munitions and AC-130s can underscore the terms of both altruistic and self-interested deals. Through intelligence, at a deeper level, the CIA teams on the ground generated and directed this intangible power, reinforced by lethal force, in concert with the broader U.S. military-political strategy. The Afghans understood and embraced this complex partnership of power. As a consequence, Taliban-sponsored tribal alliances began to unravel, as the center of gravity, within the minds of those militia leaders, shifted toward the United States and the prospect of collective victory.

Teams

To accomplish this mission, the CIA deployed uniquely capable teams into Afghanistan. These teams blended diverse talents and boasted highly experienced leaders who excelled in missions demanding independence and initiative. Despite the erosion of the CIA's paramilitary capabilities since the end of the cold war, the CIA retained a core group of these warriors. These few dozen paramilitary officers provided the backbone for the CIA teams. Many were cross-trained as operations or intelligence officers. Most, however, lacked relevant language skills, experience in central Asia, and expertise in counterterrorism. Moreover, CIA operations officers with the requisite qualifications often had limited or rusty tactical skills. A team usually consisted of an operations officer with language skills, especially Farsi/Dari, who may have had military experience. His deputy was usually a paramilitary officer. Other team members brought tactical, technical communications, counterterrorist, and language capabilities. This combination of personnel with the right leadership proved successful.

The team leaders were all senior officers at the colonel or general level. Gary Schroen, a fifty-nine-year-old SIS-3 who spoke fluent Farsi/Dari, led the first team into Afghanistan; it arrived in the Panjshir on September 27. This was analogous to the U.S. military deploying a three-star general to lead an eight-man A-team. Another team leader with advanced graduate study in Islam and central Asia, who spoke fluent Russian and Uzbek, had vast experience in the area. Yet another, who spoke Farsi/Dari, was a cultural anthropologist intimately familiar with the tribes of the region. The average age of a CIA team member in Afghanistan was forty-five, with more than twenty years on the job. Experience mattered, because these men had to plumb the depths of political and cultural dynamics to understand the environment. These CIA officers needed to map the human terrain of their patch in Afghanistan, while understanding and contributing to the larger strategy. They needed not just skills but knowledge rooted in virtue and judgment developed through experience. They especially needed to know themselves, because this was the first and most important reference point in measuring the complex psychological, social, cultural, and political variables that swirled around them. The GPS provides a good analogy. When deployed into the field, the teams used a GPS, and their first point of reference was their position. Only then did they start fixing allied and enemy positions. The same was true of the psychological, cultural, and social environment; these officers needed first to know themselves, then to understand others, build empathy, acquire deeper intelligence, make decisions, and take action. For example, CIA officers challenged Afghan warriors to fight a common foe, to avenge the deaths of September 11 victims and Afghan martyrs Ahmed Masood and Abdul Haq, brutally murdered by al-Qaeda. CIA officers collected deep intelligence and invoked a common honor to build alliances. Significantly, these culturally sensitive and professionally disciplined officers also harbored and nurtured a cold, visceral determination to kill the enemy. This focused passion needed no translation for their Afghan allies.

These experienced teams demonstrated a special kind of courage. With confidence in their leadership, they ignored political risk and embraced the courage of responsibility. While less clear and less recognized, this type of bravery was critical to the victory in Afghanistan. Their courage enabled these leaders to make decisions and move forward with speed and confidence. Each team, with unprecedented responsibility, complemented each other.

Team members had tactical responsibilities but made decisions with strategic consequences. This was especially true because of the CIA command structure, purposely designed to deal with the unique tribal environment and enhance networked decisions. Afghanistan is not a nation-state in the conventional Western sense but a fractured, shifting jumble of tribal and clan networks. Intelligence collection and war are very local matters. The CIA, therefore, did not assign an overall chief of station for Afghanistan, not in the beginning. Instead it initially deployed seven semiautonomous teams that operated in a network under the command of a single headquarters office within the CTC. Each team understood its strategic objectives within the overall plan, but each had the widest latitude in its tactics and operations while keeping other teams informed. They could thus maintain maximum flexibility in order to understand and adjust as local variables changed. For example, a team could deploy reconnaissance elements of two officers at will; no operational permission or review was required. There was no requirement for close air support. No approval was needed to hire a local. The teams could reconfigure and recombine with U.S. military partners or Afghan allies at a moment's notice. The team leaders and members operated in a manner that took full advantage of their experience, initiative, and local knowledge. Only after all the major Afghan cities had fallen in December 2001 and a nascent national government had begun to form did the CIA assign a chief of station—a senior operations officer who had led the CTC's effort against al-Qaeda for the previous three years. In sum, the teams performed as self-organizing networks, linked by a single chain of command to a single headquarters office.

Intelligence

In contrast to the decentralized, networked command structure, the intelligence reporting system was extraordinarily centralized but also networked. Each team generated intelligence reports that would reach other teams, the military commands, CIA stations around the world, analysts, and policymakers. There was plenty of intelligence. In the first six months CIA teams, using laptops in the dirt, often in combat conditions, produced almost two thousand HUMINT disseminations. This is an extraordinary number of reports, surpassing during the same period geographic divisions with more than a score of permanent stations. Significantly, the CIA fused these reports with all other sources of intelligence, from imagery to other HUMINT to SIGINT to overt Foreign Broadcast Information Service cuts. The CIA operators and analysts worked together in this fusion process; this real-time melding of operations and analysis proved essential, because analysis supported not only CENTCOM and policymakers but also the operator who was collecting intelligence and waging covert war. The CTC office, relying on the entire intelligence community, strived to push fused, value-laden intelligence to CIA teams in Afghanistan.

Integrated all-source intelligence sharpened operations through the constant validating and reprogramming of each source. An unvetted HUMINT source could be under the coercive influence of the Taliban, but the comparison of his reporting with other sources could prompt an investigation and the rejection of his information. SIGINT could provide the details of a true conversation of a militia leader pledging support to a Taliban commander, but a HUMINT source could claim that the same militia leader was lying to the Taliban and truly intended to defect. Imagery could provide indications of enemy camps; HUMINT sources could therefore be deployed in the area and SIGINT sensors redirected. An unvetted HUMINT source could prove his worth and thus receive more sensitive tasking if his information was corroborated. For example, CIA officers tasked volunteer sources to report on areas already understood, as a test of their intentions. In one case, an outstanding long-time Afghan source provided exact targeting information and, seized with the mission, rejected the CIA's repeated orders to evacuate the enemy area before U.S. air strikes commenced. Joint direct-attack munitions igniting secondary explosions of Taliban–al-Qaeda military targets further validated his information and his courage. Thanks to superior imagery and a perfect expression of U.S. air power, the asset survived. He earned special CIA recognition and reward.

The fused intelligence produced specific dynamic targeting for the U.S. military. This was conveyed in phone-video–teleconference-video feeds to CENTCOM. The CTC generated an electronic map with multiple overlays of data that tracked CIA teams, U.S. military deployments, allied Afghan forces, enemy locations, and no-strike zones. This was done nearly in real time. The CIA pushed the data as fast as possible. U.S. pilots in particular responded with precision and great flexibility. On more than one occasion U.S. aircraft veered away from enemy camps at the last moment because the CIA could not contact an asset exposed to the air strikes. The CTC maintained a duplicate electronic map via a link in CENTCOM, so military commanders knew what the CIA knew. Moreover, the CIA welcomed detailed military personnel into the CIA operations structure, on the teams, and in CIA headquarters. A select few CENTCOM and Special Operations officers even had direct access to source-sensitive databases and operational cable traffic. The protection of sources and methods, of course, is fundamental to the intelligence business, but effective operations need compartments with the right people on the inside, including analysts and warriors. These military partners were fully integrated into the CTC and provided invaluable guidance for all aspects of targeting and operations. Special Forces General Mike Jones, assigned to the CTC, played a key leadership role. CIA liaison officers were also posted at CENTCOM, air force commands, and throughout U.S. military commands in central Asia.

The CIA's partnership with the U.S. military was the foundation for the kinetic war, and the integral link of intelligence to military operations reached new levels. In one case a CIA HUMINT source reported the possibility that an enemy convoy would be departing a small village at dawn. The navy deployed a P-3 surveillance aircraft that picked up the three suspect vehicles. The navy handed off the coverage to an unmanned aerial vehicle (UAV) that tracked the convoy. In response to this imagery, a small team composed of U.S. military personnel, CIA operatives, and Afghans blocked the enemy's escape into Pakistan. This one encounter forced the enemy's convoy deeper into Afghanistan, allowing sufficient time for navy SEALs to reach the convoy by helicopter. While the UAV provided live video coverage, the SEALs executed a classic L-shaped attack. All seventeen Chechens died in the brief firefight. There were no U.S. casualties. The success of this mission reflects the success of all-source, fused, flexible, and networked intelligence geared to the tactical customer, in this case a navy SEAL team.

The field partnerships, however, faced bureaucratic challenges. U.S. military forces carried the baggage of standard operating procedures, whereas CIA teams often developed initiatives on an ad hoc basis. CENTCOM sometimes thought CTC leadership ill informed about their teams' exact tactical intent or, worse, reluctant to share detailed plans, while the CTC wondered why CENTCOM appeared so bureaucratic and rigid. Worse still, parts of the Department of Defense (DoD) sought to gain control of critical resources and exert political bureaucratic power in the midst of the conflict. Some in the DoD and CIA questioned the entire plan, predicting disaster such as the Soviets encountered in Afghanistan in the 1980s. But forceful intelligence generated speed and momentum and, with strong field leadership from the CIA and CENTCOM, eventually success.

Intelligence collection and analysis also played the critical role in policymakers' strategic decisions. A remarkably flat command link enabled intelligence and strategic decisions to flow two ways in only minutes, thus enhancing the impact of the intelligence.[7] For example, the national command authority would often listen to an intelligence brief from a CIA headquarters officer in overall command of the teams, and then debate key points. The officer would in turn inform team leaders of the policy context through informal dialogue or more formal intelligence requirements, usually within the hour. The political importance of Kabul as a capital and unifying symbol of a new Afghan state was one policy issue. The viability of a Pashtun leader and a Tajik-dominated military in a new Afghanistan was another. The expectations, capabilities, and roles of neighboring allied countries were yet another consideration, the dangers posed by Iran, another. By understanding the strategic context, team leaders could make better operational judgments and collect more relevant intelligence. These teams, sensitive and responsive to the policymakers' needs, reported reams not only of intelligence but of quality intelligence. The dramatic compression of the intelligence cycle at the tactical and strategic levels throughout the Afghan war benefited everyone, collectors, analysts, and customers alike.

War

As expected, the war evolved in three phases. The first ended in early December 2001 when the Taliban collapsed as an organized fighting force and al-Qaeda forces dispersed into their sanctuaries. Because most of the targets were large, relatively static enemy concentrations and infrastructure, the intelligence collection for military action was relatively clear. The second phase, from early December 2001 until April 2002, focused on al-Qaeda sanctuaries. This included the battles of Tora Bora that winter and Shaikot the following spring. Because the targets were fewer in number, more mobile, and operating in specially selected areas, the United States needed more specific tactical intelligence. The difficulty grew because al-Qaeda had chosen its sanctuaries well: high mountain terrain close to the Pakistani border. Moreover, Afghan allies much preferred to fight for their village or valley; they were less inclined to engage a trained enemy hidden in a fortified redoubt. An ethnic Tajik or Uzbek Afghan is much less useful in Pashtun territory, as is a Pashtun not from that particular clan. Al-Qaeda leveraged their relationship with their Pashtun allies in the southern and eastern part of Afghanistan in seeking refuge. This intelligence nut was harder to crack. The CIA located the sanctuaries and managed to infiltrate Afghan assets, who marked out enemy locations. This, combined with other intelligence means, led to overwhelming but imperfect victories. In Tora Bora the U.S. sacrificed power for speed. CENTCOM and the CIA understood the limitations of Afghan allies but also appreciated the need to attack with alacrity. Moving U.S. forces into the area would simply take too long. Intelligence fixed the enemy, including al-Qaeda leadership. Afghan allies, encouraged and supported by the CIA and U.S. Special Forces, were deployed into blocking positions around Tora Bora. U.S. airpower, guided by a five-man joint team calling in strikes, did the real damage. The U.S. captured a key al-Qaeda sanctuary, destroyed weapons and munitions, recovered valuable intelligence, and killed hundreds of the enemy and forced others to flee to Pakistan, where scores more were captured. Osama bin Laden, however, escaped.

When criticized by London for his unorthodox method of warfare, T. E. Lawrence (Lawrence of Arabia) said of his indigenous allies, "Do not try to do too much with your own hands. Better the Arabs do it tolerably than that you do it perfectly. . . . Actually also, under the very odd conditions of Arabia, your practical work will not be as good as, perhaps, you think it is."[8] The same reasoning applied to the U.S. victory at Tora Bora.

The battle at Shaikot three months later, Operation Anaconda, was a more conventional, more "complete" U.S. victory, because more U.S. and coalition forces were directly engaged. The press coverage was also greater. The CIA provided intelligence support in this battle. HUMINT determined the enemy's area of concentration, but

HUMINT could not determine the enemy's tactical positions or defensive plans. Traditional U.S. military reconnaissance and direct engagement often determined al-Qaeda's location. Given the extreme terrain and dispersal of enemy forces in caves and canyons and poor weather, traditional imagery provided limited value. The enemy's communications discipline improved after press reports of U.S. tactical SIGINT efforts at Tora Bora; therefore, SIGINT was less useful in Shaikot. The CIA nevertheless collected unique intelligence to support the warfighters. For example, the CIA deployed unilateral Afghan assets with modified GPS devices into the Shaikot area to mark key sites and routes. The agency illuminated enemy positions for strike aircraft; on one occasion this included marking a target for a French Mirage that blunted an enemy attack on isolated U.S. troops. Perhaps as many as eight hundred enemy combatants died in this battle, but others, including some al-Qaeda leaders, escaped. What the United States had gained in power by waiting for weeks to build up its forces, it lost in speed.

The third phase of the war had actually been in progress throughout the campaign but gained exclusive focus after Operation Anaconda: the search for high-value targets such as Osama bin Laden. The CIA had in fact been hunting bin Laden in Afghanistan for years. Although he was spotted briefly, there was no immediate shooter or clear authority to complement the sensor. The CIA and U.S. military did kill al-Qaeda's number-two man, Mohammed Atef, and other terrorist leaders. Man hunting has always posed difficult intelligence challenges, especially in hostile environments. General Pershing chased Pancho Villa in northern Mexico for many hard months, with no success. Nazi war criminals eluded capture for decades. Carlos the Jackal dodged his pursuers for years, until he crossed paths with the CIA's Cofer Black in Sudan.

Future War

The transformation of war from large standing armies to microtargets armed with WMD will challenge the United States, even more so if conventional doctrines prevail. As enemies disperse into smaller units under cover of more complex, possibly vertical urban environments, the importance of HUMINT will grow. The enemy target might be a two-man terrorist cell, with firearms plus a chemical agent, in a third-floor apartment. Technical collection, especially if this cell exercises tradecraft discipline, may offer nothing. Only a local HUMINT source might have access to the target. Of course, as in Afghanistan, the best intelligence emerges from multiple sources from various collection disciplines. Such microtargets will confound larger technical systems unless they are fused into HUMINT structures and products. It is important that technical systems enhance HUMINT. Intelligence on microtargets in counterterrorist war will be increasingly transitory. There will be no time to waste, because a single terrorist, perhaps with his own agenda, can move at will at any moment. In this kind of warfare the United States will need to integrate the various sensors with the various shooters, all in the right combination, so that action is precise and immediate. The intelligence operatives, or sensors, will also need to understand the strategic consequences of such tactical missions and must factor this into collection and reporting. Sensors must support the shooters, and both must support the policymakers.

Greater emphasis on interdisciplinary intelligence teams will become the norm, especially in counterterrorist war. Such teams may require traditional sensors and shooters reinforced by biotechnicians who can track and defeat bioweapons. They may require operators who can launch and control mini-UAVs armed with special MASINT sensors. Or they may need financial analysts who can crunch data at the point of field collection and provide immediate feedback to other teams hacking into terrorist bank data on another continent. Technology, however, should not drive these operations or determine broader strategy at the expense of experienced, risk-taking HUMINT collectors on the ground. While we assess the operational impact of technology from our American perspective, we must be cognizant of other views. We seek moral comfort in long-distance, technically buffered killing, but we loose the tactile sense of the human battlefield.[9] Distance and remote technology may reduce physical risk and protect our consciences, but it impedes the development of empathy in the collectors and warriors who must understand the human variables. The United States cannot ignore the most powerful force on the battlefield: the human condition of friends and foes.

HUMINT and covert action will be unilateral, bilateral, and/or multilateral. U.S. intelligence must forge increasingly interdependent links to a multitude of nonstate partners. In Afghanistan the United States relied on a wide range of allies far from the conventional formula of interstate relations. U.S. operations in Afghanistan were supremely multilateral, supplemented by unilateral sources and unilateral action. Each reinforced the other.

One of the most important lessons of the Afghan war of 2001-2 is how intelligence enabled the calibration of covert action and war, a war that conformed to broader U.S. policy and endowed the victors with legitimacy. The United States achieved military and political success in Afghanistan and in the process boosted its global political standing. The world likes a winner, but only if the battle is just, the fight fair, alliances strengthened, and the victor humble. The calibrated operation served the United States in the military sense in part by recruiting ambivalent foes into allies against intransigent enemies. It also achieved global strategic objectives, in that calibrated U.S. power demonstrated to the world that the United States respects the "preferences of other societies . . . an indispensable element in maintaining the peace," according to Philip Bobbitt. In *The Shield of Achilles* Bobbitt writes, "Legitimacy is what unites the problems of strategy and law at the heart of epochal war."[10] Excepting the already radicalized parts of the Islamic world, the global public viewed the U.S. action in Afghanistan as legitimate, because of the September 11 attacks but also because covert action and war, guided by deep intelligence, incorporated the Afghan people into the fight. The skillful teams in Afghanistan transcended their tactical engagements to help confer legitimacy on the United States in the eyes of the world. This is no small thing. Robert Kagan notes, "The struggle to define and obtain international legitimacy in this new era may prove to be among the most critical contests of our time. In some ways, it is as significant in determining the future of the U.S. role in the international system as any purely material measure of power and influence."[11]

The Afghanistan war also revitalized the American way of war. "Boldness and prudence, flexibility and opportunism, initiative and tempo, speed and concentration, force multipliers, and intelligence," are the elements historian David Hackett Fischer sees in George Washington's winter campaign of 1776–77. These elements "defined a new way of war that would continue to appear through the Revolution and in many American wars."[12] The American warriors in Afghanistan demonstrated these same traits, upholding the legacy of their founding fathers' independent, entrepreneurial spirit.

Counterterrorist war will require a stronger CIA capable of deploying experienced teams into terrorist sanctuaries, whether in the hinterlands of Somalia or the complex urban jungles of Karachi, to collect quality intelligence and, as directed by the national command authority, execute covert action. And the intelligence and covert action must always support U.S. policy, whether reflected in a diplomatic demarche or a joint direct-attack munitions strike. At the same time, the United States should not expect CIA paramilitary officers to substitute for U.S. military forces; the CIA mission is different, requiring broader, more strategic orientation. The CIA mission also requires espionage and tradecraft. U.S. commandos need to focus on the tactics of killing terrorists; CIA officers need to focus on the intelligence that supports the operation and provides policy context for the ramifications of such killing.

The U.S. military will need to improve its responsiveness, flexibility, quickness, and stealth. According to the *Weekly Standard*, in part because of the influence of conventional military leaders, "Prior to 9/11, these [Special Forces] units *were never used even once* to hunt down terrorists who had taken American lives."[13] In counterterrorist wars like in the one in Afghanistan, conventional forces will support Special Operations Forces, turning decades' worth of doctrine on its head. But the United States should not expect these brave warriors or other elements of the military to collect nontactical intelligence or direct covert action. Regrettably, the ongoing debate, outlined in an excellent article by Jennifer Kibbe in the March–April 2004 issue of *Foreign Affairs,* is more about politics than about mission. Intelligence operatives and fighting soldiers both bring special skills and complement each other; this lesson of Afghanistan should not be lost in the scramble for resources, power, control, and bragging rights. We need the CIA and the military to work together as directed by the policy masters they serve.

Robert Kaplan wrote, "Not only should the CIA be *greener* (that is, have a larger uniformed [*sic*] military wing), but the Special Forces should be *blacker*."[14] The 9/11 Commission's recommendation to strip the CIA of its paramilitary covert-action capabilities is a bad idea.

The policy community will need a more dynamic, more robust diplomatic aid corps, geared to engage provincial, even tribal, political leaders and to support the construction of legitimate societies defined by local needs, not American (mis)perceptions. The dismissive criticism of support to "warlords" in Afghanistan ignores the obvious: local leaders hold the power and define political reality. Nevertheless, with time, patience, and hard work, perhaps a national Afghan society based on something stronger and more stable than local tribal legitimacy will emerge. In the meantime, U.S. political representatives, like CIA and military operatives, must engage these nonstate actors, especially those in the hinterlands. In the end, counterterrorist war is more about providing opportunities and hope for the dispossessed in terrorist sanctuaries than about just killing the enemy. As Eliot Cohen argues, "U.S. policy abroad has been effectively militarized, at the expense of a State Department whose collective strength has rarely matched the quality of individual diplomats."[15] In Afghanistan, military strikes needed immediate support by more than transitory covert actions, which in turn needed overt policy manifested at the local level, not just United Nations conferences in capital cities.

Finally, the Afghan war shows us what America can achieve — a victory based upon the enduring lessons of the ancients, deep intelligence, and the right people, the right partnerships: technicians and spies, collectors and advisors and policymakers, sensors and shooters, riflemen and pilots, Americans and Afghans. This victory, like any other, is also about leaders. We must therefore seize its lesson of bold leadership and learn from those brave Americans who were deployed in Afghanistan during the grief-ridden autumn of 2001, who struck the enemy with nuance and fury, with intelligence and war.

Notes

All statements of fact, opinion, or analysis expressed are those of the author and do not reflect the official positions or views of the CIA or any other U.S. Government agency. Nothing in the contents should be construed as asserting or implying U.S. Government authentication of information or Agency endorsement of the author's views. Where appropriate, this material has been reviewed by the CIA to prevent the disclosure of classified information.

1. Richard Clarke, *Against All Enemies* (New York: Free Press, 2004). See also National Commission on Terrorist Attacks upon the United States, staff statements, 2004, available at www.9/11commission.gov/staff_statements.htm. Both provide accounts of U.S. initiatives in Afghanistan before September 11, 2001. Although Clarke's account is egocentric and subjective, he successfully outlines U.S. efforts. The statements by the commission staff capture (and miss) some of the history and note the critical importance of intelligence.

2. Carl von Clausewitz, *On War,* trans. and ed. Michael Howard and Peter Paret (Princeton: Princeton University Press, 1976); John Keegan, *Intelligence in War* (New York: Knopf, 2003).

3. Sun Tzu, *The Art of Warfare,* trans. Roger Ames (New York: Ballentine Books, 1993), 120.

4. Ibid., 157.

5. Ahmed Rashid, *Taliban: Militant Islam, Oil, and Fundamentalism in Central Asia* (New Haven: Yale University Press, 2001). Rashid provides an excellent account of this operation in his discussion of the rise of the Taliban.

6. Robert B. Strassler, ed., *The Landmark Thucydides* (New York: Touchstone, 1998).

7. Eliot Cohen, *Supreme Command* (New York: Free Press, 2002). Cohen illustrates the critical importance of civilian leadership during war and the importance of policy's driving military strategy. During the Afghan war, CIA intelligence and CENTCOM briefings to the NCA helped in this regard.

8. T. E. Lawrence, "27 Articles," *Arab Bulletin,* August 20, 1917.

9. Dave Grossman, *On Killing* (New York: Little, Brown, 1995). Grossman provides a penetrating psychological analysis of conflict, exploring how men naturally seek distance and technology to ease the hard task of killing.

10. Philip Bobbitt, *The Shield of Achilles: War, Peace, and the Course of History* (New York: Anchor Books, 2002), 334.

11. Robert Kagan, "America's Crisis of Legitimacy," *Foreign Affairs* 82 (March–April 2004): 67.

12. David Hackett Fischer, *Washington's Crossing* (New York: Oxford University Press, 2003), 375.

13. Richard H. Schultz Jr., "Nine Reasons Why We Never Sent Our Special Operations Forces after Al Qaeda before 9/11," *Weekly Standard,* January 26, 2004, 19.

14. Robert Kaplan, "Supremacy by Stealth," *Atlantic Monthly* (July–August 2003), 79.

15. Eliot Cohen, "History and the Hyperpower," *Foreign Affairs* 83 (July–August 2004): 61.

ELEVEN

Managing HUMINT
The Need for a New Approach

Burton Gerber

A FEW YEARS AGO a cartoon in the *New Yorker* depicted several executives around a conference table looking at a chart with a sharply downward trend line. The man pointing at the chart is saying, "The dip in sales seems to coincide with the decision to eliminate the sales staff."[1]

This cartoon is a good metaphor for what happened to human intelligence (HUMINT) in the 1990s, when officials in the executive branch and Congress reduced appropriations for HUMINT programs and for personnel associated with those programs. Confronted with the intelligence failures associated with the September 11 disaster, many in Congress and the White House, in both the previous and the current administrations, wondered why HUMINT did not do a better job of collecting connectable dots on al-Qaeda's planned attack on America. Furthermore, most of these intelligence officials and politicians, who now openly blame this budget shortfall for our paucity of intelligence on al-Qaeda's intentions prior to September 11, failed to reveal to the American people the potential consequences of taking the cuts during the 1990s, when the decisions were being made.

As they left office in 2004, both former Director of Central Intelligence (DCI) George Tenet and former Deputy Director for Operations James Pavitt elaborated on the consequences of cutbacks in HUMINT resources in earlier years. Pavitt complained of "budgets not big enough and policy attention not forceful enough" in the 1990s, leading at that time to a 30 percent decline in funding for the Central Intelligence Agency (CIA)'s HUMINT programs in the Directorate of Operations and to personnel reductions of 20 percent.[2] Former DCI Tenet testified to the 9/11 Commission that when he became DCI in 1997, "the infrastructure to recruit, train, and sustain officers for our clandestine services . . . was in disarray." Tenet further stated that in 1995, the year he became Deputy DCI, there were only twenty-five new case officers graduating from the agency's case officer training program, meaning that the CIA was not even replacing those retiring and resigning.[3] Crucially, these personnel cuts meant that fewer case officers were available to recruit foreign spies and direct their intelligence production. According to government officials, the CIA had fewer case officers serving abroad than there were Federal Bureau of Investigation (FBI) special agents assigned to New York City alone.[4]

As most observers, including the 9/11 Commission, now acknowledge, rebuilding the U.S. human intelligence cadre is of crucial importance to the nation's security. Even the current increase in the hiring of new case officers only partially mitigates the problem. New officers need to learn clandestine and technical techniques and acquire language fluency before their first tours abroad. It is usually only during the second overseas tour that a case officer can be considered full-service. The issue is not simply whether to increase human intelligence but how to do so. A strategy must be developed and sustained for ensuring that the best people are hired, trained, equipped, and retained, so that the U.S. government can maximize the effectiveness of human intelligence over the next several decades.

Toward a Strategy for Rebuilding Human Intelligence

In fighting terrorism, "accurate intelligence is absolutely essential," said Senator Carl Levin, ranking Democrat on the Senate Armed Services Committee.[5] The challenges of terrorism and nuclear proliferation mean that intelligence failure, or even inadequacy, threatens the safety of the United States and its allies. HUMINT will have to contribute the lion's share of intelligence on terrorism and a substantial part of intelligence on proliferation issues. The U.S. intelligence community and its officers must correct deficiencies, improve coordination, develop innovations, and attract the very best in American minds and courage.

HUMINT will have to build on what it has done right and overcome the impediments that caused it to falter. The test of how well it is doing will be in its product — in how well it contributes substantially to U.S. efforts to counter terrorism and the proliferation of weapons of mass destruction while preserving our capacity to recognize and to surge against the next dangerous adversary. Intelligence officers must bring their skills of agility, deception, and manipulation to these tasks, while increasing their comfort with technology and their willingness to work with other agencies in the military and in law enforcement. They will need to develop new techniques to ensure that information, training, and resources can flow across bureaucratic boundaries. They must be imaginative in cover development, including nonofficial cover, working with both government and private-sector providers.

Working Transnational Targets: HUMINT's Special Attributes

Countering terrorism — recruiting sources, uncovering plots, and understanding how terrorist organizations develop and grow — is chiefly a HUMINT task. Signals intelligence (SIGINT) provides some, but diminishing, intelligence, as terrorists learn through analysis or leaks in Western media how they must counter Western eavesdropping. And imagery intelligence is usually not valuable against this target. If we are to fight and counter terrorists and similar transnational adversaries, such as international organized crime, HUMINT must be our focus. The U.S. government needs an approach to rebuilding HUMINT that capitalizes on the best tradecraft of the past while designing new capabilities for the future. Doing so requires an appreciation of HUMINT's unique attributes.

COMPARATIVE ADVANTAGES

HUMINT is very different from intelligence collection programs based on acoustic, imaging, or other technical sensors. While these collection systems are expensive to build and maintain, they can be refocused relatively quickly on new enemies and new threats once deployed. Refocusing HUMINT assets is a much longer process.

Former U.S. Representative (and 9/11 Commission vice chairman) Lee Hamilton has given a good description of HUMINT's dimensions. He notes that HUMINT is cheap in comparison with technical collection systems, but very hard to retarget and protect.[6] Case officers spend years building up and maintaining their skills. In doing so, they make commitments to agents and render themselves necessarily vulnerable to counterintelligence services and terrorist organizations.

Most outside observers would be amazed at how little HUMINT actually costs compared to other intelligence programs and defense weapons systems. Yet the CIA's HUMINT capabilities have always been lean. In the CIA's Directorate of Operations, officers with the necessary language and area skills may not exist or may be deployed against other targets; the platforms from which these officers operate, whether official installations or nonofficial cover systems, may not be in place and may have to be built. And once all these aspects come together, the officers must still start from scratch to build relationships with potential targets they can recruit, over time, as spies for the United States.

In addition, HUMINT works best when its logistical support anticipates rather than chases after collection priorities. The CIA ought not to repeat its earlier mistake of closing stations in small countries just because those countries appear insignificant today. The collection of intelligence on transnational threats such as terrorism and terrorist cells needs to be done worldwide; there should be no "safe havens." Today's lowest-priority countries may become of crucial interest to U.S. policymakers in a few years or even months—as was the case during the war in Bosnia in the 1990s, when Sarajevo was transformed, in intelligence terms, from a backwater into a major diplomatic venue in a few months' time. Having an infrastructure in place also speeds up the intelligence community's ability to answer policymakers' questions or execute their instructions. Therefore, it would be prudent to ensure that HUMINT has a broad enough base to engage targets worldwide, whether threats emerge in the unsteady world of the African veldt or in the settled European metropolis. A larger global infrastructure would allow

HUMINT to surge when and where necessary, with officers skilled in language and area knowledge crucial to gaining intelligence through espionage and related means.

HUMINT's greatest asset has always been people. Good HUMINT tradecraft, at least as the U.S. has practiced it since World War II, has involved case officers who, in recruiting and managing agents or spies, must be both imaginative and detail-oriented. A working definition of HUMINT case officers' tradecraft might be knowing operations and the operational situation in detail; integrating that knowledge into the physical, political, cultural, and security environments in which they operate; practicing how to conduct themselves and their agents in that context with appropriate technology; and thinking through and preparing for potential consequences.

A case officer must thus not only be familiar with the operational environment but be able to deal with ambiguity, the hallmark of diplomatic and intelligence work. He or she must be able to think independently, work precisely, and always tell the truth when dealing with his or her agency and the U.S. government. And the case officer must do all this with his or her agents while engaging in written and oral communication in a foreign language, often on complicated scientific and technical subjects, political issues, economic trends, and personal matters of extreme importance to the agent, and must command the various clandestine tradecraft techniques that serve as the basis for the case officer–agent relationship. Training case officers is therefore an intense, demanding task. The changing operational environments case officers encounter mean that they are always learning to adapt tradecraft to local situations.

In sum, while brains and academic achievement are important factors, college grades are less important than traits intelligence officers usually call "people skills" or "sales-closing" ability. What makes a good case officer are such attributes as being comfortable in meeting new people, handling new situations, being able to assess persons in terms of motivations and needs, and, finally, manipulating those persons who may be able to satisfy American intelligence requirements into accepting recruitment.

These skills are not spread evenly across the case officer community, and some case officers will be better at handling spies recruited by others than doing the recruitment themselves. Both kinds of case officer continue to be vital to HUMINT programs.

NEW OFFICER REQUIREMENTS

Although the classic case-officer system has enduring requirements, intelligence agencies that screen applicants need to focus on some of the more unusual attributes of espionage as practiced in other societies and at other times. Otherwise they may concentrate predominantly on a model that may not be suitable in many corners of the world or for some of the targets they will be pursuing.

The international environment of the twenty-first century requires new emphasis on a specialized and demanding subset of some of HUMINT's core elements. For example, new forms of cover may need to be designed for the use of penetration and "sleeper" agents who can gain direct access to criminal and terrorist groups. Of course, such new cover programs must not eclipse the old. Although some outside observers complain that case officers under official cover spend too much time at cocktail parties—a method used during the cold war but one not likely to generate leads on terrorists or terrorist supporters—the U.S. government still has significant interest in the intentions of foreign governments for purposes of influencing them to join coalitions, countering unwelcome diplomatic initiatives, and anticipating duplicity. Taking the war to the terrorists involves fighting on someone else's turf; therefore, collecting intelligence on the viability of strategies and targets generally requires intelligence on the capacities of the states that make up the battlefield. Furthermore, national security interests encompass more than countering terrorism. Case officers still need to recruit sources on older and more traditional targets, which have merit both in themselves and as springboards for information on terrorism, weapons proliferation, and the like.

Of course, even when the diplomatic venue was the principal way to meet potential sources, it was never the sole means. American intelligence officers recognize that the terrorist target requires new dimensions. Creating and using platforms other than official cover has long been an American intelligence practice and needs to become an even more dominant one. Setting up nonofficial cover platforms is difficult and requires significant cooperation and assistance from outsiders. This form of cover also brings more risk than the more traditional types, but intelligence collection for the future demands absorbing some of these risks and making even more imaginative use of such means.

This chapter will address those HUMINT issues that are crucial to the agility and productivity of HUMINT in the future. These issues may be grouped into four categories: ethnic diversity, language skills and attendant security matters; recruitment profiles and policies; promotion policies; and training—particularly training that fosters ethics and leadership within HUMINT cadres.

Ethnic Diversity, Languages, and Security Constraints

Critics have charged that the CIA Directorate of Operations is made up chiefly of white males from elite schools. For example, in the summer of 2003 an intelligence officer told a reporter that just 2 to 4 percent of CIA officers are from non-European ethnic groups. He wanted to see this number raised to 20 percent, and it needs to be—not for reasons of political correctness but because the intelligence programs of the United States would be enhanced if it were.[7] For years the agency has tried, with varying degrees of success, to enlarge its corps of female, black, Latino, and Asian American officers, recognizing that members of those groups bring keen insights and talents into the recruitment and handling of foreign sources. Charges of excessive homogeneity miss the point that the CIA has tried to increase diversity but has found it extremely difficult to do, for reasons addressed below.

Still, more needs to be done to increase ethnic representation in areas of special interest. In today's intelligence world the focus on the Middle East, central Asia, and east Asia makes it important to enlist persons of those ethnic backgrounds. Such new officers could have welcome area knowledge that would significantly expand the capabilities of overseas stations.

Fostering foreign language ability is a tandem goal and remains a challenging task. The agency is hiring people fluent in foreign languages, but it needs to hire even more. The various intelligence agencies have tried a number of systems over the years to provide bonuses and/or salary supplements to those who achieve and maintain fluency in certain languages at required levels. Those programs, when administered wisely, are imperative.

In testimony before the Senate governmental affairs committee in September 2000, the vice chair of the National Intelligence Council (NIC) outlined the need for such agencies as the National Security Agency (NSA), the Foreign Broadcast Information Service, the CIA, and the Defense Intelligence Agency (DIA) to have employees able to track events in Russia, China, the Arab world, Iran, Korea, and central Asia. She added that the agencies "would also ideally want to be able to task on short notice workers with excellent language skills in relatively small places — Burundi, East Timor, Bosnia, Kosovo — where problems can lead to U.S. engagements."

The problem is that the intelligence community is not able to anticipate the needed distribution of geographical expertise or language facility except in the most serendipitous instances. The NIC vice chair recognized the problem herself, adding that the intelligence community "often lacks the foreign language skills necessary to surge during a crisis — such as Serbo-Croatian — for the buildup to the NATO bombing of Serbia." Conceding that the problem is a difficult one, she called for the intelligence community to set foreign-language priorities for the most important regions and countries, adding that "the Community's language capability should be proportional to and not exceed the collection and analysis tasking it supports."[8] Unfortunately, the intelligence community has not proved much more adept than the rest of the government in determining the intersection of U.S. strategic interests with future crisis areas of the world (Afghanistan, Sudan, and Somalia are examples), so the problem of matching language officers to crises persists.

Although this suggests that the intelligence community needs a more ethnically diverse workforce, trained in languages or families of languages such as Farsi/Dari/Tajik, there are constraints on achieving this within the Directorate of Operations. Some traditionally minded intelligence officers have complained that foreigners who are targeted for recruitment by CIA as spies may be uncomfortable engaging in an operational relationship with American case officers who are not white males. They claim that a potential foreign target for recruitment might have a legitimate fear that the ethnic American case officer is not really an American case officer at all but a provocateur from the target individual's own home country's security service trying to test the target. Such fears have been allayed in the past through imaginative operational techniques that cannot be discussed here. There is no reason why the fears can't be overcome in these newer instances as well. Unless the case officer is operating under cover as a non-American, which, as discussed above, may be an increasingly necessary *modus operandi,* the essential quality that the case officer—male or female, and of whatever ethnic background—brings to the table is his or her "Americanness," becoming the link for that target to the power, influence, prestige, and resources of the United States.

There remains the question of whether American intelligence, particularly given its conservatively biased screening, testing, security, and clearance processes, can reach the goal of a more ethnically diverse workforce. While CIA and Defense Department HUMINT programs post their officers overseas to engage foreigners and ultimately recruit some of them as spies, security elements of these agencies often take a conservative view toward granting security clearances to applicants who are most familiar with foreigners and life abroad.

The issue of security is a significant one. Security investigators and authorities must do their best to ensure the loyalty and reliability of those applying for and working within the intelligence community. The counterintelligence threat to the United States has not diminished with the collapse of the Soviet Union and the Warsaw Pact. A number of countries and movements, including terrorist organizations, wish to do the United States and its citizens harm. At the least, they want to monitor United States activities that they perceive as affecting their own national security. So the granting of a security clearance still involves a great deal of careful work in determining an applicant's suitability and loyalty.

At the same time, security authorities and their supervisors should recognize that many of the people U.S. intelligence needs to hire for highly classified positions will necessarily have extensive foreign experience and foreign contacts. Some security authorities, at least in the initial stages of the clearance process, seem uneasy about an applicant's foreign travel, work experience, and relatives. Close connections with foreigners raise suspicions, though the most qualified applicants will often be those who by definition have such connections. Undue caution about such persons will hamper our efforts to obtain information on threatening targets such as terrorist groups, Iran, North Korea, and others.

Of course, security processes do more than subtly reinforce ethnic homogeneity. If there is one feature common to almost all complaints about security processing in the intelligence agencies, it is the length of time between the initial interview and hiring. CIA managers and other supervisors have urged speedier processing and in some instances have gotten results. But in most cases applicants are expected to wait at least six months, often longer, for a security clearance. Some applicants cannot or will not wait through the seemingly interminable process, and the agency loses many good prospects as a result.

Former CIA analyst Richard L. Russell has complained, as have others, that the procedures for security clearances in the intelligence community are too restrictive. He quotes the 1996 Brown Commission report that CIA analysis lacks "nourishing" contacts with outside experts, and that this is partly due to the "onerous security requirements—particularly the polygraph examination and the requirement to submit subsequent publications for review."[9] Although CIA and other members of the intelligence community value the polygraph, both because it has proved its worth in counterintelligence and security investigations and for its deterrent effect, there may be other ways to allay some of the critics' concerns — perhaps by giving limited, short-term clearances to experts on certain subjects that would not require the polygraph.

When the polygraph is required, it should be administered swiftly and the results announced speedily so that clearance can be granted in a more timely fashion. Ultimately the intelligence community should, with outside experts, review the effectiveness of the polygraph in all such circumstances, balancing the value of that tool against the other needs and requirements of the government so as to assure that it has the highest-quality employees, whether they are permanent hires or outside experts.

Of course, simply urging bureaucrats to speed up the process is unlikely to succeed. Studying and initiating new kinds of clearance procedures, based on the models of successful companies and programs, might. Intelligence agencies might be able to learn something from NASCAR pit-crew procedures — streamlining the process to the point where they do everything essential and nothing nonessential, and do it simultaneously and in a cooperative fashion so as to get the employee on the track quickly.

Recruitment: Assessing Risk Propensity and Related Skill Sets

The first building block in ensuring HUMINT success is the case officer. How are today's case officers different from their predecessors, and how can greater numbers of qualified individuals be encouraged to join the ranks? Compensation is seldom the deciding factor in intelligence community employment. What these jobs primarily offer are excitement, opportunities to demonstrate initiative and gain early responsibility, a sense of service to the nation, and the job satisfaction that comes from these things. Given concerns that younger workers are taking a more skeptical view of long-term employment with *any* organization, it is essential that intelligence agencies reinforce their appeal. The bureaucratic practices of the cold war period probably won't be attractive to this younger, highly educated, and technically adept generation.

The same general principle applies to the State Department, whose Foreign Service officers also have a huge role to play in overt HUMINT collection. Extensive and accurate diplomatic reporting enables clandestine collection programs to concentrate on those important national security objectives that can be achieved only through clandestine effort.

Although many of the skills required during the cold war era remain relevant for case officers of the present and future, others are new, or at least more important, given the nature of terrorists and international criminal networks. The target having changed from the Soviet Union/Warsaw Pact to terrorists, nuclear proliferation, and rogue states, the CIA must be ready to reexamine its traditional case officer profile. Former DCI Robert Gates recognized this when he complained to a reporter in 1999 that the CIA's screening tests—psychological and otherwise—make it very hard for those with extraordinary talents to get in. Gates told the reporter about the need for Azeri speakers and his delight when the agency found a candidate fluent in Azeri. But the individual "didn't write English very well . . . and he was rejected because he didn't pass our English test." Gates commented that he had thousands of people who wrote English, and no one who spoke Azeri.[10]

A quality essential in a good case officer is willingness to take risks. The activities involved in recruiting and working with agents, or acting unilaterally in difficult, maybe even dangerous environments, can present extraordinary risks. Officers have to be comfortable with what that entails: the ability to assess risk, reduce it when possible, overcome threats, and bring an operation safely home.

In their risk taking, operations officers must be confident that they have the support of their supervisors. But they do not always have such support, particularly when political events or personalities intrude into the collection program. Operational reversals rightly call for review or investigation, and sometimes in such circumstances the reviewers or investigators concentrate with brilliant hindsight on what they imagine the case officer should have known, instead of acknowledging what the circumstances were at the time. Mistakes must be identified and corrected, but investigators and reviewers need to assess the facts and circumstances known at the time by the officer in the arena, not what should have been known in a perfect world.

A sophisticated operational program understands risk, exploits it, and, when problems develop, seeks to refine or correct risk without looking for scapegoats. Several observers, including former CIA employees, have complained that CIA officers are too cautious and not willing to take risks. While these critics were making these charges, CIA officers, along with U.S. military intelligence and Special Forces personnel, were in Afghanistan overthrowing the Taliban and taking out significant al-Qaeda cells, seeking and providing vital source-protection information to U.S. forces in Iraq, and working terrorist targets in such dangerous places as Pakistan and Southeast Asia. CIA and military officers are not averse to taking risks. If the use of penetration and "sleeper" agents increases, even longer-term risks will be assumed.

There is some merit in these criticisms of risk aversion when it comes to the effects of former DCI John Deutch's 1995 order addressing the recruitment of persons who might be guilty of human rights violations. While they did not prohibit the recruitment of such sources, the Deutch guidelines, according to contemporary published reports, required field case officers to get waivers from very senior levels in CIA headquarters before recruiting agents with a history of assassinations, torture, or serious criminal activities.

The problem, of course, is that any good source on terrorist operations will fit the description of the unsavory individual whose recruitment the guidelines are designed to delay, if not prevent. Terrorists and their supporters are involved in human rights violations. And even though, under the Deutch guidelines, CIA officers did not abandon their duty to pursue sources who could report on terrorism, it is reasonable to assume that their efforts suffered a "chilling" effect. Operational tempo is bound to slow when scrutiny is going to be sharper, and when case officers know that colleagues have been reprimanded for actions dating back many years, as happened in 1995 under Deutch.

Surprisingly, Deutch's guidelines remained in force until almost a year after September 11, until George Tenet lifted them in 2002. Douglas Jehl of the *New York Times*, reporting in May 2004, quoted former CIA general counsel Jeffrey Smith about the matter. "In retrospect," Jehl reported, "Mr. Smith said he regarded the guidelines as a mistake." Acknowledging that the CIA is now encouraging case officers to take risks, Smith said that the guidelines demonstrated "the folly of trying to manage intelligence activities by looking at scandals in the rear view mirror. We tried to fix one problem and created another one."[11]

Skill sets and risk propensities that are factored into hiring profiles clearly need to be brought up to date. The CIA was created in 1947 on a military model, with the hierarchical structure expected in such an organization. CIA officers enter the service as the functional equivalents of second lieutenants and, through achievement and length of service, advance through the ranks. The CIA expects its officers to sign up for a career and rewards them appropriately. But the Directorate of Operations sets an upper age limit of thirty-five for entering officers — a limit with both positive and negative consequences. For example, there is very little opportunity for lateral entry by persons who have achieved success or experience in other fields before deciding to join the agency. As a result, CIA officers, like their military counterparts, experience common education, training, assignment procedures, and reward for merit. They share a common culture, which is valuable when working as individuals and as team members. Colleagues and supervisors know what to expect from each officer.

But the new demands on HUMINT suggest that this traditional approach needs a closer look. The agency suffers when it refuses men and women of achievement with exceptional language skills, accomplished in business and other fields, and familiar with overseas environments, merely because they are over the age limit. Such persons could perhaps serve for a limited time, five years or so, to bring fresh perspectives and needed talent to the job.

This is not to suggest that the agency should rush to rely more extensively on lateral-entry employees with established careers. Such people have been acculturated in other employment models and may not easily share the ethos of the CIA. They may expect higher relative pay and allowances than career agency employees, accustomed to U.S. government pay and allowance scales.

Still, there are strong reasons in the current world situation for U.S. intelligence agencies to examine their employment restrictions. Former Deputy Director of Operations James Pavitt, in his testimony to the 9/11 Commission in April 2004, said in regard to the war on terrorism that "the American people . . . must realize that this is a campaign with no clear end in sight, a campaign that will continue to demand our attention, and our partners' assistance, and the full commitment of American resources and tools of national power."[12] That warning suggests that the CIA, too, could examine its practices and be ready to find fresh organizational as well as operational ways to initiate more flexible personnel screening, clearance, and hiring procedures.

Retention and Promotion

A key factor in any organization's system is who gets promoted, and how. Organizations want to show that their systems are based on merit and that employees are evaluated fairly with respect to each other. The method of measuring merit is crucial to employee satisfaction and retention. The high value of expertise among operational cadres and employee morale remain important personnel issues for the future. What metrics does the organization use, are they used fairly, who judges those metrics, and do those metrics indeed represent what the organization most clearly should reward?

Metrics will no doubt have to vary according to mission. For example, case officers recruit and manage spies. The number of recruitments would therefore appear to be the most important measure of success. But comparative skills are not easily evaluated by a simple numerical system. The quality of the spy is also an important consideration, as are the difficulty in finding, assessing, manipulating, and recruiting him or her and the difficulty of working in operational environments that present totally different challenges to spy operations. Moreover, spy recruitment is often a team effort, and the quality of the reports officer or a targeting specialist from the directorate of intelligence may heavily influence the importance of source reporting. How, then, does one rank the skills at which case officers need to excel and evaluate them in an individual case? The system needs to pick the best, both to reward them and to provide incentives to others.

Agent recruitment and handling should be considered near the top of the list, but managers need to ensure that they also reward those who protect systems and sources, devise and implement new operational procedures or techniques, and acquire valuable intelligence information for policymakers (even if the officer did not recruit the reporting spy). Successfully managing a productive clandestine asset is itself a very high accomplishment.

The U.S. House of Representatives, in the Intelligence Authorization Act for Fiscal Year 2003, expressed concern that CIA and DIA had not taken appropriate steps to emphasize regional expertise and language capability in HUMINT. "Currently individuals get promoted based on their broad and often general knowledge in wide-ranging areas while those who would appear to stay focused on one area or even country are not, in the Committee's view, being given the credit or rewards deserved."[13]

Case officers have for a long time faced this dilemma: whether to concentrate on one language, one nation, or one area and risk being considered too narrow in their focus, or whether to become a generalist, prepared to serve equally well in Europe, Asia, Africa, and the Middle East. Not surprisingly, experience suggests that language fluency and detailed knowledge of an area's political, cultural, and historical situation, and thus its operational context, are more likely among those who spend years in an area than among those who have two- or three-year tours. Longevity in place may be worth rewarding as an investment in the future.

Furthermore, employee evaluations must do more than reward those who are producing quality intelligence and developing fresh operational approaches; they must also identify employees who fall short. Ignoring lackluster achievement deprives the U.S. government of return on investment, lulls an employee into thinking he or she can get by without full effort, and risks alienating officers who do work to their fullest capacity.

Substandard performance in many instances can be improved if supervisors work vigorously to identify the situation, provide necessary counseling or retraining, and establish benchmarks to measure progress. The more serious issue is how to confront inferior performance that resists improvement. Employees who have accumulated significant sensitive information may be a risk if suddenly fired. Intelligence managers often handle this problem by transferring such employees to another office or program, a solution that only passes the problem along to someone else and may also exacerbate it. Confronting cases where dismissal is the best solution requires taking a whole-team approach, in which operational, personnel, and security managers together assure that sound decision making minimizes the risk of adverse behavior.

Training: Ethics and Leadership

In a 1999 conversation with a *New York Times* reporter, former CIA general counsel Jeffrey Smith referred to a vital component of CIA personnel management and training: ethics. He said: "The management of the Agency must always worry about finding that extraordinary rare individual who has the talent to deal in the deceptive and manipulative and keep his or her own moral ballast." [14]

The ethical dimension of espionage and intelligence work is that much more important because of the secret nature of clandestine activity and the protections secrecy could afford wrongdoing. Training in ethics should be based on a framework that stresses moral reasoning, not case studies, as case officers and other intelligence professionals are often faced with ethical dilemmas when they are alone, for example when meeting an agent or engaged in a covert action, when there is neither opportunity nor time to seek guidance from superiors. Smith's concern about "moral ballast" might be a watchword for such training. Intelligence leaders have ethical responsibilities to understand the dangers and difficulties their employees face, to assign them to programs that truly reflect national security interests, and to assure that they have every opportunity to bring ethical issues to their supervisors.

Intelligence officers have an ethical responsibility to handle their agents in a way that protects sources as well. This is not just something that can be added on to other tasks or programs. It is at the core of the intelligence business, because of the responsibility that the case officer and his or her superiors bear on behalf of the recruited agent. A case officer's responsibility is to do everything possible to keep the agent alive and, if the agent is threatened, to remove him or her from danger. This not only fulfills the solemn promise to the agent but sets an example for others who may be considering whether or not to cooperate with American intelligence. As policy people and intelligence professionals debate such questions as the relative merit of "need-to-know" versus "need-to-share" approaches to teamwork, they must also remember that at the front of every successful HUMINT operation is a man or woman risking life and perhaps family members' lives to acquire that information.

The centrality of ethics to the HUMINT enterprise underscores the related requirement to foster sound leadership skills in all training programs. In intelligence organizations, as in any bureaucracy, strong leadership is a key factor in ensuring success. It does not grow naturally from the bureaucracy, nor do intelligence officers acquire it automatically through their work. While some men and women bring leadership skills to the job from their earlier experience, particularly from the military services, intelligence professionals are often placed in leadership positions with no prior experience of what is now demanded of them.

Leadership is not management, which is another skill. As is said in the armed forces, one does not manage men into combat, nor does one manage officers in a crisis. One leads them. Leadership means identifying and rewarding initiative and élan, even in the most junior officers. It also means ensuring that decisions are made when they must be. Not making a decision is itself a decision. Sometimes postponing a decision is necessary, but the actor must know that postponement is also a decision. General Colin Powell noted that a leader seldom has all the information he may think he needs to make a decision. Powell proposes that once he has between 40 and 70 percent of the information needed for a decision, he is in the zone for making a "gut" choice with a good probability of success.[15] Intelligence organizations must prepare their officers for leadership roles, provide them adequate training, identify those officers most capable of leading, reward them, and use their examples to influence others.

An illustration of leadership comes from the movie *Apollo 13*, when the crew faced monumental system failure and could not make the necessary repairs to ensure a safe return to earth. The Houston mission leader announced dramatically to his co-workers, "Failure is not an option." Of course saying it didn't make it so; but what then transpired in the film illustrates how leaders react under such pressure. First, the mission leader assembled a team, ensured that they correctly identified the problems, considered solutions, and queried them about what could go wrong. The mission leader instructed the crew in the spacecraft as to what to do. As the astronauts followed those instructions, the leader and his team followed up and reviewed them, making midcourse corrections as necessary.

Focusing on what is really important instead of what might be nice to do is a crucial leadership skill. In Iberia in 1812, Wellington complained to the British Foreign Office about instructions to provide an inventory of supplies and equipment. He responded that he saw two alternatives: "I shall pursue either one with my best ability, but I cannot do both: 1) To train an army of uniformed British clerks in Spain for the benefit of the accountants and copy-boys in London, or, perchance, 2) To see to it that the forces of Napoleon are driven out of Spain."[16] It is the leader's responsibility to recognize when action must take precedence over other obligations. Bureaucracy can get in the way of successful leadership and problem solving. The more layers between decision makers and action officers, and the more indirect their communication, the more likely it is that leadership skills will be sacrificed for management principles that may reward conventional practices rather than daring.

Leadership, often considered an innate talent, may also be a learned skill. It can be fostered by giving senior managers a larger perspective on their mission through broadening assignments and graduate education. The CIA in particular has been insular in this respect, in that few of its senior officers have had assignments outside the organization. The U.S. military, by contrast, has ensured that its rising officers take time off from their traditional assignments to study for graduate degrees. Within its own system of military colleges, the Defense Department provides those marked for advancement to senior positions with year-long programs of study, and study not just of military subjects but of how the military fits into the modern world. A significant number of military officers also have assignments in the Congress, the White House, and throughout the bureaucracy. This gives them valuable experience to take back to their military duties.

Intelligence officers given time away from their own profession to work in other organizations or pursue academic courses gain insights into their own work and how it relates in broader ways to national security issues. These officers would not be losing a year but serving the interests of their agency and themselves for the future, able to return to their jobs with fresh ideas and renewed motivation. To achieve this objective the CIA Directorate of Operations should ensure that its most promising senior officers, before assuming important leadership positions within the agency, work for one year (subject to cover considerations when necessary) in the FBI, DIA, or other Defense Department agencies, or the State Department, thus broadening the knowledge base of both the CIA officers and the host agencies.

Leadership can also be fostered by example. Leaders recognize the problems of "change overload" and yet face up to the new requirements that will drive collection and analysis. Leadership requires resisting momentary pressures that detract from the core essentials of intelligence programs. It means ensuring that intelligence agencies are sufficiently introspective about their activities, personnel, and organization that they can identify and correct deficiencies in a businesslike manner.

Leadership also means avoiding motivational gimmickry. Every now and again, in the CIA and other intelligence agencies, there is talk about low morale — an issue about which older and retired employees may have been less concerned. Secretary of State George Marshall, responding to a complaint about morale from a senior officer, told his senior staff, "Gentlemen, enlisted men are entitled to morale problems, but officers are not. I expect all officers in this department to take care of their own morale. No one is taking care of my morale."[17] A senior CIA officer, when asked by an officer why the senior had not complimented him on his work, said, "Good is what you're paid to be; you'll hear from me when you're not." Intelligence community leaders today could not satisfy their employees with statements such as these. But good leaders show employees that their morale stems in large part from their own success and satisfaction in their jobs, not from gratuitous pats on the back.

Employees today may be more skeptical about their supervisors and leaders than earlier generations were. But they will welcome leaders who help them to succeed in their mission. The leader must demonstrate credibility, the competence to foster growth in the individual employees, the willingness to listen to and experiment with new ideas, the ability to delegate authority, and the drive to challenge bureaucracy so that it supports officers in imaginative ways.

HUMINT is risky, and the investments made in it do not guarantee success. It is not a science, and serendipity and luck are hugely important in what success HUMINT collection has. The leader's job is to ensure that his or her officers are in position with all the skills necessary, that they focus on what is most important, that they have studied the target, and that they do everything possible to make their own luck.

Proposals

To a greater degree than ever, the American people, both directly and through their elected representatives, are focused on how American intelligence is organized and how well it is doing its job. They recognize that intelligence operations are of crucial importance to their lives and safety. Since September 11, 2001, terrorism and weapons of mass destruction have become household words.

Not surprisingly, proposals for transformation of U.S. intelligence agencies and systems are flowing out of this heightened public awareness. Outsiders demand it, and many insiders realize the need for it. Practices and organizational structures that at times have been successful, sometimes spectacularly so, failed to protect the United States on September 11 and did not provide adequate information about the weapons programs of Saddam Hussein's Iraq.

Intelligence managers, like those in other professions, are often reluctant to accept change. They often prefer to tinker around the edges, because change is difficult in busy times and intelligence work seems to become more demanding every day. When then-DCI Casey created the counterterrorist center (CTC) in 1986 on the grounds that counterterrorist work needed better-coordinated planning and action, with analysts working near operators, the more traditional components in the CIA's directorates of operations and intelligence saw it not as an opportunity but as a threat to their turf and the people they controlled. Years after the CTC was established, there was still unwarranted tension in its work with other agency components.

Resistance to change within the intelligence agencies needs to give way to the fresh examination of problems and failures. Intelligence officers need to study more thoroughly than ever what they are doing, how they are doing it, and what else needs to be done.

Taking a lesson from the military, the CIA ought to establish formal mechanisms for "after-action" reviews. Its review of the HUMINT on Iraq would have addressed the history of that program; the selection of personnel for it; the targeting of Iraqi and other individuals for recruitment; and the benchmarks that should have been established (or, if they were established, how they were used to set midcourse corrections on a program that senior CIA officials admit produced too few agents with significant access).

This kind of after-action review should not degenerate into scapegoating, finger pointing, or naming names. It should ensure that managers and leaders dealing with other hard targets, such as Iran and North Korea, have systems designed for success, the means to establish frameworks for espionage operations based on real examinations of other programs, and the data to adjust programs to maximize quality and ensure best practices. Other HUMINT managers should receive summaries of the practices that lead to success and reduce the risk of failure. Truly sensitive operational details need not be compromised in such disseminations.

Intelligence leaders and managers should develop, again using formal after-action studies, programs on how to hire, train, deploy, evaluate, and promote employees. For the most part, improving these systems does not depend upon legislation. It does require open and honest review and thoughtful, concerted action aimed at creating an agile work force. One way to increase the likelihood of success in this endeavor is to include at least one outsider, not a business consultant but a person of achievement in business, politics, or education in the review team. Such an outsider, having a fresh perspective, could ask questions that might not occur to those who are too close to the work.

A commitment to use the best results of these reviews would, of course, be essential. There is a strong tendency in American politics and government, faced with failure or crisis in an organization or program, to reorganize, to draw new lines, to seek quick fixes — or, alternately, to study the issue and prepare a report that no one will ever implement and few may even read.

It is difficult in any organization to transfer money from established programs to new initiatives. This is especially true in the U.S. government, which has the curious and perhaps outdated mechanism of building budgets from the base up. Each year executive departments and the Congress make the assumption that what was funded before — personnel, logistics, operational programs, and infrastructure — will continue at the same or increased levels, with relatively minor adjustments. Operational initiatives, when the Office of Management and Budget and the Congress agree, are then authorized and funded built on that base. Competition for so-called new money is intense, but chiefly between competing new initiatives, not generally between new initiatives and established programs.

Developing initiatives is a hallmark of CIA operations. Imaginative officers and leaders identify and recognize challenges and propose solutions. But they may pay too little attention to what needs to be cut or significantly altered within the base budget, thus freeing up money for new initiatives. It will be exceptionally daunting to do a thorough "scrubbing" of what is built into the intelligence base. But at a time when the whole makeup of American intelligence is under review and new threats to America loom, the scrubbing must be done. Here too intelligence professionals must draw on the experience of the best in the American private sector, which typically is more aggressive in organizational innovation than government bureaucracy can be.

Intelligence, HUMINT and other programs, will never get it all right or complete.

That is the nature of the world intelligence professionals work in. What they can ensure is that their work in informing policymakers and operational and military commanders is always focused on quality, accuracy, and integrity, using the best available integration of human and technical programs.

Notes

1. The cartoon was by Leo Cullum and appeared in the April 22, 2002, issue of the *New Yorker.*

2. James Pavitt, "Change and the CIA," *Washington Post,* August 6, 2004, A19.

3. Douglas Jehl, "Answering Call to Duty at the CIA," *New York Times,* May 11, 2004, A20.

4. Ibid.

5. Senator Carl Levin, speaking on September 13, 2004, Paul C. Warnke Lecture in International Security, Council on Foreign Relations, Washington, D.C.

6. Vice Chairman Lee Hamilton, talk given at International Spy Museum, as reported in Association of Foreign Intelligence Officers (AFIO), *Weekly Intelligence Notes,* May 10, 2004.

7. Steve Hirsch, "CIA Recruiting in High Gear," *National Journal,* August 29, 2003, 2636–37.

8. Ellen Laipson, vice chair, National Intelligence Council, "Foreign Language Training in the Intelligence Community," statement before Senate Governmental Affairs Committee, September 14, 2000, available at www.ndu.edu.nsep/.

9. Report of the Commission on the Roles and Capabilities of the United States Intelligence Community, *Preparing for the 21st Century: An Appraisal of U.S. Intelligence* (Washington, D.C.: U.S. Government Printing Office, 1996), as quoted in Richard L. Russell, "Intelligence Failures," *Policy Review* (February 2004), available at www.policyreview.org/feb04/russell.html.

10. Tim Weiner, "Spies Wanted," *New York Times Magazine,* January 24, 1999, 36.

11. Jehl, "Answering the Call to Duty."

12. James L. Pavitt, testimony before the National Commission on Terrorist Attacks upon the United States, April 14, 2004, available at www.9‑11commission.com/hearings/hearings10/pavitt_statement.pdf.

13. U.S. House of Representatives, *Intelligence Authorization Act for Fiscal Year 2003,* 107th Cong., 2d sess., 107–592 (July 18, 2002), 16.

14. Weiner, "Spies Wanted."

15. Quoted in Oren Harari, "Quotations from Chairman Powell: A Leadership Primer," *Management Review* 85 (December 1996): 34.

16. Sign posted in British government office, observed and copied by the author.

17. Quoted in Dean Rusk, as told to Richard Rusk, *As I Saw It* (New York: W. W. Norton, 1990), 131.

TWELVE   Intelligence and Homeland Defense

HENRY A. CRUMPTON

AMERICA'S HOMELAND will grow increasingly vulnerable to foreign threats unless the U.S. government develops robust intelligence systems to complement homeland defense and thereby promote sustainable homeland security. These threats emerge both from a growing array of sophisticated enemies and from the consequences of modernization and globalization. The gravest danger rests at the nexus of existential terrorism and weapons of mass destruction (WMD). It is possible, even probable, that in the near future a single operative armed with a bioweapon could infiltrate the United States, that a terrorist group could simultaneously detonate radiological "dirty" bombs in American cities, or that a nation-state could wage war against the U.S. infrastructure, perhaps even through cyberspace.

Traditional macrodefensive efforts, including heavy reliance on law enforcement as intelligence collectors inside the homeland, will provide only partial protection and in some cases may actually be counterproductive. The U.S. government can combat these foreign threats through accurate, timely, and relevant intelligence, enabling homeland consumers of intelligence to respond with precision and speed. The success of U.S. intelligence at home will increasingly depend on a new form of internal collection against specific enemies and on the forging of a deep partnership with the American nation, from local police forces to private enterprise. To this end U.S. intelligence must learn more about American institutions as partners while seeking to educate the American people about intelligence.

U.S. intelligence and the American public must also both resolve a paradox. Intelligence must adhere to fundamentals of its craft, secretly protecting sources and methods while reaching beyond its traditional boundaries to build interdependence with American society. For their part, American citizens need to guard law and democracy fiercely, while seeking to understand and support internal intelligence collection against foreign enemies. If it is done correctly, domestic intelligence will not undermine democracy or civil liberties; if not, intelligence structures will devolve into pseudosecurity mechanisms that serve the ruling powers at the expense of citizens.

The challenge, perhaps, is less about striking a balance between intelligence and civil liberties than about building synergy between the two. U.S. intelligence needs cohesive leadership plus a centralized and locally networked domestic structure in order to work with the American public in identifying foreign threats. This domestic structure needs deep, interdependent links with the U.S. external intelligence structure. And U.S. intelligence and the American public need the understanding, support, and leadership of the executive branch and the Congress — not cynical political machinations that undermine intelligence efforts and partnerships. The threat to the United States is unprecedented, and so must be the transformation — in fact, the construction — of U.S. intelligence in the homeland and its relationship with the U.S. government and the American people.

Homeland Vulnerability

The *9/11 Commission Report* flatly states that America "has many vulnerabilities."[1] This is because the nation-state system is evolving into a more complex structure, novel threats are emerging, more sophisticated weapons are available to adversaries, modern infrastructure is more fragile, and America relies on a deeply fractured and rudimentary domestic intelligence community, one that has growing but still insufficient links to the U.S. external intelligence systems.

Given the growing complexity and interdependence of our political world and the rising importance of nonstate actors, the U.S. government will be less able to control global entities and events that spawn threats to the homeland than it has been in the past. During the cold war and earlier, we could engage nation-states in diplomacy and forge treaties. The United States could fight, army against army. We could wage small wars and counterinsurgencies elsewhere — in Central America, the Philippines, Asia, and the Barbary Coast.[2] With secure borders, large oceans as moats, and an offensive capability abroad, the United States could shield the homeland. That era is over. In reference to the post–September 11 national security environment, John Lewis Gaddis remarked that the terrorist threat "exposes a level of vulnerability that Americans have not seen since they were living on the edge of a dangerous frontier 150 years ago."[3] This historical context made the terrorist attacks of September 11 even more shocking.

This increased vulnerability is in part an unintended consequence of a unipolar world and globalization. Professor Eliot Cohen contends that as the world's sole superpower, the United States poses as a colossus engendering a "swirl of hostility . . . to all it embodies, and, indeed, to the very fact of its existence."[4] Growing pockets of disenfranchised global citizens will seek retribution against the status quo, often symbolized by the United States. Philip Bobbitt, in *The Shield of Achilles*, argues that the nation-state system is undergoing a transformation. He believes that five global trends are responsible: the recognition of universal human rights, the growth of WMD, the rise of transnational threats, the emergence of a global economic regime, and the development of a global communications network.[5] All these elements point toward a vastly different, shifting world that presents unprecedented challenges, often in the form of dire threats and, at the same time, unique opportunities.

Globalization, of course, also brings many benefits, including enhanced economic integration and unprecedented growth, cyberwebs that facilitate U.S. communication with a global community, and transportation channels that bring millions of foreign businessmen, tourists, students, and future citizens to the United States.

While these are overwhelmingly positive trends for the United States, they also present new opportunities for hostile forces to hitch a ride on these growing interdependent links and slip undetected into the country. Unlike our enemies of old — battalions backed by artillery — these new enemies are individuals or teams armed with inconspicuous weapons, maneuvering secretly within the massive, complex global exchange. From an intelligence perspective, these threats can be viewed as microtargets. Examples include a pathogen carried by an international traveler, an encrypted computer virus breaching the border through cyberspace, a team of terrorist insurgents infiltrating the country, one at a time, by posing as legitimate businessmen, or homegrown enemies that gravitate to the inspiration or money of a foreign power. In a global society an idea or an inspiration — be it Jeffersonian democracy or terrorist ideology — respects no boundary; witness al-Qaeda's recruitment of American, European, and Australian citizens.

Some of these microtargets are possessed by a ruthless, destructive determination that magnifies the threat and defies conventional countermeasures. These enemies wage asymmetric war, relying heavily on terrorist tactics. Their target is not necessarily the U.S. military but also the American infrastructure and people. They seek to use terror as a political weapon, but not for traditional geopolitical gain such as territorial sovereignty. Instead, groups such as al-Qaeda view terror as both a means and an end. Terror establishes their identity, and the more America suffers, the more their identity and success grow. Such threats are generally not manifested in conventional conflict, where intelligence means calculating the traditional enemy's order of battle, where gross force needs gross intelligence. There can be no treaties in this type of terrorist war. At the tactical level, there can only be specific identification and specific action to capture or kill the enemy. Counterterrorism strategy, by contrast, encompasses a much broader set of objectives: vanquishing enemy leadership, denying sanctuary, and addressing the root causes of terrorists' discontent by employing all the tools of statecraft — especially an effective overarching foreign policy.

The magnitude of the threat grows in direct proportion to the destructive force and the value of the target itself. If armed with WMD or if leveraged with U.S. infrastructure, such as hijacked aircraft as missiles, terrorists can wreak massive economic and political havoc. The worst scenario may involve the use of a viral weapon. The destructive force of nuclear, radiological, or chemical weapons in the hands of a terrorist group could be catastrophic yet contained, while a biological attack with a contagious pathogen against which we have few or no defenses could kill vast numbers of Americans. Recall the bubonic plague, which killed one-third of Europe's population in the fourteenth century, probably exacerbated by Mongol invaders catapulting infected corpses into besieged cities.[6] Modern terrorists devoted to existential conflict seek to inflict similar destruction, and the means to do so are multiplying.

In his 2004 "worldwide threat" briefing to Congress, the director of central intelligence (DCI) asserted that al-Qaeda views the United States as its main enemy and sees the use of WMD as a "religious obligation."[7] According to the captured mastermind of the September 11 attacks, al-Qaeda leader Khalid Sheik Mohammed, al-Qaeda also sought to deploy the bioweapon anthrax in the United States: "the mission was assigned to a Malaysian named Yazid Sufaat, who has a degree in biochemistry from California State University." Fortunately, Sufaat was captured in Malaysia in 2001 and remains in custody there.[8] What other al-Qaeda operatives, with similar education and familiarity with the United States, have undertaken similar missions? Such threats challenge current U.S. intelligence capabilities and by extension U.S. strategy itself. Microtargets now pose macrothreats to the homeland.

While nonstate terrorists may pose the most immediate threat, state actors also seek to develop and enhance their microsized, macroimpact weapons. And, of course, these weapons can be aimed at homeland infrastructure and American civilians. Retooled foreign militaries, such as a nuclear North Korea, have growing capabilities. The isolated and desperate leaders in Pyongyang may opt for terrorist tactics as they have in the past, such as the assassination of seventeen South Korean government officials, including the foreign minister, in a 1983 Rangoon bombing.[9] Iran, the primary sponsor of Hezbollah's terrorist apparatus, has invested billions of dollars in a clandestine nuclear program for more than twenty-five years, and Iran cooperates closely with North Korea in nuclear weapons development.[10] Intercontinental ballistic missiles are not the only delivery system. Consider a nuclear weapon stored in an automobile's trunk or sealed in a container delivered to the port of Los Angeles, and note that only 2 percent of all cargo containers entering U.S. ports are inspected.[11] The human and economic consequences of a nuclear explosion in the port of Los Angeles would be incalculable.

A computer virus is another microtarget for U.S. intelligence. Potentially hostile intelligence and military services, such as China's Ministry of State Security and the People's Liberation Army (PLA), may launch cyberattacks to subvert U.S. capabilities. One emerging PLA doctrine, articulated in a 1999 document titled "PLA Colonels on Unrestricted Warfare," stresses the need to develop and deploy cyberweapons and other nontraditional means against China's enemies. The doctrine argues that China's offensive capabilities should be aimed at an enemy's infrastructure, such as its computer systems, banking infrastructure, and trade mechanisms.[12]

This type of doctrine blurs the line between military and civilian weapons and targets.

And it is more than a doctrine. According to the *Wall Street Journal,* in an article quoting a retired aide to the PLA's chief of staff, "the PLA has opened an information warfare center and is training special units in these skills."[13] As early as 1997 the U.S. Defense Advisory Board warned that U.S. computer systems are so vulnerable that the country could face "an electronic Pearl Harbor" and that Russia and China have advanced "info-war" capabilities.[14] The National Security Agency (NSA) "estimates that more than 120 countries now have computer attack capabilities."[15]

Highly sophisticated intelligence services, even those of erstwhile allies, may infiltrate and subvert the domestic political system by recruiting key U.S. politicians or their staff. A single foreign operative planting a seductive seed, cultivating and ultimately influencing or controlling a U.S. political leader, presents a microtarget with potentially long-range destructive consequences, especially if this covert action is linked to a foreign strategic plan that includes terrorist tactics. Foreign intelligence services also seek to infiltrate private U.S. companies and steal secrets across the spectrum: military, scientific, trade, cyber, banking, and biographical assessments of individuals selected for recruitment. According to the annual Central Intelligence Agency (CIA) report to Congress, in 2003 more than ninety foreign countries operated offensively within the U.S. homeland.[16] Given its growing power and sophisticated espionage, developed over millennia, China probably poses the gravest counterintelligence and potential military threat to America, and this threat is increasingly unconventional. Russia also works with great professionalism to steal and exploit America's secrets.

Yet nations are not the only entities that pose a counterintelligence threat. In a globalized world in which nonstate actors assume an ever-greater political role, they also assume intelligence tactics heretofore practiced only by nations. Hezbollah, al-Qaeda, narcotraffickers, Nigerian crime syndicates, and other nonstate enemies seek intelligence about U.S. plans and intentions aimed against them, or information on U.S. infrastructure as a target for exploitation or destruction. How foreign powers, both state and nonstate, leverage stolen American secrets presents a growing threat, whether using American technology to create more lethal weapons or attacking vulnerabilities in a fragile national infrastructure, which grows more dependent on the microchip and the rest of the world every day.

The Military Homeland Security–Industrial Complex: A Defensive Posture

Although America is vulnerable and has much to defend, there has been some progress since September 11, 2001. The United States initiated "the most extensive government reorganization in the past fifty years"[17] in creating the Department of Homeland Security (DHS). The 9/11 Commission has raised the issue of intelligence and homeland defense to a new level of national consciousness. But in reference to homeland security, President George W. Bush is correct: this is only "a beginning."[18]

There are bound to be false starts and wrong turns. To minimize them, the United States should resist the lure of using conventional measures against unconventional threats. The American penchant for tangible macrodefense, technological answers, and big-money projects can generate an appetite in a military-industrial complex that expands to include homeland security. This American cultural proclivity, reinforced by special interests searching for the billions in profits to be made from the DHS and other intelligence agencies, will pose major challenges in the absence of strong leadership and a clear vision.

That is a general caution; there are two other areas of concern. First, excessive defense brings unintended negative consequences that may far outweigh the expected benefits. Infringement of civil liberties, expanded military authority at home, restrictive immigration policy, and a siege mentality are examples. Second, the comfort of conventional defense provides a false sense of security and in fact may detract from the pressing need for a domestic intelligence structure aimed at hostile foreign targets. This is an important distinction: the U.S. does not need a domestic intelligence structure for domestic suspects; this should remain the exclusive purview of U.S. law enforcement. Domestic-based foreign intelligence collection and analysis are critical to constructing the right defense. This domestic foreign intelligence structure, of course, can also enable offensive law enforcement initiatives in the homeland and U.S. responses abroad, ranging from diplomatic incentives to military strikes. In other words, capital expenditure for tangible defensive measures is required, but not at the expense of an overall offensive/defensive strategy driven by intelligence.

The July 2002 "National Strategy for Homeland Security" outlines the mission of the DHS, an organization of twenty-two separate agencies with approximately 180,000 employees and a security mission defined primarily as defensive. The strategy document notes that "intelligence and law enforcement agencies focus on the detection and disruption of each individual threat," and that the DHS should "focus on longer-term protective measures."[19] The crux of this strategy rests on correlating America's vulnerabilities with foreign threats and developing countermeasures.

This general strategy as defense is sound, but the new threats also warrant a discussion of offense. The *9/11 Commission Report* implies this in some of its recommendations, such as the recommendation that America engage the Muslim world and build coalitions.[20] The United States can develop this strategy in part through foreign intelligence collection in the homeland, a critical step in forging a synergistic security policy for U.S. leadership of the global community. But foreign intelligence at home is more than the "detection and disruption of each individual threat."[21] Foreign intelligence collection, at home and abroad, is a means of understanding the enemy and the battlefield, whether in America's heartland, the east African littoral, or cyberspace. Foreign intelligence continuously updates the map that can guide U.S. decision makers, who ultimately must choose the routes we take and the weapons of statecraft we employ.

Many defensive measures, of course, are required and will be accepted. Americans will abide by new security procedures at airports. They will spend their tax dollars on enhanced security at laboratories, ports, and sporting venues. They will embrace more effective law enforcement. Americans may even sacrifice some degree of privacy for greater protection; the country has a history of such sacrifice, although we must not risk "jettisoning [civil liberties] when we get scared."[22] The Patriot Act and other legislative measures, such as the Intelligence Authorization Act for Fiscal Year 2004, have sparked serious debate among responsible citizens.[23] This is good. Americans will not and should not tolerate any abrogation of due process of law; Americans can be proud when the judiciary reminds the executive branch of this sacrosanct responsibility.[24]

Americans are wary of a role for the military in homeland security and law enforcement, as legislated in the 1878 Posse Comitatus Act.[25] Yet with the establishment of the Department of Defense (DoD) Northern Command, the U.S. military increasingly views the homeland in terms of its operational command. If the country faces assault from foreign armies, Northern Command will have a clear mission, but against emerging microthreats at home its role raises more questions than answers.[26] Mobilizing thousands of troops may indeed help after a calamity, but it will not prevent microtargets from slipping into the country, a new domestic battleground to which the U.S. military is poorly suited. Of course, the NSA, the National Reconnaissance Office, and the National Geospatial-Intelligence Agency, which currently exist under the Defense Department umbrella, should function outside it if they are intended to serve the nation's broad strategic needs and not just departmental intelligence agencies.

Elements of the U.S. military other than Northern Command have sought to assert their role in the homeland. The *Wall Street Journal* reported that the Defense Department appears to be seeking a "domestic spying and enforcement" role, in part to defend military installations within the United States.[27] The U.S. military's traditional counterintelligence elements, especially those of the individual services, do have legitimate and critical roles in protecting the integrity of their personnel and operations, as well as those of civilian defense contractors. But the military's offensive foreign intelligence collection, and investigative measures in the homeland against a broader range of targets, could pose constitutional questions. The Defense Department's now defunct total information awareness (TIA) program, under the direction of retired admiral John Poindexter, is an example of military expansion into domestic intelligence and law enforcement.[28] And the Pentagon continues to explore other avenues to accomplish the TIA goals of U.S. data-mining, as noted in a March 2004 report from the Defense Department's technology and privacy advisory committee.[29] Moreover, the U.S. military should focus on foreign conflict, given its full and crucial agenda abroad, as reflected in the ninety-one major deployments or engagements of the twenty-five years *prior* to September 11 and the strain on resources caused by the ongoing engagements in Afghanistan and Iraq.[30]

An excessive defensive posture in the homeland by any U.S. department or agency can weaken the nation, and not only in terms of civil liberties but also in opportunities lost. Immigration policy is one example. Harsh visa restrictions deny America the world's best minds, who come here to work in universities, laboratories, and business. An executive of one American company complained that these restrictive measures have undercut the company's international recruiting strategy and forced it to move more research and development programs abroad.[31] Criticizing immigration barriers to international intellectual power, former CIA director and current president of Texas A&M University Robert Gates wrote, "protecting our security requires more than defensive measures; we have to win the war of ideas, too. . . . Beyond the risk to economic, scientific, and political interests, we risk something more: alienating our allies of the future."[32] America has always welcomed the world's risk takers, those with the courage to immigrate and to contribute to American wealth and innovation. The Statue of Liberty symbolizes this great ideal.

America's strength depends upon the free flow of ideas and people throughout the nation and the world. This is partly what Joseph Nye has called America's "soft power . . . getting others to want what you want . . . [it] rests on the ability to set the political agenda in a way that shapes the preferences of others."[33] America cannot forfeit soft power in the pursuit of hard-power answers. An overly defensive posture hinders America's receptivity, impedes global partnership, and ultimately makes the homeland weaker. Robert Hutchings, former chairman of the National Intelligence Council, wrote that the current war against terrorism is "not a clash of civilizations, but rather a defense of our shared humanity and a search for common ground, however implausible that may seem now."[34] The United States should indeed think more about the "defense of our shared humanity," especially if our current defense means blocking the world's best minds from joining American universities or the world's best businessmen from contributing to American enterprise.

Homeland defense must be measured and calibrated, through the use of quality intelligence, to preserve and to enhance American "soft power." The complexities and interdependence of the world requires that we adapt. The world will respond to America's soft power, to America's understanding and empathy, in tandem with U.S. statecraft's hard power, applied with precision when and where necessary.

Law enforcement — not military force or covert action — is statecraft's hard-power tool in the homeland, and intelligence must support this customer. The DHS in particular faces a monumental mission. These law enforcement challenges will grow, given the global, interdependent, and vulnerable position of the United States. The DHS and all U.S. law enforcement need focus sharpened by intelligence. For example, the DHS must know where to increase border patrols and where to concentrate customs investigations to defeat strategic threats in the form of microtargets.

Of course, the DHS cannot attempt to screen all entries into the country with equal vigor, not when approximately 330 million noncitizens enter the United States every year and "another 500,000 or more enter illegally without inspection across America's thousands of miles of land borders."[35] The terrorist operative posing as an illegal immigrant in search of work is a far more important target than the thousands of illegal immigrants seeking greater economic opportunities. Without intelligence, the DHS will never have the resources to defend America. This is not only an operational imperative but a budgetary one: intelligence enables homeland defenders to use limited resources effectively and saves taxpayer dollars.

This reliance on heavy defensive measures in the domestic arena has another negative aspect: it clouds the value of intelligence. If the growing military-industrial–homeland-defense complex believes that high-tech, macrodefensive, and ultraexpensive projects alone can defend America, then in a world of finite resources there will be fewer resources and less focus given to intelligence. As the world's only superpower, the United States must exercise discipline and restraint in its power and depend upon superior intelligence to know where, when, and how to unleash its strength, whether abroad or at home.

Domestic Intelligence: An Allergy Needing a Remedy

In her testimony before the 9/11 Commission, National Security Advisor Condoleezza Rice noted that America is allergic to domestic intelligence.[36] Historically, America has responded to the need for a domestic foreign intelligence capability in four ways. First, it has ignored it. The 2002 "National Strategy for Homeland Security," a sixty-nine-page document, devotes less than a single page to intelligence, and there is no specific mention of domestic intelligence collection.[37] The second response has been to seek ad hoc arrangements, without clear authority or oversight, which has led to political abuse as documented in the 1975 Church Commission report. The creation of the congressional oversight committees in the mid-1970s and the passage of the Foreign Intelligence Surveillance Act in 1978 have restored public confidence that any special arrangements regarding domestic collection are regulated and lawful.

The third response has been to allow small numbers of CIA officers to collect foreign intelligence in the United States, through the recruitment of "foreigners living temporarily in the U.S." and "voluntary debriefings of Americans."[38] The resource allocation for this effort, however, has often fallen far short of collection needs, especially since September 11. In April 2004 the CIA deputy director of operations, James Pavitt, said that the CIA has fewer operations officers deployed globally than the Federal Bureau of Investigation (FBI) has special agents assigned to New York City.[39] And of that small number, only a tiny fraction conduct foreign intelligence collection in the homeland through cooperative programs with U.S. citizens and businesses against legitimate foreign targets.

The fourth response rests on an assumption that law enforcement can substitute for intelligence. Raw numbers highlight this flawed notion. The FBI has approximately 2,800 special agents assigned to cover national security issues.[40] On April 14, 2004, FBI Director Robert Mueller testified that the FBI had produced 2,648 intelligence reports since September 2001.[41] That translates into roughly one report per special agent in the thirty months following September 11. This is not a criticism of the FBI, the world's premier law enforcement agency. The successful capture and prosecution of many of the al-Qaeda terrorists who attacked U.S. embassies in east Africa in 1998 is a prime example of FBI success. The criticism is of those who expect a law enforcement organization to transform itself into an intelligence service working against foreign interests, and complete such a transformation quickly. The 9/11 Commission's recommendation that the FBI do just this, with no overlapping support or external checks, is particularly flawed.[42] This unreasonable expectation puts the FBI at a disadvantage and America at risk. We cannot ignore the need for intelligence at home, create ad hoc and unsupervised entities, rely exclusively on the externally focused CIA, or substitute law enforcement for intelligence. For the world's greatest intelligence power, the allergy to domestic intelligence needs an urgent remedy.

To understand our new enemies and the world in which they operate, the U.S. should construct an intelligence system within the domestic arena. Currently we rely on a large, amalgamated community of law enforcement groups, from the FBI to immigration customs enforcement to local police departments. There are more than 700,000 law enforcement officers in the United States. But many are bureaucratically isolated, because few of the country's 87,000 jurisdictions are capable of receiving a classified report or submitting one to national security decision makers.

Nevertheless, some positive initial steps have been made. The FBI has championed a good model with the joint terrorism task forces (JTTF) in more than eighty locations. The JTTFs are examples of local law enforcement cooperation, with modest CIA participation, where information is often shared.[43] The JTTF offers a venue for field cooperation, but not necessarily for broad and deep intelligence collection and dissemination. Many JTTF members are hindered by a lack of training, technical connectivity, and incentives to collect intelligence in the strategic global context. Understandably, a JTTF focus is usually more local than global; the emphasis is seldom on recruiting sources that can provide globally relevant intelligence. From the law enforcement perspective, a source provides tactical information to prevent a crime or evidence to support a prosecution.

But intelligence collection is not about enforcing law, though it must abide by U.S. laws. Rather, intelligence collection seeks to enable law enforcement officers and all other intelligence consumers to do their jobs. And intelligence and law enforcement can be mutually supportive. In the summer of 2004 CIA briefing teams traveled throughout the U.S. to sensitize JTTF members and local law enforcement to the al-Qaeda threat and to learn about potential international leads. According to the *New York Times,* few of these local police chiefs and sheriffs had "ever met an intelligence analyst or ever received more than a dry, often uninformed intelligence bulletin containing information already made public by the news media."[44] These briefings are another step in the right direction, seeking to bridge gaps in understanding, garner mutual confidence, and thereby boost cooperation between law enforcement and intelligence.

There are other major differences between intelligence and law enforcement. Law enforcement depends upon the coercive power of the law; police use their legal power to secure witnesses and obtain information. Although testimony can be voluntary and often is, it is also required under the law. Even information collection through consensual interviews poses obstacles for law enforcement officers, because those interviewed may respond fearfully to police as symbols of coercive power. Witness the response of one American Muslim leader to the widespread cold-call interviews performed during the summer of 2004: "the FBI agents went out of their way to be low-key but the Muslims were fearful when they got the calls, worrying that they were under investigation themselves."[45]

By contrast, intelligence officers seek to forge selective partnerships and recruit sources based primarily upon collective opportunities. While manipulation of an individual's vulnerabilities or coercion may be used in the recruitment of foreign sources, these methods often fail, and when they succeed they are usually of limited and fleeting value. Some targets, of course, understand only this kind of power, rooted in intimidation and fear. But far more often, even among recruitment targets in terrorist camps, common ground and collective opportunities present the means of recruitment. Intelligence officers acquire the best information when theses sources want to cooperate, need to contribute, and seek positive reinforcement for their efforts. Prospective sources need support and confidence, not intimidation, if they are to perform the dangerous tasks requested of them. CIA operatives in the United States have no law enforcement power, a valid restriction, and they must be transparent with American people and institutions regarding their affiliation and objectives. The essence of intelligence success in the homeland is voluntary cooperation, with law enforcement playing a complementary role and employing legal intrusive means against bona fide suspects. Intelligence relationships, contrary to popular literature, are built more on interdependence and trust than on coercion.

Another critical difference is that law enforcement officers gather hard truth in the form of evidence; prosecutors and courts require this. Intelligence covers the gray areas and makes estimates, which is what the customers demand. Former senior CIA official John MacGaffin, testifying before the 9/11 Commission in December 2003, made a clear distinction between gathering information and collecting intelligence. "While the FBI correctly highlights its unmatched ability to *gather* evidence—and with it information," he noted, "there is nonetheless a National Security imperative which distinguishes *intelligence collection* from a similar, but different, function found in Law Enforcement. *Gathering* which is not driven or informed by specific, focused National Security needs is not the same as *intelligence collection* as the DCI and the Intelligence Community understand the term. This collection is accomplished not incidental to law enforcement, but by conscious, specifically targeted, operational clandestine espionage activity, whether technical, human, or a combination of both."[46]

This fundamental difference between gathering information and collecting raw intelligence stymies greater intelligence effectiveness within the homeland. Evidence cannot be a substitute for intelligence. Intelligence cannot be a byproduct of evidence, nor can it be subjected to the rigorous yet ponderous process required by courts. Any system that imposes time constraints and degrees of separation between a source and a customer dilutes, distorts, and impedes intelligence. While by definition incomplete and imperfect, raw intelligence needs to be at least minimally contextual, reasonably accurate, purposefully relevant, and, especially, timely. And what about the other information not acquired, or dismissed because it did not conform to the needs of the evidentiary case? What about the need to query sources based not on the needs of the prosecutor but on the needs of the broader intelligence consumer base?

When asked about the differences between the FBI and the CIA, an experienced special agent confided that the CIA thinks globally, the FBI, locally. He added that the CIA serves the customer, while the FBI serves its law enforcement mission. In other words, the FBI primarily collects information as evidence to support a law enforcement agenda. The CIA collects information as intelligence to support the law enforcement officer, the soldier, the diplomat, the policymaker, and other valid customers. The CIA can collect intelligence for its own covert action, but covert action by definition is an extension of foreign policy, subject to executive direction and legislative oversight.

Deputy Director of Central Intelligence John E. McLaughlin remarked that the CIA is the "only intelligence agency that has the following four characteristics: It has global focus. It is multidisciplinary. It integrates all intelligence sources. And, perhaps most important, it is nondepartmental: that is, it does not create or advocate policy. Nor is it a component of a department that does."[47] National intelligence must serve all national customers, and not fall under the potentially constrictive influence of a single agency, department, or bureau. While departmental intelligence services do provide critical national intelligence, their product is written primarily for their respective departmental masters. This is true for law enforcement, military, and diplomatic reporting.

Another difference between law enforcement and intelligence rests in the context of domestic politics and associated publicity. Law enforcement is political. Some sheriffs and judges run for office. Politicians appoint district attorneys and judges. Law enforcement leaders, for understandable political and operational reasons, hold press conferences routinely. In this manner they seek recognition, which helps them gain more resources and educate the public. Intelligence officers, by contrast, must steer clear of domestic politics because of the potential threat to civil liberties and the risk that politics will have undue influence on the product, which should be apolitical and unbiased. Moreover, the intelligence business demands secrecy for the protection of sources and methods, which conflicts with domestic political demands for publicity.

Nevertheless, despite these major differences, there are compelling reasons for law enforcement and intelligence to cooperate, to complement each other, and to overlap. First and foremost, the primary customer for domestic foreign intelligence on near-term threats is law enforcement. And law enforcement information can provide invaluable leads for intelligence officers. The intelligence collector and the law enforcement consumer, therefore, must strive for more than information sharing; they must seek interdependence.

The United States should construct a domestic *security intelligence* corps, with its own budget and personnel, preferably as part of the FBI but under the explicit direction of U.S. intelligence leadership. This would require interdependence from the outset. Moreover, there would be more political acceptance, and a quicker development of the corps, than if a totally new organization assumed command or if the FBI exercised exclusive control. To that end, and in the interest of speed, this FBI entity should be under a separate operational command, heeding the instructions of the director of national intelligence. This separate organization should be responsive to all U.S. intelligence customers, conforming to the priorities of a national intelligence strategy. A separate intelligence organization, but within the FBI, would enable the requisite symbiotic relationship with fellow FBI law enforcement colleagues in the homeland. A command structure linked to the CIA would enable interdependence between this new entity and the CIA, to include an acceleration of cross-training and cross-assignments.

One manifestation of this hybrid organization would be a uniquely strong field operative, a special agent–case officer (SACO). The SACO would be required to pass both the FBI's course at Quantico and then the CIA's course at the "Farm." Working for his direct employer, the FBI's intelligence entity, the SACO could collect against a terrorist suspect in the United States; working for the FBI's law enforcement arm, he could testify in court; and, detailed to a CIA station abroad, he could operate under an alias and in disguise in the Middle East. This kind of flexibility reflects U.S. needs in global counterterrorism operations. This domestic intelligence service, personified by the SACO, would combine the best of FBI law enforcement, to include authorities and homeland knowledge, with the best of CIA practices, to include tradecraft and global reach.

A similar concept, but one with less emphasis on FBI/CIA interdependence, surfaced in July 2003, when eight former U.S. intelligence and law enforcement officials published a proposal for a more aggressive human intelligence (HUMINT) capability in the *Economist*.[48] The 9/11 Commission endorsed a similar but far weaker version of this recommendation. The WMD Commission's March 31, 2005, recommendation for a national security service in the FBI is on the mark.[49]

Others, such as former Deputy National Security Advisor James B. Steinberg, believe that a separate intelligence entity in the FBI will fail because special agents do not value intelligence, preferring to pursue criminals, the job for which they were trained.[50] This doubt underscores the need for a separate FBI career service, staffed by SACOs, under the supervision of intelligence community leadership and linked directly to the CIA. Moreover, this new organization should focus sharply on a *security intelligence* mission, one limited to counterterrorism, counterintelligence, international organized crime, and cybercrime, especially in the homeland. These four national security concerns play to the FBI's relative strengths. And these types of enemies in the homeland are especially susceptible to the law enforcement tools wielded by the FBI.

Broader foreign intelligence acquired within the homeland, however, should be the responsibility of the CIA, given its relative strength and expertise in such areas as international economics, foreign policy, war, and emerging strategic technologies. And this is lawful. "Under Executive Order 12333, signed by President Ronald Reagan, the CIA is permitted to secretly collect significant FI within the U.S. if the collection effort is not aimed at the domestic activities of U.S. citizens and corporations."[51] In other words, this expanded system would stress comparative advantages while creating checks and balances within a collaborative, overlapped structure. And the checks and balances are critical, because they keep us honest: the exclusive law enforcement arm of the FBI should have no intelligence functions, just as the CIA should have no law enforcement authorities. The SACO, operating in a global law enforcement and intelligence environment, would gain strength from both the FBI and the CIA while operating under the constraints of each. The SACO would need to have exceptional capabilities in order to earn the respect of both the FBI and the CIA and to understand and accept the relevant authority, whether in the law enforcement or intelligence realm.

Another challenge for intelligence in homeland defense is to bridge the gap between domestic and foreign operations. Existing links need to be reinforced and new links forged. Simply put, in addition to the development of SACOs in a new FBI subagency, more CIA officers need to be working with the FBI's JTTFs and elsewhere in the homeland. More than ever, enemy activity in Karachi could have immediate consequences in Houston. Solutions to new threats may be found in the networked dialogue between intelligence collectors and law enforcement personnel deployed throughout the world. An FBI legal attaché in Latin America, a CIA officer working with a JTTF, a DHS/immigration agent on a U.S. border, a SACO in an FBI field office, and a military special operations officer detailed to a CIA team in Afghanistan could collect and connect pieces of the puzzle that reveal the next attack. Transnational threats are growing, and we must rapidly expand our emerging interdependent structures of intelligence and link them to customers, especially in the homeland. The 9/11 Commission noted that "the American homeland is the planet."[52] U.S. intelligence systems should conform to that reality.

The United States needs to identify and track increasingly destructive microenemies in the homeland and abroad and then constantly fuse, analyze, and feed the intelligence to homeland customers for action — especially at the local level. The National Counter Terrorism Center and the terrorist screening center are examples of where information is shared and stored, but building responsive databases and producing analysis for the decision makers are insufficient. U.S. intelligence collectors need operational analysis and targeting guidance so that collection can be refined. U.S. law enforcement, as a critical intelligence customer, needs both raw intelligence and analysis, to provide leads in context and to support strategic planning. Other domestic customers, among them municipalities, civil defense, public health, scientific research, and cybersecurity, need intelligence to suit their particular needs. For their part, these customers will need to learn the strengths and weaknesses of intelligence, providing requirements and feedback while demanding the best service possible.

It is critically important that, while information and analysis must be centralized, management of collection operations must not. The field command, whether in the homeland or abroad, should have the responsibility and authority to act in a timely and decisive manner — using local intelligence/expertise, global intelligence/analysis pushed from the center, and strategic guidance from leaders oriented to strategy.

Reinforcing or building organizations that can fuse and analyze intelligence and set and manage strategic policy goals across departmental fiefdoms is essential. But conferring upon any central entity the "authority of planning the activities of other agencies," as recommended by the 9/11 Commission, could prove operationally calamitous.[53] The 9/11 Commission further notes that North Atlantic Treaty Organization (NATO) joint planning serves as a good example for a proposed national counterterrorism center; yet NATO needs months of preparation before taking action, as in the Balkan or Afghan deployments.[54]

Fast, flexible microtargets demand intelligence coverage often measured in minutes and hours, not weeks or months. Field command of intelligence operations, within strategic parameters set by the policy center, can provide such coverage. In the homeland or abroad, field intelligence operational command should be reinforced, not undermined by distant managers encumbered by multidepartmental conflict and compromise. The United States should encourage intelligence and law enforcement leaders in the field to build interdependent networks among themselves and to act decisively, rather than harness them to a distant, centralized, layered system of operational planning. We must, of course, hold field leaders to the highest standards, with reasonable oversight reinforced by rewards and sanctions. Consumers of intelligence require quality and timely intelligence, and this intelligence must serve the nation's security, not just the political masters who confuse risk management and effectiveness with personal control.

Partnership with America

U.S. intelligence and other American institutions need each other to defend the homeland through a strategic partnership, one that matches America's potential with foreign intelligence collection opportunities at home and abroad. And this must lead to greater responsiveness and warning from U.S. intelligence to the homeland. The United States is itself now the target, the battlefield, and in some cases, paradoxically, a resource for its enemies. Because America grows more vulnerable, U.S. intelligence and security organizations must be prepared to warn more Americans and American institutions about threats. Because of conflicting levels of compartmentalization, mangled bureaucratic responsibilities, and convoluted information flow, the U.S. government's warning system is ineffective. In January 2004 the CIA Center for the Study of Intelligence issued a conference report, "Intelligence for a New Era in American Foreign Policy," an excellent example of the intelligence partnership with American academia that called the warning function of U.S. intelligence "chaotic."[55] America is vulnerable and the U.S. intelligence and security organs must embrace the responsibility for collection and warning.

U.S. intelligence faces daunting tasks and major obstacles to its expanding mission. It needs help from the American private sector. While threats are growing, so are the collective opportunities to defend the homeland. American private interests and U.S. intelligence need to explore and to capitalize on these opportunities together. While an increasing number of Americans appreciate the need for U.S. intelligence, especially after September 11, 2001, U.S. intelligence and the U.S. government more broadly sometimes fail to appreciate the value of strategic intelligence partnerships with greater America. In the technical arena this is less often the case, given the government's dependence on American industry for satellites and other intelligence tools. A good example of this kind of partnership can be seen in the success of In-Q-Tel, "a private, independent, enterprise funded by the Central Intelligence Agency . . . to identify and invest in companies developing cutting-edge technologies that serve United States national security interests."[56] U.S. intelligence analysts might work with academia, and intelligence collectors might seek cover or background information from American business.

But there is more to be done. In a strategic sense the U.S. private sector can help guide U.S. intelligence into unfamiliar areas and new ways of doing business. This kind of collaboration makes sense for at least four reasons. First, U.S. intelligence needs to cover more topics than ever previously considered, and the number of topics is grow-ing. Subjects include WMD, delivery systems, biotechnology, telecommunications, foreign tribal cultures, demographics, diseases, environmental geography, and many others. Even if such topics range from the core target, such as a terrorist cell or a foreign espionage ring, the environment in which they operate, the tools and weapons they employ, and the objects of their focus are things that U.S. intelligence must understand. These topics are increasingly interrelated, as one would expect in a global society. U.S. institutions and individuals can collectively cover far more ground in these vast areas of knowledge than the U.S. intelligence system can on its own.

Second, the complexity is growing. A scientist or engineer understands bioweap-ons or nanotechnology far better than an intelligence officer does, yet U.S. intelligence must understand and appreciate these things as elements for collection. No matter how smart or studious the intelligence officer, the scientist who works such complex issues every day will always have the greater expertise.

Third, because of globalization, foreign links to the United States are growing, and microtargets can bury themselves in this flow across U.S. borders. U.S. intelligence needs help in understanding these links and uncovering enemy forces. U.S. intelligence can exploit these links, with the help of American citizens, to reach enemy targets abroad.

Fourth, the world evolves rapidly and America usually sets the pace. Through a part-nership with public- and private-sector decision makers at home, U.S. intelligence can stay better informed about security requirements and vulnerabilities and move faster to meet them. Enemies, especially nonstate microtargets, are exceedingly quick and flexible. U.S. intelligence must stay ahead of the enemy.

Reaching out to America's private sector to forge a partnership may prove challenging, but not because Americans are naturally unreceptive. On the contrary, despite some am-bivalence and misunderstanding, the number of leads and overtures from private Ameri-can citizens to the intelligence community and law enforcement is significant and grow-ing. America wants to find and destroy al-Qaeda and other enemies who are planning the next horror. In 2003 more than 130,000 Americans applied for employment with the CIA. Much of the U.S. public, now under increasing threat, supports U.S. intelligence. In fact, a growing percentage of CIA reports originate in a broad range of American partners. The challenge rests more with U.S. intelligence, under informed executive leadership and constructive legislative oversight, to understand private-sector partners and construct the right interdependent links. Political scientist Seymour Martin Lipset has described America as "the most religious, optimistic, patriotic, rights-oriented, and individualistic" nation in the world.[57] U.S. intelligence needs to capitalize on the strong character of the nation. And the nation needs to support U.S. intelligence.

We must also guard against infringing America's civil liberties. In 1781 Alexander Hamilton wrote that nations, "to be more safe, at length become willing to run the risk of being less free."[58] During the Civil War President Abraham Lincoln suspended habeas corpus for security reasons. During World War II President Franklin Roosevelt incarcerated thousands of Japanese Americans. Given this history, modern commentators are understandably concerned about the balance between civil liberties and security requirements, and many imply that the latter are, ipso facto, draconian and Orwellian in scope and intent. There is an assumption that civil liberties and intelligence inhabit a finite world and play a zero-sum game, where one must be sacrificed for the good of the other.

Sun Tzu, the ancient Chinese military strategist, provides a different view. In *The Art of War,* he stresses the paramount importance of intelligence and remarks, "the expert in using the military subdues the enemy's forces without going to battle."[59] In other words, superior intelligence combined with superior strategy can achieve victory with less cost on the battlefield, perhaps avoiding battle altogether.

Superior intelligence and superior strategy, founded on a partnership with greater America, can also achieve victory with minimized cost to civil liberties at home. Superior intelligence is, among other things, precise. Such precision, attained through networks of well-placed sources and sharp analysis, is not about spying on Americans. Such precision, in fact, is the opposite of intrusive surveillance systems. When working effectively with American institutions and private citizens, intelligence can be more precise than it can without such a partnership. Its collection need not violate civil liberties, but rather can present an opportunity for Americans to exercise those civil liberties through a free and conscious decision to cooperate, to uncover enemies in the homeland and abroad.

In *Carnage and Culture,* Victor Davis Hanson stresses that free will, and the creative independence and initiative that go with it, are the keys to the Western way of war.[60] The same argument can apply to intelligence operations; when successful, they encourage disciplined creativity, initiative, and risk taking. These traits will become more important in the fast-paced networked campaigns against the transnational enemies of the United States. All of these qualities are rooted in free will. Sun Tzu wrote, "He must use the principle of keeping himself intact to compete in the world. Thus, his weapons will not be blunted and he can keep his edge intact."[61] U.S. intelligence and homeland partners must seek to keep America "intact" and not allow enemies to diminish the collective character, the source of collective strength that provides the sharpest weapon: a citizen imbued with patriotism, independence, and free will. Those engaged in this debate need to explore the symbiosis of civil liberties and intelligence operations, not just the potential conflict.

There are daily examples of tactical cooperation: the FBI establishes a surveillance post in a business across the street from a suspect terrorist, the CIA requests intelligence from a business executive after a trip abroad, DHS inquires about infrastructure security, or

NSA signs a contract for a technical upgrade. The onus is on U.S. intelligence and security leadership to think more deeply about the strategic value of nongovernmental American partners in the intelligence collection arena — and not just domestically, but globally. And U.S. intelligence must determine who in America to engage, and how.

The executive branch, with congressional oversight, needs to support such a strategic partnership. This is a tough assignment in an environment wracked by multiple wars, tactical domestic emergencies from one threat after another, and rancorous internal debate about the future of U.S. intelligence. These things seem to compress time, crowding out any deep strategic discussion about a partnership with America. Commissions, including the bipartisan 9/11 and Iraq WMD Commissions, have recommended a centralized and powerful chief of U.S. intelligence, now the director of national intelligence. The focus of such commissions has been to rationalize the roles and responsibilities of the various U.S. intelligence organs and develop and implement a cohesive national intelligence strategy. Absent from this discussion, however, is the role of greater America as an intelligence partner, as part of the strategic offense, not just a potential victim in need of warning.

Such a partnership will not work without the support of government leaders, yet this support is often conspicuous for its absence. In fact, U.S. leaders have at times restricted the debate in favor of immediate political benefit. Members of the intelligence oversight committee will acknowledge CIA success in private and encourage more risk taking, while castigating the agency in public. When asked why, one committee member admitted that such public criticism plays well with constituents. This cynical attitude undermines the nation's efforts to strengthen its intelligence system and misinforms Americans. U.S. leadership cannot expect tactical intelligence perfection, especially in a context of strategic policy failure.

In-Q-Tel President Gilman Louie asked why CIA officers seem willing to risk their lives but not their careers. The main reason, perhaps, lies in their greater fear of humiliation than of death. In an enduring detrimental political environment of blame and shame, intelligence officers may be induced to avoid professional responsibility, yet they routinely embrace physical danger. Some intelligence veterans admit privately that the political pitfalls of Washington are more daunting and more complex than the bullets and bombs in Iraq or Afghanistan. Intelligence officers need support and leadership from their political masters. Most American ambivalence toward intelligence is rooted in genuine ignorance, unchallenged by self-absorbed U.S. intelligence agencies and distorted by politically driven misinformation. The nation can no longer afford this destructive dynamic.

U.S. intelligence does not have all the answers, nor do American institutions and private citizens kept at a distance. Together, however, we have a chance to chart the global terrain, uncover enemy forces, defend the homeland, and realize our potential to create a safer interdependent world.

Notes

All statements of fact, opinion, or analysis expressed are those of the author and do not reflect the official positions or views of the CIA or any other U.S. Government agency. Nothing in the contents should be construed as asserting or implying U.S. Government authentication of information or Agency endorsement of the author's views. Where appropriate, this material has been reviewed by the CIA to prevent the disclosure of classified information.

1. National Commission on Terrorist Attacks upon the United States, *The 9/11 Commission Report: Final Report of the National Commission on Terrorist Attacks upon the United States* (New York: W. W. Norton, 2004) (hereafter *9/11 Commission Report*), 364.

2. Max Boot, *The Savage Wars of Peace: Small Wars and the Rise of American Power* (New York: Basic Books, 2003). The author provides a historical perspective on America's many small military engagements throughout the globe over the course of two centuries.

3. John Lewis Gaddis, "Kill the Empire! (or Not)," interview, *New York Times Book Review,* July 25, 2004, 23.

4. Eliot Cohen, "History and the Hyperpower," *Foreign Affairs* 83 (July–August 2004): 58.

5. Philip Bobbitt, *The Shield of Achilles: War, Peace, and the Course of History* (New York: Anchor Books, 2002), xxii.

6. *New Standard Encyclopedia,* vol. 3, s.v. "black death."

7. Statement by DCI George J. Tenet, U.S. Senate Select Committee on Intelligence, "The Worldwide Threat 2004: Challenges in a Changing Global Context," August 24, 2004, available at www.cia.gov/cia/public_affairs/speeches/2004/dci_speech_02142004.html.

8. Robert Block and Glenn R. Simpson, "U.S. Tries to Divine al Qaeda's Next Move," *Wall Street Journal,* July 12, 2004, A4.

9. "North Korean Agents in Rangoon 1983," Armed Conflict Events Data, available at www.onwar.com/aced/data/kilo/korea1983.htm.

10. Terrence Henry, "Nuclear Iran," *Atlantic Monthly* (December 2003): 44–45.

11. John Mintz and Mike Allen, "Homeland Security, a Polarized Issue," *Washington Post,* June 27, 2004, A6.

12. Federation of American Scientists, "China Nuclear Forces Guide," 1999, available at www.fas.org/nuke/guide/china/doctrine/unresw1.htm. This article is based on a translation and summary by the U.S. Embassy in Beijing (November 1999) of the book *Unrestricted Warfare,* by Qiao Lian and Wang Xiangsui, both PLA colonels.

13. Charles Hutzler, "The New Weapon in China's Arsenal: Private Contractors," *Wall Street Journal,* July 16, 2004, A6.

14. Graeme Browning, "Infowar," *National Journal* (April 22, 1997), available at www.govexec.com/dailyfed/0497/042297b1.htm.

15. Ibid.

16. CIA Counterintelligence Report to Congress, 2003 (classified, except paragraph cited).

17. Office of Homeland Security, "The National Strategy for Homeland Security" (2002), available at www.whitehouse.gov/homeland/book/nat_strat_hls.pdf.

18. Ibid., vii.

19. Ibid., 18.

20. *9/11 Commission Report,* 375.

21. Ibid.

22. Michael Ignatieff, "Lesser Evils," *New York Times Magazine*, May 2, 2004, 48.

23. Andrew P. Napolitano, "Repeal the Patriot Act," *Wall Street Journal*, March 5, 2004, A14.

24. *Rumsfeld, Secretary of Defense v. Padilla et al.*, 03–1027 Sup. Ct. (2004).

25. Robert Block and Gary Fields, "Is Military Creeping into Domestic Spying and Enforcement?" *Wall Street Journal*, March 9, 2004, B1.

26. Christopher Bolkcom, Lloyd DeSerisy, and Lawrence Kapp, "Homeland Security: Establishment and Implementation of Northern Command," *Congressional Research Service* (2003), RS-21322.

27. Block and Fields, "Is Military Creeping into Domestic Spying?"

28. Gina Marie Stevens, "Privacy: Total Information Awareness Programs and Related Information Access, Collection, and Protection Laws," *Congressional Research Service* (2003), RL-31730, 3. TIA, sponsored by DoD's Defense Advanced Research Projects Agency (DARPA), was designed as a broad data-mining program of information in the United States.

29. Department of Defense, technology and privacy advisory committee, *Safeguarding Privacy in the Fight against Terrorism* (2004).

30. Center for Defense Information, "U.S. Military Deployments/Engagements 1975–2001," available at www.cdi.org/issues/USForces/deployments.html.

31. Conversation with author, Washington, D.C., summer 2004.

32. Robert Gates, "International Relations 101," *New York Times*, op-ed page, March 31, 2004.

33. Joseph S. Nye Jr., *The Paradox of American Power: Why the World's Only Superpower Can't Go It Alone* (New York: Oxford University Press, 2002), 9.

34. Robert Hutchings, "X + 9/11," *Foreign Policy* (July–August 2004): 72.

35. *9/11 Commission Report*, 383.

36. Condoleezza Rice, "Transcript of Rice's 9/11 Commission Statement," CNN.com, May 19, 2004, available at www.cnn.com/2004/ALLPOLITICS/04/08/rice.transcript/.

37. Office of Homeland Security, "National Strategy for Homeland Security," available at www.whitehouse.gov/homeland/book/nat_strat_hls.pdf.

38. Dana Priest, "CIA Is Expanding Domestic Operations," *Washington Post*, October 23, 2002, A2.

39. David E. Kaplan, "The No-Good, Down-Home Spookhouse Blues," *U.S. News and World Report*, August 2, 2004.

40. John MacGaffin, testiony before the National Commission on Terrorist Attacks upon the United States, December 8, 2003, 5, available at www.globalsecurity.org.

41. Robert S. Mueller, director of the FBI, testimony before the National Commission on Terrorist Attacks upon the United States, 10th Public Hearing, April 14, 2004, available at www.9-11commission.gov/hearings/hearing10.htm.

42. *9/11 Commission Report*, 423–24.

43. Interview with Gary Bald, FBI special agent, in "Ask the FBI: The Joint Terrorism Task Force," *USA Today*, June 20, 2003, available at www.usatoday.com/community/chat_03/2003-06-20-bald.htm.

44. David Johnston and Douglas Jehl, "CIA Sends Terror Experts to Tell Small Towns of Risk," *New York Times*, July 18, 2004, A13.

45. Mary Beth Sheridan, "Interviews of Muslims to Broaden; FBI Hopes to Avert a Terrorist Attack," *Washington Post*, July 17, 2004, A8.

46. MacGaffin, *Security and Liberty,* 4.

47. John E. McLaughlin, "DDCI Address to Business Executives for National Security Annual Forum," June 23, 2004, available at www.cia.gov/cia/public_affairs/speeches/2004/ddci_speech_06242004.html.

48. Robert Bryant et al., "Special Report: America Needs More Spies—Intelligence and Security," *Economist,* July 12, 2003, 44. This article, written by six former senior U.S. intelligence officials, outlines a similar plan for a new domestic intelligence and security service.

49. Commission on the Intelligence Capabilities of the United States Regarding Weapons of Mass Destruction, "Report to the President, March 31, 2005," chapter 10, recommendation 1, available at www.wmd.gov.

50. Dan Eggen, "Intelligence Unit for FBI Is Proposed," *Washington Post,* June 4, 2004, A21.

51. Priest, "CIA Is Expanding Domestic Operations."

52. *9/11 Commission Report,* 362.

53. Ibid, 406.

54. Ibid.

55. CIA Center for the Study of Intelligence, "Intelligence for a New Era in American Foreign Policy," conference report, September 10–11, 2003 (Washington, D.C.: Central Intelligence Agency, 2004), 3.

56. In-Q-Tel, "Corporate Overview," available at www.in-q-tel.org/news/attachments/Factsheet_MAY%202004.pdf.

57. Seymour Martin Lipset, quoted in Michael Barone, "A Place Like No Other," *U.S. News and World Report,* June 28, 2004, 38.

58. Alexander Hamilton, "The Consequences of Hostilities between the States," *Federalist Paper No. 8* (1781).

59. Sun Tzu, *The Art of War,* trans. Roger Ames (New York: Ballentine Books, 1993), 111.

60. Victor Davis Hanson, *Carnage and Culture* (New York: Anchor Books, 2001).

61. Sun Tzu, *Art of War,* 112.

THIRTEEN Intelligence Analysis

Management and Transformation Issues

MARK M. LOWENTHAL

FORMER DIRECTOR OF CENTRAL INTELLIGENCE (DCI) Richard Helms once told the staff of the House intelligence committee that the Central Intelligence Agency (CIA)'s Directorate of Operations was "where you got into trouble." Helms explained that the very nature of the directorate's work — espionage and covert action — was inherently more dangerous both to intelligence officers and politically. Thus there is no little irony in the fact that the recent controversies surrounding the intelligence community have largely centered on *analytical* issues: the degree of warning prior to the September 11, 2001, terrorist attacks and the issue of Iraqi weapons of mass destruction (WMD). At the same time, most of the recommendations that have been made recently to "reform" (that is, reorganize) U.S. intelligence have had little to do with managing intelligence analysis better or responding to the supposed "lessons" of September 11 and Iraqi WMD as they relate to analysis.[1]

We therefore have a serious disconnect between what seems to be the agreed set of "problems" within the intelligence community and the solutions being offered to solve them. This is not difficult to understand, as it is much easier to legislate structure than it is to legislate process, especially when dealing with something that is largely intellectual in nature. We are thus left with the impression that if there are to be "reforms" in intelligence analysis they will come largely despite or after the passage of any legislation, and largely on the impetus of the intelligence community itself. This may not be entirely bad. A number of legitimate issues regarding analysis that predate both September 11 and Operation Iraqi Freedom have been highlighted by the recent controversies. These issues include:

- Deriving useful long-term lessons from September 11 and Iraq;
- Examining the use and utility of national intelligence estimates;
- Current versus long-term intelligence;
- Competitive versus collaborative analysis; and
- Crafting a reasonable standard for evaluating intelligence.

But underlying these better-known issues, to which we will return at the end of this chapter, are two sets of equally important issues that reinforce analysis across the board: managing the process of analysis and managing the analysts themselves. If these two issues are not handled successfully—often on a daily basis—then the outcome of the issues derived from September 11 and intelligence failures on WMD in Iraq will not matter. The desired goal, finished analysis that is of use to policymakers, will not be achieved as often as desired unless attention is paid to both issues. It is important to understand the general parameters of these two management tasks—what the stresses and strains are and what the range of choices are for responding to them—before one can delve into the specific analytic issues that receive more political attention today.

Managing Analysis

If we accept the idea that intelligence is a process of which analysis is only one phase (albeit the most important one), then we can readily understand that all other phases of the process—requirements, collection, processing and exploitation, production, dissemination, and feedback—have to be strong in order for analysis to be successful.[2] Each phase of the intelligence process presents its own unique challenges, but these are beyond the scope of this chapter. Recognizing and remembering this interdependence will have to suffice.

It is also important to remember that at all times intelligence analysis is being managed at multiple levels: the head of an agency (the head of the CIA, the director of the Defense Intelligence Agency, or DIA); the head of analytic components (the CIA's deputy director of intelligence; the assistant secretary of state for intelligence and research); or the head of an analytic unit, either broad (the CIA's Office of Terrorism Analysis) or narrow (such as a regional or functional division, branch, or group). To a certain degree, the analytic issues described below are applicable at each level of management. They will tend to aggregate as one goes higher in the organization, requiring repeated tradeoffs.

The key issues in managing analysis include understanding policymakers' intelligence needs, allocating analytic resources, and selecting analytic products. These are, of course, interconnected. The decisions in each area affect and are affected by the decisions in the other areas.

Policymakers' Intelligence Needs

Simply put, there are not enough analysts to cover every conceivable issue. There has to be some basis on which managers decide where to put their resources. This is often called "priorities," which actually has two components: policymakers' needs and intelligence requirements. Policymakers' intelligence needs are not necessarily the same thing as formal "intelligence requirements" as defined in U.S. policy documents. Such intelligence requirements are longer-term expressions of areas or issues that policymakers have determined to be of importance or of interest. Although intelligence requirements should be the subject of review on a regular basis and also may change, they are more strategic in nature. Policymakers' intelligence needs, on the other hand, may have a more current emphasis and may be at some degree of variance with intelligence requirements.

For example, terrorism and WMD proliferation are possible intelligence requirements. But if the president is about to travel overseas for an important negotiation, or there is an election or a coup in a major state, then the policymakers' needs are somewhat different. Therefore, analytic managers must have an understanding of the longer-term intelligence requirements (whether they have been stated explicitly or not) as well as planned or unplanned events that will also need to be analyzed.

It is also important to keep in mind that policymakers will react to events simply because they are of interest, and this can result in tasks as well. These are often, although not always, expressed in the course of morning briefings, which most cabinet-level and senior departmental policymakers receive.

Therefore, there is a recurring demand on analytic managers to determine which issues are going to require analysis and which are not. Events that can be anticipated (trips, negotiations, elections) are obviously less stressful than those that cannot. In those cases, some analysis can be prepared in advance, easing the burden as the event nears. But events that either are not or cannot be anticipated (a coup, a surprise attack) put a different kind of stress on the analytic management system.

Again, one must keep in mind that we are describing analytic management decisions that take place at multiple levels within the intelligence community, at larger and larger aggregations as one goes up within the organization. More senior levels may simultaneously question or alter decisions made at lower levels regarding which policymaker requirements and needs receive attention.

The key challenge in this phase of analytic management lies in ensuring that the right issues or areas receive attention. There is tension between current and long-term needs and requirements. As noted above, intelligence "requirements" tend to be more strategic and therefore long-term. Policymaker "needs" tend to be more immediate and therefore more current.

Intelligence analysts and analytical managers have said for decades that they are most interested in producing long-term strategic analyses. But the reality of intelligence analysis has always come out differently. The competition between current and long-term analysis has always been difficult, with the advantage most often going to current intelligence. This is understandable given the immediacy of these issues for the policymaker. There is another factor as well. Policymakers consistently express little interest in certain types of strategic analysis. The onus for the relative emphasis given to current versus longer-term intelligence does not lie entirely with the policymakers, however. The reality is that *both* groups of participants in the process, policymakers and intelligence officers, tend to emphasize current intelligence to meet policymakers' needs.

An important recent development has been the increase in Congress's role as an intelligence consumer, not just as the recipient of briefings or of analyses produced for executive-branch policymakers, but as an intelligence customer in its own right. This development raises a host of management issues. First, the intelligence agencies are part of the executive branch. Their primary raison d'etre is to support executive policymakers. Managers may face a choice between serving executive policymakers and serving Congress, either when both branches want intelligence on a single issue or when both branches require intelligence on issues that may not be identical but that call on the same groups of analysts. Neither policy group will be inclined to wait. The natural instinct of the intelligence community will be to serve the executive first, knowing full well that Congress may inflict some sort of penalty as a result. (We are talking about Congress as a unified entity when, of course, it is divided by parties, one of which will be supporting and one of which will be attacking the president and his policies a great deal of the time.)

Analytic managers recognize the importance of Congress both for political reasons and as the source of all future funding. Thus there are strong inclinations to be responsive to Congress. Congress's interests will often (but not always) parallel those of the executive, although Congress (including members who tend to support the president) may want a slightly different question analyzed. Analytic managers also recognize that some members may use intelligence analysis as a means of taking issue with executive-branch policies or decisions. This will obviously put the intelligence community in an awkward position. The separation of powers notwithstanding, there is no graceful or politically acceptable way for the intelligence community flatly to refuse a congressional request. Should congressional demands for unique intelligence support increase (as they are likely to do), analytical managers may have to choose between satisfying either executive-branch or congressional needs on a timely basis. Some members of Congress will probably accuse the intelligence community of "politicizing" intelligence by refusing to be responsive. The issue will become politicized even if the motives originally were not.

Analytic Resources

Analytic resources are an important component in managing analysis, although they may not be directly related to the decisions noted above regarding policymakers' needs. This again reflects the dichotomy between intelligence requirements, which can be planned for, and unexpected situations or short-term needs.

Let us return to the situation described above. Terrorism and WMD proliferation are intelligence requirements. They are long-standing and long-lasting issues that are of importance to a broad set of policymakers at all levels. Therefore, analytic managers make sure that they have some level of effort on hand to respond to these issues. Suppose the president has a foreign negotiation coming up. Analysts with expertise in the countries he will be visiting and the bilateral issues likely to arise can begin working in advance on analyses that will support the president and his party on the trip. These analyses will include background profiles on foreign leaders as well as background papers on the nations and issues. Suppose there is an election scheduled in a major country. Analysts working on that country are also preparing, and perhaps also writing about possible outcomes and their effects in advance of the election itself. And then a coup occurs, creating instability in a nation where many Americans reside; a major international health crisis occurs somewhere; a world leader dies unexpectedly.

It is important to understand that there is no reserve analytic capability. There are no analysts "sitting on the bench," waiting to be called upon. All analysts are engaged. This simple fact reduces the manager's choices greatly. Where are the analysts coming from to support the unexpected event? There are actually two questions being asked at this point: Which issues can be set aside or given less support, at least for a short period? Which analysts have the greatest expertise for the unexpected issue?

There are never complete lulls in the intelligence business, although there are periods that are less stressful or less demanding than others. Much depends, again, on the degree to which increasing or suddenly changing analytical demands can be anticipated. But much also depends on the knowledge and expertise of the analytic workforce and the ability to tap its knowledge and expertise as needed.

Another crucial point that must be understood is that there is a gap between the *requirement* that the intelligence community "know something about everything" (as a senior policymaker once put it) and the community's *ability* to do just that. This ability is sometimes called "global coverage," which is a dangerously misleading concept. There will always be issues or nations that receive little or no attention. This has always been true. But when analytic managers talk about sustaining "global coverage," they inadvertently create the false impression that each issue or nation can be adequately analyzed on demand. This is not so and it never has been. Indeed, it can be argued that talk about "global coverage" is actually harmful because it creates a false impression of capabilities that may be found wanting when called upon.

At the same time, however, the intelligence community has no ability to decline to analyze an issue. The community cannot say either "We don't do that issue" or "We have no ability to do that." *Someone* has to answer the mail, although the situation may not be optimal. Again, much depends on who is in the analytical corps and how much is known about them. To be sure, there have been instances in which intelligence offices have resisted shifting resources to an issue that they held to be less important, or have resisted expanding the circle of policy offices that they served. Even in these cases, however, the ultimate result has most often been to expand support. This will become an increasing problem as the Department of Homeland Security (DHS) is more firmly established and grows as a customer. Indeed, one senior intelligence official mused that at some point DHS may come to rival the Defense Department in terms of its intelligence-support requirements. Assuming that there is no higher authority that will deny requests for intelligence support in the post–September 11 world, the problems of intelligence managers will simply increase.

The "who" issue depends both on who gets recruited and on what their experience is at the time of recruitment or as acquired on the job. Recruitment is somewhat problematical as it is largely a "seller's market," that is, you can only hire the people who show an interest in the job. Agencies can and do advertise when they have specific needs, and they send recruiters to colleges and universities, but neither of these methods guarantees that people with the desired skills will respond.

This has changed slightly with the creation of the Pat Roberts Intelligence Scholarship Program, or PRISP. Named for the chairman of the Senate Select Committee on Intelligence (SSCI), this pilot program gives the intelligence community money to recruit against specific critical needs by offering scholarships that must be repaid by eighteen months of service for each year — up to a maximum of two — of financial support. Each analytic component receives a certain number of positions and dollars for recruitment. Students cannot apply for these scholarships, which are offered by recruiters. The expectation is that most PRISP recruits will stay in the intelligence community once their required period of service has been completed.

Analysts' experiences will also vary. It is highly unusual for any analyst to stay with only one or two issues for an entire career. As will be discussed in more detail below, analysts are not infinitely interchangeable in terms of the jobs for which they are best suited. The key point here is the importance of developing the intelligence community's ability to record and recall these varied experiences and expertise on demand. Until 2003 the community had no such capability. Analytic management was anecdotal at best; it fell to managers to recall who might have worked on a given issue in the past and to hope that they were still available.

In 2003 the assistant director of central intelligence for analysis and production instituted the analytic resources catalog (ARC), a database that contains the skills and past expertise of analysts in all agencies and components. The ARC is not used for the day-to-day assignments of analysts; this remains the prerogative of each component's analytical managers. Rather, the ARC allows the assistant director for analysis and production to compare current skills and assignments with the president's intelligence priorities, and also affords a means of identifying analysts whose skills may be needed to respond to unexpected contingencies. ARC data are updated annually.

Obviously, the ARC does not solve the "global coverage" issue, but it is a highly useful means of identifying analytic "gaps." Not every analytic gap is going to be filled by new hires. There will always be issues for which a decision is made to apply minimal resources, if any. In other words, some issues or nations are always "at risk," that is, they are not receiving very much analytic attention. This has certainly been the case over the past ten years, as the intelligence community has shrunk by some twenty-three thousand positions across all occupations and specialties because of declining or stagnant budgets. It will continue to be true even as Congress appropriates funds to increase intelligence capabilities.

What happens if an issue arises for which there are few — or no — analysts with applicable skills or experience? The usual recourse has been to turn to people with analogous skills, knowledge, and expertise and have them do the best they can as they "catch up" to the specifics of the new issue. It would be useful if the intelligence community had a reserve of analysts that it could call upon, especially for those areas that tend not to receive analytic attention on a regular basis. Congress actually passed legislation in 1996 creating an intelligence community reserve, but nothing has been done to implement the system. Ideally, such a system would be composed of both intelligence community veterans who had retired or resigned and outside experts who either had or could quickly be given clearances.

The most important point to keep in mind regarding analytical resources is that even under the best of conditions, the intelligence community will never have global coverage (meaning that all issues and nations have an analyst assigned to them, even if only as part of their portfolio) or global expertise (meaning that somewhere in the intelligence community there will be an analyst with the requisite skills, knowledge, or expertise for every issue or nation). First, there are not enough analysts. Second, analytical managers will always want to put more analysts on the issues of greatest concern or urgency. They will never have the luxury of assigning analysts to issues or countries that are quiescent or dormant, "just in case" they suddenly require attention. Therefore, it will always be necessary to have some system to catalog skills and to fill gaps. And every year there will be moments when the attention given to some issues will have to be curtailed or abandoned as crises erupt somewhere else.

Analytical Products

Finally we come to the question of analytical products. This is the least demanding of the three management issues. First, the intelligence community has a range of products to cover various policymaker needs. These are fairly routinized and well understood by managers. The managerial choices here consist largely of choosing the right product to get the right amount of intelligence to meet policymakers' needs within a specified timeframe. One must take into account how much intelligence is needed, the urgency of the need, and the degree to which the policymaker already has sufficient background on the issue.

Not all intelligence products are equal, however. Different products involve different production or management costs, and policymakers also express fairly consistent preferences for certain types of products. Daily briefings, which are actually combinations of briefings and the presentation of written products and sometimes more raw intelligence items (intercepts, human reports, images, etc.), are probably the most important analytical service for a variety of reasons. First, this is the most frequent interaction that senior policymakers (cabinet members and their deputies) have with the intelligence community. Briefings occur five or six times a week. Second, briefings provide the best opportunity for discovering what issues are uppermost on policymakers' minds. Third, briefings are the ultimate expression of current intelligence, closely tailored to meet the needs of each policymaker and give greatest emphasis to the most pressing issues. Fourth, policymakers consistently rate briefings and short, tailored analyses as the intelligence products they most prefer.

This raises the thorny issue of policymaker preferences and how influential they should be in shaping intelligence community responses — in other words, the question of relevance. To what degree should the community simply "give them what they want," as the best means of preserving access and putting out important and needed intelligence? Or should the intelligence community take the time, and spend the political capital, to attempt to shape policymakers' preferences? Clearly, not every issue can be analyzed adequately within the scope of an early-morning briefing. Both intelligence officers and policymakers recognize this. But there is a fairly consistent decline in policymaker interest in intelligence community products as they get longer and more removed from more current issues.

There is no correct answer; there is only a choice. As a rule, the intelligence community has, for the past several years, put its greatest emphasis on shorter, more current products. This not only reflects the recognized preference of policymakers; it is also a result of the United States' having been at war since 2001. War is a current intelligence experience, especially a war being fought against small groups, as opposed to a nation-state.

Beyond the daily intelligence briefings, there is a range of analyses that tends to get longer and offers more depth until one arrives at national intelligence estimates (NIEs). This middle range of analysis between short briefings and NIEs depends on the nature of the issue and the needs of the policymakers. Many analytical products in this range are produced for lower-level officials — assistant secretaries and their deputies; office directors, etc. Finally, NIEs are the most detailed (and often the longest) analyses, representing the views of the intelligence community on an issue and signed by the director of national intelligence, who gives the NIE his imprimatur.

NIEs actually encompass a range of purposes. Some examine the potential or likely direction of a certain issue, often several years into the future. Other NIEs represent the intelligence community's state of knowledge and known gaps on certain issues, and are a way of taking stock across the community on an issue of importance. Still other NIEs are written as a means of "forcing" analytic components to come to grips with a certain issue, usually one that has been difficult and perhaps controversial. These are all worthwhile purposes for intelligence community analyses, although some in the community have argued that they are not all truly NIEs per se and that perhaps some product differentiation should be made between the true estimative analyses and the other products that are also called NIEs.

There is a legitimate argument to be made that longer products, such as estimates, also serve other useful purposes, including bringing together the community's views and uncertainties on a given issue, or writing them so that the larger intelligence community (and not only analysts) can be better informed about an issue. But these goals will always be secondary to the issue of keeping policymakers informed.

NIEs have often been controversial. In 1962 the NIE on Cuba and the Soviet Union dismissed the possibility of Soviet missile deployments until DCI John McCone, who disagreed with this analysis, successfully argued for additional collections, which produced new intelligence that caused experts to revise their assessment and change the NIE. During the Vietnam War there were strong differences over the enemy order of battle and the degree to which military success was being achieved—expressed, in this case, in the remaining enemy strength. In the mid-1970s a group of outside experts faulted the NIEs on Soviet strategic forces, arguing that they focused too much on capabilities and not enough on Soviet intent. Finally, the lack of an NIE on the terrorist threat in the years prior to the 2001 attacks and the NIE on Iraqi WMD in 2002 have both been heavily criticized by investigating groups.[3]

One of the critiques of the terrorism NIEs, of which there were two in the years prior to 2001, is worth considering. The staff of the Kean-Hamilton Commission noted this (in staff statement 11, read publicly on April 14, 2004) and concluded that little strategic analysis had been done on terrorism prior to the attacks. This critique assumes that NIEs alone constitute strategic analysis, when strategic analysis can actually be presented in any number of ways, and sometimes by a single agency rather than the entire community.

Managing Analysts

The issues involved in managing the analytic workforce are not that different from those involved in any other professional group: recruitment, training, career management, retention, and motivation. The main issue involved in recruitment has already been noted: the ability to find analysts with the desired skills from among an almost entirely volunteer population. But there is, behind this issue, the larger question of how one determines what skills are needed. As noted above, the intelligence community now has the ARC database, which allows managers to compare current assignments, acquired knowledge, expertise, and skills against intelligence priorities. But recruitment decisions are still made on an agency-by-agency basis, which reflects the fact that each agency has specific requirements for its specific policymakers (the president for CIA; the joint chiefs of staff and secretary of defense for DIA; State Department officials for the Bureau of Intelligence and Research, or INR) that may differ somewhat from broader national intelligence priorities.

Training is an important but difficult area. The main issue in training, at least for new hires, is to acclimate them to the intelligence community and give them at least the basic skills they will need. Some of this goes fairly well; some does not. Analysts are trained in stovepipes; that is, each analytical component trains its own analysts. At some level this is understandable. Agencies have specific policymakers for whom they work, subtle differences in style and even in usage. These need to be learned if an analyst is going to be successful in his or her home agency. But it also means that at the very outset of the analyst's career he is thinking more about his home agency than about the broader intelligence community. Indeed, analysts do not go into community-wide courses until they are fairly senior, by which time there will be little chance of engendering true community officers.

The second major problem with initial training is that analysts do not come away with a very good sense of what happens in collection. Indeed, even senior analysts exhibit a surprising amount of ignorance about what happens in collection as a whole or in specific collection disciplines. The net result is analysts who are less perceptive about what they receive or do not receive from collectors and who may also be more passive when seeking new intelligence. The collection system works or does not work for reasons they will never understand, and they come to accept this.

It has been suggested that both of these training problems can be addressed, in part, by putting analysts from all agencies in combined classes for at least part of their initial training—sort of an IC 101. This would give them all a better sense of what happens in other analytic agencies as well as in the collection disciplines.

Beyond what one might call "intake" training, the issue becomes murkier. Midcareer training is not as coherent as initial training. Much depends on the analyst's initiative and the supervisors' willingness to allow analysts to go "out of the line" for more training. The normal instinct of a manager will be to keep as many analysts in the line as possible—especially during more stressful or demanding periods. This, however, can be a somewhat shortsighted decision on three grounds. First, it tends to alienate the analyst. Second, there is never likely to be a "good" time to allow analysts to leave their accounts. Third, it denies the analyst the ability to improve his or her skills or learn new ones.

Training has also been affected by changes in what types of analysts the system is trying to develop. For many years the goal was to develop "intelligence generalists." The emphasis here was on generic skills rather than on substantive areas of expertise. It was believed that it was possible to develop a cadre of analysts who could work on almost any issue based on their skills. In the mid-1990s the trend shifted. Senior managers believed that not every analyst could work on every issue and that it was preferable to develop analysts who had good general skills but greater substantive expertise in several specific areas.

At this point we have shifted from training into career management, and the two are intertwined. Again, career management has not always been one of the analytical corps' greatest strengths; it has tended to be somewhat haphazard and idiosyncratic. Part of the problem is that there have always been two career progressions going on simultaneously, each of which has different attributes and skills. The first is the continuing development of the analyst. The goal here is to develop analysts who think and write better, who develop keener insights into the issues on which they are working, who can take on more complex and more vexing intelligence analysis. At the same time, the analytic corps also needs managers to supervise larger groups of analysts as one goes up the management ladder. The skill sets required here are somewhat different. Clearly, one wants a manager who understands and has achieved some level of mastery over analytical tasks. But, beyond that, various management skills and people skills will be required. This second set of skills is not related in any meaningful way to analytical skills. For many years, however, the only way to achieve promotion was to become a manager, whether or not one had management skills. The analytical corps was, in effect, giving higher preference to management skills than to analytical skills. This has been ameliorated, somewhat, in the CIA by the creation of the senior analytical service (SAS). The SAS consists of analysts who have been promoted to senior ranks on the strength of their analytical capabilities, but who have opted out of the management track for whatever reason. Still, the highest ranks will go to the most senior managers. This also makes sense, as they will have greater responsibilities.

To return to the changing trends in analytical career management, the earlier phase, that of the intelligence generalist, meant that analysts moved from one account to another more quickly, perhaps every several years. When the trend began to go in the opposite direction, the time spent on accounts increased.

Most managers also recognize that, in addition to training, most analysts will also benefit from assignments beyond their home agency, either overseas at an embassy, in another intelligence agency, or in a policy agency. Again, this imposes a cost on the manager, as it takes the analyst out of the line.

Retention is to a very great extent the sum of the parts that have gone before. Analysts, like other employees, will stay if they feel challenged, if their careers are progressing well, and if they feel they are receiving the proper amount of attention from their superiors. Retention is an extremely important issue now for the intelligence community, as the workforce is "greening," not "graying." The last big buildup of intelligence capabilities took place under DCI William Casey (1981-86), during the Reagan administration. Many of the people hired in that period have reached the twenty-year mark or more and have decided to retire. At the same time, hiring has again increased in the aftermath of the ter- rorist attacks. The net result is an analytic corps that is younger and less experienced than before. Former CIA Deputy Director of Intelligence Jami Miscik captured this fact when she noted that 40 percent of analysts in the directorate of intelligence had worked for only one DCI, George Tenet, who resigned after exactly seven years. The analytic work force can mature only if retention is kept high.

Every institution wants motivated employees. In the case of the intelligence com- munity, the main motivations are the call to public service and the "allure" of the job. Beyond that are the customary motivators like promotion, other forms of recognition, and travel. But some are peculiar to intelligence analysts. A major motivation is seeing one's analysis go forward to a policymaker. This is of major importance to analysts, re- gardless of their seniority. For more junior analysts, the amount of satisfaction derived from this accomplishment is inversely proportional to the amount of time that a paper spends in review. Few papers will ever get published as quickly as an analyst would like, but there was a period, in the CIA at least, where the numerous levels of review had a strongly negative effect on analysts. These layers have been reduced, which helps, but the general desire to get the paper out as soon as it leaves the analyst's printer will always remain high.

But here the issue of current versus medium-length or longer-term analysis arises once again. There are some who fear that the emphasis on current intelligence has cre- ated an unspoken divide between those who contribute to the flow of current intelli- gence and those who do not, the latter implicitly having a lower status. This is the sort of unanticipated result that can have a debilitating effect on morale and motivation.

Therefore, before we get to the "transforming" issues for analysis, here is a synopsis of the larger management issues always lurking in the background:

- Managers must decide, often daily, which issues will receive analytical attention and which will not. These decisions will be driven by the more immediate policymakers' needs and the longer-term intelligence priorities or requirements. There will always be issues, some of which are also likely to demand attention at some point, that do not receive very much analytical attention, if any at all.
- The ability to answer the most pressing or urgent needs mandates the existence of a system that offers managers insights into the skills sets within their organization. This has been solved to a great extent in the ARC, but its utility depends on manag- ers' willingness to use it. The ARC does offer useful insights into the degree to which resources match requirements.
- Recruitment of those analysts whose skills are most needed remains problematic. The PRISP scholarships, described above, will ameliorate the problem of the "seller's

market," but only partially. It will not be possible, financially, to make such a program the basis for all analysis recruiting.

"Transforming" Analysis

The past several years have been one of the most bruising periods for intelligence analysis since the creation of the modern intelligence community in 1947. As noted earlier, much of the controversy centers around two largely analytical issues: the terrorist attacks of 2001 and Iraqi WMD. Of the two, the Iraqi WMD issue is much more important in terms of "transforming" analysis. As horrific as the September 11 attack was, the issues it raised for analysis are much less profound than are those of Iraqi WMD. No investigation has yet found the one or two or more analytical flaws that might have prevented the September 11 attacks. This is not to say that processes could not have worked better, but the *assured* ability to discover by either collection or analysis the *tactical* information that was needed — the date, time, and place of the attacks — did not exist. Terrorist groups do not provide the kind of strategic warning that nation-states do on occasion.[4] This is not to suggest that aggressive collection and spirited, insightful analysis will never yield results against terrorists. They will, as our post–September 11 experience has proved; but it will never be foolproof.

Iraq, on the other hand, goes to more serious issues in terms of the day-to-day work of analysis. Although at this writing the work of the Iraq Survey Group is still under way, we clearly have not found — in terms of stockpiles of weapons and a ready infrastructure — what we had expected to find. The obvious question is: Why not?

One reason appears to be the scanty collection in Iraq at the time the estimates were being written; another is the failure to challenge widely held assumptions. Interestingly, the one charge that appears to have been completely debunked is that of politicization. Although some voiced concerns on the eve of the war about the number of times Vice President Cheney went to the CIA for briefings on Iraq, neither the CIA ombudsman nor the Senate Select Committee on Intelligence found any signs that policymakers affected the analytical judgments.

If we accept the validity of the two criticisms noted above — collection and assumptions — what transforming lessons can we learn from them? The collection issue is interesting in that it raises important questions about how we do analysis. Just as analysts cannot very well ignore an issue that policymakers want analyzed, they also cannot say, "We have no collection on that, so we're not analyzing it." Quite simply, analysts are expected to analyze despite the paucity of collection. Indeed, since it is widely recognized that there will never be perfect or complete collection on any issue, there is always going to be some part of analysis that is based more on analytical experience and judgment than on solid information.

There is nothing wrong with this, as long as the analysis makes clear the freshness, nature, and quality of the collection upon which it is based, which may not have been the case on the question of WMD in Iraq. But there is also the danger that the argument over the nature of collection and the resulting analysis may be going in an altogether different direction — what might be called an evidentiary requirement for analysis. In other words, unless the intelligence community has a high degree of certainty as to its collection, its analysis is going to be held suspect. We will go from the concept of analysis, which accepts uncertainty as part of its work, to a standard of "proof."

Again, the onus is on the analysts to make clear the basis for their work and the degree to which it rests on intelligence sources — and gives some sense of those sources' reliability — and the degree to which it is based on analytical judgments. But it is unlikely that any useful analysis can be written under this more demanding standard.

The assumptions issue is thornier. It goes to the issue of "tradecraft," that is, teaching analysts how to be analysts. Part of tradecraft is corporate: learning the writing style, learning which sources are which, getting grounded in how the community works. Part of tradecraft is professional and ethical: values, standards, expectations, ethics.

Analysts are expected to challenge assumptions and to ask difficult questions. But this may not be enough. In the case of Iraqi WMD it would have been extremely difficult to find anyone in late 2002 or early 2003 who assumed that Iraq did *not* have WMD. Not only the United States, but also the members of the United Nations (UN) Security Council and their main inspector, Hans Blix, all assumed that WMD would be found in Iraq. The debate in the Security Council was over the best way to discover them and remove them, not on whether or not they existed. This assumption had fairly sound bases: Iraq had WMD in the past and had used them. We could not account for all of the WMD that Iraq admitted to in 1991 and then said had been destroyed. Iraq's refusal to admit inspectors — with 500,000 hostile troops poised on its border and in the face of continued international sanctions — all strongly suggested a state that had something to hide. As one senior intelligence official asked in the aftermath of the Iraq war: "Tell me *analytically* and *intellectually* how we would have come to an opposite conclusion?"

Added to this was the time pressure involved. The Senate, in requesting the prewar estimate, said it needed the NIE in time for its vote, three weeks away, on granting the president the authority to use force against Iraq. The speed with which the NIE was produced then became a source of criticism, despite the senatorial mandate, a contrast to the usual complaint that NIEs take too long to be written and published.

Still, there are lessons to be learned from the Iraq experience, in terms of how assumptions and contrary questions are phrased, review procedures, and briefing procedures. Again, none of these guarantee that a similar problem will not arise in the future. Like the famous saying about soldiers being ready to fight the last war, the intelligence community has to derive lessons and remedial steps that will meet the next issue, not just the last one.

At the time of this writing, the intelligence community is still learning its "lessons." It would appear that many of them involve managerial and review safeguards and trade-craft. But the intelligence community, unlike its military colleagues, has no institutional-ized capability to learn from its mistakes, no system through which it can assess both its successes and its failures. This is not to suggest that intelligence analysis and military operations are the same, but the ability to determine how close one is to the ideal is ex-tremely useful and worth examining as one way to transform intelligence analysis.

Stepping away from the immediacy of September 11 and Iraq are the other issues noted at the beginning of this chapter. The first, closely related to Iraq, is the utility of NIEs, which has already been discussed above. There is a strong case to be made that the intelligence community should examine this specific product to determine how widely it is used, by whom, and for what reason.[5] There has not been a serious examina-tion of the NIE process since the tenure of DCI William Colby (1973–76), who replaced the Board of National Estimates with the current national intelligence officer system. As noted above, there are several reasons to write NIEs, but informing the most senior policymakers may not be the most important.

The issue of current versus longer-term intelligence is related to the NIE issue. No one can deny the importance of "close-in support" to policymakers, but, as discussed above, this tends to reflect the policymakers' immediate needs at the cost of their longer-term interests. This is entirely an intelligence management issue. Policymakers, if they were asked, would never agree to a reduction in their immediate support.[6] Therefore, it is up to intelligence managers to look at the amount of effort going into the various types of products and services they provide and ask themselves if the balance (meaning distribution, not an even split) is correct.

The ramifications of this review go beyond product distribution and analyst em-phasis. The ability to conduct serious research on a topic is tied directly to the ability to spend more time on a paper than is typical of current intelligence. As a result of the cutbacks of the past ten years, the community's ability to do research has dropped dra-matically. This has an interesting self-reinforcing effect. The less comfortable analysts are about writing longer, more in-depth papers, the more likely they will be to gravitate to current intelligence.

The solution here again rests with managers. They have to show that they value longer-term intelligence by encouraging it, asking for it, and rewarding analysts who produce it. It would also be useful to return to the practice of requiring that analysts write one research paper every year. This would be important for both its practical and symbolic effect.

The tension between collaborative and competitive analysis also reflects the cut-backs in analytic resources over the past ten years. The community does much less competitive analysis than it used to. Competitive analysis, at one time central to U.S. intelligence, was based on two premises. The first was that various senior policymakers needed unique intelligence support of their own, even when working on the same issue. Consider the period prior to the Iraq war. Secretary of State Colin Powell's main emphasis was on diplomacy in the UN and with U.S. allies, garnering support and making the U.S. case that war was justified and necessary. Secretary of Defense Donald Rumsfeld's main concerns were preparations for combat and the ability of the coalition to defeat Iraq quickly and decisively. President Bush was concerned about both of these and other issues as well. Thus we have multiple intelligence agencies working on the same or similar topics for their specific customers: CIA for the president; DIA for Defense (civil and military); INR for State. In addition, other departments—Energy, DHS—have their own intelligence components, as does each of the military services.

The second premise was that on issues of national importance these various components would bring their distinct points of view to an issue, increasing the likelihood that all aspects would be considered—that their analyses would "compete." However, as the number of analysts decreased, this became something of a "luxury." Indeed, there has even been an increase in specialization among agencies. Increased emphasis has been put on "collaboration," that is, sharing analysis—a useful working habit but not one that is likely to produce the sharper analysis sought in competition.

Some of the increased specialization stemmed from the particular interests of agencies' policymakers. For example, human rights issues are of greatest interest to the State Department and therefore a higher priority for State/INR than for other agencies. Some of it came about by direction. In one of the best-known examples, after the 1991 Gulf War the CIA was ordered to cease bomb-damage assessments, largely because of the military's dissatisfaction with the analysis it received. This was to some extent a problem of miscommunication rather than inability, but the CIA still lost the right to continue this line of analysis.

Of the two approaches, collaboration and competition, it is the second that has suffered. This is not to say that competitive analysis has disappeared entirely. It still occurs in NIEs and in other products, but certainly not as extensively as was true in the 1980s. One of the surest antidotes to "groupthink," which the SSCI claimed was one of the faults in the Iraq estimate, is more and better competitive analysis. Again, this depends on managers who ensure that some part of their growing resource base is trained in, devoted to, and rewarded for competitive analysis.

We come finally to what is perhaps the most important and most volatile of the transforming issues facing analysis: the need for a reasonable standard by which to judge it. Here again we face the effects of the September 11 and Iraqi WMD issues. The belief among certain sectors of the public that it should be possible to identify the intelligence flaws that led to September 11 is understandable, even though it is misleading. It would be comforting to think that if we could just identify these flaws, then no future attacks would occur. We would all like to go back to the comfort of the world we knew on September 10. But even with all of the findings of the joint inquiry and the 9/11 Commission, there has been no such discovery.[7] Still, September 11 is widely seen as an intelligence "failure," even though few can point to exactly what it was that failed.

The issue of a reasonable standard becomes more important when we turn to the Iraqi WMD issue. The statement of David Kay, the first head of inspections in Iraq, that "we were all wrong," has become accepted wisdom despite its own inaccuracy. That, indeed, has become the unstated but desired standard for intelligence: either all right or all wrong. To some extent this is a matter of deliberate political hyperbole on the part of certain critics of U.S. intelligence, but it has begun to stick in the minds of the press and the public — two very important audiences. Most observers of intelligence understand that such a standard is unreasonable, largely dooming the community to being wrong most of the time, for it is rarely "all right." But continuing damage is done to the credibility of the intelligence community when this is repeated over and over. There is also a penalty to be paid within the community. Analysts and analytical managers may become reluctant to take risks if they fear that every time they get it less than "all right" they will be subject to a political inquisition or pillorying.

What is the answer? It probably would be useful to have a true national debate between the executive branch and Congress, and perhaps with knowledgeable segments of the public as well, as to what constitutes a reasonable standard for intelligence analysis. This would have to be done separately from the ongoing legislative reform process. The preferred result of such a debate would not be some precise standard, because that is not achievable. It might be some broad and general agreement as to what can reasonably be expected from intelligence analysis in general and perhaps in some specific areas where analysis has proved more difficult, such as WMD. This would not relieve intelligence from trying to do its best at all times, but it would remove the politically charged issue of "intelligence failure" for the slightest deviation from perfection. There would not be precise rules of the road, but it might be possible to come up with an agreed standard or standards (depending on the issue) by which both branches could assess the efficacy of analysis.

Transforming Analysis

As I have written elsewhere, if we knew with certainty what made one analysis so much better than another, we would write better analysis more often. There is no recipe or formula. Analysis remains, at its heart, an intellectual process within a bureaucracy. This is not the best model for regular success. Neither is trying to transform analysis when it is under attack and when the entire structure of U.S. intelligence is being revised.

I have not, up to this point, defined what I mean by "transformed" analysis. The definition may depend on who is doing the defining, but in my view it means improving the ability of intelligence to help policymakers reduce uncertainty and make decisions. This may not seem very "transformational," but it certainly is necessary, as it goes to the core of what analysis is about.

To sum up, this chapter has identified eight issues that are central to transforming analysis. Three are generic in nature, regardless of the temper of the times: dealing with conflicting priorities; managing analytic resources; and managing the analytic process. Five reflect the aftermath of September 11 and Iraqi WMD: deriving useful lessons from those two incidents; reexamining the utility of NIEs; adjusting the balance between current and longer-term intelligence; fostering more competitive analysis; and creating a reasonable standard for evaluating intelligence analysis. These are all important, but if pressed to rank them in order of importance, I would choose the first set over the second, for its three issues address the analytic process for the longer term. But, if pressed to choose one over all the others, I would choose the last: a meaningful national discussion on a reasonable standard for evaluating analysis. This one step would be most likely to defuse (if never entirely) the political atmosphere that now surrounds and undercuts intelligence analysis. If we could achieve that one step — which would be a transformation of the political atmosphere in which analysis takes place — we could then turn our full attention to the first three issues with a greater chance of success.

Notes

1. See Richard A. Posner, "The 9/11 Report: A Dissent," *New York Times Book Review*, August 29, 2004, 1.

2. Mark M. Lowenthal, *Intelligence: From Secrets to Policy*, 2d ed. (Washington, D.C.: CQ Press, 2003), passim.

3. The most scathing reviews of faulty intelligence on WMD in Iraq came from the U.S. Senate Select Committee on Intelligence, in its *Report on the U.S. Intelligence Community's Prewar Intelligence Assessments on Iraq*, 108th Congress, July 7, 2004 (available at www.gpoaccess.gov), and the Commission on the Intelligence Capabilities of the United States Regarding Weapons of Mass Destruction, "Report to the President, March 31, 2005" (available at www.wmd.gov). Criticism of British intelligence on the same issue can by found in a report by a committee of privy counselors (the Butler Committee report), *Review of Intelligence on Weapons of Mass Destruction* (London: Stationery Office, July 14, 2004). See www.butlerreview.org.uk.

4. There is a huge body of intelligence literature on the issue of surprise attack and the failure of the party being attacked to discern warning signals. See, for example, Roberta Wohlstetter, *Pearl Harbor: Warning and Decision* (Stanford: Stanford University Press, 1962); and Richard K. Betts, *Surprise Attack: Lessons for Defense Planning* (Washington, D.C.: Brookings Institution Press, 1982).

5. Interestingly, NIEs are the only intelligence analysis mandated by law. The National Security Act states that the National Intelligence Council will produce NIEs "for the Government."

Note this last phrase — not just for the executive. Assuming this provision survives the current reform efforts, as is likely, any reexamination of NIEs will have to keep this provision in mind.

6. This raises an oft-discussed issue — the fact that for most policymakers intelligence is a "free good," that is, one for which they bear little or no direct administrative or financial cost.

7. I purposely omit from this analysis the inane charge that the intelligence community failed to "connect the dots," surely one of the most simplistic and inaccurate portrayals of analysis ever uttered. Indeed, as one intelligence manager noted, in the case of the September 11 attacks the community was accused of not connecting the dots, and in the case of Iraqi WMD it was accused of connecting too many dots.

FOURTEEN

Congressional Oversight of
Intelligence after September 11

L. BRITT SNIDER

SINCE THEIR CREATION in the mid-1970s, the congressional intelligence committees have labored in relative obscurity. Because their work has usually involved classified information, most of it has taken place behind closed doors. Nevertheless, they
have managed to agree on a public authorization bill for intelligence each year since
their creation, and from time to time they have held public hearings and issued public
reports about matters they have looked into. As a result, these committees have gained a
reputation over time for doing solid work and taking an enviable bipartisan approach.

In the years following the terrorist attacks of September 11, however, the committees have
found themselves in the glare of the public spotlight in a way they had not been for some time.
Not only were the issues they were dealing with suddenly center stage in the mind of the public, the committees found themselves in the middle of controversies that had the potential to
affect, perhaps even determine, the outcome of a presidential election, and their stewardship
of the oversight function was, for the first time since their creation, coming under attack.

What had theretofore been the committees' hallmark — bipartisanship — suddenly
seemed to go out the window. What had always been their strong suit — expertise and
competence — suddenly seemed in short supply. Indeed, with respect to the terrorist
attacks of September 11 and the run-up to the war in Iraq, it appeared they had failed
to focus on the right issues. After a quarter-century of proving themselves, at a time
when the country most needed an objective, authoritative assessment of its intelligence
capabilities, the committees did not seem the ones to provide it. At a time when, by all
rights, they should have been at the forefront of reform efforts to prevent the same kind
of intelligence failures from happening in the future, and broadening and solidifying
their oversight responsibilities vis-à-vis other committees, they found themselves on
the defensive, struggling to regain the stature they had labored so long to achieve.

Background: How the Congressional Intelligence Committees
Operated before September 11

It was not until the mid-1970s that Congress decided that it had better get serious about
intelligence oversight. The cozy arrangements of the past had allowed U.S. intelligence

agencies to pursue a number of activities without the knowledge or acquiescence of the Congress—activities that in hindsight appeared dubious if not illegal.[1] To provide for greater awareness of, and involvement in, the work of intelligence agencies, each house created a committee dedicated to intelligence oversight: the Senate Select Committee on Intelligence (SSCI), created in 1976, and the House Permanent Select Committee on Intelligence (HPSCI), in 1977.[2]

At the same time, there was considerable apprehension in the Congress—and even more in the intelligence community itself—about whether the committees would be able to carry out their mandates. Given the volatile experiences of the Church and Pike Committees, the two investigating committees whose work led to the creation of the select committees, many wondered whether Congress, a political institution, would be able to oversee intelligence work without exposing its secrets (and thereby ending it). In the mid-1970s no other country in the world had allowed such scrutiny of its intelligence services by the legislature.

The standing committees in each house whose jurisdictions overlapped with those of the two oversight committees were also concerned, albeit for different reasons. While they were willing to cede primary jurisdiction over the Central Intelligence Agency (CIA) to the intelligence committees, they retained jurisdiction over intelligence activities in the departments and agencies they controlled. They did this not only to protect their turf but also as a hedge against the possibility that the newly launched experiment in oversight might go badly.

Both houses saw the new committees as "special creatures." To begin with, both were "select" committees, whose members were appointed by the leadership of each house rather than by the party caucuses. Both bodies believed that extraordinary care should be taken in deciding who served on these committees. Members appointed to them would serve fixed terms rather than indefinitely, as they did on other congressional committees, in order that they not be co-opted by the agencies they were overseeing and so as to expose more members of Congress to the intelligence business.

Both houses also saw the need for the intelligence committees to operate in a bipartisan fashion. While the Senate adopted specific measures to foster bipartisanship on its committee and the House of Representatives (historically a more partisan institution) chose a more conventional approach, the floor debate preceding the vote in the House nonetheless made clear that both sides expected the oversight committee to operate in a bipartisan way.[3] Intelligence should not, they recognized, become a political football.

For the most part, over the ensuing quarter-century, both committees adhered to this model. While each had its share of partisan squabbles, the majority and minority acted in remarkable concert compared with other congressional committees. Differences between the parties rarely made it into the news. The majority and minority on both committees worked together to produce legislation and issue investigative reports that usually commanded support from both sides of the aisle. Party-line votes, whatever the issue, were rare.

The oversight function clearly benefited from this bipartisan approach. Not only were the committees able to accomplish more, intelligence agencies were encouraged to be more forthcoming with them. Indeed, without some expectation that their information would not be used for political purposes, intelligence agencies would have been far more reluctant to share it over the years. Partisanship on the oversight committees is, after all, fundamentally a security problem for the agencies, undermining the trust that is essential to making the system work (regardless of the laws on the books).

Also key to making the system work is the perception that the oversight committees know what they are doing. Intelligence agencies expect to be held accountable for their decisions as well as for the results they achieve (or fail to achieve). But they expect the committees' criticism to be informed and fair. If the agencies perceive that they are pawns in a game of political "gotcha," their tendency will be to pull back into their shells. On the other hand, if the committees are perceived as knowledgeable and constructive (however demanding or skeptical they might be), the level of candor and cooperation will inevitably rise.

From the outset, both committees recognized the need to educate their members as well as to hire and retain staff with expertise in the field. Indeed, for the first twenty years of their existence, both committees made concerted efforts to keep professional staff who had demonstrated the knowledge and skills needed for the oversight function, regardless of the staffers' party affiliation. As a result, the "professionalism" of the intelligence committees' staffs was lauded repeatedly over the years by the members of both houses.

Appointment to the intelligence committees came to be seen as a "plum" assignment. Senators and representatives who served on the oversight committees were seen as people "in the know," privy to the secrets and inner workings of the executive branch. The leaders of the committees, in particular, were looked to not only by their parent institutions but by the public and news media as well, as authoritative spokesmen on a variety of national security issues.

Suffice it to say that by the turn of the century the experiment begun with some trepidation in the mid-1970s appeared to have worked. There had been a quarter-century of congressional oversight, and the sky had not fallen. The committees had demonstrated the capability and intent to protect the classified information that was shared with them, and had, for the most part, carried out their duties in a responsible fashion. They had provided not only the resources needed for intelligence work but the policy support as well. What the intelligence committees of the U.S. Congress had managed to achieve had provided the inspiration, if not the model, for democratic governments around the world.

Problems Apparent after September 11

In the aftermath of September 11, however, with the glare of the public spotlight upon them, problems within the intelligence committees became manifest. Oversight had become more political than it used to be. In the years immediately preceding the attacks, the committees had apparently failed to focus on the right issues. Gaps and ambiguities appeared in the scope of their jurisdictions that had not been appreciated before, and, for the first time, their stewardship of the oversight function was challenged.

DEBILITATING PARTISANSHIP

It was apparent by the late 1990s that the House and Senate were themselves becoming more partisan institutions. Even in areas like defense and foreign policy, where political consensus had been relatively easier to achieve during the cold war, it now seemed harder for Congress to get things done; debates were more rancorous and mean-spirited; and each side seemed to go out of its way to skewer the other and keep it from having its way.

The intelligence committees themselves were not immune to this partisanship.[4] While there was an obvious need to "pull together" after the attacks of September 11, which both committees did,[5] as time wore on and their oversight activities took on greater political significance, it became more difficult to maintain harmony. While the two committees undertook an unprecedented joint inquiry into the intelligence community's performance prior to the events of September 11 — and were ultimately able to obtain approval from the membership of both committees for a final report that was issued in December 2002 — by the end of this process, political friction was clearly evident.[6]

It was the ensuing war in Iraq, however, that brought partisanship on the committees to hitherto unforeseen levels. This was hardly surprising, since, for the first time in their history,[7] the committees found themselves seized with issues that were likely to have a direct bearing upon a presidential election. The intelligence judgments that had ostensibly prompted President Bush to wage war on Iraq, i.e., that Iraqi ruler Saddam Hussein possessed weapons of mass destruction (WMD), which Bush in turn had used to persuade Congress and the American public to support the war, turned out to be wrong. Both committees recognized that they were obliged to find out why. But in the highly politicized environment of an election year, it turned out to be very difficult to separate the responsibility of the intelligence community for this disconcerting failure from the responsibility of the president.

On the SSCI the divisive question arose of whether the committee would limit itself to looking either at the actions of the intelligence community (the preference of the Republican majority), or at how the prewar intelligence was used by the White House (the preference of the Democratic minority). After battling over this issue for several months, the majority had its way and limited the scope of the inquiry to the actions of the intelligence community. This led the Democratic vice chairman of the committee to request a memo from his staff asking what the minority's options were, in terms of expanding the scope of the committee's investigation. Someone on his staff drafted such a memo and apparently left it on his or her desk, where it was pilfered by another member of the staff—presumably on the majority side—and subsequently given to a conservative television commentator who used it to lambaste the Democrats on the committee.

Never had this happened before. Previous partisan disagreements on the two committees had always been handled internally. Never had internal memos been leaked to the press for political reasons. To be sure, the memo in question was a political document. It showed that the minority had already made up its collective mind in terms of White House culpability on the subject of Iraqi WMD and was intent on doing everything in its power to keep the issue alive before the next election.

While memos of this sort were commonplace elsewhere on Capitol Hill, they were rare for the SSCI, and this one led to a political uproar. The committee's vice chairman went on television the next day and refused to take responsibility for the memo or concede that it was improper. Members of the committee from both sides of the aisle then took to the Senate floor to denounce each other. Editorials appeared in the conservative press excoriating the Democrats and demanding that their staff director be fired. Then, in what surely must be the lowest point in the history of the committee, a columnist for the *Washington Post* in effect accused the Democratic vice chairman of lying when he refused to take responsibility for the memo, citing information to the contrary that he acknowledged had come from the Republican chairman.[8] It appeared that the chairman of the SSCI had, for the first time in the committee's history, gone to the press to launch a personal attack on the vice chairman. For the remainder of the congressional session, the committee found it difficult to conduct its affairs. In a telling and unprecedented action, the Senate majority leader stepped in and suspended the committee's ongoing inquiry into prewar intelligence, and the committee met again only once, to consider the conference report on the annual intelligence authorization bill.

When Congress reconvened in January 2004, a semblance of normalcy returned. The committee began to meet again and, to its credit, reached agreement on a plan that would allow it to proceed with its investigation into prewar intelligence on Iraq. The agreement was announced jointly in February without rancor or recrimination, and while its political overtones were apparent (the performance of the intelligence agencies would be examined first, and the question of how the Bush administration used the prewar intelligence would be deferred until later), the announcement nonetheless seemed to signal recognition by both sides that, for the good of the institution, they had to present at least the appearance of being able to work together. Clearly, though, the wounds that had been opened a few months earlier continued to fester. As the chairman of the committee told the *Washington Post* in April, "We're in danger now of seeing the politicization of the whole intelligence issue. What really worries me is this 'gotcha' business."[9]

On the HPSCI, things may have been better, but not by much. Although the committee had been run in a relatively evenhanded way for the previous seven years by its Republican chairman, Porter Goss, by the time Congress reconvened in January 2004 it was apparent that bipartisanship had seriously broken down, leading the ranking Democrat on the committee to lament: "Bipartisanship has become the hardest [to achieve] since I've been on the committee, and I'm very, very sad about it. This is a serious change. If these intelligence committees can't do it, no one can do it."[10]

Indeed, in the weeks that followed, Goss made unusually partisan statements criticizing the putative Democratic presidential nominee's views on intelligence as well as questioning the veracity of one of the president's most vocal critics.[11] It was subsequently reported that the ranking member herself had come under fire from certain Democratic colleagues for not taking a sufficiently hard line against Goss, viewed by Democrats as going out of his way to protect the president.[12]

One consequence of this growing partisanship was that the HPSCI was unable to produce a committee report similar to its Senate counterpart on the prewar intelligence on Iraq. The ranking Democrat on the committee was quoted as saying that she had sent four letters to Goss requesting that the report be completed, but he had ignored all of them.[13]

Unfortunately, the partisan bickering did not end there. When Goss brought the committee's annual authorization bill to the House floor on June 23, 2004, he took the occasion to hold up a poster criticizing the Democrats' putative presidential nominee for advocating cuts to the intelligence budget in years past.[14] Not surprisingly, his remarks prompted angry counterattacks from the other side, and Democrats on the Senate intelligence committee let it be known that they would oppose the nomination of Goss to replace George Tenet, who by this point had announced his intent to resign as director of central intelligence (DCI).[15]

For a while this negative response from the committee Democrats appeared to doom Goss's nomination, but in August 2004 the White House decided to nominate him anyway. He would have to endure criticism, they undoubtedly calculated, but in the end would have the votes needed for confirmation. Indeed, this proved to be the case, but the ferocity of the Democrats' attacks on Goss—citing his political machinations over the previous year to raise doubt about his ability as DCI to remain independent of partisan politics—was unexpected and undoubtedly soured the process for the nominee. Listening to these attacks, as well as the politically motivated statements by Goss that had prompted them, one could only marvel at the degree to which partisanship had come to infect the work of the two committees. Once held up as models of how congressional committees should work, they now seemed no different from the rest.

For some observers, this rancorous partisanship called into question the committees' fitness to conduct full and fair investigations. Citing the growing politicization of the intelligence committees in particular but commenting upon Congress as a whole, one critic wrote: "The downward spiral of congressional inquiries into partisan bitterness has undermined Congress's fitness to give the public the answers it needs. . . . More than any other factor, it is the mutual imputation of bad faith by Democrats and Republicans that has deposed Congress from its place as our lead investigator of official malfeasance. It is not that all investigations of the past have been free of hard-edged partisanship, but that partisan gain has now become the standard by which they are measured."[16]

For either party to use the intelligence committees to achieve a political advantage, however, only undermines their authority and effectiveness. It makes the job of oversight more difficult and weakens the committees' standing with the public and within their parent bodies. In one particularly telling action, when the Senate leadership had to decide, in August 2004, which committee should develop the legislation needed to carry out the reorganization of the intelligence community recommended by the 9/11 Commission, they turned to the Committee on Governmental Affairs rather than the SSCI. Indeed, the chairman and vice chairman of the SSCI found themselves on the sidelines, offering amendments to the Governmental Affairs proposals (and having many of them rejected) rather than controlling the process themselves. For the SSCI to be relegated to this inferior position with respect to a major piece of legislation suggests more than anything else a lack of confidence on the part of the Senate leadership in the committee's ability to work in a productive bipartisan manner to produce a bill.

Nothing will make a greater difference in terms of enhancing the effectiveness and credibility of the oversight committees than restoring bipartisanship to their operations. But this is easier said than done. While rules that promote bipartisanship are desirable,[17] history has shown that policy and procedure will give way if the members and, to a lesser (but still significant) degree, the staff, choose to take a partisan course.

The best way to prevent this is to appoint members to the committees, and hire staff, who are not excessively partisan — in other words, people who have demonstrated an ability to work collegially with members on the other side of the aisle and who understand the importance of such collegiality to the intelligence oversight process. While identifying these qualities in prospective members and staff admittedly involves subjective judgment, the leadership in each house certainly knows who their most partisan members are, and the committee staff directors (who have the key role in hiring staff) also can get a good sense of this from their applicants' records and recommendations. A track record of excessive partisanship should simply disqualify a congressperson or staffer from serving on the committees.

Both committees should also adopt a single, "unified" staff structure rather than continuing the traditional "majority/minority" staff structures they now have. Under this kind of structure, everyone but the staff directors and their deputies would be hired by the committee as a whole and would work for the committee as a whole. A variation on this sort of system was employed effectively by the SSCI for the first twenty years of its existence and was instrumental in promoting a bipartisan approach to its work.[18]

Whatever the staff arrangements may be, however, the leaders of the committees ought to ensure that the operations of the committees are, for the most part, transparent to the members on both sides. The interests and views of the minority should be taken into account by the majority and accommodated when they can be. Differences that arise between the two sides ought to be aired immediately and forthrightly within the committees themselves and not fought out in public. Appearance is crucial here. Unless the intelligence committees are perceived as bipartisan by their respective houses, as well as by the American people, they will not be seen as credible overseers or as authoritative proponents of change. Instead, partisanship will undermine everything they try to do.

FOCUSING ON THE WRONG ISSUES

While the attention of the country was initially focused on the actions of the intelligence agencies after September 11, as time passed it became increasingly apparent that the oversight committees themselves had not focused sufficiently on the threat posed by al-Qaeda or on U.S. readiness to forestall a domestic terrorist attack. The *Washington Post* reported in April 2004, for example, that the Senate intelligence committee had held only one hearing devoted to al-Qaeda and its leader, Osama bin Laden, in the months prior to September 11, despite the fact that the committee had access to intelligence coming in during the spring and summer of 2001 suggesting that an attack against U.S. interests somewhere in the world could well be in the offing.[19]

Although the two committees' joint inquiry into September 11 did not address the performance of the congressional players,[20] the chairman of the SSCI at the time conceded that the "committee could have and should have given more attention to the emerging threat [of terrorism] and assessed how our intelligence community was making the transition from the Cold War into the new era."[21] In a similar vein, a former HPSCI member, commenting on the committee's performance prior to September 11, said that the committee had spent so much time worrying about budget issues and keeping up with current events that its oversight role over U.S. counterterrorist efforts had "almost gone away."[22] The fact is, both committees received voluminous intelligence information concerning bin Laden and al-Qaeda for years before September 11 and did relatively little to alert their colleagues or the public at large to the threat they posed. Nor did the committees delve deeply into how the intelligence community was dealing with these threats until after the attacks occurred.

For these and other failings the oversight committees were ultimately taken to task — for the first time in their history — by an official inquiry of the U.S. government. Describing congressional oversight as "dysfunctional," the 9/11 Commission stated: "In recent years, traditional review of the administration of programs and the implementation of laws has been replaced by 'a focus on personal investigation, possible scandals, and issues designed to generate media attention.' The unglamorous but essential work of oversight has been neglected, and few members past or present believe it is performed well." Commenting on the role of Congress generally before September 11, the commission judged that "the legislative branch adjusted little and did not restructure itself to address changing threats. Its attention to terrorism was episodic and splintered across several committees. Congress gave little guidance to Executive branch agencies, did not reform them in any significant way, and did not systematically perform oversight to identify, address, and attempt to resolve the many problems . . . that became apparent after 9/11."[23]

To remedy these problems, the 9/11 Commission recommended either that the two intelligence committees be combined into a single joint committee, or, if they were kept separate, that they be given authority by their respective bodies to authorize and appropriate the funds for intelligence each year. This latter option was seen as empowering the intelligence committees at the expense of the armed services and appropriations committees by minimizing if not eliminating the involvement of the latter committees in the annual appropriations process.[24] While both options ran counter to the way each house traditionally operated,[25] the 9/11 Commission insisted that unless the current congressional oversight arrangements were significantly changed, none of the changes they were recommending for the intelligence community would work.[26]

Coincidentally, as criticism began to be leveled at the oversight committees in the spring and summer of 2004, both issued public reports that were unusually harsh in their appraisals of the intelligence community's performance. In June the HPSCI issued a public report accompanying the annual authorization bill that, among other things, described the CIA's Directorate of Operations as "dysfunctional" and faulted the agency for spending a disproportionate amount of its effort on counterterrorism and the ongoing war in Iraq.[27]

Then, in July, the SSCI issued a 511-page report on the performance of the intelligence community with respect to the prewar assessments on Iraq that was considerably more substantive but every bit as scathing.[28] The report meticulously analyzed all of the evidence available to the analysts who put together the October 2002 national intelligence estimate (NIE) on Iraq's WMD capabilities, which had been the most authoritative assessment done by the community before the war and which had concluded, among other things, that Iraq "is reconstituting its nuclear program" and "has chemical and biological weapons"—judgments later proved wrong.

The committee concluded that the analysts responsible for the NIE had "mischaracterized" the available intelligence, blaming a "groupthink" mentality that had caused them and their superiors to give undue credence to evidence that fit their existing predilections. Instead of setting out what they actually knew and did not know, the committee found, the analysts reached conclusions that were not justified by the evidence. Also coming in for criticism was the failure of the CIA's Directorate of Operations to mount unilateral human collection operations in Iraq after the United Nations inspectors left in 1998. The committee blamed this particular failure on "a broken corporate culture and poor management" and said the problem could not be fixed by additional funding or personnel.[29]

Whether or not such harsh criticism can or should be seen as a defensive response to the mounting criticism of the committees' own performance, it was the source of considerable consternation within the intelligence community. DCI George Tenet called the HPSCI's criticism of the Directorate of Operations "absurd" and "ill-informed."[30] Official reaction to the criticisms leveled by the SSCI with respect to the Iraq NIE was more muted, but Deputy DCI John McLaughlin noted at a press conference that the SSCI had asked for the NIE in question and had given the CIA less than a month to produce it. He pointed out that the primary mistake had been failure to highlight caveats about the key judgments set out at the beginning of the estimate (such caveats were provided in the body of the estimate, but they were not emphasized). McLaughlin asserted that it would be wrong to infer from this particular lapse that there were "sweeping problems" within the intelligence community.[31]

In private, intelligence officials expressed greater resentment, wondering where the SSCI had been before the war. The committee, they noted, had access to the intelligence that formed the basis for the NIE before the war but never bothered to look at it when it might have made a difference. Both committees, in fact, accepted the judgments set forth in the NIE without making an independent critical examination.[32]

However valid the criticism of the committees' recent performance—whether before September 11 or concerning the war in Iraq—it does appear that the committees failed to focus adequately on the issues that turned out to matter most. This needs to change. It is not terribly difficult, one suspects, to discern where the focus of intelligence agencies will be for the foreseeable future. The war on terror, both at home and abroad, is likely to be their principal preoccupation for at least a generation. Intelligence agencies will also be concerned for the foreseeable future with the proliferation of weapons of mass destruction and with keeping them out of the hands of terrorists or hostile regimes around the world. While the intelligence community will be expected to cover a host of other issues, these topics will get the lion's share of attention.

The oversight committees ought to structure themselves and organize their activities to get at the issues and problems that impede the intelligence community's performance in these critical areas. While it might well be useful to restructure the program and budget procedures of the intelligence agencies so as to provide the committees a better view into these areas, oversight cannot be simply a matter of reviewing the agencies' annual program and budget submissions. Nor should oversight rely solely on current events briefings to indicate where the systemic problems are. The committees need to dig more deeply than that. They need to dedicate staff and, ideally, members to exploring these areas in a thorough, systematic way.[33] They need to find out what the intelligence agencies are doing about the problems of particular concern, where the shortfalls are, and what, if anything, can be done to address them.

And if they believe major change may be called for, the committees ought not to shy away from pursuing it, even if it means tangling with other committees or raising difficult issues. If the committees believe, for example, that major organizational reform (e.g., creating a National Counter Terrorism Center) would remedy a serious shortfall they have identified (e.g., the analysis and dissemination of intelligence on known or suspected terrorists within the United States), then they ought to press forward with such reforms, regardless of whether such action would bring them into conflict with other committees. Too often in the past they have shied away from pursuing macrolevel change,[34] fearing that working out the particulars with other committees would be time-consuming and rancorous. But the legislative process is exactly that, and if the committees are willing to put in the time and effort to achieve accommodations with the committees of overlapping jurisdiction, change is usually possible — perhaps not everything the intelligence committees would like to see, but needed change nonetheless.

A similar point can be made with respect to solutions that are perceived as too difficult to achieve. Too often the committees are leery of taking on issues they perceive will be difficult to work out because they are controversial. Neither committee, for example, chose to look seriously at the domestic roles and responsibilities of intelligence agencies in the aftermath of September 11, recognizing that allowing intelligence agencies greater latitude in rooting out terrorists within the United States would be controversial and require a great deal of effort, given the limitations and conditions that would be needed to satisfy civil libertarians.[35] In fact, certain intelligence agencies, notably the CIA, did assume a greater domestic role after September 11,[36] and the committees apparently decided that the preferable course was simply to acquiesce in the agency's more aggressive approach without undertaking a time-consuming critical review. This may have been the politically expedient way of dealing with such situations, but it is also an abdication of the committees' oversight responsibilities.

To be sure, the oversight committees cannot be on top of everything. The intelligence community is too large and complex, and the committees' capabilities too limited. They must choose the areas in which they want to be most active, and those should be the areas where the performance of U.S. intelligence agencies is most critical to the nation's security.

JURISDICTIONAL GAPS AND AMBIGUITIES

Apart from what is needed to improve the performance of the intelligence committees, it became apparent after September 11 that there are also gaps and ambiguities in the congressional oversight structure that need to be addressed.

The most significant of these involved the oversight of domestic intelligence efforts against terrorism. Prior to September 11, principal responsibility for these activities rested with the Federal Bureau of Investigation (FBI), which was subject to oversight by the judiciary committees (principally for its law enforcement functions) as well as by the intelligence committees (principally for its intelligence functions). The intelligence committees were also responsible for overseeing intelligence activities within the United States by elements of the intelligence community other than the FBI. Oversight of non-intelligence elements of the U.S. government involved in protecting against terrorism, e.g., the Department of State, the Customs Service, the Federal Aviation Administration, was spread among a variety of congressional committees. After September 11, a new department—the Department of Homeland Security (DHS)—was created to consolidate many of these nonintelligence functions.

But the new department did not include intelligence elements from the FBI or from the intelligence community itself. Nevertheless, it was given responsibility to serve as the governmental focal point for intelligence involving potential terrorists. Not only was it supposed to have access to all the intelligence produced by the intelligence community, it was supposed to have access to all information produced by nonintelligence agencies of the government, as well as the private sector, that might bear on the terrorist threat to the United States.[37]

In the House of Representatives, a new select committee was created to oversee the activities of the new department. In the Senate, no new committee was initially created. Instead, the Committee on Governmental Affairs assumed overall responsibility for overseeing the DHS, with the SSCI retaining concurrent oversight of its intelligence activities.

To make matters worse, from an oversight standpoint, the new department for various reasons had a difficult time implementing its responsibilities in the intelligence area. Stepping into the void, the CIA and FBI created new entities and undertook new functions that appeared to assume certain of the roles intended for the new department—actions the new department did not appear to contest—that blurred even further what the intelligence functions of the new department were or were apt to become.[38] This necessarily left open the question of which committee or committees were responsible for oversight. If the DHS intended to defer to the FBI and intelligence community in terms of executing the intelligence functions it had been assigned by statute, it would mean a decreased role in this area for the new select committee in the House as well as the Governmental Affairs Committee in the Senate, in favor of an increased role for the intelligence committees.

Incredibly, this crucial jurisdictional issue has yet to be resolved. While the Senate did act, in October 2004, to rename the Governmental Affairs Committee the "Committee on Homeland Security and Governmental Affairs," and specifically gave it oversight over the DHS minus several of its key components (e.g., the Transportation Security Administration), nothing was done to delineate the specific responsibilities of the renamed committee and the SSCI where the oversight of intelligence relating to homeland security is concerned.[39] If there is one aspect of intelligence oversight that matters most to the American people after September 11, it is the oversight of intelligence activities designed to protect the homeland from future attacks. Yet, more than three years after September 11, responsibility for such oversight remains divided and ambiguous — a recipe, if there ever was one, for inaction and failure.

The congressional committees involved in the creation of the DHS, together with the intelligence community, need to go back to the drawing board and reconsider, in light of what has happened over the past three years, which intelligence functions, if any, should continue to reside in the DHS and which in the intelligence community. Whether the intelligence elements of the DHS should be considered part of the intelligence community also needs to be reevaluated in light of the functions assigned. From there it should be possible to assign specific responsibility for oversight within the Congress, and such oversight should include not only identifying shortcomings in the collection, analysis, and dissemination of intelligence related to homeland security but also whether such activities pose an unwarranted threat to the civil liberties of American citizens, an aspect of oversight that has gotten short shrift in recent years.

An unrelated area of jurisdictional ambiguity that became apparent after September 11 was the involvement of military personnel, especially Special Operations Forces, in covert operations against terrorists. Existing law provides that covert actions normally require written approval by the president (who must find them necessary to the national security) and prior notice to the two intelligence committees.[40] But the law exempts "traditional military activities" from its purview. Congress had previously taken the position that "traditional military activities" included covert operations that might be undertaken prior to an "imminent" military operation, e.g., inserting persons who did not appear to be military personnel to recruit local sources and carry out other activities to "prepare the battlefield."[41]

The war on terror, however, and in particular the use of military personnel to hunt down terrorists in Afghanistan, raised the question of whether use of military personnel (who would not be identified as such) to hunt down or eliminate known or suspected terrorists would constitute covert action (and therefore require a presidential finding and notice to the intelligence committees), if such operations were carried out as an end in themselves rather than in preparation for an overt military operation. Some have contended that President Bush's direction to use all necessary actions in the war on terrorism obviates the need for specific presidential approval and notice to the committees where covert actions of the military are concerned,[42] but, as of this writing, the issue has yet to be resolved. The question needs to be answered, however, if only to ensure that subsequent operations of this sort do not lead to blame and recriminations later on. Covert actions undertaken abroad that involve the use of lethal force, whether carried out by the military or by the CIA, inherently raise issues that Congress needs to know about and be given an opportunity to weigh in on, if only because of their implications for U.S. security.[43] Although the intelligence committees have a statutory charter as well as an internal infrastructure to receive and consider such reports, whether they are made to the intelligence committees or the armed services committees is less important than making certain that such reports are made to some congressional committee. The worst of all possible worlds is the current situation, in which neither the military nor the affected committees are certain what their responsibilities are.

EXPERTISE AND STAYING POWER

In the wake of the *9/11 Commission Report,* published in July 2004 — and in implicit agreement with the 9/11 Commission that the congressional oversight of intelligence has not been as efficacious as it should have been — both houses of Congress appointed special task forces to examine the existing arrangements and consider what should be done to improve them.

Where the intelligence committees were concerned, foremost among the changes under consideration by both task forces was the elimination of term limits for service — eight years for the SSCI, and eight years for the HPSCI (over a period of twelve years). Not only had term limits diminished the level of sophistication and institutional memory resident in the committees, but they tended to discourage ordinary members (who were not the leaders of the committee) from devoting the time to learn the intelligence business while serving (knowing that their tenure was limited). Exacerbating the problem was the arcane, technical nature of much of the intelligence business. Simply understanding the functions of the various agencies involved and their relationships with each other could be a daunting task for members whose schedules allow them little time for such pursuits.

Also undermining the institutional effectiveness of the committees has been the frequent change in their leadership. In the past ten years, the SSCI has been chaired by five different senators, four of whom have served for two years or less. The HPSCI has been more stable in terms of its leadership in recent years, but the stability of leadership on both committees pales in comparison to other committees. Not only is it difficult to mount and sustain committee initiatives over a short period, frequent changes in leadership inevitably also mean frequent changes in key staff positions, which in turn often mean disruption and change of focus at the working level.

There has also been a noticeable trend in the past ten years toward appointing members for political reasons rather than to ensure, as it was originally conceived, that seasoned, "responsible" veterans of the legislative process be those chosen to serve.

Finally, there is the ongoing struggle to hire and retain qualified staff. While both committees recognize that staff expertise is essential to dealing effectively with the ever more complicated nature of the realm they oversee, members often prefer to bring in staff they know and trust even when others may have more expertise. They also sometimes hire people who, while knowledgeable about the intelligence agencies, are not familiar with, and do not take kindly to, the ways of the Congress (excessive partisanship, in particular, has driven many away). Occasionally people with agency experience come to the committee staff bearing grudges, or use their positions to do the things they have always wanted to do. Finding staffers who know the subject matter and can approach it objectively is difficult enough. But finding such people who also know how to work the Hill has been virtually impossible. Such skills have to be developed, and this takes time. Yet staff development has often been cut short or sidetracked by changes in the staff leadership or by unexpected changes in the committees' workload. Moreover, neither committee has a training program; employees are simply expected to learn as they go.

THE SENATE task force reported first, and on October 9, 2004, toward the end of the 108th Congress, the full Senate approved a series of amendments to the charter of the SSCI based on the recommendations of its task force.[44] Among other things, term limits for committee members were eliminated. From now on, service on the committee would be of indefinite duration and subject to the same vagaries as service on other Senate committees. In addition, the number of senators on the committee was reduced from seventeen to fifteen, and the majority and minority leaders were given authority to appoint the chairman and vice chairman, respectively, as well as the members of the committee from their respective sides of the aisle.[45] The majority party will have eight members, the minority party, seven. The resolution also provides specifically for the creation of a subcommittee on oversight, whose chairman and vice chairman will be appointed by the chairman and vice chairman of the full committee.

As far as the staff is concerned, the majority is authorized to hire 55 percent of the staff and the minority, 45 percent. The resolution also provides that, within these percentages, each member of the committee can hire one member of the staff to serve as his or her designated representative, subject to the security requirements and rules of the Senate.

While these changes were understandably touted as "really quite significant" by senators on both sides of the aisle, there is less to them than meets the eye. While eliminating term limits for members of the SSCI should prove to be important in the long run, it will still take time and effort for members to develop the desired expertise. Reducing the number of members from seventeen to fifteen only brings the size of the committee in line with the original requirements of Senate Resolution 400, which from the beginning has provided for a one-vote majority between the two parties. Providing for appointment of the chairman and vice chairman by the majority and minority leaders, respectively, rather than by the party caucuses is new but probably reflects the reality of what usually occurred anyway within the party caucuses. Moreover, unless the Senate leadership exercises this authority in a way that promotes bipartisanship and competence in the committee's leadership, it will not improve oversight. Similarly, while mandating the creation of a new subcommittee on oversight may be desirable, unless its members and staff are dedicated to plumbing in depth the issues that matter, the subcommittee could become little more than window dressing.

As far as the new staff arrangements are concerned, the Senate appears to have returned largely to the system that was in place for the first twenty years of the SSCI's existence, whereby each member was allowed to hire a "designee" who would be his or her representative on the staff and at the same time work for the committee as a whole. While the ratio of 55 to 45 percent was not formally in place in the early years, it comes close to approximating the split that existed during that period. (The ratio between majority and minority staffs in most congressional committees is roughly 66 percent to 33 percent.) Returning to a "designee" system will not in and of itself improve the expertise of the committee. To the contrary, it may mean, at least for the short term, that expertise is lost. (It can be anticipated that staff will be brought on because of their personal relationship with members rather than their expertise in intelligence.) The test will be whether the "designees" actually enter into the work of the SSCI (or see themselves solely as representing their members), and whether they stay aboard for the long haul. The elimination of term limits for members should help this problem, but only time will tell. Although the Speaker of the House of Representatives indicated in the fall of 2004 his intent to take up changes to intelligence oversight arrangements, during the next Congress, as of this writing, such changes have yet to be agreed to.

The congressional intelligence oversight committees play a valuable role in American democratic government. In a world that operates largely in secret, they are the only outside check of any consequence, operating not only as surrogates for their colleagues but as representatives of the American people as well. But the committees are more than simply a check on ill-advised actions by the executive. They often are in a position to bring about change, or serve as a catalyst for change, that cannot be readily achieved within the executive branch itself. Perhaps at no other time in our history has it been more important that these roles be performed effectively.

As a result of September 11, the anxiety level of most Americans has grown. They feel vulnerable to terrorist attacks in a way they never had before. The war in Iraq has not helped matters. Not only have many Americans come to realize for the first time the degree of hatred and animosity toward the United States that exists in the Muslim world, many feared that the war would only feed this anger and increase the likelihood of terrorist attacks against them. And while Americans appreciate that they cannot be told all the things that their intelligence agencies are doing to prevent such attacks, they want to believe that someone knows and is asking the right questions—the hard questions—on their behalf. They also want to believe that the intelligence agencies are doing what needs to be done. They would like to think that oversight by the congressional intelligence committees actually works.

Since September 11, however, Americans' confidence in the system has been shaken. They are disgusted by the political bickering they have witnessed, and they look for a credible, authoritative voice to tell them what to believe. In other words, they want a return to the bipartisanship and professionalism that used to characterize the work of the two committees.

Indeed, until the committees reestablish themselves as credible, authoritative voices, their role as overseers and producers of change within the intelligence community is going to suffer. While the Senate has recently taken steps to strengthen its oversight arrangements, and the House is presently expected to follow suit, organizational and procedural change alone will not be enough. Unless and until there is a genuine commitment to bipartisanship among members and staff, as well as a genuine seriousness of purpose to tackle the intelligence issues whose solution is crucial to the security of the country, the oversight committees will not regain the stature they once had.

Notes

1. These included the widespread collection of information on the political activities of U.S. citizens during the Vietnam War era, drug tests on unwitting citizens, and plotting assassinations of certain foreign leaders.

2. The Senate Select Committee on Intelligence was created by S. Res. 400, 94th Cong. (1976). The House Permanent Select Committee on Intelligence was created by amendment to Rule X of the Rules of the House of Representatives (1977).

3. See Frank J. Smist Jr., *Congress Oversees the United States Intelligence Community, 1947–1994*, 2d ed. (Knoxville: University of Tennessee Press, 1994), 214–17.

4. One of the more blatant examples of partisanship came during the March 1997 confirmation hearings of Anthony Lake, President Clinton's national security advisor, whom Clinton

nominated for director of central intelligence. After several days of political badgering by the Republicans on the committee, Lake withdrew in disgust.

5. Both committees participated in the development of what were seen as the legislative "fixes" for the September 11 attacks, e.g., the passage of the Patriot Act and the creation of the Department of Homeland Security, and also provided additional resources to the intelligence community.

6. The Republican vice chairman of the SSCI filed an "additional view" of 135 pages in which he lamented the failure of intelligence community leadership, i.e., the failure of DCI Tenet. Two other Senate Republicans criticized the report itself, saying that it had been put together in such a way that they could not "vouch for its contents."

7. During the 1988 presidential election, the committees considered the issue of candidate George H. W. Bush's involvement in the Iran-Contra scandal of the Reagan administration, but the evidence was not substantial or compelling enough to make it a viable issue in the campaign.

8. Robert Novak, "Memo Splits Intelligence Committee," *Washington Post,* November 17, 2003.

9. Senator Pat Roberts, quoted in Dana Priest, "Congressional Oversight of Intelligence Criticized," *Washington Post,* April 27, 2004, A10.

10. Congresswoman Jane Harman, quoted in Dana Priest and Walter Pincus, "Hill Probes Faulty Iraq Intelligence," *Washington Post,* January 30, 2004, A16.

11. See C. W. Young and Porter Goss, "Need Intelligence? Don't Ask John Kerry," *Tampa Tribune,* March 12, 2004. Also see Porter Goss quoted in Ethan Wallison, "Goss Questions Truthfulness of Clarke's 2002 Testimony," *Roll Call,* March 25, 2004, 1. Goss suggested that former White House counterterrorism czar and Bush critic Richard Clarke may have lied in previous testimony before the HPSCI.

12. Alexander Bolton, "Goss Defends Pace of Intel Report as Dems Cry Foul," *The Hill,* July 13, 2004.

13. Congresswoman Jane Harman quoted ibid.

14. Alexander Bolton, "Rep. Goss Has No Chance of Heading CIA: Roberts," *The Hill,* July 14, 2004.

15. As Chairman Roberts put it: "The (Goss) trial balloon went up, and Senator Rockefeller [the vice chairman of the SSCI] got out his BB gun and popped it out of the sky." Quoted in Bolton, "Goss Has No Chance of Heading CIA."

16. Ross K. Baker, "9/11: Where's Congress?" *Washington Post,* April 18, 2004, B4.

17. The resolution establishing the SSCI contains several such provisions. One provides that the majority on the committee will have only a one-vote majority. Another provides that the ranking minority member of the committee will be the vice chairman, who will preside in the absence of the chairman. The rules of the committee provide that the majority and minority sides will both have access to information in the possession of the committee. The rule establishing the HPSCI provides for a majority of two among its sixteen members.

18. Under the "unified staff" concept, the chairman and vice chairman of each committee would be permitted to hire the senior staff, but other hires would be agreed upon between them and subject to the approval of the entire committee. I am obliged to note that in an article I wrote in 2001 for Duke Law School, I endorsed the concept of majority and minority staffs, arguing that in an increasingly politicized environment, they were the best means of protecting the minority's rights. Having watched the deterioration of bipartisanship over the past three years, however, I now believe that having separate majority and minority staffs contributes to the problem rather than eases it.

19. Priest, "Congressional Oversight of Intelligence Criticized."

20. House of Representatives Permanent Select Committee on Intelligence and Senate Select Committee on Intelligence, *Joint Inquiry into Intelligence Community Activities before and after the Terrorist Attacks of September 11, 2001*, 107th Cong., 2d sess., 2002, S. Rep., 107–351. In their additional views to this report, Republican Senators Kyl and Roberts specifically cited the failure to address the performance of Congress as a shortcoming of the report, and Senator DeWine lamented the fact that the oversight committee had not focused its attention on the limitations of the Foreign Intelligence Surveillance Act (FISA) insofar as conducting surveillance of suspected terrorists was concerned.

21. Senator Bob Graham, quoted in Priest, "Congressional Oversight of Intelligence Criticized."

22. Tim Roemer, ibid.

23. National Commission on Terrorist Attacks upon the United States, *The 9/11 Commission Report: The Final Report of the National Commission on Terrorist Attacks upon the United States* (New York: W. W. Norton, 2004) (hereafter *9/11 Commission Report*), 105–6.

24. Ibid., 419–21.

25. Neither of the organizational options offered by the commission is compelling, in my view. One intelligence committee, rather than two, would probably reduce the oversight capabilities of the Congress rather than enhance them, and it would be unwise to vest the authorization and appropriation power in the same committee. Indeed, one committee must have the entire appropriations picture so as to ensure that what the authorizing committees may do fits into the federal budget framework as a whole.

26. *9/11 Commission Report*, 420.

27. House Permanent Select Committee on Intelligence, *Intelligence Authorization Act for Fiscal Year 2005*, 108th Cong., 2d sess., 2004, H. Rep., 108–558.

28. Senate Select Committee on Intelligence, *U.S. Intelligence Community's Prewar Intelligence Assessments on Iraq*, 108th Cong., 2d sess., 2004, S. Rep., 108–301.

29. Ibid., 14–26.

30. George J. Tenet, director of central intelligence, to Porter J. Goss, chairman, House Permanent Select Committee on Intelligence, June 23, 2004, available at www.cia.gov/cia/public_affairs/press_release/2004/pr06242004.html.

31. Transcript, press conference of John E. McLaughlin, deputy director of central intelligence, July 9, 2004, available at www.cia.gov/cia/public_affairs/press_release/2004/pr07092004.html.

32. One does wonder whether the committees do not owe this to their colleagues, if not to the country itself, before the Congress votes to go to war largely on the basis of intelligence reports.

33. Creating subcommittees dedicated to these issues is one means of achieving this focus, but whether subcommittees are created or not, staff (apart from the budget review staff) should be devoted to them.

34. For example, both committees endorsed the creation of a director of national intelligence in their joint report on the events of September 11, issued in December 2002. Neither, however, moved such legislation out of committee in the years that followed. It eventually came about in December 2004, not as a result of action by the two committees but rather as part of the intelligence reform legislation prompted by the report of the 9/11 Commission.

35. Interestingly, the director of the National Security Agency, Lieutenant General Michael Hayden, in his public appearance before the committee's joint inquiry, specifically raised this issue, saying, "Just tell me what you want me to do." Individual members did not take up his challenge, however, and their final report was silent on the issue.

36. After September 11, the CIA stationed dedicated analysts around the United States to support the joint terrorism task forces established by the FBI. The agency, in conjunction with the FBI, also formed the terrorist threat information center to support the FBI's domestic anti-terrorist operations.

37. See *Homeland Security Act of 2002,* U.S. Public Law 107–296, 107th Cong., 2d sess. (November 25, 2002), secs. 201–2.

38. See Justin Rood, "Cast in a Major Intelligence Role, DHS Is Mostly a Spectator," *Congressional Quarterly,* February 20, 2004.

39. See S. Res. 445, 108th Cong., 2d sess., sec. 101.

40. *National Security Act of 1947,* U.S. Public Law 253, 80th Cong., 1st sess. (July 26, 1947), sec. 503, as amended.

41. U.S. House, Conference Report on H.R. 1455, 102d Cong., 1st sess. (July 25, 1991), H. Rep. 102–166.

42. For a detailed discussion of this issue, see Jennifer D. Kibbe, "The Rise of the Shadow Warriors," *Foreign Affairs* 83 (March–April 2004): 102–15.

43. See Helen Fessenden, "Intelligence: Hill's Oversight Role at Risk," *Congressional Quarterly,* March 29, 2004.

44. See S. Res. 445, 108th Cong., 2d sess., sec. 201.

45. See "Senators Offer New Oversight Structure," *Washington Post,* October 5, 2004, A4.

Meeting the Challenge: Action Now

JENNIFER E. SIMS AND BURTON GERBER

THE CENTRAL PURPOSE of this book has been to illuminate the ways in which U.S. intelligence capabilities can be significantly improved by adjusting policies and practices rather than institutions and structures.* It is less a book on organizational reform than one on methods. Of course, new methods may give rise to structural reforms, as suggested in Henry Crumpton's chapter on homeland defense or Donald Daniel's chapter on denial and deception. But with function placed before form in the foregoing analyses, we have sought to offer ideas for future intelligence managers regardless of where they sit institutionally.

Our work has been, of course, contemporaneous with the two commissions and the reform legislation and, we believe, tracks well with those efforts. Perhaps most important, however, our work is distinguished from the aforementioned commissions and legislation, both because it was done exclusively by "practitioners" of the intelligence business and also because we had no particular demons — approaching elections, commission deadlines, or political scrutiny of the process — pressing at our backs. The unique qualification we bring to the table is that each of us, to one extent or another, has been "part of the problem." The conclusions we have each identified in our respective chapters arise from the crucible in which more than three hundred years of our collective professional experience and dedication collided headlong with the tragic failures of September 11 and Iraqi WMD.

Of the authors' ideas that resonate most sharply, five seem particularly important:

- Fostering agility by clarifying and streamlining chains of command, permitting risk management at lower levels of command, and encouraging partnership among civilian agencies and between them and the private sector to speed up these agencies' acquisition of collaborative intelligence technologies.
- Enhancing the interagency teamwork overseas through increased chief of station and chief of mission authorities, and using a similar approach for domestic operations at the state and local level.
- Using the strengthened national leadership in the office of the director of national intelligence (DNI) to coordinate budgets and programs, including open-source col-

---

* John MacGaffin contributed significantly to this concluding chapter, both with his ideas and with written input. We gratefully acknowledge his contribution, particularly to the domestic intelligence section, while absolving him of any responsibility for the overall result.

lection, with those agencies not formally part of the intelligence community but critically linked to it, such as the Department of Energy, the National Laboratories, and the Department of State.

- Eschewing Department of Justice leadership of domestic intelligence.
- Addressing counterintelligence challenges by, among other things, developing greater capacity to undertake offensive measures.

Agility and Teamwork

Of all the reforms suggested in this volume, the need for improved agility and teamwork is the most pressing. The capabilities adversaries may employ to gain asymmetrical advantage are mobility and stealth. By operating within the bounds of civil society and by using modern technology and commercial encryption, they may cluster quickly, coordinate secretly, and strike with little warning. U.S. operatives countering such adversaries need to be equally mobile and to have intelligence that keeps pace.

In our current networked world this mobility requires, in the first instance, decentralized and empowered decision making accompanied by clarity of command. Interagency teams of collectors, operators, and analysts in the field need to be able to share what they know and make decisions quickly based on all-source intelligence, including national collectors. Management of risk—to operations or to sources and methods—must be delegated down the chain of command and accepted as part of a process in which intelligence is destined for use. At the same time, users at all management levels need to assume responsibility for intelligence losses as well as gains. When careful use of intelligence nonetheless requires compromising sources, and thus temporarily diminishing estimative capabilities, policymakers and congressional appropriators need to restore lost capabilities before true failure—that is, loss of a decisive information advantage over the adversary—does occur.

In this and other ways, the behavior and decisions of intelligence users and congressional oversight committees are critical to the enterprise and its long-term health. For example, a decision to engage in covert action may expose sources or skew the reports from agents who have a stake in the outcome. If the covert action then fails, the sources may be lost. Similarly, tapping a source repeatedly for information before a critical event or decision can lead to that agent's exposure and eventual loss. Yet not doing so can cost a decision maker his critical advantage. Such decisions on use and loss are familiar to seasoned intelligence officers and involve values that lie at the core of the profession. Ethical conduct and sustained agility require intelligence users who appreciate the full dimensions of risk, are ready to take some risks themselves in delegating decisions and allocating scarce collection resources, and are willing to accept responsibility for the losses—be they in the decision or the collection realms—when they do occur. Congressional committees overseeing the process should not hold intelligence, an executive-branch function, hostage to political disagreements over how those risks were weighed or decisions made in the aftermath of policy failure by denying the funding needed to restore lost capabilities.

That said, risk taking must be disciplined. Authors of many of the chapters in this volume mention the value of instituting lessons-learned exercises. While these exercises exist in certain agencies, they need to be more disciplined, focused, and informed by outside perspectives. Furthermore, we endorse the concept of "lessons while learning" in which intelligence professionals systematically review and revise as they go, learning and adapting to new challenges in real time. Of course, such flexibility requires a mind-set somewhat liberated from regulations and procedures. Although some will find such an approach objectionable in high-risk endeavors, the question is not whether there will be risk but where one wishes to take it. Training can instill good judgment and an introspective capacity for self-correction; it cannot eliminate the risk that mistakes will be made—only that they will not last once recognized.

Agility also requires sharing of information and coordinated action at all levels of the decision-making process. It will be tempting for the DNI to try to enforce this requirement for teamwork from the top down. The recent commissions on both September 11 and Iraq have recommended an enlargement of DNI authorities to achieve these ends. Too much direction and oversight from the top, however, may squash initiative, imagination, and agility rather than encourage them. Leadership may at times require restraint.

In our view, the solution rests in the field. Chiefs of station who run human intelligence and other clandestine operations in their respective countries should continue to act as the field representatives of the highest U.S. government intelligence authority and thus retain responsibility for coordinating activities of all intelligence agencies in their respective countries. This coordination role has been allowed to atrophy over the years, making teamwork more difficult than it should be. The chief of station's role must be strengthened and bound more closely to the mission of the ambassador and regional commander. At the same time, chiefs of station should not have multiple masters. For field operations they should coordinate with the ambassador and, when necessary, the regional combatant commander, but on all intelligence matters, whether human intelligence (HUMINT) or multi-INT, they should report to a single Washington-based authority. Separating the hats traditionally worn by the director of central intelligence (DCI) should not lead to overlapping reporting chains for those implementing intelligence policy in the field.

Ambassadors, in turn, should be understood as managers of critical collection assets and customers of intelligence in their own right. The State Department and the Central Intelligence Agency (CIA) could aid them in their coordination function by detailing senior intelligence analysts to selected embassies to work with ambassadors and chiefs of station in the area. In this way the State Department's Bureau of Intelligence and Re-search (INR) could help ensure that intelligence available to the secretary of state is also available, as required, to the appropriate officials on the country team and vice versa. Such analysts could help make embassies truly synergistic intelligence centers, collect-ing, processing, and using all-source information for field-based operations, even as threats and opportunities change. As part of this effort, Foreign Service officers should be augmented in number to increase the reporting on foreign developments.

The idea of strengthening overseas teams and asking them to help prioritize targets as these targets change contrasts sharply with the idea of establishing Washington-based centers. Such mission-based centers will see their futures in the persistence and the magnitude of the threat they are created to counter, risking the rigidifying of intelli-gence enterprise at the top. They will tend to dig in bureaucratically, making it harder to foster an ethic of sharing across mission areas. And such sharing is particularly crucial as targets, agendas, and thus missions change — a prerequisite to effective warning of surprise attack. The expected success of the National Counter Terrorism Center must not lead to the bureaucratic calcification that may result should the "centers" solution proliferate. The best way to counteract this result would be to ensure that country teams and their domestic counterparts remain focused on changing threats and opportuni-ties, not on single-mission objectives.

An appreciation of the critical role ambassadors, embassies, and, by extension, the State Department as a whole play as facilitators of worldwide operations should raise the stature and importance of budgeting and programming for this department—a mat-ter that requires the DNI's urgent attention. Even as intelligence agencies and national security managers look to increase nonofficial cover, the role of American embassies in foreign policy and national security programs will remain essential. If the Office of Management and Budget, the Congress, and State Department officials themselves would regard the U.S. government's overseas facilities as ground-based platforms for critical national security operations — as important in their own right as space-based platforms — then perhaps the ongoing struggle to ensure they are properly funded, augmented by the latest technology and communications gear, and staffed with enough high-quality personnel would be eased.

But such steps to enhance the agility of official presence in the field are not enough, particularly for the purposes of warning. Breadth in official coverage must be matched by depth if the intelligence community is to enhance its capacity to warn. Here imagi-nation and experimentation are needed. For example, a cadre of deep-cover intelligence officers loosely tethered to regional stations could be deployed for many years at a time to learn the social and cultural fabric in which they are immersed. These officers would help refine requirements, collect information from the "street," and provide perspec-tive during crises. In rare circumstances, they would support military or diplomatic operations. They would thus be encouraged to be analysts as well as collectors, actively shaping their own missions. As they take the pulse of a region, such officers would not need to focus exclusively on adversarial circles such as Islamists, terrorists, or criminal groups. They could also perform positive functions, albeit covertly, as doctors, agricultural experts, or educators. While their purpose would be to improve strategic and tactical warning on a regional basis, such officers would aid the societies in which they work through the transfer of skills, knowledge, and resources.

Of course the emphasis on deep-cover officers with nonofficial status would require new approaches to the placement of such individuals. It would be essential not to act in ways that might compromise established nongovernmental and AID-related organizations. Such balancing of objectives can and must be accomplished. Detailed understanding of social, cultural, and economic issues of likely target areas is not possible in crisis mode. It requires attention in the strategic sense, before the crisis arises.

Of course, direct intervention in a crisis simply underscores the value of deep-cover officers. Nowhere, perhaps, are agility and teamwork more needed than in the conduct of paramilitary operations. As Henry Crumpton has written, deep intelligence permits the enlistment of local forces to support U.S. or multilateral operations. Binding selected local leaders or groups to U.S.-run operations provides the flexibility needed for engagements in unknown territory. Done wisely, such associations help to secure victory through psychological association of U.S. objectives and military plans with local agendas and historical precedents. Although the 9/11 Commission has argued for transferring authorities from the CIA to the Special Operations Command, whether "sensor" or "shooter" is in charge of operations, ensuring teamwork at all levels is crucial. Certainly the CIA must remain in the business of sustaining the network of contacts and the operational infrastructure to carry out its responsibilities in the paramilitary domain. Intimate knowledge of social fabric, cultural dynamics, and history constitute the agency's comparative advantage and, as an integral element of activities from covert action through proxy war and direct intervention, must be encouraged. For this reason we do not see any gains in shifting the structure and authorities for paramilitary operations to the Defense Department, as the 9/11 Commission has proposed.

The complement to such agility in the field is the need to achieve agility in decision support within the United States. The DNI needs the authority and the responsibility to identify those decision makers who need intelligence at all levels of government and to act decisively to provide it. This objective complements what has been the director of central intelligence's long-standing responsibility for protecting sources and methods and thus limiting distribution. However, the long-standing burden placed on the decision maker to demonstrate "need to know" should be modified. Intelligence must now move rapidly to new users, particularly on the home front, who will need it before they know they do, and will have access to critical information before they understand that it is critical. The office of the DNI should train new and prospective users of intelligence, forge partnerships with the private sector to automate the sharing of data during crises, and establish liaisons with those first responders who find their need for intelligence fluctuating enough that they need a "411" number for national-level support and information handoff.

Agility also requires a capacity for innovation. The private sector's rapid advances in intelligence-related technologies are increasingly of a systemic nature. Hospitals, water-treatment plants, and landlords are investing in inferencing engines tied to wireless networks of sensors to help them manage inventory, monitor operations, and anticipate and respond to crises. In this way, firms are partnering with customers at the local level to create "smart" solutions for managing complex missions.

Unfortunately, busy U.S. government decision makers are often in the dark about these new commercial alliances and the opportunities they hold for federal partnering. During the next domestic crisis, federal officials may at last realize the importance of intelligence generated in the private sector. Without access to it — ideally automated in a way that minimizes the need to interfere with first responders — those decision makers will be frustrated. With access to it, they might be able to master or even anticipate the crisis before it happens and save valuable time. Imagine, for example, how important it might be to have advanced information-processing systems in place, together with a protocol for protecting individual privacy, that would allow hospitals, public utilities, and building managers to share information about an unfolding attack involving the release of anthrax, a radiological device, or the contamination of water supplies. The DNI needs a staff dedicated to learning about private-sector initiatives of these kinds and finding ways to build on them.

Federal decision makers are also unlikely to envision the technological requirements of missions made plausible through commercial advances. But in the current acquisitions system, the premise is that government officials know what they require and levy those requirements on the private sector through the contracting process. The DNI should consider developing an approach that incorporates a "catcher's mitt" for system-wide solutions to intelligence needs, particularly on the civilian side. Companies that believe their commercial systems or innovations might be relevant for intelligence activities should have a place to bring them for vetting. In turn, the office of the DNI should have personnel dedicated to ferreting out promising technologies in the commercial realm and buying them, or subsidizing their employment, at the state and local levels.

Agility also demands investment in the processing and exploitation of data with both strategic and immediate needs in mind. Here the creation of new centers dedicated to current intelligence may make things harder. Their organizational boundaries could in effect trap expertise within them — a phenomenon the Iraq WMD Commission has usefully referred to as their "gravitational pull." Instead, networking should be emphasized among translators and primary analysts at collection agencies and all-source analysts involved in strategic and tactical support within and across issue areas. Highly effective analytic units do this as a matter of course with daily meetings at which they share developments in each mission area that might affect others. The DNI may thus be able to encourage the best of both worlds by requiring all national-level centers to establish a norm of cross-mission intelligence sharing. In addition, the DNI can work to ensure that all-source analytic capabilities are optimized for both immediate and strategic objectives but not artificially divided along these lines. Otherwise the strategic picture cannot evolve with all the pieces of the puzzle that current intelligence can provide. And current intelligence would remain uninformed by the gathering storms that only strategic analysis of intelligence may reveal.

Finally, there will never be enough analysts with the right mix of area and language knowledge and sufficient experience to meet all surge needs. Commitment across intelligence agency lines to developing the cadres able to handle quick-reaction issues as well as studying and writing about longer-range problems will enhance policymakers' ability to meet the threats of the less structured enemy we now face.

Leadership

Leadership is often understood as a capacity for action, as decisiveness. This is indeed one quality a commander must have. But leadership also involves the wisdom, insight, and courage to avoid quick action when restraint is in order. Leadership is also about clear-headed vision and a capacity to embrace failure and innovation as two sides of the same coin. In intelligence, unlike in boating, the captain ought not to go down with the ship; he ought to repair the ship, deploy lifeboats or buy commercial craft, and complete the mission anyway. That is his responsibility. Creating the teams to innovate, lose a boat, and purchase anew is the essence of intelligence leadership. It cannot be backward-looking but must look forward and be mission-oriented.

Leaders will thus need to challenge conventional wisdom — especially of the post–September 11 sort. Although a number of the contributors to this volume believe that intelligence failed badly both prior to the September 11 attacks and with regard to Iraq's weapons of mass destruction, our collective intent has been to focus less on past mistakes than on future requirements, informed by what we have learned from the important work of the 9/11 Commission and the commission on Iraq's weapons of mass destruction. National tragedies and miscalculations of this magnitude properly capture our attention; but they cannot, alone, tell us what needs to be done in the years ahead. Significant as transnational threats such as terrorism and proliferation are, there are other, state-based challenges that deserve our continuing and persistent attention, such as the rise of China, the nuclear plans of North Korea and Iran, the stability of Pakistan, the health of Russian and Ukrainian democracy, and the implications of political change in states in the Middle East. These traditional intelligence challenges, together with the need for overt and clandestine collaboration with other governments on counterterrorism, argue for strengthening official cover — not, as some have suggested, for its weakening, in the rush to restructure human intelligence. Translating the shocks of September 11 into balanced proposals for a revived intelligence community will require appropriate resistance to some new ideas, even as others are embraced.

Indeed, it will take strong leadership to ensure that the post–September 11 intelligence capabilities of the U.S. government do not become fixated on terrorism alone. Terrible as this threat is, especially if linked with nuclear weapons, strategies to counter it and to prevent equally unwelcome outcomes (such as a nuclear and ballistic-missile-equipped North Korea or Iran) emphasize the need for a balanced and focused approach to requirements under strong leadership. The requirements process, as Jim Simon's chapter has explained, must be transparent, flexible, and tied in tightly with the needs of intelligence users.

An effective requirements system would attain its flexibility by balancing four tasks: filling gaps in collection that analysts and deep-cover officers encounter in the course of their work; discerning decision makers' needs as national security policies evolve; following up on needs identified by domestic (first responders) or foreign operatives while embedded in the field; and satisfying the peculiar needs of intelligence managers who must both support the warning function — a responsibility the DNI must exercise even when policymakers discount the likelihood of surprise — and design collection systems for future decision makers. In our view, no single element in this four-part balance should trump the others. Current decision makers, no matter how powerful, should not have the capacity to skew a collection asset so much to their immediate needs that they rob the system of its capacity to provide warning of policy failure or to counter significant threats likely to crystallize after they leave office. It is in the management of this politically sensitive requirements system, particularly as it affects the intelligence agencies' budgets, that the DNI may find his greatest powers and Congress may need its most effective oversight mechanisms.

To achieve the kind of leadership suggested above, the office of the DNI is now responsible for ensuring the programmatic cross-walking and strategic planning of intelligence missions across agencies. The DNI, benefiting from the insight into budget execution that the 2004 legislation affords, must exercise the power not only to determine where intelligence dollars will be spent but also where they will *not* be spent. In the world of finite dollars, the question of "where from" is ultimately much more defining than the ability to decide "where to." Anyone can say — as almost every U.S. intelligence department head has — that he will add additional resources to some aspect of the war on terror. But the new resources are seldom "additive," and it usually falls to someone else lower down the command chain to decide where those resources will come from.

Instead, it should be the DNI's role to ask whether an intelligence organization should do less on China or less on Russia while it does more on counterterrorism. This office should set the standards for doing less as well as more.

Furthermore, the DNI should have in his most senior councils representation from agencies not formally within the intelligence community but critical to its operations, such as program managers within the Department of State responsible for buildings, communications, and human resources, and the Department of Energy's national laboratories. The DNI should include these representatives even if they do not manage any programs that are part of the formal intelligence budget process or that he directly controls. He should chair a subcommittee of the National Security Council to coordinate the budgets of these agencies with those of the formal intelligence community. The Office of Management and Budget not only should attend but should adopt a similar method of cross-walking among related accounts instead of considering programmatic analysis strictly along agency lines. Because problems in coordinating programs are a chief source of interagency friction, this one step in programmatic coordination could do more for intelligence sharing than the creation of any single mission center or set of centers. In fact, the extent of government programs implicated by such a strategy suggests that the leadership of the intelligence community must always use interagency diplomacy and negotiation to succeed. It is simply not possible to entrust one individual with complete authority over all U.S. government intelligence functions.

Similarly, the DNI will need to take on the difficult issue of open-source collection. This is an area that has long been stifled by security concerns and leadership failure. For too long the use of open-source intelligence tools has been hampered by counterintelligence objections. Analysts need unfettered access to these materials. Of course an adversary may learn what the U.S. government is most interested in by monitoring its use of journals and magazines, but there are easier ways than penetrating the intelligence community's huge and growing database of open-source materials. This is also a domain where collaboration with transnational, nongovernmental, and international organizations may make sense. Of course, as with any intelligence endeavor, counterintelligence training should be as much a part of managing open-source collection as of any other collection discipline.

In sum, the new DNI must have wide-ranging programmatic authorities. Without them, there is little chance that the intelligence community will make the changes in policies and practices, either within its own organizations or in the collective, that are required. Because the 2004 reform legislation was intentionally vague on the personnel and budget authorities of the DNI, he must seize on the first significant challenge in these areas and seek a more explicit statement of authority, either by executive order or by statute. The issue is too important to be left in limbo.

Leadership will also be crucial for binding the inherently diverse cultures of disparate U.S. intelligence agencies into effective teams for the purposes of strategic analysis, tactical warning, and overseas operations. At times, cultures must be forced to change. But usually, it seems to us, cultural differences are strengths that can be used to good advantage. Cultures evolve from mission and reflect the qualities that set standards for recruitment in a particular discipline. The more stringent the discipline's requirements, such as in special operations or in the CIA's Directorate of Operations, the more pronounced the common cultural characteristics of those successfully performing the mission. Cultures do, of course, affect cognitive screens that can help one see clearly or impede vision. Mixing cultures helps expose biases either way. Effective leadership involves truly understanding and valuing the cultures involved, capitalizing on the strengths each brings to a mission, and, where necessary, bridging differences to get maximum collective output. Building into training programs the expectation that cultures will not be scorned but rather employed synergistically across the intelligence domain, including agencies not part of the National Foreign Intelligence Program, is important for preventing "groupthink" and sustaining morale.

Domestic Intelligence and American Democracy

Perhaps nowhere is the need for agility and leadership more critical than in the difficult domain of domestic intelligence. Whether law enforcement or intelligence should be the tool of choice against terrorism and other forms of foreign threat within U.S. borders is an issue that was neither clarified nor resolved by the 9/11 Commission or the reform legislation. This question was, in fact, obfuscated. In our view, American law enforcement is intentionally a reactive tool. The law enforcement investigator seeks to determine whether elements of a crime are present and whether they can be associated with a given suspect or a given set of facts. Law enforcement becomes proactive only when a suspect threatens to break the law. For intelligence, which must warn, that is simply too late. Intelligence collection seeks to understand those indications of hostile intent that may be cause for alarm. It does not matter whether or not a U.S. statute may have been violated. The focus is possible catastrophic damage, not violation of law. Whereas law enforcement may be too slow, intelligence—from a civil liberties standpoint—may be too fast and too intrusive. Herein lies the domestic intelligence conundrum.

Although the Department of Justice and the Federal Bureau of Investigation (FBI) maintain that the constitutional rights of U.S. persons will be protected only if they (DOJ and the FBI) maintain control of domestic intelligence collection, we believe this argument does not accord with past or present practice. For more than a decade, Executive Order 12333 has provided the rules for intelligence agencies with regard to U.S. persons. The attorney general participated in the development of that executive order and has authority to take action whenever its provisions are breached. Foreign intelligence collection, even when done domestically, must be done by those who have the necessary experience and substantive knowledge. Agreeing with this principle, the WMD commission proposed that non-law-enforcement activities against terrorism and other foreign threats conducted domestically be directed by the new DNI, just as he directs those same activities abroad. Such activities should receive the same Justice Department oversight and safeguards for protection of U.S. persons' constitutional rights and privacy as currently apply to U.S. intelligence activities abroad where U.S. persons are involved. But these non-law-enforcement activities do not require DOJ direction or supervision on a day-to-day basis.

In sum, we remain concerned that civil liberties are most at risk when law enforcement agencies assume the character of intelligence agencies. If the Justice Department and FBI assume responsibility for domestic spying, how will Americans be assured that they will not overreach in the domestic intelligence domain? The American people have long resisted the confluence of federal powers to arrest, to spy, and to use force. These federal powers must be kept separate even as we face the enormous task of fighting terror at home.

Henry Crumpton, in chapter twelve of this volume, lays out a path whereby proven intelligence skills and competence can be brought to bear quickly against this problem. A domestic intelligence service could combine the best of law enforcement, especially homeland knowledge, with the best of CIA, to include tradecraft and global reach. Just as Executive Order 12333 lays out the rules that ensure that CIA and other foreign intelligence collectors observe constitutional protections of U.S. persons in their activities abroad, a similar regime, transparent to Congress, the executive branch, and the public, can be developed with the full participation of the Department of Justice and state and local law enforcement. With the constitutional rights of U.S. persons protected, there is no need to remove foreign intelligence collection from its home and saddle it with management and direction by law enforcement authorities.

Counterintelligence

Whatever intelligence collection systems the United States deploys, and whatever the degree of their analytic and technical excellence, intelligence agencies and organizations without solid counterintelligence (CI) programs will not succeed. American interests are worldwide, involving exchanges with, and intelligence activity directed against, a large number of foreign nations. Not every foreign nation has an intelligence collection service, but almost all have active security organizations and CI agencies.

The United States will be among the first targets of these foreign organizations, because they need both to defend themselves against American intelligence and to learn what they can about U.S. interests through recruitment of American sources. Foreign intelligence services are also likely to use liaison channels to attempt to influence U.S. decision making whenever possible. Strong counterintelligence capabilities become increasingly important as liaison relationships proliferate and deepen. This is because good CI and associated security programs can reveal seemingly productive intelligences exchanges to be manipulative exercises in deception. Ineffective counterintelligence can undermine and even negate the achievements of transformed intelligence agencies and personnel, putting American defense at risk. Just as we argue for new scrutiny of all aspects of intelligence collection and analysis, so we believe that the intelligence community must take the lead, with the support of policymakers, to enhance CI, both offensively and defensively.

In March 2005 President Bush approved the "National Counterintelligence Strategy of the United States," which makes clear that CI must provide strategic input for policymakers, helping them to understand why, where, and how our adversaries will attack us. The new strategy makes explicit the indivisibility of national intelligence and counterintelligence efforts. Ensuring that intelligence professionals of all organizations pay heed to the president's national counterintelligence strategy will be an important task for the DNI, working with the president's national counterintelligence executive.

The modern counterintelligence challenge resembles in many ways the transnational threat communism posed at the start of the cold war. Then as now, the question of how to balance our defense against adversaries and the preservation of civil liberties is crucial. One way to accomplish this goal is to invigorate counterintelligence efforts overseas. Intelligence community agencies need to do a better job of successfully penetrating foreign intelligence and counterintelligence services and terrorist groups. In the past, when American services succeeded in this assignment, not only were American defenses enhanced but intelligence collected from such penetrations assisted policymakers in deciding on courses of action not strictly related to CI or security issues. Spies recruited by American intelligence agencies in those hostile services and groups have reported not only on the intelligence and security activities of their nations and organizations, but also on the efforts they have made — both successful and unsuccessful — to penetrate American institutions and secret programs. However, when American services have failed in this regard against certain hostile countries or terrorist groups, the result has been wasted opportunities, ignorance of the targeted country, and, of course, physical assault on the American homeland. A counterintelligence program without the benefits of offensive measures will be second-rate by definition.

A valuable art in offensive counterintelligence is deception. As Donald Daniel argues in chapter eight, the American CI effort must include not only the withholding of information from those who wish us harm but also deception programs designed to mislead and confuse actual and potential enemies. Deception, done well, need not distort official representations of government policies to the public but can convey misleading information through the adversaries' more trusted sources of information, such as its spies or its technical collectors. The United States currently has inadequate capabilities for the formulation and use of such deception techniques, despite the talents embedded in its political culture. This deficiency in turn affects the U.S. ability to detect the deceptions of others. New efforts in this regard should be high on intelligence leaders' agendas.

Finally, the counterintelligence challenges posed by technological change are also growing rapidly. Private-sector innovation is providing the core technologies both for government-wide networking and for managing infrastructure such as railroads, electrical grids, and air traffic control. As Jim Gosler explains in chapter six, these technologies, created by firms with multinational reach, may involve their own sleeper "agents," ready to switch from benign to pathological status at the instigation of overseas hackers. Developing an effective capability to exploit this technological loophole in collection endeavors must be accompanied by an equally vigorous effort to manage it from a defensive standpoint.

Action Now

Of course none of these reforms will be truly transformative unless the mechanisms for congressional oversight are strengthened and improved to ensure consistent and informed programmatic reviews and fair, ethical, and supportive oversight of the U.S. intelligence process. The notion of "lessons while learning" should be embraced by the congressional oversight committees. And it is in Congress that the critical juncture between overseas and domestic intelligence operations must be both encouraged and carefully monitored. Leadership skills in Congress are, in other words, as important as those in the executive branch. With all the changes anticipated in the process of programming and budgeting of intelligence within the executive branch, Capitol Hill must streamline its committees to permit agile authorization and coordination of intelligence programs across intelligence and nonintelligence agency lines. This may be, at the end of the day, the most important and transformative idea we have to offer. Unfortunately, achieving better programmatic decision making may be the most difficult challenge we face.

Yet we feel there is room for optimism. As Ernest May points out in chapter one, the United States is blessed with a great capacity to innovate and to adapt its institutions to new requirements even when crises are not occurring. During the 1950s the intelligence community continued to consolidate and innovate for the purpose of countering an adversary determined to remain extraordinarily secretive. Exploiting advances in science, technology, and engineering, the U.S. government launched massive, expensive, and highly productive technical collection programs and consolidated them in the National Security Agency and the National Reconnaissance Office (NRO). In the 1970s the intelligence community adapted to the requirements of more stringent oversight. Additional structural and procedural changes were made in the 1990s, with the creation of the National Imagery Agency, the decision to commercialize imagery, the expansion of intelligence support to Congress, and the move toward greater openness, such as the declassification of the NRO and certain imagery technologies for purposes of improved accountability.

Innovations also occurred, albeit quietly, at lower levels of U.S. intelligence in the form of collaborative enterprises such as national intelligence support teams, which proved so crucial during the first Iraq war, and their civilian reflection, the diplomatic intelligence support center, which aided diplomacy during the Balkan conflict. That the U.S. intelligence community generated such changes through teamwork and timely action is testimony not to its rigidity but rather to a capacity for flexibility that has received, in our view, too little attention. The issue now is whether we can seize this moment of opportunity and public interest to expedite progress without doing harm. Strong national leadership, agile enterprise, effective congressional partnership, and innovation in all intelligence programs are reform issues requiring most urgent attention.

The American intelligence community has reached middle age, while terrorist organizations, weapons proliferators, and nations that mean America harm have fielded agile teams with whole new playbooks. We must recognize and adapt to this reality now, without destroying or undermining American strengths, because if the enemies succeed in their attacks against the United States, the threats to American civil liberties and democracy will only proliferate.

CONTRIBUTORS

HENRY A. CRUMPTON, a 24-year veteran of the CIA's Clandestine Service, led the CIA campaign in Afghanistan from September 2001 until June 2002. He was chief of the CIA's National Resources Division from August 2003 until May 2005. He is the recipient of the Intelligence Commendation Medal, the George H.W. Bush Award, the Sherman Kent Award, and the Distinguished Intelligence Medal. He earned a bachelors in political science from the University of New Mexico and a masters with honors in international public policy from Johns Hopkins University's School of Advanced International Studies.

DONALD C. F. DANIEL is a professor in the Security Studies Program, Walsh School of Foreign Service, Georgetown University. He previously was special advisor to the chairman, National Intelligence Council, Milton E. Miles Professor of International Relations at the Naval War College, and research associate at the International Institute for Strategic Studies (London) and at the United Nations Institute for Disarmament Research (Geneva). He is the author or editor of seven books on strategic affairs and peace operations. Dr. Daniel's latest book is *Leveraging for Success in United Nations Peace Operations* (co-edited with Jean Krasno and Bradd Hayes). He has written more than sixty articles, the latest — an analysis of the future of the Bush doctrine — published in the summer 2004 issue of *Defence Studies*.

BURTON GERBER, a retired CIA operations officer, served as chief of station in three communist countries over a thirty-nine-year career. A graduate of Michigan State University, Mr. Gerber is a member of the Council on Foreign Relations, the Royal Society for Asian Affairs (London), and the board of visitors of James Madison College of Michigan State University. He is a Knight of Malta. He has received the CIA's Distinguished Intelligence Medal along with other awards. In retirement he lectures on ethics and public policy and the ethics of espionage.

JAMES R. GOSLER is a Fellow at Sandia National Laboratories. His areas of interest include information operations, information assurance, nuclear weapon security, cryptography, critical infrastructure protection, terrorism, and space superiority. He regularly assists the Department of Defense, the intelligence community, and the National Academies through his participation on numerous boards and panels. Previously he was a visiting scientist at the National Security Agency, the director of the Clandestine Information Technology Office at the CIA, and commanding officer of three units in the U.S. Navy Reserve over a twenty-nine-year period. He is the recipient of several awards, including Lockheed Martin's NOVA Award, the director of central intelligence Director's Award, the CIA's Directorate of Operations Donovan Award, and the U.S. Navy's Legion of Merit. He received his M.S. in mathematics from Clemson University.

MARK M. LOWENTHAL is president and CEO at the Intelligence and Security Academy, a national education and consulting firm. He is also vice chairman of the National Intelligence Council for Evaluation. He previously served as staff director of the House Permanent Select Committee on Intelligence and as deputy assistant secretary of state for intelligence. Dr. Lowenthal has written eight books, including a novel. His textbook *Intelligence: From Secrets to Policy* (CQ Press, 2000) is used in intelligence courses across the country. Dr. Lowenthal received his Ph.D. in history from Harvard University. He is also an adjunct professor at the School for International and Public Affairs, Columbia University. In 1988 Dr. Lowenthal was the grand champion on the television quiz show *Jeopardy!*

DOUGLAS MacEACHIN served from March 1993 through June 1995 as the CIA's deputy director for intelligence, heading the agency's analytic component. In the fall of 1995 he joined Harvard University's John F. Kennedy School of Government, where until recently he served as senior research fellow. Mr. MacEachin received his B.A. from Miami University of Ohio, at which time he was commissioned as a regular officer in the U.S. Marine Corps. In 1962 he returned to graduate school in Miami, where he received his master's degree in economics.

JOHN MacGAFFIN heads the international security company AKE LLC, is a member of the Center for Strategic and International Studies (CSIS) Global Organized Crime Project, and serves on the Defense Science Board Taskforce on Homeland Security. In 2002 he was a member of the DSB Taskforce on Intelligence in Support of the War on Terrorism. He is also a member of the CSIS Project on Transnational Threats and the advisory board for the CSIS Project for Multilateral Information and Intelligence Sharing for Terror Threats to the Transatlantic Region. He serves on the CSIS private sector advisory group and, most recently, as a consultant to the National Infrastructure Advisory Council. Mr. MacGaffin served with the CIA for thirty-one years, for some of them as chief of station in several overseas locations. At the time of his retirement he was associate deputy director for operations — the second ranking position in the nation's clandestine service. After leaving the CIA he became the senior advisor to the director and deputy director of the FBI. In 1998, at the behest of the secretary of defense, the director of central intelligence, and the director of the FBI, he chaired a commission charged with restructuring the national counterintelligence system.

ERNEST R. MAY is Charles Warren Professor of History at Harvard University. In 2003-4 he was senior adviser to the 9/11 Commission. His publications include *Strange Victory: Hitler's Conquest of France; The Kennedy Tapes: Inside the White House during the Cuban Missile Crisis* (with Philip Zelikow); *American Cold War Strategy: Interpreting NSC 68; Thinking in Time: Uses of History for Decision Makers* (with Richard E. Neustadt); and *Knowing One's Enemies: Intelligence Assessment before the Two World Wars*. He is a member of the board of visitors of the Joint Military Intelligence College and of the DCI's Intelligence Science Board. From 1986 to 2000 he directed a program on intelligence and policy at Harvard, and he serves on the board of directors of the Belfer Center for Science and Technology at the John F. Kennedy School of Government.

AMY SANDS is the dean of the Graduate School of International Policy Studies at the Monterey Institute of International Studies. She formerly was the deputy director of the Center for Nonproliferation Studies and a Monterey Institute research professor. From 1994 to 1996 she was assistant director of the intelligence, verification, and information management bureau at the U.S. Arms Control and Disarmament Agency (ACDA). She received ACDA's Distinguished Honor Award and the On-Site Inspection Agency's Exceptional Civilian Service Medal. Before joining ACDA, she led the proliferation assessments section of Z Division (Intelligence) at the Lawrence Livermore National Laboratory. Dr. Sands is a member of the Council on Foreign Relations and the International Institute of Strategic Studies. She holds a B.A. in political science from the University of Wisconsin and earned her M.A., M.A.L.D., and Ph.D. from the Fletcher School of Law and Diplomacy.

JAMES MONNIER SIMON JR. served from 1999 to 2003 as assistant director of central intelligence for administration, a position to which he was appointed by President Clinton and confirmed by the Senate. His responsibilities included policy and budgetary oversight of the intelligence agencies and chairing the mission requirements board. After September 11, 2001, he served as senior intelligence official for homeland security. A career analyst, he was responsible for some years for managing the CIA's collection requirements. After retiring from government in 2003 he founded Intelligence Enterprises, LLC, and was recently named director of the Microsoft Institute for Advanced Technology in Governments. He serves on the boards of U.S. Airways Group, Inc., and United Devices, Inc., as well as on numerous governmental advisory groups. He has received numerous awards, including the Distinguished Intelligence Medal. Mr. Simon has a B.A. from the University of Alabama and an M.A. from the University of Southern California. He has written extensively on military history, intelligence, and homeland security and has lectured at universities and military colleges in the United States and abroad.

JENNIFER E. SIMS is a visiting professor and member of the core faculty of the Security Studies Program, Walsh School of Foreign Service, Georgetown University. She has served as deputy assistant secretary of state for intelligence coordination and as the Department of State's first coordinator for intelligence resources and planning. Previously she served as Senator John Danforth's defense and foreign policy advisor and as his designee to the Senate Select Committee on Intelligence. She is the recipient of the national intelligence community's Distinguished Service Medal and is a member of the International Institute of Strategic Studies. Dr. Sims received her B.A. from Oberlin College and her M.A. and Ph.D. from Johns Hopkins School of Advanced International Studies, where she has also taught. Her publications include *Icarus Restrained: An Intellectual History of Nuclear Arms Control, 1945-1960*, as well as numerous articles on arms control and intelligence.

L. BRITT SNIDER served as counsel to the Church committee, the special committee created by the Senate in 1975 to investigate alleged improprieties by the U.S. intelligence community, and subsequently worked on the resolution creating the Senate Select Committee on Intelligence. He served as general counsel to that committee from 1987 to 1995. From 1998 until his retirement from federal service in 2001, he served as inspector general of the Central Intelligence Agency. Mr. Snider is a graduate of Davidson College and the University of Virginia School of Law.

INDEX

actionable intelligence, 26

adaptability, and U.S. intelligence institutions, 9–10

Afghanistan: history of intelligence collections in, 163; phases of war in, 174–75; Soviet invasion of, 122, 124, 132n14; and strategy of intelligence collections in, 164–69; and use of collection teams in, 169–73. *See also* al-Qaeda; bin Laden, Osama; Taliban

Africa: and 1998 embassy bombings, 120; and post–cold war policy change, 4

after-action reviews, 195–96

agents, sleeper, 184

agility, and intelligence capabilities, 260–65

air power: and Afghanistan, 168; and World War II, 98

all-source analysis, and the INR, 59n31

al-Qaeda: and the FBI, 91–92; and history of intelligence collections in Afghanistan, 163; and information analysis, 126; and strategy of intelligence collections in Afghanistan, 164–69; and use of intelligence collection teams, 169–73

al-Shifa, and U.S. attack on pharmaceutical plant, 70–71

Ames, Aldrich, 141

analysis: management of, 221; and products, 226–28; and resources, 223–26; transforming of, 232–36

analysts, managing, 228–32

analytic resources catalog (ARC), 225–26, 231

ARC. *See* analytic resources catalog

Armed Forces Security Agency, 11

Arms Control and Disarmament Agency, 45

art, and intelligence practices, xiii, xvin5

Berlin, and disco bombing of 1986, 5

Beslan, and September 2004 terrorist attack, 23

bias, conservative, and the American intelligence cycle, 41–46

bin Laden, Osama: and covert action against, 84, 85; and information sharing, 119–20; and Inmarsat communications system, 79–80; and strategic denial and deception, 143; and World Trade Center bombing (1993), 5. *See also* al-Qaeda; September 11 attacks; Taliban

Blix, Hans, 233

Bosnia, and post–cold war policy change, 4

Brezhnev, Leonid, 124

budgets: and cuts for embassies, 44–45; and neglect of open sources, 38–39; and relations between the CIA and State Department, 46–47

Bureau of Intelligence and Research (INR): and all-source analysis, 59n31; and budgets, 44, 45; history of, 11; and intelligence collections, 38; and intelligence support, 51–53; and teamwork, 261–62; and technological challenges, 8

bureaucracy: and competition, 41–46; and the intelligence cycle, 40–41; and program budgets, 46–47; and stovepiped intelligence collection, 48–49

Bush, George H. W., 256n7

Bush, George W., ix, 202, 235, 242, 252

Carter, Jimmy: and SALT-II, 124; and Soviet invasion of Afghanistan, 122

Casey, William, 11, 230–31

Central Intelligence Agency (CIA): and budgets, 46; and clandestine service, 7; and the cold war, 10; and collection management, 56; compared to the FBI, 209; creation of, xiv; and democracy in the former Soviet Union, 36; and directorate of science and technology, 29; and domestic intelligence, 206; and Executive Order 12333, 211; and faulty focus, 248; and human intelligence cutbacks, 180; and information collection requirements, 151; and information technology, 100; and In-Q-